JOURNEY ON A DUSTY ROAD

Memoir of a missionary surgeon's twenty-year career in Nigeria

Dr. William David Ardill

CreateSpace

Printed by CreateSpace, An Amazon.com Company
© 2015, 2016 by Dr. William David Ardill. All rights reserved
Second Edition

ISBN-13: 9781517320898
ISBN-10: 1517320895

Cover design: Mary Ellen Krieger, Kelkē Design
Cover photo: © Dreamstine.com, Michal Bednarek

Unless otherwise noted, Bible references from *New American Standard Bible: 1995 Update*. LaHabra, CA: The Lockman Foundation, 1995.

*The names of patients and some Nigerians in Christian work have been changed to protect their identity.

DEDICATION

This book is dedicated to my dear wife Dorothy who has supported me through our ups and downs. I admire her wonderful love and rapport with our children, her compassion for the unfortunate, and her love for me and the Lord Jesus.

I also want to acknowledge and thank my four amazing children - Marie, Heather, Anna, and David. This book is really written for them. I hope it is a reminder of their home in Nigeria, a partial explanation for the decisions we made that affected them, and provide some insight into the joys and tribulations we faced as their parents during the Nigeria chapter of our lives. Our sudden departures, our absenteeism as parents, our irritability during times of stress, and the public nature of our lives when we were in the States are rooted in our deep desire to participate in the clear proclamation of the Gospel of Jesus Christ in Nigeria.

ACKNOWLEDGMENTS

This book is the compilation of some of my experiences over the past 20 years serving as an SIM missionary in Nigeria. Interestingly it is also the 10th anniversary of an incident that changed my life profoundly, shaped my understanding of the nature of God, and solidified my love for my wife and family.

It would be impossible to thank all who have had an impact on my life and been formative influences in my maturing and growth as a person, father, missionary, and surgeon. At the top of the list is my dear wife, Dorothy, who has ridden the roller coaster with me and never left my side. As the best thing that ever happened to me, I owe her my profound gratitude for her faithfulness and support through the good and tough times.

My parents have always been supportive of our missionary calling, and I am grateful for their prayer support and encouragement during the many years I have been on the field.

In preparing this book I am grateful for the editing help of Ruth Carlson, Sid and Jean Garland, Tittle Abader, Carmen McCain, Ron Rice, Jamie Janosz, Karen Keegan, Dee Parker and Heather Ardill. Their insights, suggestions, and keen literary perspectives were invaluable. I also wanted to recognize Mary Ellen Krieger for her terrific design work on the book cover.

To God I owe my life and any measure of happiness and success I may have enjoyed as a husband, father, missionary, and surgeon.

TABLE OF CONTENTS

The fishermen know that the sea is dangerous and
the storm terrible,
but they have never found these dangers sufficient
reasons for staying ashore.
- Vincent Van Gogh

Safety does not depend on the absence of danger.
Safety is found in God's presence, in the center of
His perfect will.
- T.J. Bach

Be strong and courageous.
Do not be terrified.
Do not be discouraged.
For the Lord *of* God is with you wherever you go.
Joshua 1:9 (Our son David's version)

BEGINNINGS

In the shade of the large mango tree in the center of a remote village in the desperately hot backwater of northern Nigeria near the town of Roni, a pith-helmeted missionary drenched in perspiration was preaching the simple gospel message of Jesus Christ. No one farmed in the heat of the day, so a mixed crowd of villagers, who were mostly animists and Muslims, gathered to hear this white man tell his stories. The young missionary had barely finished when an old dirty farmer clothed in rags and drooling the orange spittle of the cola nut slowly made his way from the back of the crowd to the front. He gently grabbed my father by the lapels of his coat and inquired,

"Did you say God had a son?"

"Yes," my father answered, pleased that the man had grasped the essential truth in his message.

"And you said his name was Jesus. And you said he came to die for my sins?"

"Yes."

"And when did you say this Jesus came to die for our sins?"

"Two thousand years ago."

In desperation he grabbed his coat tighter and pleaded with my father, "What about **my** father, and **his** father, and **his** father? Why didn't anyone come and tell them about God's son Jesus?"

My father had little to say, but quietly replied, "I do not know. But I am here now to tell you about Him." This was the calling of my father to go to Africa as a missionary, and it became my life's calling to proclaim Christ to those in desperate need of a Savior.

My parents left their home in Northern Ireland to attend Moody Bible Institute. They joined the international mission agency SIM and served in Roni, Nigeria, for several years before being transferred to Jos. My sister Sharon and my two younger brothers, John and Jim, and I were born and raised in Jos.

As a young boy, I was interested in science and especially medicine, so my mother arranged for me to observe various aspects of hospital life. I remember "helping" in the laboratory and learning to look into a microscope to see the red blood cells and various microorganisms in the stool specimens. Later the x-ray technician showed me how to take x-rays and develop film in the dark room. These experiences at Bingham Hospital were a wonderful exposure to medicine, and I was excited to be learning so much in a real hospital environment at such a young age.

After my experiences in the laboratory and x-ray as a boy, I remember asking if I could watch an operation. The surgeon was working at Evangel Hospital, so I watched him remove a thorn from a little boy's hand. The boy was asleep under anesthesia; but as the surgeon put the knife to his skin and cut the skin open, I felt very light-headed and ran from the room to avoid passing out and falling on the floor. After getting some fresh air, I worked up the courage to go back in and watched the rest of the case. The surgeon was very kind and explained what he was doing as he went. So much for my auspicious start in surgery!

In 1967 when the Biafran War was starting, we left Nigeria for our furlough in the United States. My parents decided not to return to Nigeria because my sister was graduating from high school and was interested in going to nursing school. Since we did not have relatives in the United States, they felt it was important to be able to help her during this big adjustment in her life. SIM had asked my father to join the SIM USA administrative team, so we moved to New Jersey. I graduated from Belleville High School in 1970 and, in preparation for medical school, did pre-med courses at Ursinus College in Collegeville, Pennsylvania. Graduating four years later, I went to Columbia University in New York to complete my pre-med studies to enter medical school. Two years later I was accepted at George Washington University School of Medicine in Washington, D.C., and finished in 1980.

During my senior year of medical school, I had the opportunity to go to Liberia and work at the SIM ELWA Hospital in Monrovia for two months. I was there during the coup d'état of Samuel Doe against President Tolbert so had an exciting time. My experience as a medical student affirmed my desire to become a medical missionary, and I returned to the United States motivated for a career as a medical missionary.

I went to Baylor University Medical Center in Dallas, Texas, for my residency in general surgery. While a third-year resident in 1983, I went to Jos and worked with several American surgeons at Evangel Hospital for two of the greatest months of my residency. It was an amazing experience for a budding young surgeon. Every morning at 7:30, we would look at the list of cases for the day, they would ask me which ones I wanted to do, and I would get a room for the morning to do "my" cases. I learned the valuable lesson that as long as you have a good book with pictures of the procedure, you can operate on any part of the body when you are trained in the basics of good surgical principles and technique. I ventured into body cavities and dark places I never imagined I would enter as a general surgeon and loved every bit of it. I kept a daily log of the cases I did and came back with an experience my resident colleagues envied. This experience was more confirmation from God that I should continue on my course to become a medical missionary. I was not sure where I would end up, but I knew God would make that apparent when His time was right. I completed my residency in 1985 and joined SIM.

My first assignment was at the ELWA Hospital in Monrovia where I had gone as a medical student. The missionary surgeon had just moved to the United States and they needed a general surgeon. I was delighted to return there and enjoyed four years of fruitful ministry at ELWA Hospital. I was working extremely hard as the only surgeon, had little time off, and few opportunities to train Liberian staff in surgery. There was some tension among the missionary physicians and, although the location on the beach was incredible, I was not as happy as I wanted to be.

The Lord brought Dorothy Hostetter into my life in the summer of 1987. She had finished her degree as a medical technologist and was interested in going to China as a medical missionary. China was still closed to Western missionaries, so she was working as a women's dorm resident director at Moody Bible Institute in Chicago. She was recruited to come to Liberia with a team of students to work in various SIM ministries. She was assigned to work in the laboratory for six weeks. She had always wanted to scrub in on surgery cases. When I invited her into the Operating Room, she jumped at the chance and we fell in love over an open abdomen! I thought she was beautiful and funny, and I wanted to share my life with her. We fell madly in love, and by the end of the six weeks decided we wanted to get married. Nine months later in March 1988, we were married in Chicago and then returned to Liberia together in January 1989 to work at ELWA hospital.

We both became heavily involved in a variety of ministries on the compound and in the city of Monrovia. I was the hospital administrator and medical director in addition to my surgical responsibilities. We were both on call at the hospital and were exhausted much of the time. Many days we spent so little time together we were like ships passing in the night. In spite of our hectic schedules, we anticipated spending the rest of our missionary careers in Liberia. The hospital was growing and the future for our ministry in Liberia looked bright.

In December 1989, Charles Taylor, a former member of the Liberian government who was removed for embezzlement and then became a Libya-trained guerilla fighter, invaded the northeast corner of Liberia with a band of rebel soldiers in an attempt to overthrow the regime of the Liberian President Samuel Doe. As the rebellion moved down through the country towards Monrovia, SIM began evacuating missionaries. In June, the fighting was outside Monrovia and most of the SIM missionaries had left the country. Dorothy was resolved to stay with me and help at the hospital until the local newspaper showed a picture of the heads of three men who had been beheaded in the village next to the hospital. Dorothy suddenly realized she needed to leave and in a matter of days had left on the last commercial flight out of the country. I stayed for another two months to manage the hospital, do surgery as needed, and help care for the 20,000 refugees who came to our compound. The last ten of us SIM missionaries eventually also left the country after a major gun battle between Charles Taylor rebel soldiers and the government forces on our mission compound. We drove into Ivory Coast and then to the SIM headquarters in Abidjan along the coast. I made it back to the United States at the end of the summer in 1990, and Dorothy and I decided to stay in the United States until the situation in Liberia improved.

Our last few months and departure from Liberia were traumatic and took a toll on me emotionally. I suffered for months with difficulty concentrating, flashbacks, inability to make decisions and depression. Later, I realized I had been suffering from post-traumatic stress disorder (PTSD). Due in part to my condition, we decided, after a short debriefing at the SIM headquarters in North Carolina, to settle in Dallas for an extended furlough. We would remain in Dallas, waiting until God gave us clear direction for our next assignment.

Our time in Dallas was a season of healing and recovery from our traumatic Liberian war experience in 1990[1]. Through

---

[1] Ardill, William, *Where Elephants Fight: An Autobiographical Account of the Liberian Civil War,* 2002.

a recommendation from Don Meier, a Baptist missionary general surgeon on furlough from Nigeria, God provided work for me as a surgeon at the VA Hospital in Dallas. God also blessed us with a beautiful daughter, Marie. Our consideration of places for a future ministry now included Marie's needs and our expanding family commitments.

After six months in Dallas, we were ready to explore various opportunities for service in Africa. Some counseled us, "You have already done your thing for God; why don't you stay in America now and help support others to go?" However, we had a strong conviction that God still had more work for us to do in Africa. It became apparent that the war in Liberia would go on for a long time, so we began considering other options. One hospital we considered was the Evangel Hospital in Nigeria where there was a urologist who wanted a general surgeon to come and help him.

Since I was born and raised in Jos, which is in the Middle Belt of the Nigeria, I was familiar with the culture of Nigeria, a little of the language in that region and some of the issues that the mission and church were facing. As a surgical resident in 1985, I had visited Evangel Hospital for two months. And, although I had a great experience professionally learning a variety of surgical procedures, I thought it unlikely I would return to Nigeria.

Dorothy and I prayed, asking our family and friends to join us in asking for God's clear guidance. In addition to my familiarity with the hospital and country, we both felt it was the best place for our second assignment for several reasons. One of my frustrations in Liberia had been the lack of a training program and teaching opportunities at ELWA Hospital. In contrast, Evangel Hospital had a strong family practice residency program to train Nigerian physicians. There was a terrific mission school in Jos called Hillcrest School. Anticipating that our family would grow, we would not need to send our children far away for their schooling. Another advantage was that English was a major trade language, so our transition would be quicker and easier. We could function in our home and in the hospital from the start with only English. Another real plus was the location of Jos. It was on a plateau 4,000 feet above sea level making the climate more comfortable than the humid tropical heat of coastal Liberia and the dry roasting heat of the desert to the north.

The call of God to serve in Nigeria, though not involving a vision or dream, was unmistakable. Dorothy and I had a mutual peace in our hearts that God was directing us to serve Him in Nigeria at Evangel Hospital. Intellectually, Dorothy and I believed we made a good decision, but emotionally we never felt the same sense of a call we had in Liberia. We moved forward with the light God had given us and trusted Him as we began our move to Nigeria.

COMING HOME

March 1992

It all seemed familiar but still so much was new. I was returning "home" eager to share with my wife Dorothy all the places of my childhood. She had heard stories from my parents and me about the country where I was born and raised until my parents left in 1967 during the Biafran Civil War. I was anxious to show her the places we had travelled, our house, my childhood school, and to share the special memories of my youth.

Right now, however, Dorothy's heart was consumed with preparing for our life in Nigeria. We would need a four-year supply of baby clothes and toys, kitchen gadgets and spices, clothes and underwear. More often than not when we made shopping trips to Wal-Mart or Costco and pulled up with three full shopping carts, the clerk would ask in wonder, "Is that all for you?" Because of our experience living in Liberia as missionaries, Dorothy thought well ahead and prepared for most contingencies. "What does a four-year-old want for Christmas?" Dorothy pondered as she gazed at Marie.

Moving in the United States is hard enough, but it does not compare to the challenge of moving abroad. The list of tasks seemed endless. Our to-do list also included sorting all our earthly possessions and then packing the items in each room for the garage sale, storage, or Africa. We also packed the piles of donated medical supplies and equipment. To get this all accomplished by our departure deadline in six months, we set up a schedule of tasks that needed to be done.[2] On more than one occasion, I complained about the large number of boxes because of the hassle of getting through the airports but also the work of packing them all. "Dorothy, do we really need four saucepans?" Dorothy protested, "Getting some of these supplies in Nigeria will be impossible." Although Dorothy feared my mother would side with me, my mother always sided with Dorothy saying, "Oh, Bill, that would be great to have in Nigeria."

It became clear to me that I was losing the battle.

My father, Trevor, helped me pack the boxes and understood the art of packing a cardboard box to fit airline maximum specifications. To meet the maximum allowable weight of 70 pounds required having an array of things of different size and weight in front of you on the floor and carefully placing an item in the box and then surrounding it or stuffing it with the right mixture of sundries. It was easier to pack the boxes on the bathroom scale than to pick the box up and set it on the scale every few minutes to see if it was overweight.

Dorothy and I developed a tradition of doing things "one last time" before leaving. This included going to favorite restaurants, eating special foods we would not enjoy in Africa and going to a theater for one last movie. Our favorite "last" was going to a local supermarket and gazing longingly at each shelf trying to fix in our memory those wonderful things we knew we would not see for a long time. Passing the aisle-long stocked freezer of ice cream, Dorothy asked, "Can we get a small carton of Hagan-Daz Raspberry sorbet, please?" How could I resist? These Safeway final excursions became a tradition we remember fondly.

---

[2] Ardill, William. "Practical Tips on Preparing for Home Assignment." Evangelical Missions Quarterly

(2005). EMQOnline.com. EMIS. Web. 9 Jan. 2011.

Interestingly, grocery stories had been our most feared place upon re-entry from the field. They induced panic when faced with too many choices of toilet paper, toothbrushes, and food. Shortly after arriving in the U.S., I remember going into a store to buy a toothbrush and, after about 30 minutes of examining all the choices in a 4-shelf 20-foot wide section of the store, I came back out to the car empty-handed.

Dorothy asked, "Which one did you buy?"

"I couldn't decide. There were too many choices."

So embarrassed by my physical and mental reaction to the excess of the United States, I left the grocery store without a toothbrush because of decision paralysis.

These transitions are something a missionary gets used to but never fully expects – even when they repeat the process. For us, a familiar but distasteful part of missionary life is the "hellos" and "good-byes" that become commonplace both in your home and adopted country. When we came to Dallas after being evacuated from Liberia because of the civil war, we knew a few people in the church I had attended when I was a surgical resident five years earlier. But, aside from my brother John and his family, we knew very few in that big city. Over the next 18 months, we had made many friends. Now we had to say good-bye to these new friends.

Some we hoped to see again when we returned to the United States in four years, some we hoped to see if they came to visit us, and some we knew we would never see again until heaven. I always had a difficult time saying goodbye to my parents. I would weep in the dark of night thinking about them. Leaving this time was different, however, because I had my best friend with me – my wife Dorothy – and our darling daughter — the center of our universe. Having emotional support I needed made a world of difference.

Our preparations were now complete, or as complete as they would ever be. We felt we had recovered from our traumatic Liberia war experience and were healed emotionally and spiritually. We had a renewed sense of God's call and direction for our lives. We had the support and encouragement of family members and hundreds of friends. We had done everything we possibly could to prepare for the day of our departure. Our hearts were full with mixed contradictory emotions of excitement, anxiety, happiness and fear, hope and panic – all barely contained inside our tired bodies. We were ready to go and just needed to do it!

We left the airport in Dallas on a British Airways jet Monday, March 16, 1992, the day after my birthday, headed for London. Our ongoing British Airways flight arrived in the northern city of Kano, Nigeria, at 8 p.m. When we stepped out of the plane, the 100° F temperature hit us like we were opening a hot oven door. We abruptly realized we were really in Africa, on the edge of the Sahara Desert, and, as I teased my wife, "We aren't in Kansas anymore, Dorothy!"

An SIM missionary met us and helped get our boxes through customs. I changed some U.S. dollars into the local currency called Naira, and we headed to the SIM Guesthouse. From the moment we stepped inside the airport, we were immediately struck by the number of people everywhere, all men, who were generally loud and did not share our sense of personal space – crowding, pushing, yelling, and grabbing whatever we were carrying to "help." After getting through the inside gauntlet, we faced a new crowd of mostly beggars in the parking lot, all asking for help as we battled with the porters who helped carry the bags to the car and then their demands for "something." Despite the bedlam, we were thankful and excited – we had arrived in Nigeria after months of planning and praying.

Having lived in Liberia for four years, we were not surprised by many of the sights, sounds, and smells in Nigeria. The road to the Guesthouse was covered with lots of potholes! It was already dark, so we could not see much beyond the immediate buildings along the road. There were motorcycles everywhere cutting in front, beside and all around us. No one was heeding the traffic lights, including our driver, for fear you would get rear-ended or get robbed if you stopped. The air changed from still hot air at the airport to a breezy hot air coming through the van windows. After maneuvering a deeply pot-holed dirt road just in front of the SIM Kano Eye Hospital, we eventually pulled into the Guesthouse compound and unloaded our carry-on bags into our rooms.

Dorothy gasped when she saw the interior. My heart sank. "Stark" may be too kind a word to use to describe our dingy room. There was one sheet on the bed and one threadbare towel. Several vintage pictures with Christian themes from the last century were crookedly hanging on the dusty walls along with an old calendar showing the faces of several past Nigerian church leaders. On the dresser was a bicycle pump style bug spray can for killing the ubiquitous mosquitoes, a candle, and box of matches for the inevitable nightly power blackout. The bathroom had a dirty, moldy cracked cement bathtub with a bucket of water set in it because there was often no water coming from the faucet.

On the sink was a bottle of drinking water because the tap water was not safe to drink. The paint job was awful with different shades of color highlighted by the brushstrokes and peeling edges but did little to camouflage the roaches and ants scurrying out of sight when the single bulb incandescent light hanging from the corrugated metal ceiling went on. Rust colored dust clung to the rough patches of the wall, smoke spots revealed where the kerosene lanterns normally rested, and the dead bugs splattered on the walls testified to the inadequacy of the insecticides and the accuracy of a former tenant.

The crib for Marie was nothing more than a slatted wooden frame box with mosquito netting on all sides that had so many holes and jagged edges we hoped the mosquitoes were as tired as we were. Marie did not sleep well and neither did we, but at least we were in Nigeria and we hoped things would be better in Jos. Although we didn't speak much that night, I later told Dorothy, "After seeing the dilapidated bug-infested room at the Guesthouse,

I almost got back in the van to go back to the airport and get back on the plane to London!"

Things in the morning were better. After a good breakfast, we set out for the five-hour trip by road to Jos. Nigeria actually looked less forbidding in the daylight! Several things were striking. Nigeria is nestled on the windowsill of the Sahara Desert, so during the winter dry season the northern wind blows dust that makes the air look like fog and covers every flat surface with a fine powdery dust. This thick harmattan makes the sky so hazy you cannot see the sun and sometimes obscures things as near as a few hundred feet away.

The countryside was dry and dusty, too, having had no rain for six months. The streets were jammed with motorcycles and bicycles. The local cargo trucks, called "lorries," were loaded above the top of the rails, so that they often leaned to one side under the burden of their loads. The taxis in Kano were beat up old cars made to look a bit younger with a bad coat of green paint and a yellow stripe along the sides. Everyone was dressed in flamboyant African garb, but the women were especially colorful usually wearing bright head-ties (head scarves), blouses, and skirts that to our Western sensibilities did not match. The roads were bordered by three-foot deep, smelly, dirty, open pit sewers that drained waste products from homes, businesses, and the many market stall tables that lined the roads.

The streets were lined with markets made up of individual stalls. Each stall seemed to sell the same items in any given area, but each represented a family's entry into the African dream of prosperity and free enterprise. There were also some holdovers from the British colonial days, like the round-abouts on the roads, and the British spellings of words like "tyre," "theatre" and "paediatrics" on the sign boards. Most of the vehicles were either Peugeots or any of a number of Japanese imports and most were taxis packed to near bursting.

After a five-hour journey in a van packed with boxes and tired people, we arrived in Jos at the Evangel Hospital compound. The red laterite dusty road inside the hospital compound winds around the various hospital buildings to the senior staff quarters in the back. In spite of the lack of rain and heat, the trees were in full bloom and the place looked beautiful. We had a grand welcome by SIM missionaries Steve and Jan Arrowsmith. They showed us our three-bedroom apartment that they had worked so hard to prepare for us and gave us a brief tour of the compound.

The missionaries live at the back end of a 100-acre property that is surrounded on three sides by a privately owned polo field. Although there are a few duplexes, most of the families have three- or four-bedroom single-family houses. The buildings are all cement block with zinc pan roofs. Our apartment was in a block of four and was about a five-minute walk from the hospital. There was a dilapidated tennis court hidden between several houses.

An eight-foot perimeter wall that kept out some of the street noise and hopefully some of the thieves surrounded the entire compound. I remember during my childhood that there was no wall or fence between the houses and the polo grounds, and we often came out to the polo field on a Saturday afternoon to watch the British rugby teams play. In those days, the hospital seemed so far outside the city of Jos that by now had grown around the hospital and had changed the atmosphere from a rural environment to an urban context. This was the beginning of many flashbacks and memories of my days as a child growing up in Nigeria.

I enjoyed telling Dorothy about the significance of so many places smells and sounds as they related to my childhood. So much was the same, just bigger, noisier, and dirtier! It was hard not to compare those days and today. Most of my memories brought a comforting sense of familiarity and confidence during our early days and months in Jos.

Over the next weeks and months, we began to settle in to our new lives. We had new roles to learn, new friends, a new house, new music and food, new recreation, and new problems. We faced many of the common culture shock milestones in spite of our Liberia experience. We fought the temptation to compare that experience to this and especially wanted to avoid this trap in our conversations with other missionaries. Many people gave us advice and counsel, most of which was valuable and helped us cope. We learned the various quirks and idiosyncrasies of each of the missionaries as reported by each one but were delighted that many of these passed-on impressions were not true. We enjoyed developing our own new friends and tried not to be influenced by other people's prejudices about people, both Nigerians and missionaries.

The first year would be our biggest adjustment and present many lessons and trials that eventually served us well. We had to face many difficult challenges, but we were at our new home and eager to learn how God would use us and mold us.

COMPOUND LIFE ON THE PLATEAU

I n many areas of the world, a common wall surrounds a group of houses called a "compound." Sometimes the compound is owned by a company to house employees, sometimes it is built by a non-government organization (NGO) or mission agency, but often it is just a group of houses owned by a landlord who builds the wall for security purposes. Major cities in Nigeria like Lagos are almost entirely "compound-ed." Driving around the city you see mostly compound walls and not the individual houses where people live.

All the SIM houses in Jos were on compounds – the Pharmacy compound, the Niger Creek compound, Crescent Hill compound and the Evangel Hospital compound. The Evangel compound surrounded a polo field on three sides. The field was used for polo games during the Christmas season, political rallies when elections loomed, trade fairs at least twice a year, Christian crusades and Muslim rallies, and as a rallying point for army operations. Conveniently for us, the polo ground served as a buffer from the noise and security risks of neighboring developments. But the compound could not always prevent problems. Sometimes people would sneak over the walls by climbing bordering trees or stepping onto adjacent buildings.

Our compound housed both missionary and Nigerian hospital personnel. Most of the missionary houses were clustered at one end of the property. In some ways this compound housing arrangement interfered with the missionaries' efforts to develop neighborly relationships with the Nigerian staff. But, for orientation of new missionaries and for communication during times of crisis, it was an advantage.

The SIM missionaries who started the hospital in the 1970s built most of the houses within our compound. The houses were cement block with corrugated asbestos or zinc roofs. Although the floor plans were originally similar, with the additions and renovations that had taken place since their construction, they were now quite different. Although some were duplexes with small yards, most were single-family houses with large yards containing fruit and vegetable gardens.

The difficulty of compound living is compounded by the close proximity of the houses. It seems the more the residents have in common the more everyone knows everyone else's business. When we lived in Monrovia, Liberia, on the ELWA compound, it was like living in a fishbowl. There was little privacy and few secrets. Some interdependency is necessary because of the common hardships of the residents. People rely on each other to help with house repairs, car problems, utility frustrations, babysitting assistance, shared security resources, and sometimes shared water and power.

In the Evangel compound we helped each other with problems, shared security personnel and Internet resources, looked after each other's houses, and visited each other as often as we felt comfortable. We not only worked at the same hospital, but we enjoyed spending much of our social time together as well. There were, indeed, cultural and generational differences, but there was also openness and a sense of community. Dorothy often dropped by a neighbor's house if she needed more powdered sugar to finish making a cake or some other ingredient she ran out of for cooking. Chuck Truxton brought over the bounty of his garden including grapefruit, blackberries, and even home-grown and home-roasted coffee beans.

Early in our Evangel life we invited all the missionaries on the compound over to our house for a family birthday party. Dorothy made a big cake and everyone enjoyed watching the kids open their presents, eating cake, drinking a "mineral" (soft drink), helping with games outside in the yard, and catching up on news. As our children grew older, these parties were more about inviting school friends than our fellow missionaries, but we still invited our neighbors for the cake part of the evening. In middle and high school the children usually had sleepover parties, which meant no one in the house slept well and we were all exhausted the next day. I finally got smart and would go to our neighbors, the Truxtons, when the girls had sleepovers, so I could get some peace and quiet.

We had a custom on our compound that when a family arrived or was leaving, we would take turns having the family over for dinner. This would reduce the burden of cooking on the arriving or departing family and give us the opportunity to say our greetings or goodbyes. We got to know the favorite dishes each missionary mom liked to serve, and our kids looked forward to Aunt Bev Truxton's ice cream truffle dessert or laboratory technician Rick Naatz's chocolate silk pie. When Dorothy was a stay-at-home mom with small children, hospitality became an important part of her life, and she looked forward to these meals as an opportunity to meet new missionaries for some adult talk.

Easter was a big event at our house. Dorothy gathered baskets and plastic eggs over the years, and we would host a mega-Easter egg hunt for all the missionary kids on the compound. The older kids placed about 150 plastic eggs filled with candy around our yard, and then we unleashed the little ones to find the hidden eggs. There was great excitement hunting for the eggs, and, surprisingly, we lost only a few eggs every year. Our gardener would sometimes find the ones we had missed, since, as hard as we tried, there were always a few missing at the end of the hunt.

These festivities within the compound reminded me of my childhood as a missionary kid. I remember celebrating Halloween at Kent Academy. We dressed up in costumes with a parade and party. One year I was transformed into a monkey baseball player and another year, ironically, I dressed as a nurse! In retrospect, it baffles me that the missionary community celebrated Halloween. It is not understood or celebrated in Nigeria, and could be particularly confusing for the animist people in the local villages.

In our compound, we would go to a fellow missionary's home for what they called a "Hallelujah Party!" The kids made their own creative costumes since they did not have the luxury of purchasing one from a local Wal-Mart or costume store. One year, our son David taped together blank sheets of paper the size of a walking billboard and then copied both sides of a Cheetos snack bag onto the paper. He was the largest bag of Cheetos I have ever seen, and he was so proud of making it himself. Heather wore a small box around her waist covered with blue paper. Wearing blue leotards, a swim cap, and goggles, she went as an ice cube. Anna draped a mosquito net around her and was "Mosquito Lady" or "The Ghost of Mosquitos Past!" What a hoot it was to see our kids use their creative imagination to fashion these one-of-a-kind costumes!

Thanksgiving is not a Nigerian holiday, so the Americans and Canadians organize a get-together and eat a lot of food without the after-feast Macy's parade or American football games on television. If we missed the big gathering in Jos for the Americans, we would invite single missionaries to our house for dinner complete with homemade pumpkin pie and chicken. Yes, chicken, not turkey. Much to our surprise, however, before Thanksgiving one year I found a huge turkey in the birdcage in our back yard. Our Nigerian friend Kingsford gave it to us to thank us as a Thanksgiving gift for our friendship and kindness to his family. Wow! We listened to the gobbling all night, then the next day the pardon was revoked, and the turkey met a timely end in our freezer.

One Nigerian custom among Christians that we have appreciated is the "home visit." If there is a big event in someone's life - a death, birth, a major trip - friends will come to your home as a group to pray with you for God's special presence. During the various crises in our family, hospital and church, friends would pay us a "home visit" to extend their sympathies and pray with us. It is a beautiful custom that embodies the body of Christ caring for one another during times of hardship. For example, when a hospital staff member's father died I drove the hospital management team to visit him and his family. The hospital chaplain spoke briefly and then prayed for the family, encouraging them with the prayers of the hospital staff. These times of prayer were a good reminder of the depth of spirituality in the African church and of the community found in the Body of Christ. Visiting the home of a friend at significant family events like weddings, funerals, sickness, and a new baby was an important cultural expression of sympathy and kindness.

Most foreign missionaries and business people employed Nigerian staff to do the majority of the cooking and cleaning. Some also had a gardener and driver. With the heavy rains during the rainy season and the incredible dust drugging the dry season, cleaning the house and clothing was a major daily endeavor. Cooking was also time-consuming since most meals were made from scratch and many missionaries canned vegetables throughout the year. Those who did not have help with the chores often could not have ministries outside the home for lack of time and energy. We wrestled with this common practice of having people work for you in the house. With domestic help there is sometimes the unwanted perception of aristocracy. There is also the real sense that having help in your home invades your privacy. We also worried that the people back home who supported and prayed for us might misunderstand and think we were either living too opulent a lifestyle or were living in the last century with domestic slaves. It took us awhile, as new missionaries, to realize how helpful house staff could be, how much they appreciate the work, how to treat them with dignity, and how this practice was accepted and even expected in both the Nigerian and expatriate communities.

Unfortunately because we were novices in this area, we had several bad experiences with hired help during our first six months in Nigeria. One after another, the women we hired stole either money or jewelry, and we had to let them go. These were painful experiences, and we naturally reacted by being hesitant to hire anyone, setting our expectations higher each time. We ended up having a better idea of what kind of person we were looking for and being wiser in our selections. One good idea we happened upon was to solicit the help of a local church leader who could vet applicants for us and recommend a known upstanding church member in the local congregation.

Dorothy taught the cook to make the evening meals, can vegetables and tomato sauce, make granola and potato chips, bake bread and cookies, and shop each week in the market for groceries. We also hired a woman to clean the house and help with the laundry. This included sweeping away the never-ending dust during the dry season, cleaning the louvered glass windows in every room, and helping with other household chores. The gardener tended the flowers, gardens, and bushes, picked the fruit, swept the walkways and driveway, and had time to plant a small vegetable garden of his own.

Compound life meant we had a safe place for our children to play. And, our children benefited from having playmates within the same compound. When I built a go-kart for David, the compound kids all came for a turn. When we invited the Nigerian horse handler to bring a horse to our house so the kids could ride, the rest of the compound kids showed up for the fun. We bought a used trampoline from SIM dentist Dr. Steve Porter, and it also became an attraction for the kids to come and take turns bouncing each other around.

Sunday mornings in Jos unfortunately were a time of frustration and a clash in cultures. There were several churches in our neighborhood, so the Sunday morning preparations for the service and the subsequent four-hour services adhered to the stereotypical loudness of everything else in Nigeria. Each Sunday morning we gravitated to the opposite side of our house in order to communicate with each other and function without getting a headache from the noise.

In addition to the Sunday morning bedlam, the polo field adjacent to our compound was a public gathering place. So every event generated a huge amount of noise, traffic congestion, and chaos in our neighborhood. Below are a few examples from my journal of our reactions to the weekend activities on the polo field.

October 2007

> We are suffering a bit today from hearing loss. Over the weekend a Christian group held a crusade on the polo field next to the hospital compound. They often arrange the loudspeakers, so they point in our direction. This time they also positioned additional speakers around the perimeter of the field, so not only was it at a deafening decibel level, there was a delayed echo of every syllable and utterance. The noise started with the usual microphone checks and then practicing on Saturday at 2 p.m. and continued until 10 p.m. Dorothy took the kids to a neighbor's house that was a bit quieter, but because I was on call I was not comfortable leaving the house. The noise started up again on Sunday afternoon, and finally the amplifiers were silent at 9:30 p.m. In spite of closing the windows, curtains and doors, it was so loud we could hardly talk in our house. We tried headphones, earplugs and finally turned up our own TV

loud enough to drown out most of the noise, which ranged from good singing to off-key screaming, to yell preaching and a smattering of group tongues speaking and antiphonal chanting and singing. So today the silence was deafening, and we are getting back our equilibrium. In the past, if we had wind of a crusade, we would go out of town to Miango, but I was on call, so I was stuck in Jos.

October 2008

My ears are still ringing and my headache just left this morning. On Saturday a large group gathered at the polo grounds beside the hospital compound. They were Muslims who had come from all over Nigeria for a fundraising ("launching") for two new Muslim schools. I don't remember ever seeing a crowd so big. They came all day Saturday and packed the roads around the polo field and hospital. What normally was a 10-minute drive to the school took over 30 minutes. Several groups had LOUD loudspeakers going all day preaching and teaching until 2:30 a.m. Sunday morning. Then they started up again at 5:45 a.m. Sunday, so not only could we hardly think because of the noise, we got little sleep. Along with the crowds, merchants gathered with their wares – cloth, shoes, hats, and all sorts of merchandise and set up their shops along the road medians, the sides of the road and any empty spot near the meeting place. They finally finished up on Sunday afternoon and left the streets littered with trash since most of these venues have not only no provision for rubbish but no toilet facilities either. We were thankful it was only one night of no sleep and that there were no incidents of either violence or incursions on our compound. Instead of being angry at how much our peace is disturbed, I try hard to remember they are an important reason we are here and we, indeed, live in a fallen world where we are to be light and salt.

November 2008

All week there has been a trade fair next door on the polo field. What this means is the polo field has small plywood houses all over it with merchants from all over town creating a new market next door to us. An added attraction is a huge stage where music groups and artists present their "music" every night. Many of the merchants also have music blaring all day from their stalls and when you throw in the Muslim call to prayer five times day, it makes for quite a din. We are about the closest missionary house to the action so feel we have front row seats to the cacophony. Last night the noise went to about 12:30 a.m., so I am getting some sleep only with the aid of earplugs. On top of the noise, the traffic around our area is worse than usual with everyone coming and going and trucks pulling in to drop off their goods. The motorcycle taxis are more obnoxious than usual, and we pray every time we have to go near the area. Nights are the worst, especially when there are concerts. Not only is it more difficult to see Nigerians at night that are walking along the road and running across the four lanes of traffic, pedestrians think you can see them, so they often walk right in front of oncoming traffic. The trade fair was supposed to end today, but we heard it is being extended another four days.

Just as the noise levels in Nigeria could vary in dramatic ways, the seasons brought extreme differences. The change of seasons was another amazing aspect of living on the Plateau. The rains began in late March and gradually increased their frequency from once every few days to daily. By late summer there was a heavy rain shower every day for an hour or two. In March, the showers started in the morning and then shifted into the later morning and then into the afternoon. The pattern continued until they stopped in October. Then there was no rain at all until the following March. During the dry season there was no rain, the grass all turned brown, and the landscape changed from lush green tropical forest to parched dry savannah plains. During the rainy season the winds were from the south, bringing the rain from the ocean north. In the dry seasons the winds were from the north, bringing dust and disease from the Sahara Desert. The dust formed a fog-like haze called "harmattan." The dust was unusually fine and got into everything, requiring the compulsive duster to clean several times a day. It also got into electronics, so during the winter months we kept all our electronics covered with towels. By contrast, here are my comments mid-November.

> The weather changed this week almost overnight.
> The rainy season was unusually long and we hope
> our full wells will last a long time into the dry season.
> The skies changed from the dramatic blowing clouds
> full of rain to a hazy almost fog-like cloudless sky you
> can hardly see through. You would think you were in
> a smoggy city, but it is mostly the dust (harmattan)
> even though the exhaust fumes belching from the
> motorbikes, taxis and trucks (lorries) do their part
> in polluting the air as well. So we are headed into
> about five months without rain and an increasing
> amount of dust and dry winds. These winds bring
> lots of eye diseases and meningitis in addition to
> the dusty coating of every flat surface several times

a day. We prefer the rainy season but manage to get through the dry season pretty well as long as the water in our well lasts till the rain comes in April.

By May the rains were coming more frequently, so it was much cooler, and in the evenings there was a refreshing breeze. The grass grew quickly, and the water table rose enough to fill our wells, so we could stop the bucket baths and water recycling. Here are my journal comments one summer morning.

> It reached in breath-taking splendor from the horizon to almost the zenith of the sky with mountain upon mountain of heaping billowy clouds in a myriad of gray and white shades. We stood in amazement at the cloud-filled panorama of the Nigerian sky during a sunny day in the rainy season of Jos. We never saw clouds like this in San Diego and, to be honest, we have had more rain this week than we had the whole year we were in southern California. Then there are the dark thunderclouds that precede the storms rapidly moving across the skies interrupted by the flashes of sheet and bolt lightning ripping through the dark curtain backdrop of impeding downpour. Welcome to the skies of West Africa!

The wet, slippery roads would mean more traffic and more accidents. The motorbike taxi drivers, who often don't even have a driver's license or any education on road safety, directly caused many of the trauma cases in the hospital. The general unwritten rule in Nigeria was that it was NEVER the motorcyclist's fault. Even if a motorcyclist drives into you, you are at fault and have to pay for the damages to his bike as well as your own automobile. After all, you should have moved when he was driving at you! The motorcycle taxis, called "achabas," were a huge public menace on the roads causing carnage wherever they went.

Security was a shared compound concern. Leaving Liberia during the civil war, we were more aware of the importance of good security measures, evacuation protocols and drills, and had a heightened awareness of the "prodromal" signs of impending trouble. The security situation in Jos changed dramatically during our twenty years living on the Evangel compound. In addition to the political events unfolding in the neighborhoods around us, we also faced concerns unrelated to religious or political agendas. We increasingly realized our vulnerability against armed robbers and others intent on doing us harm. Consequently, our investment in security increased. Chuck Truxton and our Nigerian friend Paul Chega led this effort, and we were all grateful for their commitment, wisdom, and cultural awareness. Nevertheless, our anxiety and stress escalated.

On Tuesday morning May 24, 2011, at 6:30 a.m., I found a Nigerian man wearing a red hoodie, smoking a cigarette, and kicking the fence where our dog is confined. I approached him to find out who he was and what he wanted. He was quite angry, demanding to see a doctor who worked at Evangel. I managed to get him out of the yard after finding out he was a nurse who worked at our hospital.

Then on Thursday he came again at 6:30 a.m. when I was at our neighbor's house in a men's prayer group. He banged on the door, waking up David and Dorothy. She locked the doors and called me to come to the house. This time I asked the three men I was praying with to join me, and again we met an angry man demanding to know where this doctor lived. The four of us persuaded him to leave, and I notified security to get him off the compound.

On Friday morning, he came again and walked right past the security guards at the security gate. They called me on the intercom phone and warned me he was on the way. I locked our yard gate and let our dog out into the yard. When the man arrived, he was furious I had let the dog out, so he began throwing stones at our dog. Fearing he would turn on me, I went inside and locked the house. Hearing the commotion, my neighbor Rick Naatz (a large 6'2" man) decided to bring his Rottweiler dog over and see if he could help! He chased the man toward the gate and along the road until the man pulled out a knife. Fortunately, the dog kept him at bay. At the security gate, the guards managed to catch him and remove his knife. He apparently had gotten a special knife and had it cursed. In his pockets were gloves and a rope, so it appears he intended to kill the doctor he was looking for. The guards kept him for several hours and concluded he was psychotic, so gave him a sedative, and took him to the university hospital where they have a psychiatric unit. Fortunately he never returned to harass us, probably because Rick Naatz and his Rottweiler dog were a formidable threat to the cigarette-smoking crazy man if he ever returned.

The missionaries as a group sometimes differed in their response to robberies and security breaches on the compound, but most of the time we shared a common concern. We chipped in to increase the height of the security wall and add razor wire, increased the number of security guards patrolling the housing areas at night, improved the steel gate guarding the entrance to the housing area of the hospital compound, fixed the road security light countless times, and installed an alarm system that triggered a siren we could all hear in times of distress. We organized contingency plans if there was another attack, set up code terms if one of us was taken hostage, installed an intercom system between our houses and made sure we all had walkie-talkies to communicate in the event of a security situation. This all required a great deal of effort and time.

It is easy to fall into the rut of always focusing on the bad things about Nigeria and life in Jos, but there were also wonderful aspects. We loved the beautiful countryside with green mountains and amazing rock formations. We were grateful for the happy and hospitable people, praying Christians who believe in miracles and a God who answers prayer. Nigeria gave us rich traditional music sung by choreographed choirs that rocked the church in praise to God, food with spices and seasonings that were delicious, creative and energetic people who were resourceful with little and thankful for what they had, ambitious young people desiring a better education, and people whose faith in a sovereign, loving God challenged our faith and improved our prayer life by their example of intercessory communion with God!

JANKWANO

As a general surgeon, having a good working relationship with the Operating Room staff was critical. Evangel Hospital had nurse anesthetists, nurses to scrub and circulate during the surgical cases, aides and cleaning staff. One of the Nigerian male nurse anesthetists named Bako had just put one of my first patients to sleep in the Evangel Hospital Operating Room, and we were draping the patient for a thyroid operation. When I looked up, Bako asked me an interesting question, "How much blood do you usually transfuse in a thyroid case?" (This was an indirect way of asking how good a surgeon I was.)

I replied, "I rarely ever give a blood transfusion during a thyroid case."

He smiled, and I knew we were off to a good start.

Even though I had been practicing surgery for six years (four of which were at the ELWA Hospital in Liberia), one aspect of coming to a new place is to figure out how your way of doing things syncs with the precedents and traditions already well established in an institution. Although reasonably confident in my surgical skills, I knew I needed to learn a lot about the Nigerian culture and the challenge of learning the hospital and medical culture at the hospital locally named Jankwano – which in the Hausa language means "red roof."

I finished my residency in general surgery at Baylor University Medical Center in Dallas, Texas. I had been doing mostly trauma surgery in a hospital in Fort Worth as I was preparing to go to Nigeria so felt a bit rusty on many of the general surgical procedures I knew I would face. The only other surgeon at the hospital was Dr. Steve Arrowsmith, a urologist. He was very excited I had arrived to do the general surgical cases. I was thrilled to handle whatever situation walked in the door and felt confident I could manage a thyroid goiter case. I did not ask for a blood transfusion for this thyroid case, and so began my surgical career at Jankwano.

Since its beginning in 1893, SIM had a long tradition of medical ministries in Nigeria. In spite of the horrific fact that many of the early missionaries died going to "the white man's grave" of sub-Saharan Africa, missionaries continued to settle in unreached towns and villages. On almost every mission station a small clinic was set up to care for those with various illnesses from dysentery to malaria and a host of other tropical ailments. Many missionary wives with little or no medical training cared for those who came knocking on their doors at all hours of the night – mothers carrying infants with fever, a woman in obstructed labor, a man with a laceration from a machete, and babies with pneumonia and tetanus. Pressing farther into the North, however, was a problem because the colonial British rulers would only allow Christian missionaries into the Muslim northern areas if they were willing to care for people afflicted with the dreaded leprosy. SIM subsequently built leprosy hospitals throughout northern Nigeria, and their outreach grew from those footholds.

In many major cities the British government built hospitals, which they turned over to the Nigerian government at Independence. In Jos, the government built a federal teaching hospital called Jos University Teaching Hospital (JUTH), and the Plateau State government built Plateau Specialist Hospital. SIM missionary Dr. Andrew Stirret conducted open-air clinics in the market for years without a mission hospital facility. As the number of missionaries increased in the country, the need for good medical care for missionaries became obvious. SIM opened a small hospital called Bingham Hospital in Jos primarily for the care of expatriate missionaries in Northern Nigeria. Named after Roland Bingham, one of the three founding members of SIM, it was staffed by SIM missionary nurses, doctors, and laboratory and x-ray technicians. There was a Delivery Room and one Operating Room at one end of the six-room semi-private ward wing. The lab, x-ray and administration offices were along the other wing of the L-shaped building. The nurses' and the doctors' houses were on the hospital compound. My sister, brothers, and I were born at Bingham Hospital.

Several of the SIM doctors with a heart for helping the Nigerians were frustrated that there was no hospital facility to serve as a local medical Christian witness. In 1957 ground was purchased on the outskirts of Jos, and in February 1959 a hospital and houses for the missionary doctors were built, and the hospital opened to care for Nigerian patients. It was named Evangel Hospital. After several years of operation, it became apparent that there was unnecessary redundancy of equipment and personnel trying to keep two hospitals open in the same city. So Bingham Hospital was closed and a wing called the Bingham Ward was opened at Evangel as a semi-private ward.

SIM doctors also saw the importance of training Nigerians in health care, so a school was started to train community health workers to staff clinics all over the middle belt region of Nigeria. Later a nursing school was started and eventually a residency program to train Nigerian physicians in family medicine.

SIM turned over the ownership and administration of the hospital to the ECWA Church in the 70s. This meant that the hospital governing board would be responsible to the ECWA church and not SIM, and the missionaries would be under the authority of the medical director appointed by the church hospital board. SIM continued to provide doctors, nursing staff and other personnel but believed it was time for the church to manage the day-to-day operations and future direction of the medical ministry.

Evangel Hospital is located inside a walled compound on a busy street on the northwest side of the city of Jos. Unlike the more common grey concrete blocks used around the rest of the compound, the front red brick wall borders the twin entrance gates and the sometimes lighted sign over the guard hut.

In front of the outpatient building, there is a large, partially paved parking lot with shack provision stores serving hot cooked food. The shops are packed with all sorts of things a patient or relative might need: snack food and beverages, toilet paper, soap, candles, matches, diapers, bottled water and candies. My girls and David liked me to bring them to these little shops for a treat since there were so few shopping options for them within walking distance of the house.

Like most mission hospitals, Evangel Hospital was built a little at a time and reflects the various ideas and needs of each period of its history. The groundbreaking ceremony was November 13, 1957. The first building was the long front (current outpatient) building which Dr. Lonnie Grant dedicated February 15, 1959. After climbing the steps to the main entrance of this building, the first room on the right is the Card Room where patients register, get their outpatient medical record cards, and where the inpatient medical charts are stored.

The outpatient waiting area is a large, dark, open room with a few translucent ceiling panels. Various offices, examination rooms, the billing office, and the dental clinic surround the waiting room. Usually a few people from out of town sleep on the benches over night since they have nowhere else to go.

We have had a few disasters at the hospital including riots and mass casualties from bus accidents, so Dr. Greg Kirschner, a family practice missionary physician, thought it would be helpful to have mass casualty training and drills to equip the staff to handle these situations more professionally and efficiently. After preparing each cadre of staff on their role in a mass casualty exercise, we organized a surprise mass casualty drill. Greg contacted a drama group from the church across the road and gave each of the 20 in the group a role to play. Some had head injuries, chest injuries, burns, or minor injuries. Others played family members of the injured, press and television personnel, or curious onlookers. They dressed in torn clothes, sprinkled with dirt and a generous spreading of ketchup. We prepared the mass casualty forms and equipment box and then set aside a Saturday to do the drill, including hiring a video photographer to film the event for our review. On the day of the drill the actors were driven to the emergency room door, the van blaring its horn and racing into the compound. The "patients" were unloaded into the hospital and the staff was supposed to begin. Some staff performed well, a few just froze, while others didn't take it seriously or didn't even show up to help. The screaming and carrying on of the actors was so realistic that the real patients and visitors in the waiting areas were alarmed and wondered why we were not doing more to rescue these dying people. After the drill, we had a group assessment time, and it was helpful to point out to the staff their strengths and areas needing improvement.

The "injection room" or emergency room at the end of this building used to be the Operating Room where I watched my first surgery as a young boy. Between the emergency room and the main entrance waiting area are the physical therapy and x-ray departments. Along the outside hallway there are benches packed with patients waiting to be attended to by the staff. Just beyond the emergency room is a separate smaller building housing the eye care department. This building was built from funds donated by a family whose son was in an ophthalmology residency when he died a few years ago. The family wanted to build an eye clinic on the mission field in memory of their son, so the Mark Lovett Eye Clinic is now a busy ministry with two ophthalmologists and several Nigerian staff.

On the way back to the waiting room is the pharmacy. A major problem in Nigeria is the problem of fake drugs on the market. It is challenging to determine which drug suppliers are reliable and selling us the real thing. If a patient is not responding well to medication, we switch to another drug or brand of the same drug because of the concern of counterfeit medications.

Next on the tour is a clinic for patients wanting to be seen by a senior physician, the crisis pregnancy ministry offices, the optical shop, and the old laboratory. Beside this building are the new laboratory building, the **PEPFAR HIV** treatment clinic, and the administration building.

Unfortunately, behind the laboratory was the refuse burn pit. This is a large pile of hospital garbage that burns or smolders like the burning fires of Hades but never seems to completely consume the rubbish. Rats, roaches, dogs, and other vermin gather around it. It was disturbing to see dogs rummaging through the garbage heap when I knew there were blood products and medical waste that the dogs were eating. A few years ago the Quality Control Committee of the hospital was upset to learn from patient exit surveys that one of the main criticisms about the hospital was the garbage, roaches, rats, and the general uncleanliness of the hospital. Subsequently a large incinerator was built near the generator building to burn the medical waste and reduce the risk of transmission of diseases and rodents in the hospital area.

The next large building on the circular tour houses the private ward, amenity ward, intensive care unit, and Operating Room. The main entrance to the building has a beautiful small rock façade and cement awning that opens into a small waiting area, doctors' library, and a nurses' conference room. The hallway to the right is the Bingham Ward, which has seven semi-private rooms. Behind the nurses' station is the four-room Amenity Ward with private rooms and more amenities.

To the left from the waiting area is the four-bed Intensive Care Unit (ICU). The next rooms on the left are for taking care of the surgery outpatients who need sutures removed, wounds drained, or a cast put on or taken off. They are always busy, and at night there are people sleeping on mats huddled under their blankets from the cold night air and mosquitoes.

Next room on the right is my office. It is a shared office for four consultants or senior attending physicians. I keep most of my surgery textbooks, journals, and some medical supplies and equipment in this office because it is conveniently close to the Operating Rooms. The next rooms are the changing rooms for the Operating Room staff and the scope room used for doing most of the outpatient scopes.

The main Operating Rooms are at the end of the building. There are also the anesthesia recovery areas, the sterilizers, area for preparing the surgical packs, and a shipping container with extra instruments and equipment. This is where I have spent hundreds of hours treating thousands of patients.

The main Operating Rooms are equipped with mostly donated anesthesia machines, automatic blood pressure machines, pulse oximeters, and electrocautery machines. The operating tables are manual because I did not want to have a table get stuck during a power outage. We converted the main Operating Room lights from using 110-volt bulbs to a 220-volt system, so we could get the bulbs locally and not have to import them from the States. We also installed a 110-volt system for each Operating Room connected to a stabilizer to reduce the damage to the instruments from electrical spikes and surges. The oxygen is still in large tanks that are wheeled in and out of the rooms as needed.

Patients are brought each morning to the anesthesia waiting area outside the two Operating Rooms where the anesthesia nurses evaluate them. After surgery, they are brought back to the same area for observation until they are stable enough to return to their rooms. This waiting area is also used for doing procedures like burn dressings done under an anesthetic delivered by a nurse anesthetist.

A key leader in the Operating Room for most of my years at Evangel was Simon Khantiok. He was making a fraction of the salary he could make working at a government hospital and doing twice the work. He worked as a nurse in the pediatric ward for many years and acquired the name Baba Yara – "father of children." He became interested in anesthesia, got his nurse anesthesia training, and became the lead nurse anesthetist and Operating Room nurse manager. We worked together for hundreds of hours doing surgical cases. He enjoyed teaching and had a godly influence on his staff and others in the Evangel community.

Simon occasionally came to me for encouragement and affirmation that it was worth it to stay at Evangel. I was always relieved that he still wanted to stay and proceeded to share from my heart and experience that we faced many of the same pressures. I believed God had given me the assignment to use my gifts to serve Him here at Evangel. I challenged Simon that if God had given him the same assignment, God would provide for his needs. I was greatly encouraged that the Lord had provided wonderful people to work with in this mission hospital, people who served the Lord sacrificially in order to be part of His Kingdom work.

The next buildings on the tour are the maternity ward, the pediatric clinic, and pediatric ward. There is always a mother or father who stays with each child since they must feed, bathe, and care for the children. The nurses dispense medication and do wound care.

The largest wards are the general male and female wards. The first ward is the 16-bed open male ward for surgical patients. This is where the majority of my patients were cared for during my tenure at Evangel. At the end of the ward high on the back wall is a television monitor, which usually has the *Jesus* film or other religious films playing. The ward has patients with orthopedic problems, urology cases, burn and plastic surgery cases, head and neck problems, abdominal surgery patients and so on. The diversity of specialties is pretty typical for a mission hospital but usually challenges the average general surgeon from the West who is visiting the hospital. The male medical ward has an open ward for patients admitted with medical problems like high blood pressure, diabetes or AIDS and several semi-private rooms for any male patients needing isolation.

The female ward is similar to the male ward in layout, but all the female surgery and medical patients are in the one large open ward. Behind the female ward is a smaller ward for the eye patients, and off the nurses' station towards the front of the hospital is the 20-bed VVF Ward. VVF means "vesicovaginal fistula" and describes a condition caused by obstructed childbirth. When women cannot deliver the baby because either the baby is too big or lying the wrong way, the constant pressure of the baby pushed against the pelvic organs by the contracting uterus causes erosion of a hole between the woman's vagina and her bladder or between her vagina and rectum. The baby dies and eventually is delivered. The woman is then left with a hole between her pelvic organs, so she is incontinent of urine or stool or both. This problem used to be common in Europe and North America until there was improved access to good prenatal and maternity care.

Because of the smell of urine from these women, they are rejected by their husbands and families and are often destitute. Some resort to prostitution, but most return to their mother's home to survive. In 1992 Evangel began a focused initiative to reach these women and help them with physical, emotional and spiritual healing. The program has helped over 5,000 women in the last ten years and has now expanded to include an extensive rehabilitation program, physical therapy, literacy, and vocational skills training. The women are given free room, board, medical and surgical care and transport money to return to their village, all through the generous gifts of many donors in Nigeria and around the world – a remarkable testimony of God's provision.

The remarkable physician in charge of the VVF Project is Dr. Sunday Lengmang. He finished the Evangel family medicine residency and expressed an interest in staying on as a trainee in the VVF program. With the help of Nigerian gynecologist Dr. Jonathan Karshima, missionary surgeons like Dr. Caroline Kirschner and others, Sunday became an expert VVF surgeon. He eventually assumed the leadership of the VVF Project. He was not only competent technically but was an outstanding leader of the group demonstrating Christ-like love and compassion to the women who came with desperate stories and tragic lives. He was respected by the staff, loved by his patients, and admired by the missionary physicians with whom he worked. He made trips to remote places in Nigeria where there was a large number of fistula patients and trained the local physicians to perform the surgery, offering to treat the complicated ones at Evangel. This networking was a huge benefit to the underserved patients in these communities and was good public relations for Evangel Hospital.

Sunday also presented the amazing work of the Evangel VVF Project at Nigerian national VVF meetings, West Africa Regional conferences, and international venues. Dr. Lengmang earned kudos internationally for his clinical work, creative holistic program, and congeniality. At an international VVF conference in East Africa he presented the unique emphasis of the Evangel VVF Project's goal to present Christ as the ultimate hope for these women. Many of the physicians at the meeting came up to him later remarking, "That is what we want to do. We want to present Christ as well. Tell us how you are doing that."

We had the privilege of getting to know his wife and children as well and have great admiration for Sunday as a husband and father. He is a wonderful example of the incalculable value of investing in young people eager to learn medicine and grow spiritually. As we watched his metamorphosis from resident to world-class leader, we are grateful for the privilege of being a part of the process of God working in his life.

Behind the VVF ward is a 30-bed hostel for women who are either waiting for their surgery or waiting to go home. The hostel has a kitchen and laundry area in addition to a small outpatient clinic, offices for the surgeons and staff, and a room for the sewing and knitting machines used in the rehabilitation vocational training.

These women are the happiest in the hospital as their faces reflect the new joy in their hearts since they have been made dry. These "dry evangelists" are the best advertising we could possibly imagine for the program since many return to their homes and tell others with this affliction where they can find help.

On the lower side of the hospital road are the laundry unit, the 200-seat Chapel of Compassion, and the generator shed which also serves as the "office" for the maintenance staff. When we arrived there was only one small generator that had been there for at least ten years. It was too small for the growing needs of the hospital and residential area, so we raised funds to purchase a larger generator. God supplied through several generous donors, and we installed a much larger 165 KVA generator in the summer of 2005. Each building on the hospital compound is indeed a gift from God as He has supplied the funds through generous donors, both abroad and within Nigeria.

In 2009, the Evangel Hospital celebrated 50 years of service. Alumni missionaries, former staff and patients, church officials and mission leaders were invited for the weekend reunion. All the celebrations were a reminder of God's faithfulness and a wonderful tribute to the hundreds of Nigerians and expatriates who have served sacrificially – all committed to the singular goal of reaching people with the saving Gospel of Jesus Christ through medical care. To God be the glory. The challenge continues for the hospital to be a Christian witness for another 50 years serving all for whom Christ died.

THE DUSTY ROAD

It is only a quarter of a mile long. I know every nuanced curve and irritating pothole. The road has never been paved. Only occasionally a few truckloads of red gravel laterite are spread over its potholed surface. In the dry season its slippery gravel top is dusty; but when the rains come, the pounding of every car tire packs the clay, deepening every pothole until it becomes "washboard."

Like a towering guard along the western edge runs a ten-foot-high cement block wall with circular, coiled barbed wire strung along its top border. Plastic bags caught in the pointed barbs flutter in the breeze like miniature scarecrows. There are a few holes in the wall that are helpful to see what is happening on the polo grounds next door, but unfortunately they also serve as footholds for small intruders. The most interesting side is the right side. After leaving our yard and turning right onto the dusty road, there are the homes of the staff and missionaries, the former Community Health offices transformed into Bingham University School of Medicine classrooms and dorms, and then the gate with its boom bar and ten-foot-high steel plate double doors.

There is a small fork in the road with the right path heading past the AIDS counseling center, laundry, red-roofed new mortuary, hospital chapel, petrol dump, rusty zinc-roofed cooking shed for the families of the women in the fistula program, and the above-ground diesel tanks in front of the generator shed surrounded by cluttered piles of spare wood, pipes and "dead" hospital equipment. Finally, as you make the last gentle left turn (this is probably the worst stretch of the road as far as potholes go), you pass the hospital restaurant or cafeteria with its crooked Coca-Cola sign and beauty salon and are greeted by the guards sitting at the hospital front gate handing out the compulsory blue plastic cards to visitors, so they can monitor for stolen cars.

If you take a left at the fork near the inner gate, which is my preferred route to the hospital, you pass to the left of the Spring of Life HIV/AIDS counseling center and the decorative red block waiting room for the maternity unit, and then the parking lot beside the Operating Room theaters and pediatric ward.

I know this road like the back of my hand and could probably negotiate it blindfolded because not only is it my commuting route to work every day but also it is the path of my morning exercise walk. I normally get up at 5 a.m., have devotions for 30 minutes, try to get some overdue emails sent and then at 6 a.m., after waking my wife, Dorothy, I don my walking clothes, running shoes and iPod for my 30 minutes of daily exercise as the sun is rising. I can do two return trips to the far end of the hospital property before coming in for a shower and breakfast with my family.

Every morning it is wonderful to see the sun rise with a pink and blue palette of colors splashed in a new pattern every day. In spite of being 10^0 north of the equator, it is so cool on my walks I normally wear a sweatshirt and occasionally a bright red winter down jacket. I love the quietness of these morning moments before even the birds are awake. On the horizon I see the outlines of the city buildings with the minarets of the mosque silhouetted against the rising sunlight.

Recently there have been more cell phone towers that I call "horizon pollution." Another activity I am drawn to is picking up nails along the way hoping to save someone from a bad day having to visit the local "vulcanizer" to patch a tire puncture. I am greeted on the road at dawn by a few regular early risers: two Nigerian housewives with loads of pots, pans, firewood, and oil skillfully balanced on their heads. They are making their way from their homes to their appointed spots along the main road to cook *kosai* (bean cakes) and yam slices for those needing a fast food breakfast on their way to work. Occasionally I meet a family practice resident or intern wearily returning to their apartment after a night on call, hoping to take a shower and catch a quick bite to eat before the morning report meeting and the new day's challenges.

I know all the guards at the inner gate with their different working styles. Some stay in the guardroom, and I have to call them to let me through. Others vigilantly wait for my arrival and open the massive gate for me to pass on my appointed rounds. Then on mornings when I am doing surgical cases, I stop in at the Operating Room to check and see who was admitted for elective surgery, so I can list the order I would like to do the cases and make sure they are ready. The women on duty are at the end of their night shift and are sometimes resting on the stretchers in the Recovery Area or are doing their final mopping and cleaning before going home for a rest.

This dusty road is not just a well-trodden path for me because it's my way to work; it is my "getting mentally and spiritually ready for the day" time. I vary my iPod selections between sermons, surgical continuing education topics, and music. I must admit I do love a few NPR podcasts like "Prairie Home Companion," "Car Talk," "Fresh Air" and "Foreign Correspondent." Another favorite audio "breakfast for the brain" is a selection from a Christian view of culture series. My musical taste varies from classical to the jazz of Michael Bublé and a wide range of Christian music.

Most importantly this morning quiet time is my review with God of my day ahead – the surgical challenges, the difficult personalities I must face, the thorny issues in our mission or challenges I face on various committees and boards. As I reflect and wait, God often works in my heart and mind to soften my position, calm my heart or even give me a new idea or exciting project or ministry to meet a need. In prayer (sometimes even out loud), I adore God's greatness and majesty, confess my shortcomings and sins, give thanks for His blessing me so richly with a wonderful wife and four amazing children, then close in supplication asking for His help with the many challenges of living and working in Africa with the relentless stresses of life and the intermittent tension and anxiety of trauma in our family or the community.

In the quiet of those twilight hours I can sing, shout or whisper to the Lord the deepest longings of my heart knowing He alone hears my cry. He sometimes calms my heart, but I know at least He has heard and He knows what to do. So the road is familiar, the sights not especially exciting or interesting, but it is significant to me because of the inter-heavenly process that takes place every morning at 6 a.m. on that dusty road.

A REAL SURPRISE

We went to Nigeria in March 1992, and that fall over the course of several weeks I began feeling unusually tired and weak and noticed my skin and eyes began turning yellow. I also had severe pain in the right side of my stomach. Finally we came to the obvious conclusion I had viral hepatitis. My weakness and abdominal pain was so severe we ended up returning to the United States for several weeks for additional tests and recuperation.

Dorothy and I had decided to try to have another baby as soon as we were back in Nigeria, but my unexpected illness delayed that decision. When I began to regain my strength, we decided it was time to try for our second child. In March 1993, Dorothy suspected she was pregnant and checked with a quick pregnancy test kit she had brought from the United States. We were both ecstatic when it was positive. In calculating the due date, we figured we would have a late November baby.

It soon became obvious that there were several things about this pregnancy that were unusual, or at least different from Dorothy's pregnancy with Marie. For one thing she gained weight quickly and by seven months looked enormous, even though she had only gained 25 pounds. Prophetically, two years earlier while dining out at a restaurant one evening in the States, the hostess, who was a complete stranger, looked at Dorothy and for some reason said to her, "You will have twins some day." We took her remark about as seriously as we took the fortune cookie message we opened after the meal. When Dorothy was farther along in the pregnancy, the head of the Nursing Department at Evangel greeted Dorothy by calling her "Mama yan biyu." In the Hausa language this means, "the mother of twins." Again, we thought her comments a bit foolish.

In spite of Dorothy's huge abdominal profile, after examining her repeatedly, her obstetricians insisted she was NOT having twins. They were so convinced they refused to do a sonogram, but I decided do one anyway. One afternoon we went to my office, and I pulled out the small, old portable sonogram machine with its three-inch screen and looked for two babies. We saw only one clearly, and then there was this curtain effect with something like a hand waving behind it. We had placed a small bet with each other, and I won because we only saw one baby and it looked as if Dorothy was not having twins.

In spite of her size, Dorothy was very active throughout the pregnancy and even hiked up a volcano with the family at Miango. At about six months, Dorothy began to have excruciating pain in her groin. Her doctors examined her and decided it was not from too much exercise, appendicitis, kidney stones, or any other infection and was probably just her uterus stretching from the pregnancy. When Dorothy commented that the baby was a very active kicker, we suspected it was a boy.

Tuesday October 19, 1993

After a busy day at the hospital, I decided to go home about 4:30 p.m. Dorothy and Marie (now two years old) sometimes came and walked home with me, so I called Dorothy and asked her and Marie to meet me on the way. Marie was at a cute age, so these walks became opportunities to explore, talk about everything she discovered along the dusty meandering road, and finally run to give me a hug when she saw me. We had a leisurely walk along the dusty quarter mile road to our house. Dr. Randal Bailey (a New Zealand family physician) came by on his bicycle, and we chatted with him as we walked.

Just about halfway home, Dorothy interrupted our conversation with "My water just broke!" When I turned, I saw her with a red face and fluid running down her legs. She hurried on home while I followed at a more relaxed pace with Marie and Randal. When we got home I found Dorothy standing in the shower because she was draining so much fluid. She was puffing heavily like she was having strong contractions, so I told her to try to slow down and not push while I hurriedly took Marie to the Blyths and told her doctor, Bev Truxton, that Dorothy had gone into active labor.

By the time I got back, Dorothy was in serious labor and having even stronger contractions. When Bev arrived, I told her the contractions were three minutes apart, so she said she would meet us at the hospital. I wondered whether Dorothy should just lie down on the bed, but she insisted, "Let's go! Let's go!" Like a chicken with his head cut off trying to collect my thoughts, I gathered the bags and helped Dorothy to the car. She maneuvered into the front seat of our old white Peugeot, and I threw the bags in the back seat. As soon as I got into the car, Dorothy started puffing and panting from the strong contractions. She said she had to push and I kept telling her, "Breathe. Breathe. Don't push!" She cried out that she couldn't help it because the urge was too strong.

I was driving the old Peugeot as fast as I safely could on the potholed winding road, but when we turned the corner on the road half way to the hospital, she had another contraction and said, "I feel better now." I glanced over at her and saw a baby's head emerging between Dorothy's legs on the car seat. While still driving, I grabbed the baby's shoulder, pulled the baby out, and put the child on Dorothy's lap. I was so relieved to see the baby breathing and not looking blue. Then, looking carefully at the baby I told Dorothy, "It's a girl." I figured she was born around 5:28 p.m. in the front seat of our Peugeot car at the bend in the road. (We now call this

"Heather's Corner"!) Racing on, I finally pulled the car into the maternity hospital parking lot.

When we arrived, I ran in and got a Nigerian midwife who came and clamped and cut the baby's umbilical cord. I carried the baby to the newborn nursery for a checkup while the midwife helped Dorothy walk to the Delivery Room to deliver the placenta. Bev Truxton showed up then and we told her, "You're too late. Dorothy's already had the baby. It's a girl." She said she would stay anyway and help with the delivery of the placenta.

When Dorothy took off her dress and got onto the delivery table, Bev looked at Dorothy's large abdomen and remarked, "There must be another one." When Dorothy looked at her stomach she couldn't believe it either, but it sure looked like there was something still inside. Dorothy then told the midwife, "Go. Tell Maigida (Bill) the news." When the midwife did not move, Dorothy yelled at her again, "Go. Tell Maigida the news!" (It is not good to mess with a woman in labor!)

When the midwife came to the newborn nursery across the hall and told me there was another baby on the way, I loudly exclaimed "Kai!" (a Nigerian exclamation that can mean almost anything). Dorothy said she heard me all the way over in the Delivery Room! I rushed in and saw Bev helping Dorothy push out baby #2. I jumped in by her side as "coach" and helped Dorothy with her breathing and pushing to get #2 two out. After about 15 minutes the second one was born, also a girl. The midwife whisked baby #2 off to the nursery to get weighed and cleaned. Dorothy's total labor was 45 minutes from the time her water broke until the last twin was out. Wow! In a state of shock, we both started laughing at this surprise turn of events.

I went back to the nursery to see both girls. By this time, two of our doctors, Mike Blyth and Mark Sauerwein, arrived to check on "the" baby. They were dumbfounded. After laughing with them and taking a few pictures of the twins, I called our neighbor Robin Bailey and told her, "Dorothy just delivered twin girls." She replied, "Bill,

JOURNEY ON A DUSTY ROAD

stop kidding. How's Dorothy doing?" I again repeated, "Dorothy just delivered twin girls." She screamed in disbelief. After composing herself she agreed to bring Marie and the Blyth family to see the twins.

Dorothy was brought over to the Amenity Ward with the twins, and we got all of them comfortable. Interestingly, Dorothy had packed two of each baby clothing item in her hospital bag! The staff started pouring in to see the girls and to offer congratulations. It was both funny and exciting – all at the same time. We all kept saying "Kai. How could Phil Andrew and Bev Truxton – her doctors – and me all be fooled and completely miss the twins?" For the rest of the evening we had a nonstop line of visitors, including missionaries from all over Jos and lots of the Nigerian staff. They brought Dorothy some food and drink and everyone wanted to hold and help with the babies.

Because the phones were not reliable, I went back to the house about 7:30 p.m. to get on the HAM radio to tell our families in the United States the news. I got through to Don Hammond at Camp of the Woods in upstate New York via a HAM network and asked him to call our parents. No one answered Dorothy's parents' phone, so he left a voicemail message. In shock and disbelief, upon her return Dorothy's mother replayed the message several times.

Since our phone was not working, I went over to the Truxton's house and waited for any phone calls from our families. My mother called first from Tucson, Arizona, where she was visiting my sister. Mom and Sharon were both excited at the news and had said they had been trying for days to get through on the phone. Then a few minutes later my dad called from California. He was also excited and of course had a joke about having lots of babies.

The word of the twins' arrival was quickly spread around via Chuck Truxton, so we had a constant stream of visitors that night. Finally, we had some quiet time together and again were in wonder at the exciting thing that had happened to us. We paused to thank the Lord and dedicate the girls to the Lord. What a day!

Bev came by and checked Dorothy's blood pressure and was surprised it was 170/120! For a while we had thought about going home but then felt it better to stay at the hospital where Dorothy could be checked overnight. The bed was also higher, making it easier for her to get in and out of it. Bev ordered some IV medicine for her blood pressure and then had the nurses check her blood pressure hourly all night, so she did not get much sleep. Fortunately, the twins ate at 11 p.m. and slept pretty well until 5 a.m. We were so relieved they had a good night. Little did we know how little sleep we would be getting over the next few years!

All that evening and the next day Dorothy and I worked through our list of names for the second baby. We had one name picked out if it was a boy and one for a girl. Although Anna Louise was the original girl's name we had chosen, we decided to name the first-born Heather, as she was smaller and daintier, and chose Joy as her middle name, which described our feelings over the past 24 hours. We ended up naming our second daughter Anna Louise. Shock and amazement still had us shaking our heads.

We began to work out how we were going to cope with having twins. Since Dorothy's time was monopolized with Heather and Anna, I spent more time caring for and playing with Marie. The wicker basket bassinet we had purchased was too small for both of the twins, so we decided to separate them to keep them from waking each other up. We put Anna in the wicker basket, and Heather slept in a drawer from my bureau until we got a crib set up. Eventually they both slept in one crib in our bedroom.

Over the next few days Dorothy tried to get some rest, and I tried to spend special time with Marie, so she would not feel left out with all the excitement over the twins. Between the onslaught of visitors and the twins irregular sleeping and feeding schedule, we were both exhausted. The next two years we called, "The Blur." I remember one night getting up to get one of the girls and after she had fed, taking her back to her bed. A few minutes later I thought the other one cried, and in my fatigue I ended up bringing the same one back to Dorothy for a snack, but she was clearly not hungry!

Initially we let the girls sleep, and when one was hungry, I would get up and bring the hungry one to Dorothy. This is called the "demand" approach, but it didn't take us too long to realize with this approach we never slept! As soon as one was back to sleep, the other one woke up hungry. So we changed to a "demand-schedule" approach which meant whoever demanded the food first, scheduled the other one to eat at the same time! This allowed us to get a little more sleep. Dorothy's nickname soon became "The Dairy Queen" because of her new line of work!

As the feeding frequency decreased over the next few months, we also began to take turns sleeping in different bedrooms to allow one of us to get a little more sleep. It seemed that when one baby woke up crying, the other also woke up and cried, so it was about four years before we both were able to sleep through the night.

When Heather and Anna were in bed together, they were usually "spooning" – lying close to each other facing the same direction. So when one rolled over, the other rolled as well. Heather started crawling first, but when Anna started crawling, she crawled backwards – I guess so she could keep an eye on her sister! When they started walking, Anna did it the usual way, but Heather was in such a hurry, she would stand up and then leap forward instead of taking steps. It took her a little longer to really walk, but Heather eventually got there.

Later in the first year, when they were getting around a bit more, we would find they had switched cribs during the night and were in each other's cribs. Sometimes they would end up in the same crib. We never knew when we put them in their cribs how they would end up in the morning. One night we heard a strange thumping sound coming from their room. When I couldn't stand it any more, I wandered down the hall to their room. When I opened their door, I found Heather and Anna lying on their stomachs on the floor with a plastic bottle of baby powder. They were both giggling as they thumped it on the floor and watched the spray of powder shower all over the room. The floor and beds were covered with a fine layer of baby powder, and they were having the time of their little lives. It was so funny that we couldn't get angry with them but instead just laughed and laughed and tried to clean the mess up a bit before getting them back into their cribs.

On another afternoon, during naptime, things got unusually quiet. When you have active twins, quiet is not always a good sign. We ventured silently to their room to see if they were sleeping or if something else was going on. To our astonishment when we opened the door, they were both standing in the middle of the room covered from head to toe with Vaseline ointment. One of them had climbed on the changing table, found the Vaseline, and, after applying it generously to her hair and head, decided she needed to share the fun with her sister. We never quite figured out who was the instigator, but it took a few days of baths to get out the last of the Vaseline from their hair. Never a dull moment for a long, long time.

THE NIGERIA FACTOR

The "Nigeria Factor" is a popular topic among expatriates living in Nigeria and a part of the daily struggle of life. In a word, it is the cumulative stress of inefficiency in support services like water, electricity and phone, the irritations of careless and reckless motorbike, taxi and truck drivers, the incessant parade of people at your door begging for help, the 419ers[3] who zinged you when you least expected it, and the exasperation of how long it takes to get most things done in Nigeria. Everything takes longer. The Nigeria Factor is an undercurrent of stresses that everyone faces on a daily basis, but it seems to affect expats more. Sometimes the normal pressures of living in an adopted culture mix with the tensions of interpersonal relationships. When piled onto tired or sick missionaries, the result is a meltdown or burnout.

Cycle of Life

After being in Nigeria only a short time, I landed on a theory for accepting the vicissitudes life threw at us daily. I called it the "Cycle of Life." Usually on the first week of the month something electrical falls apart in your house causing frustration and delays, and an

---

[3] Scam artists recently known for their online and email appeals asking for help to get money out of the country.

interruption of your daily routine. We went to great lengths to avoid this with backup systems including a small generator for our house when the power failed and a 12-volt system to run lights in every room, the TV, computers, and coffee machine. Just when you get that sorted out, week two presents a problem with the water supply or plumbing; you are forced into taking bucket baths, conserving every drop until you can find the plumber. The countermeasure was a water backup system with two wells and several reserve tanks. Week three involves major car problems like the transmission or back axle needing repair. The only backup was having two cars and eventually getting a driver who could deal with these problems without causing us endless frustrations. Once I took our car to a mechanic for repair and found out he had fixed a carburetor leak by stuffing a rag around it! The last week of the month is often the worst because the attack is something electronic — the computers or video system. This drove me especially crazy, so I learned early on to back up my computers regularly and knew who in the community could rescue a crashed hard drive. Often the inciting demon was the wild electrical power surges, sometimes spiking to 400 volts, enough to fry anything attached including nearby structures.

Take heart though, because it starts all over again the next month, but not necessarily in the same order. This is the "Cycle of Life" in Nigeria! Knowing this secret did not alter the cycle, but it did help us face the inevitable with more courage and hope! As we developed backup systems, the amplitude of the waves of despair flattened a bit.

We tell people in the United States, "It takes a lot longer to live in Nigeria." The basic things in life just take longer to get done. Getting anything fixed, getting anything done in the bank or a government office, getting parts or supplies from here or abroad, getting people to change or systems to improve – it all takes longer than you could possibly imagine. For example, the to-do list of things falling apart burgeons daily. Here is a partial annotated list from a week in 2008:

- Well pump – burned out and replaced
- Ground pump – burned out and replaced
- Ground pump wiring – burned out and replaced
- Ground water tank leaking – will wait to fix when the heavy rains are over
- Security lights for the house – most burned out – fixed
- 12-volt lights in every room – 50 percent not working – still need to be fixed
- Toilet in girls' bathroom leaking – fixed this week
- Internet access at our house – still only partially working
- Clothes dryer stopped working – sent repairman to a city three hours away for parts and, after a lot of money, it is now working.
- Satellite radio speakers – not working

The good news is that our van, the washing machine, and the stove have not broken down... yet.

WATER – "Water, water everywhere and not a drop to drink."[4]

When we first arrived in Jos, the supply of city water was reasonable – meaning we got water about every other day. The first apartment we lived in had a water storage tank on a 20-foot-high tower behind the apartment block. People living in three adjacent apartments shared this water source. The two problems that surfaced immediately were that often the city water pressure was not strong enough to push the water up to the water tank, so we ran out of water regularly. The other obvious problem was that some people consume more water than others or were not as careful about leaving taps on, so we were victims of the consumption habits of our neighbors.

After about a year we moved into a much larger four-bedroom, single-family house and became masters of our own water supply – or so we thought. Over the years, the reliability of the city water supply

---

4 "The Rime of the Ancient Mariner," Samuel Taylor Coleridge, 1798.

deteriorated, getting city water about every two weeks for an hour or so and eventually no city water at all! This situation accelerated into a crisis as our family expanded and our water needs grew – diapers, multiple loads of laundry, and so on. Our first backup plan was to build a large underground concrete water storage tank. The idea was that if the water pressure was weak, an underground tank would get any water coming, even if it didn't have enough pressure to make it up to the tower tank. This idea was actually brilliant, and we ended up over the years getting more city water than anyone on the compound because of our low-pressure strategy.

It became apparent during the dry season when we were getting water every few weeks that our storage capacity was still inadequate. We worked out an organized approach to water recycling that at times was heroic. "Every drop of water can be used at least three times" became the slogan. Of course we took so-called Navy showers (turn water on quickly to get wet, then off to soap up, then on again quickly to rinse) standing in a bucket to save the water. This water was then used for shaving and rinsing hands until finally it was used to flush the toilet after a "Number 2!" Laundry water was used for several loads until it became too black to recycle, and then it was used in the garden for the few plants or fruit trees that critically needed water. Our girls became so used to not flushing the toilets that when we traveled to the United States, it seemed such a waste to flush and, much to our embarrassment, they often left the toilet unflushed — and still do in college!

When even these extreme measures left us without water, we hired a local work crew to dig a well in our back yard. The timing was critical because we wanted them to dig at the end of the dry season, so we would be sure to dig down far enough to assure us water at the worst time of the year. Two men showed up with picks and shovels and hand dug a 5-foot-diameter well down 45 feet! It was amazing to watch them sit on the floor of the deepening well and swing the pick down between their spread legs to dig down to the water table. They had carved out little footholds in the walls, so they could climb out about twice a day. They used buckets on ropes to pass up the dirt and pass down water and food. After they got to the water table, they kept digging a few more feet until we felt we had enough water in the bottom of the well. They brought half-ring molds for the sides and layer-by-layer poured concrete to form the sides of the well. This made it less likely to cave in and also protected the deeper pure water from the contaminated ground water near the surface.

A few years later when that well was not producing much water, we called our Nigerian plumber JJ to see if digging the well deeper would help, but the answer was "No." He then called in the "professionals" for help. When I arrived later to meet them, the group of three men told me they had found water in the back yard with their "thing." I asked to see the "thing," so they showed me a piece of strong wire about 18 inches long bent like the letter "L." I asked one of them to show me how to use it. He then held the wire in his hand like a handgun and walked across the yard. When he came to the place where there was water, the wire in his hand swung 90 degrees to one side. I could not believe it and thought it was a trick, so I asked him to show me the other water spots, and he did. They were not as strong and the wire did not turn as much. Then I asked if I could try it. In spite of my best efforts, the wire never turned. I called in the big guns and asked our kids to each try it. Marie and David also failed to get the wire to move, but to our amazement both Heather and Anna saw the wire move when they got near the water source.

Wow! I have no explanation for this except that I have heard of water "divining" or dousing before but had never witnessed it. Consequently, the men started digging where the wire pointed and eventually found water at about 45 feet down. Now at least Heather and Anna can add to their resume and business cards that they are "diviners."

The hospital also struggled with having adequate water for the basic functions of washing clothes and equipment, cleaning patients, and keeping the hospital hygienic. Although they had access to two different city water main lines, they had the same frustration with poor service and unreliable water supply. There were a number of hand-dug wells around the hospital property, which were helpful, but they could not keep up with the increasing demands for water. Large reserve tanks were built to increase the storage capacity when we did get water, but they were not adequate to carry the hospital through the dry season. Finally, funds were sourced for borehole wells to provide more reliable water. These sources of water were helpful for a while, but most developed problems and required ongoing maintenance. Finally, the hospital management paid for trucks to bring water to the hospital reserve tanks to allow the basic hospital functions to continue.

In spite of our brilliant planning, having enough water was a constant headache. Many nights Dorothy would get up after midnight when there was water and electricity at the same time to do the laundry. When the water came, we all ran out and made sure the valves were open to the storage tanks, so we could capture as much of the liquid gold as possible. Of course the water situation was not as critical in the rainy season, but the electricity was more erratic, so having both water and electricity at the same time was a constant challenge. During the rainy season there was always the option of sending the kids out in the blinding rainstorms to have their showers!

The other problem with water is not just its availability but whether it is drinkable. In most developing countries neither the city water nor river water is safe, so we all learned ways to purify the drinking water. At first we filtered with stone Katadyn filters and boiled large buckets of water to kill viruses and parasites and make our water safe. Later we found water filters that were so good that the boiling became unnecessary. We taught the children that the only safe drinking water was the water in the fridge that had been filtered and boiled. At each bathroom sink was a bottle of safe water to be used for brushing teeth and drinking. We sometimes suspected that the stomach ailments the children occasionally succumbed to might have been related to drinking the bath water when we were not looking. The concept of keeping healthy had huge implications for family life. Whenever one of us got diarrhea or stomach ailments, we all suffered. Typhoid fever, cholera, and all sorts of dysentery diseases are killers in Nigeria, so we took whatever precautions were necessary to stay healthy. This could be difficult in social situations with Nigerians or when you were traveling in Africa. Most Nigerians are very hospitable and will offer you a drink or food whenever you visit their church or house. I paid the price dearly when I threw caution to the wind at one church function and suffered for months afterwards from hepatitis.

So the general rule outside the house was that it is okay to drink things from a capped bottled (like Coke) or drinks that are boiled (coffee or tea). In Nigeria there are several brands of bottled pure water that are safe, but you always need to be sure the seal on the bottle has not been broken.

ELECTRICITY

The other essential commodity for most Western missionaries is electricity. Our lives seem to revolve around kitchen, office, and personal things that needed electrons flowing through them. The challenge was similar to the water issue in needing both the presence of electricity and having good quality current. The city electricity was called NEPA – Nigerian Electrical Power Authority or "No Electrical Power Again!"

NEPA produced the power for our region at a hydroelectric power plant on a large lake halfway across the country. The power was then shared around the country, and occasionally we got some. Discussions about the reasons for the irregular power were quite colorful and included acts of sabotage on the transformers, generators and power lines, stealing of the high power lines, an

DR. WILLIAM DAVID ARDILL

inadequate number of functioning generators because of lack of repair and maintenance, and planned brownouts because of corruption and prejudice against the Christians.

We learned to stop asking the "why" question and accepted it as part of life. The power was supposed to be 220 volts, but it varied throughout the day from 110 – 350 volts. Either extreme created problems. The low voltage was hard on motors and fridges, and the high spikes wiped out electronic equipment. At the hospital, the buildings were zoned on different phases to balance the load. The houses, however, were wired for only one phase. To increase our choices and improve the chance of a good line, we installed three cutout switches at our power panel. Each line had a light and meter, so we could choose the line/phase with the best current.

When we were having our roof changed a few years ago, a worker stepped on some wires in the attic causing an electrical short that resulted in a fire on the main electrical panel. We were staying next door during the renovation, but the next morning I was shocked to see a large area of the electrical panel burned with melted wires everywhere. So after you get clean power into the house, your next worry is the safety of the wiring inside the house. This took years to sort out, and just when you thought it was okay, you got shocked from an improperly grounded circuit or got a shock in the shower from a pipe that was on the short circuit! Never a dull moment.

Being from North America, we brought many 110-voltage kitchen, office, and personal items. When we moved into the larger house, I had an electrician install a 110-volt outlet in each room. Some of my most maddening moments were when I was working on the computer and using the printer and the NEPA power went out. Not only was I left in the dark with the glow of the laptop screen to comfort me, but I had also botched up the print job and lost my work.

The solution to that problem was an inverter. This little gadget converted or "inverted" 12-volt DC current from a truck battery to either 110 or 220 AC voltage. It was a sanity-saving device because the 110-volt outlets in the house were wired to the inverter; so when the power went out, the 12-volt battery kicked in and we kept on working without missing a beat. The key was that you had to have enough city power to keep the batteries charged. The backup plan for was a solar panel that I used a few times when there was no city power days at a time.

The next backup system was to have our own generator. Our little Yamaha generator or "gen" would run everything in the house except the washer, dryer, and water heaters. It was easy to start and bailed us out many times. In the last few years each of the houses on the hospital compound was wired to the hospital generator grid. When the hospital generator was on, and we had no NEPA, we could use hospital power at minimum cost. Since there were times when both the hospital generator and NEPA were off, our trusty little Yamaha generator came through.

Finally, because of my concern about having candles or open flame gas lamps in the house, in every room we installed a 12-volt light connected to the truck battery in the house. There were many times during a blackout when we did not need to run high voltage equipment and only needed a reading light. These locally made 12-volt lights were terrific, especially when you were sitting in the dark and could switch on a small light in each room. These little lights burned up regularly but were easy to replace and were a great last resort for light. So if you are in North America or Europe and turn on the light switch or turn on the tap for a drink, think of the millions around the world for whom this is a luxury.

TELEPHONE

Mark Twain was once asked to record a Christmas message on an early gramophone. This is what he said,

> It is my heart-warm and world-embracing Christmas
> hope and aspiration that all of us, the high, the
> low, the rich, the poor, and admired, the despised,

the loved, the hated, the civilized, the savage—every man and woman of us all throughout the whole earth—may eventually be gathered in a heaven of everlasting rest and peace and bliss, except the inventor of the telephone.

Nigeria has the trappings of a modern civilization, but it is only a veneer. This is never as obvious as in a discussion about the electricity and telephone services. As you drive along the roads in cites and rural areas, you see poles with wires on them that appear to be telephone and electrical wires, but they are only the illusion of such things. Even in our house, we had what appeared to be a telephone on the dresser, but it served more as a paperweight than a communication device.

There is only one company that operates the landline telephone network. It is called NITEL. I remember as a child in Jos when the first telephones were installed in the 1960s. The system required a telephone operator sitting at an exchange booth with the plug-in wires to connect each caller to his desired line. My father tells a funny story of a time he called the operator and asked for number 12. The operator hesitated a minute and then replied, "Sir, 12 is busy, will 13 be okay?" So much for an understanding of telecommunications!

By the time we arrived in Nigeria in 1992, the telephone exchanges were all automatic. Most of the missionaries on the hospital compound had house telephones. You could not make international calls with the average telephone unless you went to the telephone office downtown, paid for the call first, and then used the telephone in their special telephone booth. A few had what were called "IDD lines" — international direct dial access to anywhere outside Nigeria. When we moved into the larger house on the compound, we were pleased the house already had a telephone and a number! At that time NITEL declared they had run out of telephone numbers – "the numbers are exhausted." Anyone needing a new line had to either wait for a customer to die or buy someone else's number. People selling their number usually had a large unpaid bill, so in order to get their number, you had to not only pay them for the privilege of getting their number, but you also had to settle their unpaid bills.

The telephone bills were often not delivered and payment was confusing. Your bill often sat in the telephone company office until you came to collect it. If you were late in collecting it and paying it, they would cut off your line. Of course, when your line was cut, you had to pay NITEL a reconnect fee as well.

To make matters worse, for several years our telephone would stop working when it rained. We asked the telephone company to help us fix this problem, but the most common answer was that an underground trunk line was faulty, and they were not planning to fix it. So we told our family in the United States if they wanted to know what the weather was in Jos, give us a call. If they could not get through, it was probably raining!

A complicating factor in Nigeria as far as the telephones was the risk of lightning to computers and modems hooked up to phone lines. Of course this was not a problem in the dry season, but when the rains came, it was a serious threat. We got into the habit of unplugging the telephone line after using the computer to do email. Since others on our compound also experienced the telephone frustrations, we installed an intercom system to connect all our telephone lines to a common unit. With the new system, if a person's line was not working, they could call out on anyone else's line and receive calls. After a few hiccups the system worked well and bailed us out when our telephones were "tossed" or just stopped working.

Our telephone had not been working for several months in 2003. One day I received a hand-carried letter from the Manager of NITEL. The letter stated that I had been selected as "The Best Individual Customer of the Year 2002" in the Plateau Territory and was invited to the awards ceremony the next day at the NITEL

Headquarters. I almost laughed aloud but stuffed the letter in my trousers and in frustration decided to boycott the ceremony. After all, my telephone had not been working for at least a year.

The next morning while I was in surgery, I received a telephone call at the hospital from the NITEL headquarters asking me why I had not come to the awards ceremony. The television crew from the local station televised the event, and they were embarrassed I had not come. They wanted me at least to collect my award. I came out of the Operating Room in my scrubs and told the phone operator to tell the NITEL spokesperson that I did not have a functioning phone so thought it improper to come for an award as the best phone customer. I also had patients waiting for surgery and felt I could not just cancel their surgery because NITEL had not given me enough advance notice to reschedule the surgery. I thought that was the end of it.

The following week, out of curiosity I decided to go to the NITEL office to get my award. The manager was surprised to see me and apologized for the oversight on their part for expecting me to come and receive an award when my telephone was not working. He gave me the plaque award with my name on it and promised my telephone line would be working within the week. I guess I figured "the check was in the mail too!"

Amazingly, by the end of the week, there were NITEL workmen on our compound tracing out our telephone line to find the fault and repair it. After that our telephone worked much better, even during the worst thunderstorms. So miracles are possible when you least expect it. I proudly displayed the plaque in my bedroom as a little reminder of God's little humorous surprises.

In recent years the cell phone business has taken off like a wild fire in Nigeria. It is a perfect solution for the communication nightmare since it has fewer elements that depend on local support. It is also a status symbol that supports the Nigerians' love of conversation! So from a humble beginning of one main carrier, we eventually had a selection of half a dozen cell phone service providers. Unfortunately, they don't communicate well between each other, so many business people buy one phone for each service.

Cell phones became almost a necessity for communication. Our plumber, electrician, and welder had cell phones, and it was convenient to be able to contact them for emergency work instead of sending our driver all over town looking for them. Our house helpers had their own phones, and we are amazed how so many could afford the weekly prepaid cards with their low salaries, but they somehow managed. So we jumped the era of tortuous landlines to a wireless generation.

INTERNET/EMAIL

When email technology arrived in Nigeria, it required a reliable phone landline, which made it a challenge to send and receive email. Usually one house on the compound had a working line, so we used the "sneaker net" approach and ran over to each other's houses with our laptops or floppy disks to do email. Satellite phones also allowed email, but they were expensive. Dr. Mike Blyth set up a wireless transmitter from the satellite dish that allowed us to get email and Internet from our houses. The phone companies eventually sold "dongles" to allow laptops and computers to connect to the Internet. Each step was a giant leap forward and greatly improved our communication with our family and friends abroad.

Trusting in our new computer Internet "dongle," on Marie's 19th birthday we arranged to call her on Skype when we got to Miango for our weekend away. So at 6 p.m. I turned on my laptop and, to my dismay, there was no Internet signal at the house where we were staying. Having been to Miango many times before, I knew there was a spot at the far edge of the property on a hill overlooking a valley that had a good view almost all the way to Jos. There was usually better cell phone reception there, so I hoped we would have a better chance for an Internet signal. With laptop in hand

I dragged Dorothy, Heather, Anna and David to this spot on the edge of the Miango property. After trying to get on the Internet for a while without success, I began to get irritated at the spotty reception. We called Marie on our cell phone to be sure she was going to get on Skype, and then I decided to walk around with the laptop and look for a stronger signal. Getting up on top of a granite boulder I was surprised to get a good signal and tried Skype again. Lo and behold, we got through to Marie, and the five of us spent the next 15 minutes huddled precariously on this rock laughing and talking to Marie. We panned the computer camera around showing her our precarious perch on a rock. She took her laptop around her new apartment introducing us to her new roommates and showing us her room. It was hilarious, and we hoped an encouragement to her on her birthday. Another triumph for persistence in the face of seemingly insurmountable odds!

CORRUPTION and **EXTORTION** - "Corruption, the greatest single bane of our society today."[5]

The final aspect I must discuss is the challenge of living in a country where corruption and extortion are the norm. The stories are legendary (and true) about the corruption in Nigeria. In fact, tales abound of scams, fraud, deception, and corruption that often cross the line of credibility. The situation was so bad in the 1970s that the President issued a Presidential Decree — Number 419 — to warn the public and curb corruption. Now, every scheme, scam, or fraudulent activity bears the name "419." Unfortunately the reputation of Nigeria and Nigerians living abroad has suffered.

From the minute you step into the country to the minute you leave, you are confronted with the opportunity to get anything done for a price. Certainly not all government officials are corrupt, but there are plenty police, traffic wardens, judges, and other government officials willing to get you what you need for a price. In many

---

[5] Olusegun Obasanjo, President of Nigeria 1999-2007.

cases, they extort the public and will not provide regular services or goods unless an under-the-books fee is paid.

After one trip abroad, I went to the immigration office in Jos to check back in as we were required to do. I wanted receipts for my transactions, so I could get reimbursed by the Mission for this expense. The clerk asked for some additional money for this transaction, and when I asked for a receipt, she said she could not give me a receipt for that money. When I asked "Why not?" her reply was that it was just not done and that was the end of the discussion.

The most famous scams that have received international attention are the email or letter appeals to help a noble Nigerian get a large amount of money out of the country. The stories differ, but usually there is an innocent and well-meaning person who received this new wealth as an inheritance or from the government by mistake and desires to help the poor, help the church, or whomever, but needs to get the money out of Nigeria in order to do this. He needs your help to deposit the money abroad. Sometimes there is an appeal for a small amount of money to help process the transaction and, of course, you will receive 10 to 20 percent of the millions of dollars that will be moved out of the country. After they get your bank account number, they usually clean it out and leave you, the poor victim, penniless. In some cases, they ask you to come to Lagos to complete the transaction where you are mugged and abandoned after the transaction.

We continue to receive these emails at least once a month with variations on the general theme of money laundering and a golden opportunity to get rich quick. Unfortunately, we know some pastors and Christians in the United States who innocently got involved and lost a great deal of money. As they say, "If something is too good to be true, it usually is."

On a regular basis we face con men and women looking for an easy mark. Naïve, generous, and kindhearted new missionaries often fall prey to these folks unless warned or until they are seasoned enough to see the scheme and avoid the trap. Many con artists present heart-rending stories of poverty, disaster or a host of calamities and say they just need help with food, school fees, or whatever. It takes only a few probing questions to determine the truth of the matter, but the initial appeal is usually compelling.

In reality, there are a lot of people in Nigeria with genuine needs and it takes time and experience to learn discernment. After several bad experiences and some friction between Dorothy and me on the issue, Dorothy and I set up some basic rules to guide us in these situations.[6] We set aside a certain amount of money that we budgeted to help the poor. In most situations, we agreed to consult each other before giving out money. This spares us the embarrassment of telling the person on the spot that we can't help; it allows us the opportunity to blame the other person if we say "No"; and it helps us stay more objective rather than making decisions based on the emotion of the moment. As long as we followed these guidelines, we were okay and it protected us from the 419 schemes that abounded. If we could not help someone, we would refer them to their local pastor or friend, and then pray with them that God would provide for their need if it was in His will. This took the pressure off us to be the savior of all men and helped the needy one focus on God, not us, to provide for them.

Often the requests were suspicious or fraudulent. One afternoon a man came to our door asking for money to help pay for his wife's surgery at Evangel. I asked about his wife's surgery and not knowing of her case, I knew his story was a sham since I was the surgeon at the hospital and knew every patient on the ward.

Another issue was the Nigerian perspective on stealing. Over the years we caught people stealing: several women we had hired to

---

[6] Ardill, William, "Begging and Beggars: A missionary's dilemma," Evangelical Missions Quarterly, Vol. 36, No. 3, July 2000, pp. 328-331.

help in our house, children on the compound, and many hospital employees. The amazing thing we discovered was that often even when caught red-handed, thieves would almost never admit they were wrong or repent. There was often an excuse or simply a denial of guilt, even as they stood in front of us with the goods in their pockets, purses, or hands.

Some of the problem of stealing in Nigeria seems rooted in various religious worldviews. If you are caught stealing, lying, or cheating, God is punishing you for your sin. However, if you get away with it, God is blessing you. So the principle is, go ahead and do what you want to do, just do not get caught! Even more frustrating is the misunderstanding of forgiveness. When caught, the thief sometimes pleads for forgiveness. To him or her it means you will forget the crime, forget any punishment, and restore them to their previous standing, rights, and responsibilities. The concept of payment or retribution is missing and causes a lot of misunderstanding when you say, "I forgive you, but you are still going to jail, or you must repay what you stole." The reply is, "But I thought you forgave me?" Sin without consequences, crime without penalty, and forgiveness appears to mean forgetting both the crime and the punishment or penalty.

The "Nigeria Factor" played an important part in our lives every day. The stress level each morning when you wake up is already twice as high as the average person living in the West because you are never certain if you will have water for your morning shower, electricity to make breakfast, petrol at the hospital to run the generator for your surgical cases, safety on the roads for your children to go to school, and Internet to get that encouraging email from your parents that they are praying for you every day. Having a sense of humor helped us decipher when to laugh at the hopelessness of it all and when to engage to effect change. At times we got very discouraged; but usually after a holiday or long weekend, we mustered the energy to press on, make it better, think of another backup plan, and keep on going. We were grateful for God's grace and mercy each day, the patience of our Nigerian colleagues who took it all in stride much better than we did, and forgiving family members who also matured through our trials living in another world.

EXTRA OPPORTUNITIES

During my surgical residency, I had intentionally taken rotations that would prepare me for the wide variety of surgical challenges and nearly impossible situations I would face in an underserved area. When I took orthopedics, I learned to set fractures, not do total joint replacements. In my plastic surgery elective, I needed to learn reconstructive procedures for burn patients and not cosmetic surgery. I learned by reading surgery textbooks and atlases, from specialists who visited Evangel, and from the painful tutor called "experience." Little did I know as the senior surgeon at the hospital I would need skills in interpersonal conflict, building construction and equipment repair, hospital administration and finances, disaster drill oversight, technology for the hearing impaired and fund raising.

During my brief tenure as the medical director and throughout my tenure at Evangel, I learned how rewarding it was to improve a facility and add necessary structures and enhance patient care and services. We painted and renovated the patient wards, helped build a 20-bed ward and 30-bed hostel for the VVF patients, set up a borehole (a large ground water holding tank and overhead tank to supply water to the hospital), purchased and installed a new generator to provide for the ever-expanding hospital departments, renovated the outpatient and billing area, and made a few other renovations.

These all helped us deliver better care to the patients and were an encouragement to the staff and management of the hospital.

Another surprising aspect of the surgical work at Evangel was the ebb and flow of patients through the year because of strikes and government actions, political unrest and violence. This had enormous implications on the finances of the hospital and my daily workload. Some days were extremely busy and exhausting, but we also had days when I went to the Operating Room only to learn there was not even enough water to wash my hands, much less do surgery. I usually went home until someone could get the well pumps to work or send a truck to get water, so the surgical team could work. These days stimulated me to look for ministries outside the hospital, so I could find fulfillment in ministry that was not de- pendent on the hospital infrastructure and that allowed me to use my other spiritual gifts.

I did not realize until we were in Nigeria for some time how much I loved teaching – especially surgery and the Bible. Evangel provided a great opportunity for me to teach medical students, nursing students, Nigerian residents in Family Medicine and visit- ing residents from abroad. I enjoyed sharing with them my experi- ence and understanding of how to care for patients. The pathology we saw in patients every day made the hospital and clinic a great teaching environment. Because we were not under the scrutiny of lawyers and national accreditation bodies, we gave our students and residents great latitude and freedom as they learned proce- dures and skills.

The surgery clinics were on Monday and Thursday mornings af- ter we did teaching rounds on the inpatients with the family medi- cine residents, medical students, and visitors. Ayibo was the nurse aide in charge of the clinics, and I was privileged to have his help as a translator for my 20 years at Evangel. He had a keen under- standing of each patient's problem, including their family situation, spiritual condition, and cultural concerns. When I arrived at the clinic with my two junior doctors, Ayibo had already placed the outpatient card records in a neat pile on my desk. I pulled out for the resident doctors the cards with patients who had simple postoperative follow-ups or uncomplicated surgical problems like hernias, lumps and bumps. I often had a medical student with me to work through seeing the patients with the more complicated surgical issues. My patients ranged from newborns with congenital surgical problems to young adults and older Nigerians suffering from cancer, orthopedic injuries, contracted scars from burns, prostate and kidney problems, accident victims, and the occasional vascular aneurysm patient. Each day in clinic was a hurried journey through a kaleidoscope of medical problems. Each had a unique story. Many had traveled hundreds of miles seeking help. Many were too poor to pay for the operation, but each needed to see Jesus in my eyes and touch.

The clinic was also a wonderful classroom for medical students, residents, and visiting trainees to see interesting conditions, learn hands-on physical examination techniques, and discover the joy of making a diagnosis and formulating a treatment plan. I was continually amazed at the openness of the patients allowing these young doctors to practice on them and the wide variety of surgical pathology that showed up each week in our small outpatient clinic.

The clinic is also a place of heartache. A woman came into my office in the clinic holding a baby who had hydrocephalous (water accumulation in the brain). I explained we needed to do an operation to help the baby. I asked her to go to the "theatre" to get an estimate of the cost before taking her child to the pediatric ward for admission. After getting the price of the operation, she left the hospital because she did not have enough money. Another day two women came into the clinic; one woman in Muslim dress was holding a baby, and her friend was her English translator. Her friend was a Christian neighbor who felt sorry for her neighbor's child who had a spina bifida (congenital open spine) problem. The child already had a back wound infection and needed to be admitted to get antibiotics before the surgery. They both pleaded they had no money for an operation. After the Christian woman asked if the baby would ever walk again, I had to honestly answer "No." Sadly she left with her friend and the baby because they did not have enough money for the admission and surgery. These sad situations are heartbreaking as we strive to serve the poor, yet the hospital does not have the resources to provide free care. There used to be a Benevolent Fund to help patients who did not have the means for life-saving surgery, but this fund was insufficient to cover all the patients in need.

A man came into the clinic with a painful abdominal aortic aneurysm. I offered to help him with surgery but told him because we did not have a blood bank, he needed to come back with four people to donate blood for him. Otherwise, it is not safe to do the surgery. He did not show up for his surgery either because he could not find donors or the necessary funds. Desperately needy patients came every day hoping they would be cared for at the Christian hospital. We could only do a limited amount of free care, but it still broke our hearts to see patients walk away because they were trapped in inescapable poverty. Normally patients would ask their families to help with their hospital expenses – the African health insurance plan. Some were unable to do this, so we counseled them to ask their pastor for help or friends in the community. Many times they were able to gather the necessary funds for their surgery. Sometimes staff would tell us about a patient with a serious need and we would take care of their medical bills. Many of the hospital staff and missionaries gave generously to help patients in need.

One problem that frustrated me for years was the lack of care for the deaf and the hearing impaired. Through the ministry outreach to the deaf called Gidan Bege, I knew there were many with hearing problems in our community. Hearing aids were almost impossible to find, were very expensive (several thousand dollars), and the batteries only lasted a few weeks. The little hearing aid batteries had a short life in the tropics of Nigeria and were difficult to find at the best of times. At the Kenya medical meeting for missionary doctors sponsored by the Christian Medical and Dental Association, I learned about a solar battery-powered hearing aid from Dr. Jim Smith, an otolaryngologist or Ear, Nose, and Throat (ENT) specialist from Portland, Oregon. He offered to give me the only unit he had, so I could try it out. The unit is about the size of a deck of cards and has a small solar panel on the side that needs to be in the sun for about an hour a week to charge the battery. There is a small wire to the earpiece that can be customized for each patient to improve the clarity. I was excited I had finally found the solution to another vexing problem because it solved the battery problem, was affordable (only $100), and was designed to be durable in the tropics. Wow!

As soon as I got back to Evangel, I spread the word about the hearing aid and soon a five-year-old Muslim girl came with a hearing problem asking for help. I used the old audiometer we had lying around, and it seemed she was profoundly deaf and would not benefit from the hearing aid. I decided to try it anyway and got little reaction from her when the hearing aid was in her ear. Still optimistic, I explained to her mother and a missionary nurse how to use the hearing aid and adjust it to see if it would help Sadika at all.

A few days later the missionary nurse excitedly told me that Sadika could now hear with the hearing aid. It had been turned up so loud she had no idea what was happening and after they adjusted the settings, she heard her mother's voice for the first time! I almost cried on the spot, it was so exciting. Sadika came to see me a few days later and was already making and mimicking the sounds she heard from her mother. She still did not know the meaning of any of the sounds, but she was making fantastic progress. That is how we began the hearing aid ministry.

The Gidan Bege ministry also discovered a large deaf community in Jos. Many were Christians seeking fellowship and support with friends who had similar challenges. We met David Audu and he told us about his hearing problem. Not assuming he was profoundly deaf, I asked him to come to the hospital to be evaluated.

After a series of examinations and tests it was determined he was a suitable candidate for the solar battery-powered hearing aid. It transformed his life, and he became a volunteer staff with Gidan Bege eventually coming on as a full-time staff member at one of the outlying transition houses for street boys.

The next piece of the puzzle was a phone call from Dr. Jim Smith when we were in the States. He asked me to come to the board meeting of the organization making the hearing aids. COM Care was a Christian organization dedicated to providing these low-cost tropicalized solar-powered hearing aids to Third World hospitals. I had a terrific time meeting the Board, and we committed to setting up a hearing evaluation center at Evangel with the intent of providing the hearing aids at low cost to those who were eligible.

A few months later I got another phone call from Dr. Smith that he had met an ENT surgeon interested in medical missions. Jim recommended he contact us and consider Evangel. After a few more phone calls and emails, Dr. Joel Anthis and his wife Cindy (family practitioner) and their three children flew from Houston to Baltimore to meet us and learn about Evangel Hospital, SIM, and life in Nigeria. They continued to pursue this idea by applying to SIM.

In the meantime, Jim Smith arranged with COM Care to come with a team to provide training for several Nigerians in audiology, so we could assess who would benefit from the hearing aids. The team of three came and trained several key staff in the technique of testing for hearing problems. We now had a hearing aid that worked and staff to assess those in need, but we really needed a physician to oversee the care of these patients.

After we returned from our furlough, I was determined to build a clinic for the new ENT unit that would also serve the expanding needs of the eye unit. An eye mission organization and a private donor provided all the necessary funds, and within six months we opened the new eye/ENT unit. About a year later, Joel and Cindy Anthis came to Evangel and served at Evangel and a variety of other ministries in Jos for several years. It was a wonderful tale of how God provided the materials, the people, and the facilities to begin a wonderful ministry to a neglected segment of the population with great physical and spiritual needs.

Another of my responsibilities as a surgeon was overseeing the emergency patients who needed a surgical procedure. Most of the time when I was called to the emergency room, it was to evaluate a patient with a surgical problem. That was not always the case. A sister of one of our Nigerian friends was brought to the emergency room because she was acting crazy. A few days earlier her family had a meeting to decide on the dowry from the man who had made a marriage proposal to her. Later that evening she went to her apartment and found a cow horn with chicken feathers on it on the ground in front of her door. She panicked and began acting quite strangely. She stopped eating and could not sleep for several days. None of this came out at first during her visit to the emergency room. When another doctor asked me to evaluate her, I did not think she had a physical illness but suspected there was something spiritual or demonic going on. The cow horn was a curse on her by someone whom she knew. We asked the hospital chaplains and churches leaders to pray for her and get to the bottom of her spiritual oppression. After much prayer, by the end of the week she began to feel better. "Our struggle is not (only) against flesh and blood, but against the rulers, against the powers, against the world forces of this darkness, against the spiritual forces of wickedness in the heavenly places." (Ephesians 6:12 NASU) They certainly did not prepare me for this in medical school!

An additional responsibility and privilege was hosting visiting medical students, residents, and teams from North America and Europe. We had so many visitors that when the girls were young, they usually asked, "Who is coming for dinner?" not "What are we eating for dinner?" In 2008 a group of urologists from IVUMed spent a week with us learning about vesico-vaginal fistulas and teaching us from their experience about various tropical urologic conditions. They generously provided some equipment and were a great encouragement to our VVF team and to me with my challenging urologic patients who had urethral strictures, hypospadias, kidney cancer, and various congenital conditions. We also hosted many individual surgeons who came with expertise in orthopedics, pediatric surgery, and plastic surgery. Dr. Bob Zirschky is an orthopedic surgeon from Salem, Oregon, who came every few years with his family and with boxes of orthopedic equipment. Most valuable was his wisdom and counsel in handling the challenging orthopedic problems that resulted from trauma, infections, and cancer. I grew in my knowledge of orthopedics, our residents learned from a great teacher, and our family was encouraged by Bob, his wife Sally, and their children Kyle and Katie. Many visiting church teams came for hospital tours, often dropping off boxes of medical supplies and equipment they had collected from their local hospital in America. We stretched these donations of equipment and supplies way beyond their normal shelf life, often resterilizing disposable items to help patients who were grateful for our care.

In addition to having capable and caring staff, perhaps the hinge pin for all the surgical work was the surgical instruments, equipment, and supplies that allowed us to perform procedures. Another of my critical responsibilities in partnership with the Charge Nurse in the Operating Room was keeping the Operating Room instruments and equipment in order. Every time we were in the U.S. surgical instruments and equipment were donated to the hospital, and we did our best to round up suture, catheters, chest tubes, drains and other disposable supplies from U.S. hospitals. Much of the equipment that relied on electricity burned out because of the enormous voltage fluctuations, so that was a constant headache trying to get that equipment fixed or replaced. I believed anything with electrons flowing through it was in peril in our Operating Room.

One week I noticed that most of the surgical patients developed wound infections. After thinking through a few possibilities, I asked if the autoclave in the Operating Room that sterilized all the linens and instruments was working properly. Much to my horror I was told it had not been sterilizing correctly for the past week, and the backup autoclave had been "spoiled" for months. We immediately sent all our instrument packs to another hospital until we could get our main autoclave fixed and then put out an urgent email appealing for funds to purchase a new autoclave. People responded generously, and we were able to get another autoclave in a few months.

The British name for the Operating Room is the "theatre." It is an apt description because in many ways the drama of life and death played out in the people who were cared for in the Operating Room. Being at Evangel for 20 years allowed me to do approximately 10,000 surgical cases on Nigerians from many different socioeconomic backgrounds and tribes, as well as missionaries and expatriates from around the globe.

During days with scheduled elective surgical procedures in the Operating Room, I set the order of the cases based on whether they were "clean" or "dirty" (infected), children or adults, inpatient or outpatient, surgery or scopes, and who was available to help. Between cases we evaluated patients brought to the emergency room, did rounds on the critical patients, checked or repaired equipment, attended hospital committees, and tried to get a break for lunch. I tried to anticipate equipment breakdowns by asking friends in the U.S. to help get replacements and bringing back as much suture, surgical instruments, and Operating Room monitors as I could gather. We improvised a lot, sought local repairmen to fix "spoiled" equipment, and built in as many protection systems as possible to keep things working as long as possible. Having a piece of equipment break in the middle of a case or finding out an item was "exhausted" (no longer in stock) was disheartening, and at times patient care suffered.

At times the challenges seemed overwhelming. The surgical cases we faced were often very complex even in a modern Western medical center. I had no referral options since the government hospitals had less equipment and resources and often were closed because of strikes. The lines of waiting patients rarely got smaller no matter how many hours we worked. The indescribable poverty and hardship of so many who came to us in desperation taxed our pocketbooks and compassion. In spite of my best efforts to learn surgery, cross-cultural communication, and the local language, I was also often frustrated when I became aware of my oversights and mistakes as a result of my lack of understanding about the cultural views of health, disease, cancer, and death. After making some bold statement about a patient, I was regularly humbled to find I had completely missed the point with a patient's care decisions.

In spite of all the instruments, equipment and supplies at our disposal, we knew our trust was in God who enabled us to work, provided the healing for each patient, and should receive the glory in everything. Every day was started with prayer and each case was begun with prayer. We often stopped to ask for God's help when things looked bad, and prayed for each patient as they recovered in the wards. We saw God work many miracles in the Operating Room and on the wards. Many patients walked out of hospital healed because of God's health-giving power against impossible odds. Truly, we could say with the apostle Paul, "My grace is sufficient for you, for power is perfected in weakness." (2 Corinthians 12:9 NASU) We were thrilled to see many healed spiritually as well – coming to faith in Jesus Christ as their personal Savior. But there were times of disappointment and discouragement. There were many patients who died in our custody, were not healed, or rejected the life-giving message of the Gospel. We clung to God's assignment that each day we remain diligent and faithful to Him and leave the results in His hands.

All this added up to a roller coaster ride every week from the elation of successfully completing an impossible case to the depression of a patient dying, an operation failing, or a patient rejecting the Gospel. I went into medical missions thinking I could make a difference in Africa because God called me to serve there. I realized I had made a difference in some, but God had also changed me in many ways. SIM's motto is "By Prayer," and it is only through the prayers of my family, friends, and Christians around the world that we were able to continue through the many crises we encountered.

WARD ROUNDS

The ward teaching rounds were on Monday and Thursday mornings with the medical students, interns, and family medicine residents. Rounds provided an opportunity to review each surgical patient's problems and treatment plan and consider their spiritual needs with the team. I invited one of the hospital chaplains to join us for his or her insight and encouragement. We started in the ICU, then went on a defined route from the private ward to the pediatric ward, and finally the male and female wards. If we had time after rounds, I would treat the surgery team to a Coke and peanuts at one of the restaurant shacks in the front parking lot of the hospital. This was a helpful informal time for me with the residents, and I learned about them and other issues of the day, including politics in Nigeria and our community.

ICU

Rounds always began with the sickest patients who were in the Intensive Care Unit (ICU). The only "intensive" aspect of this four patient unit was the higher nurse/patient ratio and the presence of a machine to monitor the vital signs of a patient – one at a time! There was an antique ventilator for patients who could not breath on their own; but it was never used for fear that if the electricity went off, the patient would die.

Bed 1: Martha underwent a C-section to deliver her baby because of ongoing bleeding from her uterus. She kept bleeding so had an emergency hysterectomy in the middle of the night. By 5 a.m. the next morning, she was still bleeding, so Dr. Stacy Lemanski, the SIM obstetrician/gynecologist, urgently called me to the Operating Room to help. We took her to the OR twice that night to stop the bleeding until, after seven units of blood, we finally stopped her bleeding. The next morning, much to our surprise, Martha was awake, talking and doing extremely well. We believe in these situations God had intervened in ways beyond our power for His glory.

Bed 2: Over the weekend I admitted a visiting missionary Jim who became very sick. Yesterday we moved him to the ICU when he appeared to be going into shock. He had several other conditions including a heart problem that made his care challenging. We are not certain how he got sick or even his diagnosis, but thankfully, after antibiotics and fluids, he is doing much better today. We will be sending him overseas for more expert care as soon as he is stable enough to travel. We evacuate missionaries and other expatriates often for expert care because of traumatic injuries, heart conditions, cancer treatment, or obstetrical emergencies.

Bed 3: Several weeks ago Godwin had been stabbed in the neck in an altercation and came to Evangel for treatment. A junior doctor evaluated him, sewed up the skin over the stab wound and sent him to my clinic a few days later. He came into the hospital several days later, bleeding from the large swelling the size of a large grapefruit in his chest and the size of a tangerine on the left side of his neck. The next day we took Godwin to the Operating Room. We hoped to control the damaged artery through his chest, but because the mass in his chest was so large, we could not get near the artery. Finally, we just opened the shoulder beyond his swelling and got control of the artery just before the aneurysm ruptured. Unable to repair the severely damaged artery, we tied off the artery, hoping his arm would stay alive from other new blood vessels to his arm.

Thankfully, later in the day his arm was still warm, and by the next day it was even better. Godwin is improving each day, and we hope and pray he regains more use of his arm in the coming days.

Bed 4: During a robbery in his neighborhood, 25-year-old Joseph was shot in the head and survived. We took him to the Operating Room without the benefit of a head CT scan and removed the blood clots and pieces of his broken skull embedded in his brain. We started medication to reduce the swelling in his brain, and thankfully he is responding now and should recover.

Amenity Ward

The Amenity Ward is the single patient room ward that is often used for patients needing isolation precautions or additional privacy.

Room 1: Lassa fever is a deadly hemorrhagic viral fever like Ebola that was discovered at Evangel Hospital in the late 1960s. We still have occasional outbreaks of Lassa in our community. Many patients die since all we can do is offer supportive care. Hawa came with an unusual rash and has continued to deteriorate since arriving. She is on isolation precautions, has few visitors, but is receiving counseling by the hospital chaplains every day. A few years ago we tested the hospital staff, and over 50% had antibodies to Lassa, which meant they were exposed to the deadly virus probably while working at the hospital. Unfortunately Hawa died a few days after admission. Some survive after getting this deadly virus, but many do not.

Room 2: On Wednesday I did prostate surgery on a paramount chief from a nearby state. He has authority in his region over many village chiefs and was a well-respected Christian leader. We do not have a blood bank so ask each patient to bring in people with their blood type willing to donate for their surgery. It is challenging to communicate this in a culture where blood is associated with animal sacrifices and has spiritual significance. If we do not need to transfuse the blood to the patient, many questions are raised about getting it back or at least being paid for it. The chief was always surrounded by his court servants dressed in bright, broad-striped red and green outfits and who attended to his every need. They came to the Operating Room with him and had to be shooed out and then slept on the floor in his room every night after his surgery. Fortunately the surgery went well. He was a gracious and grateful patient and made a special effort to come and greet me every time he came to the hospital with his flag-bearing Mercedes-Benz.

Room 3: Bed 3 is empty today. At 6:30 yesterday morning I got a phone call that an SIM Australian missionary, Anne Burke, whom I had been treating for peptic ulcers was in a lot of pain. I asked her husband and the mission nurse to bring her to the hospital. She had severe pain, and we assumed it was from a flare-up of her ulcers. Shortly after getting her settled in her hospital Amenity Ward room, she collapsed. During our efforts to help her we found she had a ruptured chest aneurysm which was beyond our ability to fix. She died in the early afternoon yesterday in spite of our best efforts. I even called my vascular surgeon colleagues in Texas and San Diego for advice, but they encouraged me I had done all I could under the circumstances.

It was a sad day for the SIM and missionary community, the Nigerians who knew her and especially her husband Peter. They were scheduled to return to Australia this week for a month of holiday. The funeral service and burial will be on Saturday at Miango where SIM has a cemetery for missionaries. Everyone remembers Anne's joyful spirit, her talkativeness (especially about her children and grandchildren) and her servant heart as she served those coming to the SIM Guesthouse.

Room 4: When I saw Binda in the clinic, he had a large painful swelling behind his right knee that he said began after he had been shot seven years ago. He had an injury to his artery that had been slowly leaking and now was threatening the survival of his leg. He agreed to the surgery, so I got my instruments and equipment ready for his surgery the next day. On Wednesday I began operating on his leg first thing in the morning, hoping to get control of the leaking artery quickly, so we could repair it. Shortly after I began, the large pulsating mass burst, and blood spurted everywhere. We quickly got a tourniquet on his thigh and stopped the exsanguinating hemorrhage before it was too late. I then took three and a half more hours to find the injury, attach the new artificial artery, and hook it up to the small, inflamed artery to his lower leg. Holding our breath before rejoicing, we then checked for a pulse in his foot. I almost cried when his foot was cold, and we could not feel any pulses. I then got out my Doppler machine, which is a sensitive instrument to detect pulses, and it too was silent. Dr. Adam Lee, my new Korean surgical colleague, suggested I check my own pulse with the instrument and it was silent again! Either I was dead or the batteries were dead! I could not replace the batteries right then, so we closed our patient's leg up and prayed for a miracle.

That night I did not sleep well – I was depressed that after all our hard work our patient might still lose his leg and so continued "praying without ceasing" through the wee hours of the night and morning. The next morning I rushed to his room in the private ward of the hospital and, after finding him sitting comfortably in bed, he said he felt fine and was no longer in pain. I then pulled back the sheets and placed my hand on his right foot. Miracle of miracles, his foot was warm and he had two pulses in his foot. Wow! I almost hugged him as I rushed to tell the Operating Room staff and Adam the good news.

Pediatric Ward

Bed 1: A few days ago I operated on a two-year-old boy who had a cleft lip. When the anesthesia nurse brought the child back to his room and put him in his bed, the mother did not recognize him and told the nurse, "That's not my child." Finally after some convincing, she was overjoyed at the transformation in her boy. The little boy will be discharged today. His mother is thrilled and does a little dance of joy every time we come to check on her son.

Bed 2: Some babies are born without an anus because the rectum and anal dimple do not join. This is an emergency, so we normally make a colostomy for the newborn to allow his bowels to function. Several months later we join the normal intestine to the anus to allow the child to have a normal bowel movement. Ruth had got her new anus last week. The surgery went well, and her mother is grateful she is pooping normally now in a "nappy" (diaper).

Bed 3: Last week our driver Kingsford's son Francis was crossing the road in front of the hospital and was hit by a motorcycle. He had large cuts on his scalp and fractures of his left arm and leg. His fractured arm was placed in a plaster cast. He will be going home soon.

Bed 4: Six-year-old girl Regina was run over by a car and dragged along the road. Most of the flesh on the top of her foot was gone. First we cleaned up her wounded foot in the Operating Room, and then a few days later we lifted a flap of skin on one calf and covered the other leg wound by sewing it to the flap. So her legs are sewn together and supported with a plaster cast. Regina will stay in bed for two weeks to let the flap on her foot wound heal. Next week we will divide the flap and cover the new leg wound with a skin graft. These flaps are usually reliable and do well in spite of their barbaric appearance at the time.

Bed 5: Last week we were notified that a woman in the obstetrics clinic underwent an ultrasound that showed that her baby had a large neck mass. They were concerned this might cause an obstructed labor or the baby might be born with breathing difficulties. The delivery went well, but the baby was having trouble breathing because the large mass below his neck was pressing on his trachea (windpipe). This condition is called cystic hygroma. We took the baby to the Operating Room and after much prayer removed the mass from the baby's neck. This kind of benign tumor tends to recur, but for now the baby is recovering well, much to the delight of his mother.

Bed 6: Two babies were brought to Evangel last week for treatment. One child weighed one pound and the other was only half a pound. Both babies had some of the signs of a bowel obstruction, but I was not sure, so we waited a few days to sort out the situation. Finally, on Thursday I operated on both of them, and to my surprise they had similar problems with a blockage of their intestines. Even with my magnifying glasses on, sewing their tiny intestines was a bit like sewing two pieces of spaghetti together. The one-pound boy is doing well, taking breast milk and seems out of danger. The half-pound baby boy died a few days later probably because of his low birth weight and prematurity.

Bed 7: Spina bifida is quite common because of the lack of prenatal care and lack of necessary vitamins during pregnancy. There is arrested development of the spinal column, and the babies are born with an open spine, exposing the spinal cord and nerves. This week a child with a spina bifida problem was brought to our clinic. His mother had taken him to a local government hospital and his mother had been waiting three months for the surgery. Finally in exasperation she brought him to Evangel where we did the surgery the next day! Even though the baby will not have normal function in his legs, the parents are grateful we did the surgery to prevent infection and further deterioration.

Bed 8: Hydrocephalous is another common problem often because of meningitis. The fluid in the brain is blocked because of the infection, and the children develop heads swollen with fluid that compresses their brains. Baby Ahmadu had a plastic tube called a shunt placed in his brain and then tunneled under his skin into his abdomen to drain the excess fluid. His head size is already reducing and in a few days, if his wounds are healing well, he will go home with his relieved mother. The shunt will prevent progressive brain damage and will stay in permanently.

Bed 9: Burns from fires are a major problem in children. They often play near open cooking fires, or boiling water pots are knocked onto them. The burns are treated with open dressings and painful daily dressing changes. If the children heal without proper care, they can form paralyzing scars, which hinder the normal movement of their arms, legs, and neck. Another type of burn was caused by battery acid being thrown at someone. These burns also caused permanent, horrific scars. David was burned when his uncle threw battery acid on him in anger. He was brought to the hospital several years after his injury by the Gidan Bege staff. His neck was severely contracted, so his chin was almost touching his chest and he could hardly eat. We have done several procedures to cut through the scars and next week will do another skin graft and flap of skin to allow him to hold his head up. He is a brave boy who had undergone severe suffering and is coping with his disfigurement surprisingly well.

Male Ward
Bed 1: Last Monday at 8 p.m., the family practice resident called me to the Operating Room for an emergency case. The patient Mathias had surgery at another hospital a few days ago for twisted intestine, but it had recurred. As we were preparing him for surgery, I learned the patient was a Jehovah's Witness so would not accept a blood transfusion. Thinking he would probably need a blood transfusion, the resident wanted to send him away thinking it was unethical for us to embark on a surgical procedure with that limitation. I disagreed and said we would honor his wishes, help him with the surgery, and NOT transfuse him. We removed the enormous twisted section of intestine and gave him a colostomy. He will need to learn how to care for his colostomy but can be reconnected in a few months.

Bed 2: We have four patients in the hospital with a condition called *enterocutaneous fistula*. They all had intestinal surgery at other hospitals for various problems but have developed a leak in their intestines, so stool is now draining out of their abdominal wounds. Most come to us very sick, dehydrated, severely malnourished, anemic, and some near death. Before we fix the leak in their bowels, they need water and food, specifically protein, so they can begin healing. We don't have prepared nutritional supplement drinks available, so we improvise by using a blend of oils, soybeans, peanuts, and fish cereal. It is called "kwash pap" because it was first used in children with kwashiorkor – a form of severe malnutrition. "Pap" is any kind of mush or porridge usually made from corn or rice. It works out that one milliliter of this kwash pap is about one kilocalorie nutritionally, so we know if a patient needs a 2000-kilocalorie diet, the patient needs two liters of kwash pap a day. It is remarkable how well most of these patients do after a few weeks of a high protein diet. Some of the fistulas close spontaneously without needing surgery, but at least they are in better shape to have the surgery. In bed 2 lies a young man with an enterocutaneous fistula. He had two different "surgeries" in another hospital – for a hernia and for his appendix – and was finally sent to Evangel when stool started pouring out of his abdominal wound. Of course he was terribly malnourished with dehydration and anemia and by now was penniless. The hospital used to have a benevolent fund to help in these situations, but that fund is now empty. We will do our best in spite of this limitation to care for him.

Bed 3: Yesterday morning I operated on a man who was a tax collector for the motorbike taxi drivers. Like most tax collectors, he is not well liked. The night before last about 50 motorbike men attacked him with machetes. They cut both his hands quite badly. I spent three hours putting eight tendons in his hands and wrists back together. The key in these operations is to find an even number of tendons, match the two ends, and then sew them back together again, one at a time. He will have a challenging recovery that depends on the patient's motivation to do the prescribed physical therapy. He also had four broken bones in one hand from the machete blow. On top of all this, he is HIV+. We pray he is willing to accept treatment for his HIV, heals from his surgery, and has an encounter with the Lord during his recovery at Evangel.

Bed 4: Abubakar came from another hospital with all the skin gone from his groin to his ankle on his left leg because of a flesh-eating infection. He was also severely malnourished and penniless. Sometimes these enormous wounds are caused by snakebites or poisonous spider bites. We began to care for his wound and encouraged him to eat kwash pap to help his nutrition and wound healing. He will eventually need extensive skin grafts and physical therapy. He is so poor he cannot even afford food. Now what?

Bed 5: There are hundreds of *achabas* (motorcycle taxis) in Jos. They are like the flying monkeys in the *Wizard of Oz*: buzzing like gnats around you as you drive, flying in front of every driver, and weaving in and out with passengers hanging on for dear life. Although the government instituted a helmet law, only about one third of the drivers wear helmets, which range from plastic toy hats to painted gourds to a few regulation helmets. Of course none of the passengers are given helmets, and they are usually the most seriously injured victims in the accidents. Almost every night we have people admitted to the hospital with head injuries, broken arms, fractured legs, and some deaths.

Last week Bitrus was admitted to the hospital after an *achaba* accident with a serious head injury, including facial fractures. He did not have a motorcycle driver's license, but even though he had a seizure disorder, he borrowed the motorbike. The accident occurred because he had a seizure while driving the bike. He is fortunate to be alive and will probably leave the hospital and unfortunately will probably ride a bike again. A few days later a woman eight months pregnant was brought in with a head injury from a motorcycle accident. She was thrown from the back of the motorbike. We were trying to manage her serious head injury, but her blood pressure kept going up, so we finally did a C-section and got the baby out safely. The mom is doing better now, and we thank God she will leave the hospital alive to be able to care for her new baby.

Bed 6: Motor vehicle accidents in Nigeria are a major public health concern. Thousands of people are killed and injured each year along the highways. Robert was a passenger in a taxi that was hit and came to the hospital with a major fracture to his left lower leg. Because of the injury to his muscles and flesh, we put pins in his bones and what is called an "external fixator" to keep the bones and pins in place for the eight weeks of healing. He is learning to use crutches and will be discharged as soon as he has a second operation to cover the wound with a leg muscle flap and skin graft. His wife is bringing him food every day since we do not provide meals to the patients. After several weeks recovering in the hospital, he is anxious to get home to his family.

Bed 7: Four days ago I got a call from the family practice resident on call that a man had been stabbed in the abdomen during a robbery and needed urgent surgery. The knife had injured his intestines in about ten places and cut into a major vein in his abdomen. Fortunately, we were able to stop his bleeding and repair his injuries. Without a blood bank it is challenging to help patients with major bleeding, but we got control of his intra-abdominal bleeding quickly. We are slowly increasing his diet and activity and pray for his recovery and salvation.

Bed 8: Now a story about culture. This week Yusuf was brought to the hospital with major infected wounds on his swollen hands and an inability to use his fingers. The cause of his ailment proved surprising. Apparently his brother had a problem with infertility. Surprisingly the local witch doctor blamed our patient Yusuf (not the man with the infertility!). The witch doctor treated this ailment by tightly binding our patient's hands for several hours. This resulted in near strangulation of his hands causing serious painful wounds. We are now cleaning his wounds twice a day in preparation for major reconstructive surgery. The moral of the story may be, choose your relatives (or doctor) wisely!

Female Ward

Bed 1: Mariamu is a 30-year-old woman who was born with her bladder open on her lower abdomen. She constantly dribbled urine out onto her abdomen her whole life and had desperately gone to every hospital she could find asking for help. The only procedure I knew to help her stay "dry" in this environment was to remove her nonfunctional bladder and re-implant the ureters from her kidneys into her lower large intestine. We do this procedure as a last resort for the vesicovaginal fistula patients when other options have failed. Mariamu agreed, so after much prayer and 4 ½ hours later, I had diverted her ureters to her colon, rebuilt her "private parts," and was able to close her abdominal muscles to restore her lower abdomen to a more normal appearance. I was so thankful this complex surgical procedure went well, and she is also doing well on the ward. After 30 miserable years she is finally dry.

Bed 2: Ruth is a very special patient. Tuesday morning we made history at Evangel when Ruth underwent the first laparoscopic cholecystectomy. The equipment was donated while we were on furlough in California and now was put to good use. This is a real answer to our prayers to be able to do these procedures and use this wonderful equipment. Almost every conceivable equipment problem happened during the case, including a power outage for ten minutes in the middle of the case when we were in the dark looking at dark monitors. With persistence we got through it, and Ruth should go home tomorrow.

Bed 3: While on rounds we were asked to evaluate a 25-year-old Fulani woman who had been in another clinic for over a week because of fever and abdominal pain. She was now in a coma with a distended tender abdomen and had slow gasping breathing. I suspected she had intestinal perforation from typhoid and was in septic shock. After trying to get her ready for surgery and in spite of her having no blood pressure, after rounds I took her to the Operating Room, and under local anesthesia I drained two liters of pus and intestinal contents from her abdomen hoping it might help her. In spite of all we did, she died later in the day.

Bed 4: Last Monday a young woman named Hawa was brought in who was several months pregnant. Her ex-husband had beaten her, and now the baby was dead. She was also HIV positive. Her ex-husband denied beating her, but the family was pressing criminal charges against him. Fortunately, Hawa had no other injuries, so the obstetrics team will help her through her delivery and HIV treatment, and the chaplains will counsel her through her family crisis.

Bed 5: Although we see women with breast cancer in Nigeria, most patients present with late stage disease. Hanatu was a 55-year-old woman whom we saw in the clinic last week. She had a large fungating cancer on her left breast that smelled horrible and was beyond curative surgery. We did a mastectomy to make it easier for her family to care for her. After her family learns how to change her wound dressings, Hanatu will go home with some hormone treatment and hopefully go to Kaduna for radiation treatment. Her prognosis is poor, but she is in better shape now than when she arrived.

Bed 6: I was involved in a sad situation yesterday with teenager Laraba. She had an abortion at another facility about a year ago and developed complications, so the doctor did a hysterectomy (removal of the uterus). After that she came to see me because she started draining stool from her vagina. It turns out, she had developed a rectovaginal fistula (a hole between her rectum and vagina). I did surgery and gave her a colostomy to decrease the stool drainage. A few days ago I took her back to the Operating Room to sort out the situation in her abdomen from her previous operations. Her pelvis was so scarred I could not put her intestines together and had to leave her with a permanent colostomy. Now she would never pass stool normally through her rectum and could never get pregnant and have a child – all because she had an abortion that went wrong.

Each day after finishing ward rounds with the residents and students, I usually concluded by saying, "Let's go to the shop in front of the hospital for a Coke and peanuts before heading off to the clinic to face the anxiously waiting crowd."

THE MAIN THING

"**O**ur goal is to not populate hell with people with good hernia repairs." This was the motto I repeated when speaking in churches across the United States about our ministry in Nigeria. Although trained as a general surgeon, I was determined when I went to Africa to have a greater impact than just providing a surgical solution to physical ailments. I wanted the Main Thing to be providing a Christian witness through health care.

There is a spectrum of philosophies and ministry styles regarding the role of evangelism in medical care. Some believe the health care alone is enough of a testimony while many pair the delivery of medicine with a proclamation of the Gospel. There are also differences in individuals' calling and giftedness in evangelism. I have worked with some missionary doctors who wanted to spend more of their time in evangelism outside the hospital than in delivering medical care. Others had little interest in outside ministries and focused on good patient care. I saw my role in evangelism in the middle ground. I took advantage of opportunities to talk to patients about spiritual issues but focused more on mentoring and discipling the hospital chaplains. I felt they were better equipped in evangelism because of their understanding of the cultural overtones of these discussions and their command of the local languages.

There is also the practical need to see patients who come to the hospital and want to be seen in a timely manner. Although it would have been ideal for me to share the Gospel message with each patient, time prevented me from this practice. But I often sensed a patient needed a special word of encouragement or prayer and so took the extra time to provide counsel or prayer to a mother in tears for her child, a women who was told she would not be able to have children, or a man who just learned that his father had cancer.

The mission statement of Evangel Hospital was "The purpose of Evangel Hospital is to glorify God ... by witnessing to our patients in word and deed the saving love of Jesus Christ, providing a quality and compassionate health care alternative for our community, and training and discipling dedicated Christians to assist the Church in meeting her goals." The strategy for fulfilling this evolved over the years we served in Nigeria. In 1992 when I first started at Evangel, the hospital chaplain staff consisted of two ordained male ministers who preached daily in the outpatient clinic and then occasionally visited the ward patients in the male ward, female ward, obstetrics ward and pediatric ward. As I reflected on their target audience, I realized that it was men in the male ward, women in the female ward, women in the obstetrics ward and mothers in the pediatric ward. Three of the five wards were mostly women and we had two male chaplains. In any culture this would be a problem, but especially in African culture it is not acceptable for a male to counsel a female. I challenged the hospital administrator and the chaplains to think about this disparity, and over the next few years two female chaplains were hired and had a fantastic ministry to women and children in the hospital. We also changed their focus from primarily preaching, to bed-to-bed counseling and friendship. The goal was to counsel "every patient – every day" using a "spiritual chart" comparable to our medical chart, so each staff could see their spiritual journey and previous conversations.

Later advances in the chaplaincy included providing tape recorders to patients to hear Gospel messages in their own language and then television monitors in each ward to show the *Jesus* film and other faith-based movies. Christian tracts and Bibles in various languages were also distributed generously.

Unquestionably the most significant element of the Christian witness in the hospital was the staff in each department. Many had a passion for sharing their faith in Christ and took every opportunity to discuss spiritual issues with their patients. It was thrilling to hear their enthusiasm for witnessing and their joy in kindly caring for patients in Christ's name.

When patients came to the Operating Room for surgery, we prayed with them before they underwent anesthesia and often prayed during the case for God's guidance and wisdom. If the outcome was bad news, I often asked the chaplains to come with me to talk to the family and pray with them as they dealt with their loss or devastating news like cancer or HIV.

I also pondered on the notion that the longer patients were exposed to the Gospel message, the more likely they were to understand the message and put their faith and trust in Christ. When I served at the ELWA Hospital in Liberia, it was the practice to admit all patients for a few days for both their recovery from surgery as well as to provide the chaplains maximum opportunity to hear and understand the Gospel. When I came to Evangel, I was tempted to do that as well, but the economic toll on the patient, the need for hospital beds and other constraints made that unworkable. We did invite the chaplains to join us for our ward rounds, so they could give us a report on their counseling conversations with each patient, which helped us understand the broader issues each patient was dealing with in their recovery. Dr. Paul Ushie, a family medicine consultant, often interrupted rounds to clearly share the Gospel message with a patient whom he felt was ready to hear the Good News.

The overall chaplaincy program grew and matured to the point we began discussing starting a hospital chaplaincy program. Several of the chaplains were sent to other mission hospitals to learn from them, and we began reaching out to the local ECWA seminary for students interested in a hospital chaplaincy ministry.

Seeing spiritual, marriage, and family needs among the staff, we also encouraged the chaplains to offer Bible classes and discipleship materials to the staff. Each ward normally started the day with a time of worship and devotions. In order to provide some theological depth to these important sessions, the chaplains distributed Bible study materials to guide the discussions and address common issues. Some of the Bible study material we used in Liberia that was developed by SIM missionary Pat Shea was also helpful.

Even though I sometimes struggled with my lack of direct opportunities to share my testimony and the way of salvation through Christ with my patients, I was confident I was part of a great team at Evangel whose primary goal was to be a witness in word and deed for Christ. I offered skills and experience that drew patients to the hospital, and then we trusted the Holy Spirit to work through the preaching, witnessing of the staff, Christian literature, bedside counseling, and the love demonstrated to all regardless of tribe or ethnicity.

Wonderfully through the ministry of the chaplains and staff, hundreds made a profession of faith in Christ each year at the hospital. They all came with hope for healing. Some left cured of their physical ailment. Some were beyond our ability to help, and some died while under our care. All had an opportunity to hear in their own language the Good News that was the door to the eternal cure.

THE HOUSE OF HOPE

Amidst the crowded streets and busy shops of downtown Jos, a common sight is the groups of boys with plastic dishes begging for a "dash" or gift. When Dorothy was shopping in Jos in 1994, a young Nigerian beggar boy befriended her by always carrying her bags from each store to the car. He would follow her down the street from store to store and, though Dorothy knew very little Hausa and he knew no English, somehow they became friends. On shopping day each Monday, Dorothy looked forward to seeing this little boy about whom she knew nothing, not even his name.

Six months later, the little street boy disappeared. While shopping, Dorothy looked in vain for several weeks, but her little friend had vanished. Dorothy felt as if she had failed him as a friend. She hadn't told him about Jesus, hadn't helped him much with his needs, and now he was inexplicably gone. Her memories of him haunted her for many months as she searched her heart to know what she could or should have done differently. Who was he and where had he gone?

In June 1995, we went to a Muslim Outreach Seminar in Miango. The thrust of the weeklong conference was to inform us about Islam and ways to present the Gospel of Jesus Christ to Muslims. During the seminar, two Nigerian Muslim converts gave their testimonies.

Each explained that as young boys their parents had sent them away to live with a Muslim teacher or "malam" to learn about Islam and the Koran. Their primary goal is to memorize the Koran by age 16. Some parents wish their sons to be teachers of the Koran, and this is the first step in that process. A teacher will migrate around the country, and every time he moves, his disciples go with him. Some boys leave their parents when they are five and six years old and don't see their parents for ten years. It is an enormous sacrifice for these Muslim parents and a hard life for the young boys.

As disciples, these "almajari," as the boys are called, are under the authority and care of the teacher. Some teachers have as many as 100 boys with them, and they find it difficult to feed them, care for their medical needs, and clothe them. Because Friday is the Muslim Sabbath, Thursday is their "Saturday." The boys are sent out into the streets when they are not in school but especially on Thursdays to beg for money for food and take care of their other needs. Since one of the five "pillars" of Islam is giving alms to the poor, helping beggars is accepted in most Muslim communities.

At the Miango seminar one convert, Saleh Husseini, testified how a Christian had befriended him and shown him love and kindness that he never forgot. He showed us scars on his legs from childhood wounds, his constant hunger, and lack of basic health care as a child. As Dorothy heard the testimonies of these Muslim converts, she realized that the little shopping helper was probably an almajari boy whose teacher had decided to move to another town, so the boy had gone with him. Dorothy felt even more remorse wondering what impact she had made on this child's life, especially his eternal destiny.

After much prayer and discussion with others in Jos who had been involved in various urban outreach ministries, in August 1995 Dorothy began feeding these street boys once a week at an urban outreach office close to Evangel Hospital. Dorothy was encouraged when the Evangel Hospital chaplain, one of our house helpers, and several women from our church volunteered to come and help in this new venture. Over the next few days, she told the boys to come on Thursday for some free rice and beans. Realizing the risk in approaching Muslim children with the Gospel because of previous hostilities in Jos between Muslims and Christians, our fledgling team committed the project to the Lord for His wisdom and protection.

Our cook prepared the rice and beans in our kitchen and, after much prayer, we took the food to the meeting place. On the way our cook invited as many boys as she could find. Much to our delight, that first Thursday 17 boys came for the advertised free food. They were typically mischievous and playful but what was more striking was the ragged state of their clothes and their poor physical condition. Many had open sores and rashes, ringworm, and parasites.

Over the coming weeks the numbers grew until about 50 boys were coming regularly. Usually before the food was served, a children's video was shown to provide some entertainment and fun for the boys. Dorothy was not sure how to begin a spiritual outreach so asked the hospital chaplain to begin telling stories of the Old Testament patriarchs. Since Islam recognizes these prominent historical figures, it seemed a safe approach, especially if we could show the progressive revelation of God leading to the perfect Lamb of God.

The boys listened intently, but, much to our dismay, only half of the 50 boys returned the following week because their teacher had forbidden the others to return. It was a real disappointment. Not knowing where to turn, our team returned to showing only the children's videos, even though they were in English and most of the boys couldn't understand a word of English.

Slowly the numbers grew again and held to around 75. Another converted Muslim man heard about this ministry and excitedly told Dorothy he knew how to reach these kids. He had been an almajari boy and understood them. So, the following week, Shaba brought a chart with the characters of the Arabic alphabet and began drilling them on their Arabic script. He also taught them from their own holy book. It was amazing to see the boys as they eagerly listened to a man explain who Jesus was from the Arabic Koranic text.

The number of boys continued to grow as each week Shaba explained how Jesus was different from the other prophets. It was "school" for them but with a kinder and gentler instructor than anything they had known.

About this time several other things began to happen. Dorothy started bringing sewing needles to the Thursday lunches. As the boys ate their food, they would peel off their shirts, and Dorothy would sew up the holes in their ragged shirts. Some had more hole than shirt! Dorothy also asked a nurse from Evangel to come and evaluate some boys who had obvious medical problems. If necessary they were then sent to the hospital for free treatment of their worms, sores, infections, and malaria. The response was marvelous as we watched boys who had been lethargic and quiet bounce back as perky and alert youngsters after treatment.

The blind women in Jos are assigned a young seeing girl as a guide to help them get around town to the various begging points, to the mosque, and back home each day. After several months, a few girls who were guides for blind beggar women began coming to the Thursday lunch. Midway through the meal there was a big commotion outside when their beggar mothers came looking for them. The girls were wasting "good begging time." We told the girls to go but to come back next week with their mothers when we would feed all of them. The following week nine blind beggar women came with their guides, so another chapter in the street ministry began.

These desperate women were in need of so much — food, health care, proper hygiene, and love. They were so suspicious that they wouldn't give the volunteers their real names. The volunteers gave them food each week, and several began to braid their much-neglected hair. Sharnel Smith, an SIM missionary nurse, cleaned their filthy feet and cut their toenails. This unconditional love began to break down the walls of mistrust and suspicion, and the women began to relax and enjoy their times at the center.

A rivalry developed between the street boys and the blind beggar women and their girls. There was clearly a pecking order among the beggars, which we had not understood when we had them come together. So we changed the women's day to Wednesday, and that solved the problem of the boys harassing the blind women.

Volunteer Ladi spent time talking to the blind women, sharing the Gospel, and told them she would love to visit them in their homes. This was unheard of for blind women since the rest of the community ostracized them, and no seeing person from outside their community had ever visited them. One afternoon a blind woman led Ladi to her house, and it was one of the greatest breakthroughs in the outreach ministry.

Ladi ran back to our house after the visit and excitedly told Dorothy what had happened. "You will not believe where I have been. A place called 'Blindtown.'" In the middle of the Muslim area of Jos a large section of multi-house compounds, probably a half square mile, has been set aside for the blind in the community. They have a blind chief with his own blind elders and security guards! The adults are almost all blind, but the hundreds of children running about with snotty noses and ragged clothes are not blind. The blind governing council presides over the cripples and lepers who also reside in this remarkable community. The lepers have a king, and even the thieves have a king! The medical, emotional, and spiritual needs were overwhelming and the opportunities for ministry staggering. This was the beginning of a fantastic ministry into not only the Blindtown in Jos, but also the Blindtowns in most of the major cities in northern Nigeria.

For years the blind in Blindtown had to trek outside their community to get water for cooking and bathing. They asked for our help. We received a grant from Tear Fund and installed pipe and taps into several points in the community, so they would not have to go so far for water. In anger the Muslim leaders rebuked the Blindtown elders for allowing the Christians into their community. The elders responded, "For years you have done nothing for us.

These people care for us and our children, so we will continue to allow them to help us." Wow! What an open door of opportunity and responsibility. We got to know the chief, secretary, and elders and felt welcome any time. I often did medical consultations in the dark, dirty rooms of Blindtown residents in an effort to help some of the most desperate people I have met in my life.

So many new opportunities were opening every week that when Dorothy would come home after a long day at Gidan Bege, I would tentatively ask, "So what was new and exciting today?" She would proceed to tell me another amazing story about the new outreach to the deaf, or the wheelbarrow boys, or the motor park boys. We felt that every door we gently pushed on, the Lord flung open and asked us to move forward. It was an amazing time of blessing and opportunity.

Several missionary kids and teachers at the mission school Hillcrest heard about the street children ministry and asked how they could help. Subsequently, they sponsored a "Flip-flops for Friends" program where each child in the school brought a pair of flip-flops for a street boy. They also had a Read-A-Thon and donated the proceeds to help buy clothes for the boys. Each Thursday four missionary kids would come to the center during their lunch break and help pass out food to the almajari boys. It was a great opportunity to help missionary children learn about poverty, and the culture around them, and realize they could be involved and help.

With all this rapid growth, Dorothy realized the need for more staff and a larger facility. There were now 130 boys coming every Thursday and 40 women and 40 girls coming on Wednesdays. After looking at several sites, in the spring of 1996 the Lord led us to a two-story building in a good location close to the hospital and near the Muslim area of town. We wanted a place in a neutral zone, so the boys and beggars could come without feeling threatened by either the Christians or Muslims in the community. We also did not want the ministry to be in a church building since no Muslims would venture inside church property. We wanted the ministry to be church-centered but not necessarily church-based. With only a small amount of renovation, the newly rented building became a much better facility for the expanding program and allowed room for the growth of new ministries. We called the center "Gidan Bege" which means "House of Hope."

Ladi was hired as a full-time counselor for the women's outreach. Joseph, a recent seminary graduate, was brought on staff to help Yakubu, the hospital chaplain, with the almajari boys outreach. Although we were sorry to lose her, our house helper, Hawa, was added as a full-time cook and cleaner of the new urban center. Volunteers from local churches continued to come and became the backbone of the personal counseling and friendship evangelism strategy.

As we got to know more of the street boys, we learned there were several different kinds of children living on the streets. Some did have homes to go to at night and only begged during the day. Some either left their homes or were forced out because of divorce, remarriage or death of their parents. These boys indeed lived on the streets and survived through stealing and begging. The majority were the almajari boys who were in Koranic schools and had a place to sleep but were committed to the Muslim teacher. Some of the boys really wanted to get off the street, so we began to think through how to help them transition from the street or how to transition the street out of them. One of our single male staff started having some of the boys live with him, but we knew this was not the best long-term arrangement.

In 1996, before going on furlough, we bought a house in a small community on the outskirts of Jos, moved a staff couple into the house, and began to bring into the house the boys who had shown they wanted (to stay) off the streets. In every case, we tried to contact the boy's family. Some did not want their children back, some took their boys back after our reconciliation efforts, and for some we were unable to find their families. The boys would tell us false names and fictitious stories because of their fears and suspicions. It often took several weeks and lots of versions of the story before we finally learned the truth about why they were on the street.

The Transition House was another important step forward in the ministry. Although most of the boys were not almajari boys, they were definitely street-wise. It was a steep learning curve for us to figure out how to get the "street" out of them. Stealing, lying and cheating were a way of life, and they didn't understand the meaning of trust. The house parents had small children, and soon it became clear to them the boys were a bad influence on their children. We moved the families out and had rotating staff to supervise the street boys, which worked better. Because most of the boys were illiterate, we enrolled them in the local government schools. This was another problem because they were all older than their classmates and became the class bullies. Imagine a 12-year-old in first grade – not a good idea.

So after training our staff, we started our own home school using the Accelerated Christian Education curriculum. This allowed the boys to progress at their own pace and minimized the peer pressure and discipline problems. We were thrilled when a visiting member of one of our home churches told us he was running a Maryland state government Transition House for problem children. Mark Cruz gave our staff important training and was a big encouragement during these early days of the ministry.

We were leaving for furlough in 1996 and decided we needed an advisory board in place that would help with the oversight of the rapidly growing ministry. We had made effort to include church leaders in our plans, but there was little interest from the church leadership at this stage. A board was formed to help coordinate the ministry as new opportunities continued to arise.

After returning from our furlough in 1997, we were summoned into the SIM office to answer some questions about the beginning and future of the ministry. Apparently the church leadership believed the ministry was inappropriate in its focus on Muslims. During the frequent riots in Jos, the street boys had burned churches and harassed Christians. "Why on earth would we feed and clothe them?" the leaders asked us. They also expressed that they had not been involved enough in the strategy and development of the Gidan Bege ministry. We explained to the SIM Director how at each step of the growth of the ministry we had consulted church leaders and asked for their input and involvement. We had documented our conversations and contacts along the way and demonstrated our sincere efforts to include the church leaders along the way. At one point we had even invited the church leaders to come to the center and sit with the street boys for a bowl of rice and beans and some did. They were so amazed at this experience that we felt they would be supportive of the ministry. After intense scrutiny, the SIM leaders were satisfied and encouraged us to continue. From then on we felt SIM and the church were behind the ministry, and we prayed they would show their commitment with personnel and financial backing.

The rental property soon became too small, and the landlord began giving us headaches with huge increases in the rent. After returning to Nigeria in 1997, we began a prayerful search for another property to purchase. After looking at several in the neutral zones of Jos, we settled on a hotel with a separate restaurant and offices surrounding a courtyard. In a miraculous answer to fervent prayers, the Lord provided the $90,000 to purchase this property in three months in the spring of 1998. During the purchase process we found out the hotel had been used for prostitution, and so many women had become Christians through the outreach of our sister ministry, Urban Frontiers Ministry (UFM), they had to close the hotel. The UFM staff had often prayed for the hotel owners and that one day the property would be redeemed and used to further the Gospel. We were indeed "redeeming" the lost in many ways. Another "coincidence" was that the hotel was located on Doherty Street – sounds pretty close to "Dorothy" to me!

While on our furlough, we met a family in Dallas who were interested in a ministry to children in a Muslim context in the Third

World. After hearing about Gidan Bege they planned a trip to see if this was where the Lord was leading them. So in 1998 Peter Fretheim came to visit Jos and fell in love with Nigeria, the street children, and the ministry. Although he visited other ministries on that trip, he felt clearly led to return with his family to work with us in the Gidan Bege ministry. Dorothy felt the ministry was growing beyond her ability to manage on a part-time basis. She still had responsibilities at home and knew she needed help. The arrival of the Fretheims in 1999 was a welcome answer to her prayers.

Because Dorothy was the "mother" of the ministry, it also became a problem when she started to hand over responsibilities to Peter. At times the staff questioned his authority, so eventually Dorothy withdrew from the day-to-day work and focused on helping Peter become oriented to the culture and vision of the ministry. By 2000 Peter was fully in charge, and our role became consultants and patriarchs!

Although we envisioned growth in the ministry because of the thousands of street children and beggars in every major city in northern Nigeria, the Fretheims have taken the ministry far beyond our wildest dreams. There are now Gidan Bege staff in seven cities in northern Nigeria working with the blind and beggars. In each city the ministry looks a bit different, but there is strong involvement of the local churches with both a commitment financially and staff. The Jos center serves as the main training facility for staff that are then deployed to places where the church wants an outreach to the destitute. There are now two compounds in the Jos area for the discipling and training of the street boys in addition to the main center downtown. These Transition Houses provide a safe environment for the boys to learn to read and write, learn about the Christian walk, and have their physical and medical needs met in a loving and compassionate way.

The ministry has also expanded within the ECWA organization and is now under the mission arm called the Evangelical Missionary Society (EMS). This partnership has allowed the Gidan Bege staff to assist the EMS missionaries with medical outreaches, film evangelism through the Challenge Cinema ministry and partnering in other evangelistic initiatives. The EMS children's hostels have also benefited from this relationship, and Gidan Bege has provided considerable help to the missionary children and staff in the EMS schools and hostels.

In the early days of the ministry it was obvious that all the street children were boys. We wondered why until we learned from our Nigerian colleagues that the girls who were in similar impossible and dangerous domestic situations often went into prostitution when they left home. Girls were more valuable to fathers because they would fetch a dowry and would be helpful workers in the home until they were married. Dorothy was especially concerned with the tidal wave of AIDS that there would be an increase in the number of street girls because of so many houses with parents lost to the HIV virus.

After 2010 it was interesting that pastors and community leaders began bringing at-risk girls to the ministry asking if Gidan Bege could help them. These were girls in homes with one parent unable to cope, or child-led houses, or where there was known sexual or domestic abuse. The Gidan Bege staff immediately set aside a house in a little village about 45 minutes outside of Jos. This transition house provided a safe environment for their general education and teaching about the Christian message. Much to our surprise, before we left we learned that there were more than 100 girls staying at the village who had been rescued and kept from street life and who were being raised and discipled in a safe place.

In October 2005, Gidan Bege celebrated the ten-year anniversary of the ministry. We were privileged to attend. It was humbling and wonderful to hear the testimonies and reports of staff and new believers touched by the ministry over the past years. It was especially exciting to see Chinadu, one of the first street boys in the ministry ten years ago, now preparing to start university. We were hoping for some sort of farewell to the Gidan Bege "boys" but were not sure how that would happen. On Saturday, May 12, 2012, we drove out to the Transition House village as their honored guests. The teenage boys in the ministry had a soccer match against the boys who had gone through the ministry and graduated from secondary school. We learned these boys had formed a street boys alumni association. It was a tearful occasion but remarkable to see what the Lord had done through the vision He gave us to reach out to the children on the streets of Jos 16 years ago.

The ministry now serves more than 200,000 meals, has presented the Gospel to more than 250,000 people, has provided medical care to thousands, is shepherding over 400 street boys in various locations around the country, and has developed hundreds of volunteers and staff. It is a phenomenon beyond our dreams and brings glory to the God of compassion who sent His Son to reach the poor and destitute. It is a "House of Hope" indeed.

RESURRECTION BOY

Like the rippling of the water after a stone is thrown across its surface, we heard many stories of lives touched by the grace of God through the ministries we had started. The outreach to street children became Gidan Bege (House of Hope) and then grew to become City Ministries – encompassing compassionate care of the blind, beggars, crippled, lepers, street children, and widows. The following story is an example of a child rescued by the City Ministry staff that we had recruited and trained.

The most prominent features in the landscape around Miango were the two extinct volcanoes with their flat semicircular ring tops and blown-out sides, a favorite hiking trip for school children and families. Belched from the belly of the earth, house-sized boulders were strewn everywhere in the surrounding countryside, heaped up in piles that defied gravity and the physical laws of balance. The ash and pumice covering the terrain made this region an especially fertile area for growing *ache*, maize, and green vegetables. Most of the large farms were managed communally with groups of villagers banding together during the planting and harvesting seasons.

Unlike a number of village groups in Plateau State, the Irigwe tribe had resisted the invading northern Islamists and stuck to their ancient animist practices. This remote Irigwe village in Plateau State, Nigeria, had centuries of animist practices handed down to appease the evil spirits and stay their judgment and punishment. In the not-so-distant past, human sacrifices were offered, but pressure from the British "Christian" colonialists discouraged this practice. Now it was mostly killing animals and offering other sacrifices of umbrage. Around the countryside and especially on the tops of hills and mountains, one could easily identify the places of sacrifice. The circle of stones, the pile of rocks in the center, and the feathers or other animal parts strewn around the ground gave warning to the passerby that this was a holy place, not to be disturbed, where serious business with the powerful spirits was conducted.

A few years ago a spate of accidents and tragedies led the villagers to one conclusion: there was someone in the village responsible for offending the spirits and bringing down their wrath on the innocent tribes people in this rural hamlet. This offender had to be identified and eliminated if there was to be peace and relief from the suffering they had painfully endured. Ten-year-old Ahmadu was the one chosen as the sacrifice to the gods to rid the village of the curse and give them relief from the suffering of ongoing unexplained tragedies.

The village witchdoctor notified the elders and Ahmadu's family, including his sister and parents, who were given the news of the death sentence of their son. Ahmadu was taken bound and screaming to a place outside the village, and a noose placed around his neck for hanging. After dropping him from a branch of the hanging tree, he was abandoned to die alone. Much to the relief of the village, the curse was now considered broken, or at least until the next time the spirits needed appeasing.

Later that dreadful morning, a woman from a neighboring village on her way to her farm was horrified to see a boy hanging from the branch of a tree. She quickly cut him down with her sickle hoping he was still alive. When he began breathing, she carried his limp body to her humble, mud-daubed, thatched roof hut and began her search for a safe place where he could be cared for away from the damning glare of her neighbors. She heard of a place in Jos, a place of hope, called City Ministries and made arrangements to take him there.

After the 30-minute taxi ride along the dusty bumpy road, she found the City Ministries center in the middle of Jos and timidly went inside. The staff welcomed her and Ahmadu and promised to care for him. The Good Samaritan woman left Ahmadu in God's hands and returned to her village alone. Although weak and silent, Ahmadu did not seem to need any immediate medical attention, so they focused on helping him regain his strength. He slowly began to recover but did not speak a word for three months. Eventually he summoned the courage to tell his story to the staff who had befriended and cared for him.

Over the course of many weeks the staff shared with him the story of another One who had been cursed and killed on a tree and yet forgave those who had mistakenly judged him and sentenced him unjustly. God's love was evident in the staff as they fed, clothed, educated, and gently cared for him faithfully every day.

Ahmadu's heart was won over by the love he saw, and he gave his life to Christ, accepting God's forgiveness for his offenses against God and His offer of life and peace through the death of His Son. Ahmadu grew in confidence and began joining an outreach team of staff and older boys led by staff member Jacob to share the Gospel with others. Jacob's zeal for evangelism was contagious as he mentored the boys in how to share their newfound faith in Christ with others. The teams visited neighboring towns and villages around Jos almost every weekend.

Reluctant at first, their confidence grew as they saw the change in people's lives when they heard the Good News of forgiveness, and the boys began asking for more opportunities to share. Soon they took over the organizing, planning, and leadership of the outreaches. Ahmadu played an active role as they led many to new faith in Christ.

One day Jacob asked Ahmadu if he would like to lead a team to his Irigwe village to share the Gospel story. It had been five years since Ahmadu had been left to die hanging from a branch outside the village. Was he ready to see his family who had forsaken him? Was he ready to face his accusers who had unjustly sentenced him to die? Was he ready to look into the eyes of those men who had forcefully tied him and strung him from the tree branch to serve the forces of evil that controlled them? After some thought, Ahmadu agreed he was ready to face his transgressors.

As the team of City Ministry boys with Ahmadu trekked from Miango town and approached his village, the first person Ahmadu saw was his sister. She was aghast and amazed he was alive, writing him off as dead five years ago. Screaming with joy, she danced as she led the group into the village and called the villagers to the center square. As one back from the dead, Ahmadu saw again those who had sacrificed him to the gods. The whole village ran to see what the commotion was. Eventually those who hung him came to see what was causing such confusion, and Ahmadu faced his executioners. Horrified at the sight of Ahmadu alive and what he might do to them, they begged his forgiveness.

Boldly, Ahmadu told them he forgave them and shared the amazing story of his "resurrection" from the dead through the kindness of a woman who was a stranger. He then went on to tell them the great news of the One who had forgiven him and died for him on a tree and how his life had been transformed because of His power in his life. Sharing the simple Gospel story, Ahmadu had the joy of seeing many in his village that day accept not only his forgiveness but the forgiveness of sin God offers through the death of His Son on the cross. It was a time of rejoicing and revival over two brought back from the dead — the "resurrection" boy and his resurrected Savior.

AIMEE

I t took us a while after the twins were born to recover from the fatigue. We knew the question of having more children was in God's hands, but we believed He wanted us to have a larger family. Finally that glorious day came in early 1998 when Dorothy found out she was, indeed, pregnant. What a great answer to prayer. Seven-year-old Marie and five-year-olds Heather and Anna were excited they would soon have a baby brother or sister. It was a great time of anticipation for the whole family as we prepared the baby room, got out the baby clothes and toys, and began to face the prospect of more sleepless nights, baby gurgles, burps and giggles, diapers, and the joy of watching the girls assume the roles of big sisters. We thought it would be especially good for the twins to have someone younger to care for and not be the center of attention. For months our family anticipated with joy and excitement the arrival of the baby.

We had planned during the school summer break to visit an SIM hospital in Niger Republic where a resident doctor I had trained was a medical missionary. Galmi Hospital is in the Sahara Desert, and, although we knew it would be a difficult trip, we felt our visit would be an encouragement to Drs. Joshua and Joanna Bogunjoko. I was planning to help in surgery while Dorothy would keep an eye on the children and get some rest. She was now six months along.

Just before we left, Dorothy began expressing concern that the baby was not moving as much as she expected. She was busy with school activities, so she wasn't sure if it was just her busyness. Her Nigerian obstetrician Dr. Karshima did a sonogram that showed the baby was fine.

Neither of Dorothy's doctors discouraged us from going to Galmi. The only warning we got was from my parents in California. They questioned the wisdom of such a trip when Dorothy was pregnant. After explaining she was only six months along, they agreed it would be fine.

After getting to Galmi in early June 1998, Dorothy asked an obstetrics resident short-term missionary to do a sonogram to check on the baby. She noticed the amniotic fluid seemed low but said the baby's head, heart, and lungs seemed okay. She suggested maybe Dorothy was a bit dehydrated and encouraged her to drink more water and get more rest. Dorothy slowed down a bit and tried to drink more water. She was going swimming with the girls each morning and afternoon and took a good rest hour in the afternoons. A few days later Dorothy was still concerned, so the obstetrician did another sonogram on Sunday evening, and again the baby's heart was beating fine.

On Monday and Tuesday, even though Dorothy as 27 weeks along in her pregnancy, she wanted to get sonograms again. There was really nothing we could do if there was a problem, so I thought we should just wait until we got back to Jos. We stayed a week and then returned to Jos.

After we got back, Dorothy went immediately to the hospital for a sonogram. Dr. Truxton started out with the maternity sonogram machine and had trouble finding the heartbeat. Greg Kirschner looked in and knew something was wrong, so he got his obstetrician wife Dr. Carolyn Kirschner and came back to the house to get me. Greg told me they were having trouble finding the heartbeat, and I knew at that point that something terrible was wrong. When I got to the hospital Dorothy was crying on the examining table.

We both wept in each other's arms for a long time as we faced the awful reality our baby was dead. The baby for which we had waited so long was gone. It was the worst moment in my life. I couldn't believe it. I felt someone had ripped open my heart and sucked the breath out of me. We were shaken to the core of our beings. Our grief smothered us. I was caught off guard that the death of an unborn child could so deeply affect me and shake my faith in a loving, sovereign God. The six months of anticipation had formed invisible bonds with this child as we dreamed of her role in our family and what she would be like. All these dreams were shattered in an instant as the horror oppressively settled on our souls.

Dr. Karshima and Carolyn suggested it would be best to wait until Dorothy started labor on her own rather than inducing her. We walked home together weeping as the truth sank in. After spending a few more minutes in our bedroom alone crying and comforting each other, we called the girls into the bedroom and told them the baby had died. The baby that was a gift from God, He had taken back to heaven. They cried with us and had lots of questions about why the baby had died, about heaven, death, and God. "Maybe the baby didn't eat enough peanut butter." "Maybe Mommy didn't eat enough...." We told them there was probably something wrong with the baby, so Jesus took the baby back to heaven. Heather and Anna cried hard and kept saying, "We don't want the baby to die."

We had just gotten a lot of boxes of goodies from the United States, and I had promised the girls we could open the boxes after our family meeting. After talking with the girls for about an hour, they said, "Can we open our presents now? We'll let Mommy open her presents first." Surprisingly they seemed ready to move on, so we opened our boxes, and they were thrilled to get presents from our friends in the States. It was a good idea and helped them move beyond the grief and sadness of the baby.

Later I asked the hospital carpenter to make a coffin, got permission to bury the baby at the Miango cemetery, and made some of the arrangements for the burial ceremony. We went to Truxtons and called Dorothy's parents, but no one was home, so we left a message on their answering machine. After getting the girls to bed, the phone started ringing, and we spent the next few hours talking to our families. It was helpful and encouraging to talk to them, and they expressed their sadness and assured us of their prayers.

When I saw Dorothy looking at the clothes she wanted to put on the baby I cried. All I could say to Dorothy over and over was, "I'm so sorry. I love you." That evening Dorothy and I had more time to talk and weep together. We discussed a name for the baby, the service at the graveside, and the terrible loss it was for us. We prayed and thanked the Lord for giving the baby to us even for six months. Even in that short time the baby had brought us such joy, and we were grateful. We weren't angry with God or asking lots of "Why" questions; we were just heartbroken. It was the saddest day of our lives. We went to bed exhausted and in great pain and sadness. We slept for a few hours but both woke about 3 a.m. and couldn't get back to sleep. We decided to go to Miango for a week or so to rest, grieve, and wait for the delivery.

Over the next few days at Miango, many visitors came to comfort, counsel, and pray with us. I couldn't stop crying every time a new person came to the house, and we told them the story. Grief swept over me in waves all day. I was fine for a while and then something or someone triggered more crying. People assured us of their prayers and offered to help us in any way they could. Several who had lost children gave us long hugs, and we could see in their eyes the pain we felt as they shared their stories of grief. We were thankful for the kindness and love of many in the SIM family. As we pondered the events of the previous days, we were thankful we didn't find out in Galmi. It would have been so much harder to deal with the news in the midst of strangers. To face the long, two-day trip home with such sad hearts would have been especially difficult. The Lord's timing was good even if we didn't like what had happened. We kept saying to ourselves, "There was nothing we did wrong.

There was nothing we could have done to change the events, and there was probably something wrong with the baby."

We had to believe God was in control. He loved us and wanted the best for us. It was the only thing that kept us sane. We tried so hard to have a baby and wanted this baby so much; it was hard to face the fact the baby was gone. We were afraid to ask the questions about what was next. "Can we or should we try for another baby? Does the Lord want us to have only three children?" We were not ready to tackle those questions.

We knew the next phase of waiting would be hard, especially with Dorothy having to face labor and delivering a dead baby. This was the hardest thing we ever had to face. Every time I saw a baby, I cried inside and wished it were ours. Having our joyful children around helped as they played and seemed to move on with their lives.

On our family walk to the water reservoir one day we saw some fish in the water and a dead one on the bank. Anna said, "I wish I was a fish." The others chimed in they wanted to be fishes too and "that one [dead one] can be the baby." On our walk home, Anna said, "Daddy, I don't want the baby to die." I assured her I didn't either, but the baby went to heaven. The girls were thinking about the baby more than it appeared and were processing their grief in their own way.

After a week at Miango, we went to Jos, so the doctors could check Dorothy. She had not progressed much toward delivering the baby, and so they encouraged us to wait a bit longer. We also talked about the cause again, and they reassured us it was more than likely a problem with the baby. So we accepted that in God's providence He took the baby back to heaven. We returned to Miango to continue waiting.

We got a lot of rest at Miango and began to realize how exhausted we were from the trip to Niger and the stress of the news. As we rested, talked, prayed, and meditated, we began to feel physically and emotionally stronger. We began taking walks and hiking with the children. The sadness and grief lessened each day as we read, watched praise videos, and listened to Christian music. We were encouraged from I Peter 5 that after a little while "He will strengthen us and establish us." Scripture, especially Psalms and Lamentations, was a great encouragement. I also found comfort in journaling our experiences and emotions.

We wanted to have a ceremony to help the girls understand that death was a part of life, that Aimee was a part of our family, and was in heaven. We also desired to make a statement about our belief in the personhood of the unborn. When Lorraine Foute visited us at Miango, I asked her if her husband Bill would speak at the graveside service. When we thought of a verse to put on the program and Aimee's grave marker, Isaiah 40:11 came immediately to mind. "He will take the little lambs in His arms." It was comforting to us that in the midst of sadness the Lord could take our little one in His arms, and He was already taking care of her in heaven.

One evening about ten days after we had been in Miango, I pondered again the loss of the baby and felt extremely sad that God had allowed this to happen. I was still heartbroken. I cried uncontrollably, sobbing as I thought how permanent the tragedy was, and of how we would not have a baby. I just wept and wept. I am not sure what triggered the crying, but I was overcome with the ache in my heart.

On Monday, June 29, 1998, after being at Miango for two weeks, we packed up and went into Jos after breakfast in preparation for Dorothy's induction of labor. We called our family in the U.S. and gave them the news about our plans. We were anxious but prayed for the Lord's peace and knew we were safe in His hands.

At 2 a.m. Tuesday, June 30, 1998 we went back to the hospital. Dorothy was responding to the induction medicine and was admitted to the maternity ward. I brought a mattress to put on the floor so I got a little rest. By 8 a.m. Dorothy only had mild contractions, so Carolyn Kirschner stayed with Dorothy, let me go home, get a shower, and call the girls. A number of hospital staff visited us. One visitor prayed that if I had any unconfessed sin or had offended God in any way that He should forgive me! We felt like Job when his three "comforters" came to visit him.

I ran through in my mind a thousand times the various possible scenarios of the day. I imagined the worst complication of Dorothy bleeding and dying during the delivery. I had a short talk with the Lord and agreed if he wanted to take Dorothy, "Thy will be done." I felt so helpless, so anxious, and yet had a strange peace that God was with us through this valley. I also appreciated our doctors' calm, kind manner, reassuring us all along the process and helping us think through many of the questions on our hearts.

From 10 a.m. until about 2 p.m., Dorothy had contractions on and off. Then Dorothy said she felt like she wanted to go to the bathroom. As we helped her walk back to the Delivery Room, the baby was born in the hall. It was a girl, and the umbilical cord was tightly wound around her neck. We could not see any other obvious problems, so concluded that was the cause of her death. After wrapping the baby in a blanket, Dorothy held her, and we cried softly together. The time of the birth was 2:15 p.m., and we named her Aimee Natalie.

It was too late in the day to go to Miango for a service, so we planned the burial for the next day. This would give us time to notify friends, get a program printed, and notify our families in the United States.

I called the girls and told them about the delivery of Aimee Natalie. Heather's comment was "I always wished it was a girl!" Anna was the only one of the three who asked how the baby died. I asked the Foutes to bring the girls to the hospital, so they could see that Mommy was okay.

After the delivery we listened to Christian music, talked and rested. Dorothy was very tired so slept a little and began to unwind. Several hospital staff came to comfort us and pray with us. The ironic thing was that a Nigerian orthopedic nurse had just come to the hospital maternity ward with his pregnant wife who was 35 weeks along. She was admitted and by the evening had delivered twin boys. One man's day of joy is another's day of sorrow. We congratulated him but knew that he had no idea the sleepless nights ahead. We also rejoiced for the joy that the twins would bring them.

By 8:30 p.m., we finally left the hospital for home. The last two hours we were in the hospital, the electricity voltage dropped so low that the light in the room went out, and we sat in the darkness until it was time to leave. We were also amazed that from 2 a.m. when Dorothy was admitted until almost before we left, there was light and even water from the bathroom taps!

We got back to the house and called Dorothy's parents and my sister Sharon and told them about the events of the day. It was very comforting to hear from our family, and they were a great encouragement to us. Dorothy's Dad prayed with us. We were amazed how the Lord gave us peace throughout the day, how Dorothy's labor had been relatively short, and how she had come through so well without complications. We finally put out the lights at midnight and thanked the Lord for helping us through this tough day.

The next day we picked up the girls who had been staying with their friends and went to Miango for a few days of rest. At 1:30 p.m. that afternoon just before the burial, the SIM missionary Lee family came for a visit. Their teenage daughter had been killed in a car accident a year and a half earlier. It was a very emotional time as we hugged and shed tears together. It was so comforting to have them come for a visit because we knew their pain was so raw. We felt that they more than almost anyone understood our unanswered questions, pain, and sorrow.

We then got the girls ready for the burial service in the afternoon. I had a good talk with them to help prepare them and ask them to be on their best behavior. We walked together as a family to the cemetery. Flowers and roses were beautifully arranged all around the gravesite. Someone had made a lovely rose wreath, and there was a beautiful bouquet of roses on the coffin. I couldn't look at anyone but kept my head down and quietly wept as I walked to the cemetery. Surrounded by our loving friends, we sat as a family on a beautiful white bench in front of Aimee's coffin. Chuck Truxton led the service and did a great job. Ken Ward opened with prayer and then we sang "Day by Day"— a very meaningful song to us. Bill Foute gave a message about Jesus as our shepherd and His care of us. While the Voths beautifully sang "In the Sweet By and By," the Lord gave me a picture of the gates of heaven with a beautiful little girl waiting for me. She was saying, "Daddy, welcome home. Let me show you my home." Wow! What a great image of hope, joy, and assurance of joining our loved ones in heaven.

We had the girls each take a rose from the wreath on the coffin, so we could press them and put them in Aimee's memory album. We then slowly walked away from her grave together, hand in hand. At the reception afterwards we visited with our friends and began to unwind from the tension of the past two weeks. I felt a great burden had been lifted. Even though I was sad, I was grateful to have Dorothy back and to be able to try to get back to some sense of normalcy.

Over the next days we rested, walked, and talked about all that had happened and God's grace to us. There were several guest families with babies at Miango that week. Whenever I saw a baby, I was reminded of our loss and felt a twinge of pain in my heart. The girls took turns holding the babies, and I marveled at how beautiful, soft, and cuddly each one was.

As we were praying in bed one evening, Dorothy told me she had cried in the afternoon thinking about Aimee. She said she heard Aimee calling her and saying, "It's okay, Mommy. I'm okay." Then she started to cry and there was a flood of crying and tears. It seems our daughter's death was really hitting her just then. Dorothy sobbed as she asked why God would allow this to happen. It all seemed so unfair. I tried my best to comfort her that the Lord had been good to us, sovereign in all His ways and although I had no answers, we needed to trust Him one day at a time.

For several days Dorothy had abdominal and breast pain. They served as ongoing reminders of the loss of our baby. We visited Aimee's grave at the cemetery almost every day and realized this cemetery would have a new meaning for us. Slowly we began to feel better, and the memories became less painful and less vivid. After about ten days we were feeling physically and emotionally strong enough to return to Jos.

Several people gave us books on suffering and death. From Joni Erickson's book on suffering came the idea that God's purpose in creating us was that while on earth we should glorify Him and then when we die we would receive a glorified body to praise Him in eternity. In Aimee's case, she did not have an opportunity to glorify God on earth, but now she has a glorified body and is praising God in Heaven. What a great thought.

Other visitors shared their personal stories of grief and loss with us. Mrs. Lee shared quite openly her struggle in accepting and coping with the death of her teenage daughter in a car accident. She described her struggle, agonizing through the tough questions. In her quest to understand God's reasons for her daughter's death, she developed a trust in God, a greater appreciation of His greatness, a longing and love for heaven, and a deep love for Jesus. In reading the book of Job, she realized he also asked God the forbidden questions and God was not angry or threatened. Although at first she felt Job was too righteous a man to be an example or model for her, in seeing the honesty of his tough questions to God, she identified with him and his desire to hear from God the answer to the "why" question. At the end, Job learned to trust God even though he never understood the reasons for his suffering.

Rev. Lee explained how his pilgrimage was different from his wife's. He focused on the Psalms of David. He was impressed with David's honesty before God in expressing his feelings of hurt, abandonment, and anger. He articulated the cry of his heart and the tears during the hard times of his life. This brought great comfort knowing that even the great David had those feelings and wasn't afraid to share his innermost feelings with God.

Many came to comfort us – some with tender words and hugs and some with unhelpful, theological remarks that maybe sin in our lives was the cause or we could always have another child. The most comfort came from those who had lost a child themselves. They just sat with us as we wept. They did not offer explanations, possible reasons God would allow this, profound Scriptural passages, or pious statements. They just sat with us, and their closeness — physical and emotional — was comforting.

I knew the conversation with the Lees had been difficult. That night as Dorothy and I were lying in bed, she cried on my shoulder and expressed something that had been on my mind for some time but was hoping she had not thought of it. Dorothy was willing to accept that God had taken our child, but the thought of Aimee being strangled or suffocated to death and the suffering of that little innocent one was very, very hard to accept as coming from a loving God. I had no answer, but in tears we expressed to God our trust in Him in spite of these difficult and unanswerable questions.

In some ways, I compartmentalized my thinking about Aimee. On some of those questions I mentally closed the door, accepting that I would never know the answers this side of Heaven. It seemed okay to just leave some questions alone for fear of sinking into the abyss of despair and depression because there would be no satisfactory answers.

Over the years since Aimee's going to heaven, the pain has lessened and the wound is healing. At the moment of her death, time seemed our enemy as the seconds ticked by interminably. Our thoughts seemed painfully frozen in time as we labored to think past the next few moments. We learned that through trial there is the hope of recovery and healing in spite of the depths of despair and waves of grief. The difficult part was keeping our minds occupied on "things above" through the slow-motion aftermath until the circumstances of daily living began to dull the sharp edges of the trauma.

Many times we asked God why He took Aimee from us. It seemed a cruel thing to give a child and then take her back before we saw her first smile or heard her first words. Asking "why" was not a sign of anger towards God but represented our confusion. After many weeks of struggling, Dorothy finally realized that whatever answer or explanation God might have given us, it would not have satisfied. In His wisdom, God sometimes does not give us an answer. He wants us to trust Him even in His silence. Since we could not abandon Him, we could only trust that His purposes were good and right.

Over the next six months Dorothy and I experienced surprising, sudden, overwhelming waves of grief. We moved from crying all day, to once a day, to every other day, and now with those who have lost a child. We felt so numb we were like robots going through the motions of our daily activities. I thought I would never get over my grief with any amount of time, but gradually over the course of months and years the waves became less frequent and less intense, and we visited Aimee's grave less and less. Each time we were at Miango we set aside time for a stroll to her grave. In meditation and reflection we cleaned the leaves and sticks off the small white stones that covered her grave. We prayed and thanked God for her brief life, for our family and our marriage. Although through all our discussions and tears we never landed on a reason God allowed her to die, we rested in our deep conviction His loving plan for us was good and perfect.

Our grief increased our deep empathy with others who were in painful situations, especially those who had lost a child. Shortly after Aimee's death, one of the resident doctor's wives also had a miscarriage. We visited her and felt an emotional connection with her like we would never have experienced before. We had an understanding of how to comfort her, what to say and not say, and could encourage her with words from the credentials of experience. So as Paul has said, "Blessed be the God and Father of our Lord Jesus Christ, the Father of mercies and God of all comfort, who comforts us in all our affliction so that we will be able to comfort those who are in any affliction with the comfort with which we ourselves are comforted by God." (2 Cor. 1:4 NASU)

As the years have passed, the painful memory of Aimee's death has softened. We remember our excitement about her coming and regret we never really got to know her this side of heaven. We continue to thank God for helping us through that difficult dark valley and looking forward to being greeted at heaven's gate by a cheerful little girl called Aimee Natalie Ardill.

IN SICKNESS AND IN HEALTH

S ickness is part and parcel of life but is a more serious issue for those living in the tropics. Not only are the bugs and threats that we face sometimes life-threatening (malaria, typhoid, parasites, reckless drivers, and AIDS), but the health care specialists and facilities to handle these medical conditions are less accessible, more limited, and in some cases nonexistent.

Like many, we do a risk assessment and then attempt to limit our risk and exposure. At an organizational level, this may mean some missionaries should not go to certain areas of the world because of their pre-existing illnesses, proneness to certain illness or because of the lack of medical personnel. For example in Nigeria, we were not prepared to handle some medical conditions requiring specific laboratory tests, so these people were discouraged from coming to work in Nigeria.

We also took precautions to avoid getting sick. This was in the best interest of the Mission because it reduced health care costs, and so there was some legislation of these preventive measures. These precautions, however, were not easily enforced; people, like sheep, often went astray. Still, we encouraged boiling or filtering all drinking water, rinsing fresh vegetables and fruit in a bleach solution to kill the parasites, taking malaria prophylactic medication faithfully, using mosquito nets, wearing seatbelts when in a moving vehicle, avoiding the use of motorcycles or at least wearing a helmet, and keeping current on the recommended immunizations.

In spite of all these precautions, people still got sick, including those in our family. There are also illnesses that happen that are beyond our control. For the first six months after coming to Nigeria most missionaries struggle with gastrointestinal problems. Their bodies are adjusting to the new bacterial flora, and it just takes time to develop immunity or resistance to the new bugs. No matter how careful people are, many are "on the run" for the first few months.

After that initial illness, the next common experience was the problem of living in community. In the Hillcrest School community with 250 students and teachers, any virus that got a foothold spread rapidly in the dorms, hostels, and then homes of the children. Our children often brought bugs home and shared them with us. Some parents had the good sense to keep their sick children home, but some did not and, so the sharing continued.

A final observation was the seasonal nature of some illnesses. In the dry season, because of the winds and dust from the Sahara desert that blew for months, there were a lot of respiratory and eye problems. Meningitis was also a dry season concern, but most missionaries stayed current with their vaccinations for meningitis. The rainy season with the wet and damp conditions brought colds and flu, which were easily passed around.

As a family, we had the usual bugs and viruses over the years, but I wanted to share several of my experiences with illness that may give an insight into coping with sickness as a missionary.

Hepatitis

During our first term we attended a small Nigerian church in our community. We were the only expatriates in the congregation and thought we could be an encouragement to the pastor and members. One Sunday afternoon in mid-August 1992, we attended a "love feast" (potluck) after church in the yard of one of the elders who lived near the church in a mud-walled compound. We were given the royal treatment, which meant we had someplace to sit and were given a bottled soft drink to wash down the jollof rice and goat meat. To our surprise Marie handled the peppery Nigerian food without a problem. For some reason, they gave me a cup for my Coke and without taking much regard to the still wet cup, I poured my drink in it and enjoyed the fellowship.

My surgical colleague at the hospital, Don Meier, had come down with hepatitis for a few weeks in July 1992, so my workload as a new surgeon was heavier than I had expected. I was doing more orthopedic and subspecialty cases than I was comfortable with since Don had been the main orthopedic surgeon. A little while after the church potluck, I began to feel tired and was having abdominal pain on and off. It seemed like I was getting another stomach bug – not something very unusual. I continued to work and do surgery but often came home at noon to rest for the afternoon. I began to have abdominal cramps with vague abdominal pain and was getting weaker and more easily fatigued. Even my eye muscles started to hurt; when I turned, my eyes and my head hurt. I noticed I had a slight fever and then started thinking this was more than just a flu bug. Could I have typhoid fever? Or worse? The only relief I could get was to press a pillow against my stomach or lie curled up on the floor.

On September 1, 1992, Dorothy called Dr. Tim Park, the missionary internist at Evangel, to take a look at me. He was not sure what was going on but decided to start me on antibiotics. I was not eating or drinking much, so when I took the antibiotics I had dry heaves. Later that afternoon, I was feeling so bad I asked Dorothy to call my parents and tell them to pray for me.

By the next morning I still had no relief from the abdominal pain and Dr. Park casually commented that he thought my eyes looked a bit yellow. I did not believe it could be hepatitis since I didn't have liver pain, itching, or real jaundice. I noticed my urine was a bit darker but blamed it on the antibiotics and lack of drinking. Dr. Park drew some blood for liver function lab tests, placed an IV line to keep me hydrated, and gave me more antibiotics. I didn't object since I knew I was losing weight and could not keep liquids down. We rigged up a coat hanger suspended on a nail on the wall for the IV stand. Dorothy went into full battle mode and manned the IV night and day.

By September 3, Marie's birthday, I was looking more yellow, and it was obvious from my pumpkin color appearance and the laboratory reports that I had hepatitis. As I became more yellow, the abdominal pain eased a bit. Dorothy called my parents in the United States with an update, and we postponed Marie's birthday party. I was not able to eat or get out of bed and certainly could not work. Normal recovery is three months of bed rest. She wanted to be available to help me at any time so organized others to take care of Marie, our only child at the time, during the day.

Over the next few days and weeks, I turned more yellow, but my appetite improved and I could take a shower. I lost 15 pounds that week and, between the straggly look and the weight loss, looked like a prisoner of war. As is customary in Africa we began to have lots of visitors or well-wishers. After a few days of lying around feeling miserable and keeping Dorothy busy attending to me, we decided to go to Miango to allow me to recuperate in a quieter place where Dorothy would not have to worry about cooking and cleaning. Dorothy packed the car and drove us to Miango.

We had a restful few weeks at Miango. It was a wonderful hideaway to recuperate. I was not able to eat the normal meals for some time but eventually made the short initially impossible walk to the dining hall for one meal a day, and then gradually was able to make it to all the meals. I had persistent abdominal pain for many weeks after my diagnosis and began to worry if there was something else going on.

After consulting with the Evangel doctors and the SIM leaders, we decided to return to the United States for additional tests.

Dorothy was getting tired attending to Marie and me, and I was worried that my liver pain had persisted so long. We went to California and stayed with my parents. They arranged the appropriate medical evaluations and tests. The change, rest, and good food did us all good, and after a month I felt much stronger and ready to return to Nigeria. It took a while for me to resume my full workload in Nigeria, but after about six months I was back up to speed and had assumed all my responsibilities. Coincidently, about that time the hepatitis A vaccine became available to the public, so we hope it is now a disease of historic interest only for missionaries.

Diabetes

While on furlough in the summer of 2001, we went for a two-week vacation to a camp in upstate New York called Camp of the Woods. The girls went to the girls' camp called Tapawingo and one-year-old David had lots of fun in the nursery every morning. We enjoyed the music, teaching, and time with our family and friends.

On July 4th and 5th I noticed I was getting more thirsty than normal and was urinating a lot. It had been an unusually warm week, and so I thought it was just the hot weather. I continued to drink lots of fruit drinks and sodas to quench my thirst but kept urinating a lot. I was still puzzled and thought maybe I had a urinary tract infection. We picked the girls up from Tapawingo Island on Saturday morning and headed for Maryland. To my surprise I had to urgently stop to use the bathroom every two hours on the ten-hour trip home. This was what the girls usually did on a long trip, except this time I was the culprit. They did not ask a lot of questions, but I knew at that stage there was something wrong. I kept drinking root beer and sodas all the way home but could not believe the urinary urgency I had. I decided I would wait for a day or two before calling Sue (Dorothy's sister who is an internist) for advice.

On Monday, I felt a little better, probably because I stopped drinking the soda, and went to work. I was very tired and my thinking seemed cloudy. On Monday, July 8, 2001, I was standing in the fifth floor restroom in the Baltimore Veterans Administration Hospital (VA) where I had been working. I stared at the urine dipstick in disbelief and denial. It could not be. It just could not be. "What things other than diabetes could make me spill sugar in my urine?" I almost cried in the bathroom. I immediately got on the Internet to look up causes of sugar in urine other than diabetes. There were very few, and I got a sick feeling in the pit of my stomach.

I called Dorothy to tell her the bad news and then told one of my surgical colleagues I was not feeling well and needed to go home. I was very tired and quite depressed and my mind was in a blur. I called Sue's office and made an appointment for later in the afternoon. I went home and waited for the afternoon appointment. When we arrived, Sue's nurse looked at me and said, "You look pretty bad." He immediately took my blood for some laboratory tests. To his surprise and my shock, my blood sugar was 330 — three times normal! We sat in an exam room for a few minutes, and I began to feel the awful weight of the diagnosis of diabetes overtake me like a big tsunami tidal wave. I was depressed and incredibly sad. What were the implications for my children and wife? For me as a father? For our ministry in Africa? For my work as a surgeon? I was overwhelmed with the seriousness of the diagnosis and could only picture the horrible outcomes for many diabetics I had seen at the VA with kidney failure, amputations, and eye problems. Was that to be my end? When and how long before it all set in?

Sue came in to talk to us. We wanted to return to Nigeria in three weeks. What would be the best approach to get my blood sugar down in such a short time? She started me on insulin shots at a low dose. Sue thought after my blood sugars were normal, I would likely be fine on oral medicines. So we stopped at a local drug store, bought the insulin, and headed for home. My eyes were not focusing well and I was feeling miserable. I gave myself the first insulin shot in my stomach, but I dreaded the thought of having to do this the rest of my life to control my diabetes. After getting home, I called my mom and dad and wept as I told them I had diabetes. They were understandably surprised, but since dad had been diagnosed a few years ago, they had some practical advice and encouragement. They offered to ship an extra glucometer to me by overnight express, so I could check my blood sugars.

I cried on and off all night. The next morning I checked my blood sugar as soon as the glucometer arrived; it was still 300. I was even more depressed, and we began to think of what to do. Dorothy had been talking to a friend who also had diabetes and suggested maybe we could call her doctor for a second opinion on what to do. I wanted my sugars to come down quickly, so we could return to Jos.

I called the Diabetes Center at Anne Arundel Hospital and explained to the nurse at the other end of the line about my situation. The doctor in the office, Dr. Cantero, was an endocrinologist Sue respected, and she agreed to see me right away. Her office staff immediately checked my blood sugar and my weight, and showed me into an exam room. After hearing my story, Dr. Cantero did a brief exam but was shocked when I had numbness in my left big toe. Dr. Cantero was not too optimistic that I would be able to manage with only oral meds but wanted to help me as much as possible. She made arrangements for me to talk to her dietician later.

Dorothy and I went to a bookstore and bought about four or five books on diabetes including *Diabetes for Dummies*. I felt so ignorant and scared. Suddenly I was hungry for information on this disease. I wanted to know how to manage it, and Dorothy wanted to know how to feed me, so we could manage the diabetes by controlling my carbohydrates. We went home and began to read intently. I was so discouraged I did not call the church or tell friends right away. I called Dr. Young at the SIM medical office and asked for his prayer.

Our immediate concern was control of my blood sugars, but the next issue was the timing of our return to Jos. Was it realistic to go back in three weeks? Were we crazy? I called the VA to tell them the news and explain I would not be at work for a while. I went in after about a week when I was feeling better, and several of my colleagues tried to talk me out of going back to Nigeria. They were concerned about my health and the wisdom of going back so early after my diagnosis. One surgeon's father is a diabetic, and she had many horrible tales about his problems and serious complications. It was not exactly comforting, but I appreciated her concern. My boss said I did not have to go back to work before leaving for Africa.

The day after my diagnosis I began taking 30-minute walks twice a day around the neighborhood to drive my blood sugar down. Sometimes Dorothy, Marie, Heather, and Anna would join me. With the walks every day, my reduced carbohydrate diet, and the medicine, I lost 25 pounds and my blood sugar came down. I really felt better than before I had the diagnosis.

Dr. Cantero started me on an oral medicine Glyburide to get my blood sugar down quickly. It had the complication of sometimes driving the blood sugar down too far and producing hypoglycemia. I was concerned about being on this drug if we went back to Jos. I agreed to stay on the glyburide because Dr. Cantero felt it would get my sugars down quicker but really wanted to start Glucophage. Because our time was so short, I knew I needed to try the Glucophage for a week before we left to make sure it would be okay.

At my appointment with Dr. Cantero a week before we left, much to my surprise she suggested that I could switch to Glucophage. I almost hugged her I was so happy. I felt relieved and thankful that the Lord had answered my prayers.

Fortunately, when all this was unfolding, Dorothy's parents had offered to take the children for the week to a Christian camp called Sandy Cove. When I was not feeling very sociable, the children were not around, and I didn't have to deal with telling them why I was sick. The children had a great week especially since the camp had a great children's program.

Dorothy and I were reading the books we had bought because we felt so ignorant and were starved for information to help me cope and get on with a normal life. I was interested in the pharmacology of the drugs in treatment. Dorothy was keen on understanding the diet since she had to cook for me. We finally began to understand the basics of diet management. Since I was checking my blood sugar up to seven times a day, I began to see the impact of each food I ate on my blood sugar.

In the midst of all this, we were still trying to pack for Africa. Fortunately, I had packed about 15 boxes a few weeks earlier, and so was ahead of schedule. I was able to pack boxes occasionally, and it helped me feel better because I was burning off the sugar.

By the end of the week, I was feeling better but was struggling with blurred vision. In retrospect I can see how several things happened that were indicators that my blood sugar was high, but I did not put it all together until I began urinating frequently. Over the previous year in Nigeria I noticed my vision had changed. When we were in Texas my brother John checked my eyes and recommended new glasses. I liked them, and I was seeing fine. When we got back to Maryland, I noticed my vision had changed again. In retrospect, it was probably my blood sugar out of whack all along.

We managed to get my blood sugars under control with the medicine, diet, and exercise. I am thankful for God's grace in helping me overcome my fear of the future living with diabetes and am still learning to trust Him anew each day. We were able to leave for Nigeria on schedule.

Kidney Stones

At ten minutes after twelve on Thursday night, February 28, 2003, I was suddenly awakened by excruciating pain like a red-hot, sharp poker in the right side of my back. I could barely catch my breath and eased out of bed. After a few seconds I decided this was not a nightmare, and I needed some help, so I called out to Dorothy. She woke up pretty quickly and asked, "What's wrong?"

I told her about the pain and said I had never had such a pain and was not sure what it was. I was on my knees on the floor curled up in pain. I began to think through the possibilities that included a rupturing aneurysm, a perforated stomach ulcer, or a kidney stone. I had already had an appendectomy or that would have been on my list as well. I was too young for an aneurysm, and although it might have been an ulcer, from the absence of pain in the front of my stomach I guessed it was probably a kidney stone.

I finally asked Dorothy to call Dr. Greg Kirschner, our neighbor family practice doctor. She told him I was in extreme pain and asked if he could come over right away. I counted the seconds and minutes until he arrived, and after a few brief questions, he agreed it was probably a stone. Greg had been through this 15 times before so was the local expert on kidney stones. With that grim word, he said, "Be prepared for a few days of pain, so let's try and get you more comfortable." He took off to the hospital to get some IV supplies and drugs and returned about 20-30 minutes later with the necessary medications.

The pain was so intense I became nauseated and vomited everything that was in my stomach. It persisted for several hours, but finally the morphine and Phenergan injections gave me some relief. Over the next few days, I got little sleep because the pain came back every eight to twelve hours. It was moving down my right side until it settled in my lower back and right groin area. The only position that offered relief was on my knees crouched over the side of my bed hugging a pillow. Most of the time I had constant dull persistent pain. I could only take short breaths and became so tight and tense coping with the pain that I was exhausted. When the pain occasionally subsided, I crawled into bed and tried to rest. I had an IV in for the first few days to keep me hydrated and flush out the stone. I was also trying to drink as much as I could, but when the pain was strong, I stopped eating and drinking.

I found when I had the pain, I closed my eyes to deal with it, and my world would close down into a space with the periphery only a few feet from me. All seemed dark. I did not care about anything else. Although Dorothy had to take care of the children, I needed her help to deal with the pain, so whenever I had an attack, she heard me cry out for her or ring the bell and came running. In between the attacks, she tended to the children and household duties. She later told me that Marie did a great job taking care of the twins and David during those times.

Heather had read in her little human anatomy and physiology book all about how kidney stones were formed. She was always interested in medical things and was not afraid to ask questions. After I explained a bit more to her, she was prepared to educate her classmates about kidney stones. By the end of the day, the entire Hillcrest community knew I had a kidney stone and all about how they were formed!

By Saturday, three days after the attack started, I began to feel better but knew I had not passed the stone and was not out of trouble. I had one severe attack of lower back pain, and we could not find Greg to give me the pain shot. Dorothy dutifully changed the IV bags and gave me pain pills. Dorothy sent Anna looking for Dr. Bev Truxton. She came over and gave me the morphine shot. The morphine was about all that helped with the pain that was now constant. At the end of the week I was also having terrible acid reflux and upset stomach. I could hardly keep anything down.

Because I was ill, some friends offered to take the children to the Carnival at Hillcrest. Dorothy then told me she had invited about 60 people to Miango for lunch on Sunday for a surprise birthday party for me. My 50th! Since she could not easily 'uninvite' them, she hoped I could somehow manage to get there for lunch on Sunday. That became my immediate goal – to make it to my own birthday party. By Sunday morning, the pain had lessened, so Greg agreed to let me go without the IV. I took a bath and got dressed to go. I got into the back seat of the van but felt pain at every little bump on the road. I gripped the overhead handgrip as hard as I could and began to lift myself off the seat at each bump to lessen the blow. By the time we got to Miango, I was in agony and exhausted from the ride. I felt a lot worse than when we started and wondered if this was such a great idea after all.

After resting a few minutes in the car, I walked into the Miango Rest Home dining hall and was greeted by 80 friends singing "Happy Birthday." Wow! I was overwhelmed that so many people had shown up for a party for me. Someone had the video camera running and others were taking pictures. I could barely stand up because of the severe pain. I gingerly walked to the special chair they had prepared for me, complete with balloons and party decorations. Many came up to me and expressed both congratulations and sympathies. They had a nice big cake that Dorothy had made and a great lunch that, unfortunately, I could not eat. It was truly a great party except that I looked about 80 years old and felt miserable.

Since our missionary friend from Northern Ireland, Jean Garland, was also having her 50th birthday party, they relit the cake and she blew out the candles again. What fun! After I opened a few presents and cards, I was tired. Everyone seemed to understand, so I thanked everyone for coming and we left. I asked if I could ride in a more comfortable car on the way home, so a friend offered his air-conditioned car. I was exhausted by the time we made it home but delighted that Dorothy had gone to such trouble to arrange a party for me and that I had been able to make it!

On Monday I was having pain on and off again. I was not drinking enough water, so the IV was reinserted. We decided I needed an IVP x-ray to see where the stone was, how many there were, and if there were signs my ureter was completely blocked. Fortunately I was not having a lot of pain. It took about two hours to get all the x-rays done at another hospital. The last x-ray clearly showed the stone at the lower end of the right ureter. I was relieved we saw the stone and that there was only one.

Because my pain had persisted, I was concerned the stone was stuck. The problem was I was the only one at the hospital who could do the procedure to remove it – but not on myself! Amazingly, on Monday Dr. Randy Skau, a visiting American surgeon from another mission hospital outside of Jos, stopped by to see Greg Kirschner.

If I were to have a procedure done to remove the stone, I wanted to be sure it was done by someone who had experience. I knew that this procedure was not without risks and so was willing to go abroad if there was no one locally to do it. Randy agreed that if the x-rays showed a stone that was "catchable" he was willing to do the procedure on Wednesday.

I showed all the girls the x-rays with the stone. They seemed to enjoy learning about my problem. I saw them once or twice a day when I was not in pain and told them I would be okay but to keep praying for me. On one occasion I remember Anna looked in our bedroom wanting Dorothy, and saw me huddled over the bed crying in pain. She then ran from the room and started crying when she realized how much pain I was in. David had no idea what was going on and was his cheerful and humorous self each time I saw him. He wanted to jump on my tummy and play and wasn't happy I could not play with him.

I was in agony most of Tuesday night and spent the night on my knees on the floor until finally about 6 a.m. Dorothy called Greg and asked if I could have some morphine before the surgery. By now the pain was unrelenting, and I was in tears. I was worn down and exhausted. Greg thought it would help to have me a bit drowsy for the procedure. I had about an hour or so of deep sleep and then woke up to go to the hospital.

On Wednesday morning our driver Kingsford drove me to the hospital with Dr. Randy Skau and Dorothy. Nurse anesthetist Simon Khantiok prayed for me, and then put an oxygen mask over my mouth and nose. I remember seeing the bright OR light and then my mind went blank. The next thing I remember was hearing Dorothy's voice when I woke up.

Apparently Randy tried once to get the stone, and I jerked with pain, so Simon increased the medication and Randy tried again. On the second attempt when Randy retrieved the stone, Dr. Paul Ushie came running out of the OR and joyfully yelled to Dorothy, "They got it!"

When I woke up, I felt so drugged I could hardly open my eyes, but at least I had no pain. Over the next hours I fell in and out of a deep sleep. On Thursday morning I awoke feeling like a reborn man. I was so thankful the excruciating pain was over. Throughout the day people from the hospital and compound came to greet me and pray thanksgiving for God's grace. Dorothy and I repeatedly thanked the Lord for His grace and mercy. It was interesting that after the procedure, Simon Khantiok said to me he was glad we could get the stone out at Evangel since I would be tempted to "run away to America for treatment."

I will be forever grateful to Dr. Greg Kirschner for his patient and kind care. He was so willing to come see me at any time, day, or night, for any reason. I knew he was praying for me and really cared for me through this ordeal. Dr. Randy Skau was an angel sent from God for my hour of need. I am also grateful for the Fretheim family's willingness to take care of David every morning. Marie was amazing caring for her sisters and brother. She had a wonderful spirit.

Throughout each of my times of illness, I learned a great deal about God and about myself. How do I handle the process of pain and suffering? Do I trust it is from God and He is with me and will sustain me? Do I have to have meaning in the pain, or have I learned to trust Him? It reminded me of the suffering of Jesus and those martyred for their faith. I still don't know why God allowed me to suffer but thanked Him for the deliverance He brought through my colleagues, the serendipitous (or providential) arrival of Randy Skau, the good care of the hospital staff, and the amazing love and commitment of my wife. Praise be to God!

THE MIRACLE BABY

After the death of Aimee, Dorothy and I struggled with many questions. How many children did we want? Would we be willing to risk losing another child during the pregnancy? Could we handle a child with a major deformity or birth defect? After many late night discussions and soul searching, we decided to try for another child.

Because they were not available in Nigeria at the time, Dorothy had brought some home pregnancy test kits to Jos. In February 2000 she came out of the bathroom one morning with a big smile and showed me the little blue line on the strip. We danced with joy. God had indeed answered our earnest prayers and given us another child.

Many women at some time during their pregnancy have morning sickness. For the first time in any of her pregnancies Dorothy had "evening sickness." She also noticed this baby was an active kicker, so we wondered if maybe it was a boy. The pregnancy overall went well. Dorothy kept to a good weight gain schedule, and she was active throughout the pregnancy.

Our biggest fear was the six-month mark – the time when we lost Aimee. So when Dorothy got past that painful milestone in June 2000, we sighed in relief and thought things were going to be okay. We began talking more with the girls about all the changes in our lives with a new baby. After a sonogram evaluation about this time we learned to our delight that it was indeed a boy. We were all excited!

On Saturday evening, July 15, 2000, Dorothy noticed her hands were getting swollen, so she checked her blood pressure. It was a bit high, so she tried to get more bed rest. On Tuesday her blood pressure was high again, and when she checked her urine, she noticed she had protein in her urine, which is a sign of toxemia of pregnancy. She finally told me, and I was extremely concerned. This is a serious condition that can lead to premature delivery and even death of the mother. We were up most of the night worrying. On Wednesday morning, we told her obstetrician who did a sonogram and said the baby looked okay. Because she was only 28 weeks along in her pregnancy and Evangel Hospital could not handle a premature baby that young, we decided to go to the United States as soon as possible.

The twins were delighted that we were going back to the United States, but Marie was quite upset that she had to leave her friends and couldn't start fourth grade with them. Dorothy was started on blood pressure medication, but unfortunately it gave her a headache and vomiting. Several missionary women came over to the house to help get the children packed. They knew what clothes to pack for them and were very helpful especially since Dorothy was confined to strict bed rest and was already getting weak. Amazingly we got airplane tickets quickly for the whole family to go to Maryland.

On Thursday morning, July 20, we said goodbye to our house helpers and compound friends. It was especially difficult for the children because they did not have time to say goodbye to their school friends. We were leaving very suddenly and had no idea when we would be back. We literally walked out of the house and left all we owned, even food in the fridge, dirty laundry in the baskets, and the house as I would have left it going to work that morning.

After packing the van, we helped Dorothy lie down on the middle seat of the van for the four-hour trip north to Kano. I packed her medications in my carry-on bag and included two syringes of a Valium in case she started having seizures from the toxemia. I also had a blood pressure cuff and stethoscope to periodically check her blood pressure. She did well on the drive in spite of having intense upper abdominal pain.

In Kano we stayed in one of the ECWA Eye Hospital guesthouses where Dorothy spent the day resting in bed for the long plane ride ahead. I tried to keep the children busy and monitored Dorothy's blood pressure throughout the day. Kano was always hot, so we were thankful the electricity stayed on so we could keep reasonably cool with the room fans. I went to the airport on Friday afternoon to check in our baggage, which would make it a quicker check-in later in the evening. After a light supper we headed for the airport. We had arranged for a wheelchair for Dorothy to help her through the airport. Thankfully going through the airport immigration and customs desks went smoothly, and we almost ran out to the plane.

Once on the plane, I wanted to get Dorothy settled as quickly as possible. I prayed there would be an empty seat, so she could lie down. That position would help her blood pressure, ease her pain, and allow her to get more rest. Unbelievably, there was only one empty seat on the plane, and it was next to Dorothy, so she was able to lie down more comfortably for the 5½-hour flight to Amsterdam. The KLM airline crewmembers were very kind and helpful. I checked her blood pressure periodically, but I was very anxious to get her to more capable care.

In Amsterdam the crew arranged for an electric passenger cart to meet us at the plane and take us to the medical unit in the airport. After coming out of the dust and dirt of Africa, the clinic seemed incredibly beautiful, clean, and quiet. I needed to tell the clinic staff about Dorothy's condition but also did not want to get them so worried they would not let us back on the plane to the

United States. Dorothy felt better after the few hours of rest, and we were taken to our next flight to Washington Dulles airport in Virginia. That flight also went pretty well, but Dorothy began having more abdominal pain, and I didn't know what else to do to help her.

Upon our arrival on Saturday, Dorothy's parents and sister Sue met us with tears in their eyes and lots of hugs. We quickly headed for the hospital in Annapolis, 1 ½ hours away. Dorothy's sister was a physician in Annapolis, so had arranged with Anne Arundel Hospital for Dorothy's urgent admission. Upon arrival to the Emergency Room, the staff whisked us through the admission process and wheeled Dorothy to a beautiful birthing room. The latest fad in deliveries was to labor and deliver in the same room as long as the delivery was uncomplicated. The hospital room was luxurious and comfortable with a television, a nice big bathroom, Ethan Allen furniture, gorgeous curtains and flowers, and a bed that moved in every conceivable way to make the patient comfortable. Having come off a plane from Africa, we were especially struck with the luxury, the cleanliness, and beauty of the room.

From the moment Dorothy arrived in the room, she was hooked up to a continuous fetal monitor to evaluate the baby's condition. She also had a sonogram every day to see if the baby was handling the stress of Dorothy's preeclampsia. The analogy we were given was that the baby would stay in the womb as long as it was a safe place to stay, but if it became a hostile environment for the baby, the baby would either die or come out early. The danger of an early delivery was that the baby's lungs were still immature and not ready to function. To help with the baby's immature lungs, Dorothy was given some steroid injections to accelerate the baby's lung development. A premature infant also was at risk for lots of other problems like bleeding in the brain, deafness, blindness, and retardation. The task of the obstetrician was to keep the baby in the womb as long as it was safely possible and then deliver the baby.

I was determined to stay at Dorothy's side, so I set up a mattress on the floor in her hospital room and slept there for the first few days until it looked like she was more stable. Dorothy's blood pressure began to respond to the bed rest, reduced stress, and medications. The baby appeared to be okay, although there was concern the baby was abnormally stressed.

By the next day, Sunday, Dorothy's blood pressure had settled down and been safe all day, but she continued to spill protein in her urine. The doctor allowed her to take a shower (which she badly needed!). The baby continued to do well and was kicking vigorously with a good heart rate. A neonatologist visited and explained some of the problems a premature baby might have, carefully answered a number of our questions, and reassured us.

We were thankful for every single day the baby could mature and grow. During these days the girls were being well cared for by Dorothy's brother Bob and his wife Ellen, but our children were concerned about Mommy and the baby, especially after our experience with Aimee.

By Monday morning Dorothy's blood pressure was still okay, but the protein in her urine persisted. Another obstetrician visited and did a thorough sonogram of the baby. His main concern was that the baby weighed only about two pounds and was small for his age. This increased the risks of complications and the need for ventilator support when the baby was delivered because of immature lungs. The doctor wanted to keep Dorothy in the hospital at least another two weeks on bed rest to give time for the baby to grow. If she could not carry the baby that long, he recommended delivery. We aimed for the magic number of 32 weeks before delivery. She was now 29 weeks. Could she keep the baby for three more weeks?

Even though the girls visited us every evening, they missed us, and we wished we could spend more time with them. We were both on edge emotionally as we tried to process all the information and decisions we faced. We were on a roller coaster ride emotionally, and in light of our experience with Aimee, the uncertainty of the ending was extremely tough emotionally. Many friends from around the United States called and sent emails assuring us of their prayers. Both of us were on the edge of crying most of the day, and we appreciated the simple encouraging words, "We are praying for you."

In the early afternoon on Tuesday, the nurse noticed the baby was not reacting normally on the fetal monitor, so she called the doctor. For the rest of the afternoon we were on edge again worrying about the baby. Finally, in the late afternoon the obstetrician for her high-risk pregnancy came and reassured us the baby seemed fine. We were greatly relieved but still faced the tension of the moment-by-moment dimension of this situation. In the evening, Dorothy's mother stayed with her, and I went to the motel to be with the girls. We had a good time together for the first time in a week and enjoyed a swim at the motel pool. It was fun to be reunited after being apart for so many days.

At 11 p.m. Tuesday, Dorothy's mom called me from the hospital. Dorothy's blood pressure was climbing again, and the baby was not as responsive as earlier, so the doctor had decided to do an emergency C-section. Dorothy's mom came over to the motel to take care of the girls who were sleeping. Praying furiously, I dressed, called my family in California, and then headed urgently for the hospital. Upon my arrival, the nurses were busy preparing Dorothy for the surgery. Dorothy's dad, brother, and sister showed up, and we waited until the surgery team was ready. Dorothy started having some contractions, so again the timing was perfect.

Just after midnight Wednesday morning (four days after leaving Nigeria), I went into the Operating Room and was allowed to watch Dorothy's surgery. At 12:47 a.m. on Wednesday, William David Ardill Jr. was born. He weighed 2 pounds and 4 ½ ounces. His color was good – bright red. He cried well and was actively kicking and fussing. I went with him to the neonatal ICU where the neonatologist began a formal assessment. He was breathing well on his own.

Dorothy was taken to the recovery room for an hour and then back to her room. Dorothy and I were excited we had a boy, thrilled he was okay, and relieved the intense stress was over.

When the girls came to the hospital later in the morning, they saw their new baby brother. They were very excited to see how small he was and touch his soft skin. He was so red the girls called him "Bob" after Bob the tomato in the Veggie Tales videos.

For the next several days Dorothy's blood pressure stayed very high, so she continued to take the high blood pressure drugs. Our son David (We chose to use his middle name to reduce the confusion of being a "junior") was doing well in the neonatal intensive care unit.

By Thursday Dorothy was doing much better. She sat up in a chair and in the afternoon went to the neonatal intensive care unit to see David. With tears running down her cheeks, Dorothy saw David for the first time and tenderly held him close to her heart for an hour. They called it "Kangaroo Kare." (The mother and/or father hold the infant skin-to-skin on the bare chest for at least an hour at a session. It helps with bonding and just plain feels great!) What a joy and what a relief it was for Dorothy to see David doing so well. He sure was small! I was able to hold him for five minutes. David wasn't too thrilled with the whole idea and seemed to prefer being left alone. He settled down after a few minutes being held close to our warm skin. He got a bit tangled in my chest hair, but at least it helped him sort out who was who!

Of course a thousand thoughts flooded my mind every time I was with him. What would it be like to raise a boy? Would he like sports? Music? Computers? Medicine? Would he be quiet like Anna? Talkative like Heather? Or have Marie's sensitive heart? Does he have my "neat" gene or his mother's warm personality? Lots to ponder, lots of dreams, lots of hopes. At least now I'll have someone to go to the bathroom with me when we are at a restaurant!

In the coming days, it was emotionally draining to visit him. We were encouraged by the nurses to touch him, but when we did he cried and squirmed away. As a neonate, his nervous system was quite sensitive, so he was irritable if disturbed. One of the nurses said he had a temper, so I responded, "He's an Irishman like his father!" It was difficult for me to touch him knowing it bothered him, and yet I wanted to touch him since there was literally nothing else I could do for him other than pray. We were getting to know our son and hoping he was learning who we were in some mysterious way in the process.

Over the next few days various specialists examined David for possible problems with his vision, hearing or brain function. He passed all the tests with flying colors, and we were thrilled again at God's grace.

In spite of our family separation, the girls were doing fine living with friends and were excited when they could see David. When the girls visited David in the neonatal ICU, they loved putting on the gowns, masks, and gloves necessary to reduce the risk of infection of the babies. David was about the size of the beanbag animal named "Butch" that they gave him!

Dorothy continued to improve daily. The highlight of her day was her visit to the ICU to hold David even if for only a few minutes. He was in an incubator and had all sorts of lines and cables attached to him, so even if he wanted to escape, he couldn't get far. He had a cute, gold, heart-shaped temperature monitor on his back, EKG heart leads taped to each extremity, an oxygen monitor taped to one hand and an IV line in the other. David didn't have a sucking reflex, so he wasn't ready to take the breast milk. The doctors started giving him some calories intravenously and some lipids (fat) through his stomach tube. There was more technology with pumps and monitors attached to David than we had in the entire Evangel Hospital! Wow!

After a few days he was getting tired breathing, so they put the breathing tube in to let the ventilator help him. While at his bedside I was often reminded of how thankful we were that the Lord made a way for us to get to Maryland for David and Dorothy's sake. I got an email from one of the Evangel doctors saying how thankful they were as well since the electricity has been especially irregular, and there had been a shortage of oxygen in the hospital. We were encouraged by emails and phone calls from many who had gone through similar experiences and were praying for David and us.

Dorothy was discharged four days after her C-section. We were so glad Dorothy was back with us, so as a family we moved into a motel closer to the hospital. This arrangement was ideal because we had room maid service, breakfast served each morning in the lobby, a laundromat and a swimming pool. Since I still needed to care for Dorothy and orchestrate getting her to the hospital and the girls to various places, I didn't want to have to worry about cleaning, cooking, laundry and so on.

The first goal for David to be discharged from the hospital was respiratory — helping him breath on his own. The next goal was nutritional — getting him to take breast milk and teaching him to suck. Finally, the last goal was getting him to maintain his own body temperature. He was in a "greenhouse" temperature-controlled incubator and so was not burning any calories to keep warm. The nurses would gradually wean him off the supplemental heat to help him learn to regulate his own body temperature. Slowly David made progress in his breathing and was gaining weight.

Our daily activities settled into a routine — visiting David in the ICU every day and delivering the breast milk Dorothy had pumped for him. The girls then went off with friends to play for the day. They would soon be able to see David and touch him every day. We had dinner and family time together in the evenings. This was an opportunity to answer the children's questions and kept some semblance of being a family. Although we were busy, we had time to read, pray, and reflect on the turbulent days behind us. We knew God had been so good to us showing us His grace and mercy each day. This song brought us a renewed sense of God's peace:

> Day by day, and with each passing moment
> Strength I find to meet my trials here.
> Trusting in my Father's wise bestowment,
> I've no cause for worry or for fear.
>
> He whose heart was kind beyond all measure,
> Gives unto each day what He deems best.
> Lovingly, its part of pain and pleasure,
> Mingling toil with peace and rest.

In the next verses the author of the hymn explains the personal meaning behind those lyrics, "Every day the Lord Himself is near me with a special mercy for each hour. All my cares He fain would bear and cheer me, He whose name was Counselor and Power. The Protection of His child and treasure was a charge that on Himself He laid. 'As your days, your strength shall be in measure.' This the pledge to me He made."[7]

You know how some parents gush about the tiniest successes of their children? They act like their children are the brightest and most advanced ever. Over the next few days and weeks we were excited to tell everyone the small (literally!) steps of David as he began his pilgrimage with us. Somehow, having come through days of desperation, we clung to the smallest details to affirm our hope that all was well and God was answering our prayers. God was in the details, and as we saw them, we gained a new appreciation of the marvel of God's creativity in His creations. We were blessed by

---

[7] "Day By Day," Words by Karolina Sandell-Berg (1865). Translated from Swedish to English by Andrew Skoog (1856-1934). Music by Blott en Dag, Oskar Shnfelt (1872).

the prayers of so many that I could almost see a glow over David's incubator from the power of prayer working in his life.

As I watched David in the incubator, "Day by day and with each passing moment..." became "heartbeat by heartbeat and with each passing moment." David continued to take more breast milk each day and gain weight. We were also introduced to another problem of premature babies – a slowing of the heart or breathing. When this happened the nurse said, "Just give him a thump and it will come back." So Dorothy would give him a pat on the back, and he would start ticking along like before. We were warned about the possible heart and breathing instability for a while, but it sort of made us nervous to watch. My heart rate went up as his went down! We were thankful he was on lots of monitors and there were plenty of watching eyes in the ICU.

Most of the time David's eyes were closed (I guess like a puppy he was not ready to take it all in yet). When he strained to open an eye, it was if he were waking from a long, long slumber and was too tired to keep his eyes open so had a quick glimpse and went back to his slumber. After a few days he slept peacefully most of the time but still had his share of twitches and jerks. With our eyes glued to the monitors we watched for any signs of distress and had to remind ourselves to relax with him and leave the monitor watching to others. It was very relaxing for Dorothy to hold him Kangaroo Kare style, and he seemed pretty laid back through it all. Bonding was what they called it. I tried to discuss college options with him, but he nodded off to sleep!

On August 3, 2000, after a week in the ICU, David started making sounds like he wanted to suck. Dorothy mentioned this to his nurse who said, "Let's give it a try." He opened his little mouth wide, latched on, and began to nurse. Not much, not for long, but it was a start. Wow! It was unusual for a 30-week infant to be able to suck, so we were delighted he was doing so well.

Dorothy was on a real high after that session with David. Dorothy was also feeling well enough to spend more time with the girls, including a few shopping trips to the mall. After using a rental car for two weeks, we were encouraged when a friend in the church loaned us a car. Others helped with meals and babysitting the children, taking the girls to the beach, shopping and to pizza funhouses. We were grateful for the enthusiastic support of many that allowed us time to rest and prepare for the coming weeks.

David continued to make progress and was doing so well after a few more days that they moved him to the annex — a step down unit for the more stable children where there was less monitoring. He was weaned off the oxygen and was handling the breast milk by the tube into his stomach. It is amazing that God put all David needed in breast milk — proteins, carbohydrates, vitamins, and even some antibodies to help his immunity. He started to struggle to open his eyes, and when they finally popped open, he would gaze around wondering about all these folk staring at him and grinning. At this age he didn't really see much, but it sure made us happy to see his big blue eyes.

When Dorothy and I did get out of the hospital from time to time, I was in wonder at life in the United States. The grocery stores were an overwhelming experience and the myriad choices were staggering. The abundance of things and choices was awesome. The electricity was always on, the phones worked; there was drinkable water from every tap ... what a country! In the same paragraph that I sing the praises, I must note that I was struck by the insanity of this culture as well. As I drove down a main thoroughfare, a group of protesters marched in front of an office building with signs reading, "Abortions performed in this building!" What a schizophrenic society that we spend thousands of dollars to rescue a child like David and then consider it a matter of personal choice to kill children the same age as he was whenever it was inconvenient to raise the child. My heart ached as I thought of the horror of the abortion industry in this "civilized" country.

I marveled every moment I was with David at how wonderfully he was made by a genius, loving God whose attention to detail and beauty is incomprehensible. My, what a long way we have to go in America to restore the dignity and immeasurable value of the unborn over our own selfish agendas.

One afternoon at the hospital we had a delightful visit by an alumnus of the neonatal ICU. Ryan was born prematurely two years earlier and weighed the same as David. He was now an incredibly active and rambunctious little boy who didn't stop moving the whole time he was visiting. She gave us lots of tips and reassured us in a number of areas regarding his development. We had heard a number of stories about kids who had done well even when they were as premature as David, but it helped to talk to a mother who had been through it and to see her joyful little boy doing so well.

We were thankful for David's progress but began to face lots of unanswered questions and uncertainties: When should we go back to Nigeria? Should we go back at all? What should I be doing now? Look for work? Start our furlough now? What about packing up and leaving Nigeria properly? We wanted so much to go back but didn't want to go back until it was okay for David. It was still early to worry about these questions, but it was hard to stop the questions from coming. I felt bad that I was not working and hated the uncertainty. I went to a medical bookstore and picked up a surgery textbook, so I could do some professional reading.

We were also struggling to maintain a sense of normalcy for the girls. I had gotten stuck in the role of the bad guy. The friends who had been taking care of the girls were treating them like princesses. When they came home, I was the one who asked them to help clean up and do homework. So, I tried to get some time with them when we could have fun. One day I took the girls to a beach in the morning for a couple of hours and then miniature golfing in the afternoon. Dorothy was still spending several hours each morning and afternoon with David, so I could spring away for short trips to spend time with the girls.

After the nurses told us the goals for graduation from the ICU to home, Dorothy began in earnest working on helping David reach these goals. He was gaining weight with the feedings and was almost four pounds. He was doing fine outside the incubator and was off the ventilator, so Dorothy approached the nurse in charge with her news about his improved sucking. She gave Dorothy the tremendous news that we needed to begin the exit strategy for his discharge from the neonatal ICU. We took a class in CPR for infants, learned about the monitor for his breathing and heartbeat, and began the paperwork for discharge.

We were offered a furnished apartment, located on a beautiful creek with a canoe and dock. I worked hard to get the apartment ready and moved our things to the new place, so when David was discharged, we could begin our life as a family of six together.

My parents had come from California to help with the baby. Dorothy's parents had taken the girls for the day, so we could pack up David's hospital things quickly and not worry about the children. On Labor Day, five weeks after David was born, we said fond farewells to the terrific ICU nursing staff, put our little four-pound David in an infant car seat, and headed for the family picnic arranged by Dorothy's parents to show off our fantastic little boy and celebrate Marie's ninth birthday. When we arrived, they had celebratory balloons and cake, and everyone was very excited to see the miracle baby. He slept most of the time but was still the main attraction at the picnic.

The next weeks and months in the apartment were both fun and challenging. The screaming alarm on David's monitor woke us out of a dead sleep almost every night, and by the time we got to him to resuscitate him, he was breathing fine. Somehow it didn't frighten him as much as us. I can't tell you how many times I almost threw the monitor out the large glass picture window to the creek below. The monitor was supposed to reassure us but was in fact a real pain in the neck. So much for technology!

David slept in his little cot bedside our bed while the girls shared one small bedroom in the apartment. With an open floor format there was only one door in the entire apartment — the bathroom door. We did fine, but it was a challenge for the six of us to get along amicably in that small place for six months.

David continued to grow, and at every checkup he got good marks. He never had a problem with delayed development, retardation, or any other residual trauma from his being born at 29 weeks and 2 pounds. He indeed was a miracle baby, a wonderful gift to our family, and a happy little boy.

We had considered the possibility we might not be able to return to Nigeria if David's health was an issue. He continued to do so well that after getting the OK from his doctors, we made plans to return to Africa. We returned to Nigeria in time for Christmas at Miango and after a few weeks had a thanksgiving service in the hospital chapel to praise God publicly for David. It was a joyful service and gave us the opportunity to express to the community our gratitude for their prayers and help through this difficult experience. Interestingly, I was also finally in the African context called a "man" since I now had a son. My name changed from "Baba yan biyu" (father of twins) to "Baba Dauda" (father of David).

A REMARKABLE HEAD CASE

Since there are no enforced speed limits on the roads in Nigeria, trucks and cars fly at unbelievable speeds, trusting "the will of Allah" to help them arrive safely. The accident rate in Nigeria is among the world's worst. It is a combination of poor enforcement of basic road safety rules, vehicles on the road that are clearly unsafe, drivers under the influence of drugs and alcohol, and pot-holed roads. When you add the lack of rescue mechanic support anywhere and the increase in armed robbery incidents, driving takes on a different, more somber tone than in the West. No wonder we take prayer seriously before embarking on a trip and request a confirmatory call on arrival that all is well.

Ten-year-old Lami was walking along the road when a vehicle flying by her hit a half-circle-shaped piece of steel plate and sent it flying like a discus. It struck Lami in the head and lodged in her skull embedding halfway into her brain. Her father, a local pastor, managed to get her to the government hospital in Jos where they sat for six hours waiting to be helped. In desperation they brought her to Evangel Hospital in the middle of the night – now about 10 hours from the time she was injured.

Lami and her family lived in a little village east of Jos on the main road as you descended from the 4000-foot plateau into the searing hot plains of Bauchi State. Lami had been walking along the main tarmac road one evening around dusk. The side skirts of these paved roads are often covered with grains, peppers, or okra drying in the sun. There are also pieces of shredded tires and various parts of trucks (lorries), automobiles, and motorbikes that have fallen off or been abandoned after a roadside repair.

Getting the phone call after midnight about a girl with a metal plate stuck in her head got my immediate attention, and I raced to the hospital. Amazingly she was responsive and aware of her surroundings but had a clear weakness on the opposite arm and leg from her injury.

I had little experience removing metal plates impacted into skulls, yet knew I could not send her anywhere else that could offer better help and could not even discuss her situation with another surgeon who might be helpful. Before calling me, the resident doctors had gotten x-rays that were truly striking. The metal plate sliced into her head in front of her ear and went halfway across her skull into her brain.

After calling the nurse anesthetist and the Operating Room staff on call in the middle of the night to come to the hospital for the surgery, we gave Lami enough antibiotics to immediately annihilate any bugs in her body. We prayed fervently for God's help, the physical and spiritual salvation of this little girl, and then began the surgical procedure.

After cleaning the sand and dirt from the plate, I nibbled away the broken impacted edges of the dirty bone and then asked for something I rarely need, "sterile vice-grip pliers, please." In the United States I had bought a set of vice-grip pliers from Sears hardware store for orthopedic cases. They work well for holding bones and are a lot less expensive than the hospital-grade instruments used in western Operating Rooms.

I locked the vice-grips onto the plate and again shot a brief prayer to heaven knowing that after pulling the plate, she would either be okay or could bleed to death from ruptured blood vessels I could not control deep in the recesses of her brain. With one smooth jerk, I pulled out the steel plate and sighed in relief to see no massive bleeding from her brain wound. I cleaned up the dead brain tissue, removed more dirty bone fragments, tried to close the membrane covering the brain tissue, and then closed the scalp muscle and skin over the wound.

Her surgery went amazingly well and, in spite of the potential for infection, Lami never developed a brain abscess or wound infection. She had weakness of her left arm and leg that we prayed would improve with therapy and exercises. Her family had endless praise and gratitude for our help and for rescuing their daughter from a hopeless fate.

Again I was reminded of God's grace to her and us. Oftentimes we can help in situations beyond our expertise even with limited resources. What a privilege we have to serve people in desperate situations and be able to give God the glory.

LEADERSHIP WOES

I t seems that in mission circles, leaders and representatives are often chosen to serve on boards and committees based on their longevity overseas, not necessarily their wisdom or insight. I have been asked to serve on many boards and committees and have at times wondered why I was asked to serve. Dorothy thinks it is because I have the spiritual gift of "boards."

After a discussion between board members has raged for a while, I can see the main points and a way forward. Often, I will speak up and try to direct the group toward a resolution. Of course not everyone agrees with my assessment of the situation, but at least it is a way forward. My most frustrating committees are those led by people who cannot direct the discussion toward conclusions but instead allow the conversation to follow every rabbit trail or tangent interminably.

I also have a basic rule that when asked to lead a committee, meetings should not exceed (with only a few exceptions) two hours long. If people are prepared, most items can be handled quickly. If people are not prepared, they need to present the agenda item later when they are ready. Getting the minutes to members well ahead of the meeting and writing clear, organized minutes are other rules I like to follow when asked to serve in a leadership role.

These attributes served me well on many committees with a few exceptions. I didn't learn until much later that my philosophy was not culturally appropriate to Nigeria. It seems Nigerians like to have an opportunity to say something about a subject and want the freedom to talk as long as they want until the matter is concluded. So after I left the hospital administration and my two-hour meetings, the Nigerian who followed me often had 12-to 14-hour hospital management committee meetings. He allowed everyone to talk and share until they were all literally exhausted. I did not have the patience for that approach.

When we left for our furlough in 2001, I was serving on 12 boards and committees either at the hospital, SIM, ECWA, or Hillcrest. I was also the secretary for three or four so was busy getting the minutes done and distributed. I was spending about one week a month sitting on committees. I had to reschedule surgery dates for patients and left the surgical team carrying the load because I was sitting on so many committees. I let it out to a few key people that when I returned, I did not want to sit on boards and committees for a while. That worked surprisingly well, and upon my return I managed to serve on only a couple that I felt were a priority in my ministry.

An effective leader knows the core values of the local culture and the organization as well as knowing his own nonnegotiable principles and values. One of the most difficult issues I faced on the mission field was trying to understand which of my leadership principles were based on my personality and upbringing, which were cultural, which were biblical, and which were just plain wrong. At what point do you compromise your principles for the sake of a relationship? Is it necessary sometimes to let go of certain principles to continue in ministry? Can you function with leaders who do not hold the same values and principles? Can you serve under leaders who have a different sense of priorities in ministry?

I have wrestled with these questions for years and often wonder if I made some wrong decisions about my role in leadership along the way because of my determined Irish temperament, my proneness to resolutely hold to my principles, or, as some would say, my stubbornness. Let me share a few of those situations.

Early in my career as a missionary in Nigeria, I was asked to fill in at the hospital in the administration because the medical director was on furlough. I thought I was busy enough, but agreed since there did not appear to be anyone else willing to do the job. I received reasonable handover notes and then was led as a sheep to the slaughter in the new job. While I continued my heavy load as surgeon at the hospital, I was tasked with trying to figure out the personnel policies of the Nigerian staff, the budget, and financial picture of the hospital while endeavoring to move several building projects forward. Not having any background in finance, I found this area especially tough. I made spreadsheets to project and track the budget, read and took courses on hospital finance to understand the science of hospital management, and tried my best to keep the hospital out of debt.

My efforts to understand the finances were regularly frustrated by having an accountant who was not very capable. He did not know how to give me either an honest picture of the hospital finances or advice on what to do. In the face of an increasing hospital debt, the only solution I could see was to decrease the payroll by laying off staff. Having a lot of senior staff in the hospital who were mostly nurses, I thought the best approach was to streamline the upper echelons and train more lower-level, less-expensive staff.

As we faced the prospect of releasing staff, I made several proposals on how to reduce the number of nurses but faced an insurrection from the nursing staff. They felt they were overworked and underpaid in contrast to my perception that there were too many nurses. From my experience when we visited Galmi Hospital in Niger where one missionary nurse ran each ward, two nurses on each ward each shift at Evangel seemed excessive in light of our financial crisis. I was at a loss as to what to do, and with all my spreadsheets and projections I saw reducing the payroll as the only alternative.

Another area of struggle was understanding the cultural issues among the staff. I did my best to understand the ECWA Personnel Manual policies, but that did not get close to the real heart of the personnel issues. There were tribal tensions that I did not understand. I didn't know where to start since everyone on the staff had a tribal bias that would favor specific staff. There was an ongoing feud between the doctors and the nursing staff because the doctors generally thought that the nursing care was poor – even if we were supposed to be one of the best hospitals in the city.

Unfortunately there were no job descriptions or performance criteria, so there was little accountability or discipline. When staff was caught doing things wrong, there was little that could be done to discipline them or get rid of poorly performing staff. I tried hard to get the director of nursing to work out job descriptions, but that never happened. Staff were not willing to make critical evaluations of other employees in case some day they were promoted and would be given a bad recommendation.

There were several crucial personnel issues in which I felt I had failed during my time in the administration. There were suspicions of stealing in several of the departments like the pharmacy and medical stores. I didn't know any insiders well enough to catch the thieves, so we were forced to wait until something surfaced on its own. Eventually a man was caught who was suspected of stealing the x-ray film since the inventory and the log of the use of the films in the x-ray department never matched. We eventually went to court over his being sacked and it turned into a disaster. The hospital was poorly represented to the point the hospital's name was dragged in the mud. I was unfamiliar with the legal aspects of personnel issues and felt I had no one to confide in for counsel.

One of the administrative issues challenged my principles. The missionary who had been my nationwide supervisor in the ECWA medical department left, and a Nigerian was promoted into the position. I rarely met with him, and it was usually in a board meeting or hospital administration meeting. As I was facing the budget and personnel problems, I began to hear that he had been talking to hospital staff independently and was calling them into his office for private meetings. I learned he had been "stirring the pot" against me and my efforts. He also began using the medical department resources like the car, office staff, and supplies for his family needs. He regularly had his department driver take his wife around town to various places, used the department funds for personal use, and reacted angrily when asked to give account of these expenses.

A barrier arose between us as I watched with concern and frustration the way he undermined my authority at the hospital. The staff recognized him as my superior so jumped when he called and maybe even feared their jobs were on the line. I began to question if I could continue to function as the medical director under his leadership. My problems were temporarily solved when another crisis intervened. The missionary whom I had replaced while he was on furlough returned and indicated he did not want to take over the administrative responsibilities so asked if I would continue. This lasted a few weeks and then one day, much to my shock, he walked back into my office and said he was resuming his former role as the medical director. I didn't argue but handed him the keys and walked out, shocked and upset but somewhat relieved.

This incident shattered me. It fractured any ideas I had that I was doing okay in administration. It took me many years to deal with this hurt and thwarted my dreams of being involved in some leadership role in the future. I felt I was a failure in the way I had handled things, and his response affirmed that feeling.

In some ways it was a big relief to get back to my first love – surgery. I had always enjoyed being in the Operating Room and was glad to be rid of many of the problems that had plagued me for months. I was thankful not to have to deal with the financial crisis and personnel issues but was unhappy with the way it was handled.

Several months after this incident, this missionary had to leave Nigeria suddenly for family reasons. It was almost as if I felt the eyes of everyone turn in my direction to take over again as the medical director. After being deeply hurt, I was asked to step back into that position without feeling the support of the top administration in the ECWA medical department. When I turned it down, the Nigerian staff were shocked. No one ever turned down a promotion, especially when it came from the highest levels in ECWA. I felt I could not work under the current medical administrator of ECWA and also felt inadequate after what I had been through. This caused a huge commotion and panic since the hospital had no one to take over as the medical director. After a few days they finally asked the Director of Nursing to serve temporarily. This was unprecedented since she was a nurse, and physicians had traditionally led the hospital. The residents and doctors were not happy, but some knew how I felt. After some weeks another Nigerian physician was appointed medical director and I was soon forgotten, although I am not certain forgiven.

Being deeply hurt and scarred through this episode, I reflected long and hard if my stubborn stand had been right or if I should have been willing to serve again and done my best in spite of the undermining by my superior and the lack of support by church leaders. I wonder if Joseph in the Bible had agreed with the policies of the ungodly Egyptian Pharaoh whom he served. I wondered about other Bible heroes and leaders who had served in secular courts where there was a clash of values. Why did they stay and why was it so hard for me to stay? Was I just being stubborn or thin-skinned? Could I have been a change agent in the midst of the trouble? Could I have survived emotionally since I was already hurt and angry?

A similar episode came up a few years later with an SIM leader. In an effort to be helpful to the SIM leadership, I offered to help some missionaries understand the new SIM support scheme. My initiative was misunderstood as a threat to the administration, and

I was rebuked. Feeling hurt and unable to tell my side of what happened, I approached the person involved to make things right and again felt ignored. Unfortunately I nursed this wound for years because of my fear of getting hurt if I approached the offending party again. I began to withdraw from my involvement in mission and hospital committees and boards and was glad to be out of the situation when we went on furlough.

The good news was that my stress level was dramatically reduced, and it allowed me to be more involved in a number of other ministries I had wanted to do. I had wanted to open a new eye and ear, nose and throat clinic and was able to do that within six months. I also wanted to get a prosthetics workshop operational at Gidan Bege and was also able to get a man trained and hand that over to him. I did a lot of writing and published several articles in medical journals during this hiatus as well.

In the middle of this struggle there were a few good things going on. I had raised some funds for the hospital for capital development projects. We expanded one of the clinics, built a water reserve tank and storage system to provide better water to the hospital, painted the entire inside of the hospital wards and built pit latrines for the patients to improve the sanitation of the toilets on the wards. The staff were generally grateful for these improvements in the hospital. It certainly was easier to manage projects than people.

My administrative gifts were temporarily on the shelf. I wondered if that was right and how long my exile would last. Upon my return to Nigeria, my bitterness and anger increased. I began to pray for a change in my heart and a change in the leadership, and eventually the Lord answered my prayers. After many sessions in prayer, and reading extensively about forgiveness and the importance of releasing the other person from my emotional ransom, I finally forgave them and experienced the joy and peace of "a burden rolled away" and a clean heart.

I still meditate about what is the biblical response when you are serving under leaders with whom you have strong disagreements or differences in philosophy of leadership. If it is emotionally tearing me apart to work with someone who does not care or have interest in my perspective on the ministry, should I continue in that role or step aside and allow others who do not have the same perspective or emotional wiring to assume those responsibilities? One important tangential lesson I learned was that most of the boards and committees in which I was involved got along fine without me. No one is indispensable.

I wonder what God has for me in the future in terms of leadership roles. I have had the foundations of my self-esteem shaken as I have reflected on my past failures, hurts and disappointments. Should these be viewed as tests, or signposts to redirect me? I continue to seek God's leading and wisdom for the challenges ahead.

RONI

The 1950s was a different era in missions with a unique band of missionaries. My father and mother, Trevor and Mildred Ardill, joined SIM when they were attending Moody Bible Institute in Chicago. Although they were originally from Northern Ireland, they became members of the U.S. branch, raised their support in American churches, and received their Mission orientation at the Mission headquarters in Manhattan.

After graduating from Moody, they set sail for Northern Ireland to bid farewell to their family. My mother did not disclose to her family that she was pregnant for fear they would have forbidden her to leave. They boarded a ship in Liverpool, England, for Lagos, and then settled in for the weeklong journey. In Lagos they stayed in a guesthouse and then boarded a train for the long day trip to the SIM Headquarters in Jos.

Their first assignment in Nigeria was to learn the Hausa language at a school in Minna. This was a small village in the center or Middle Belt of the country where SIM had several missionary language instructors who ran language boot camp. They had to reach a certain proficiency in Hausa before they could be given their first real assignment in the bush. After spending six months in Hausa school, their first assignment was a village called Roni, a backwater village in the far north. Roni was in the heart of a deeply animist and Islamic area of Nigeria. SIM had established a transitional agricultural school for orphans and street children in that village. Raising these boys in a rural environment, away from the negative influences of the city, decreased the distractions and provided a more suitable atmosphere for learning about life principles, a trade, and how to develop a relationship with the Lord Jesus Christ — a person they had heard of in Islam but did not recognize as God's Son. My parents taught classes in their newly learned Hausa language for 18 months and became actively engaged in the ministry of the school. Because my mother was a nurse, she also opened a clinic to help Nigerians in the community and boys' school with medical problems. I recall my mother's stories of helping villagers with desperate wounds or being called to a distant village to help with the delivery of a woman in obstructed labor. The impact of loving medical care was enormous in a region so under-resourced regarding health care and clinics.

My father had run his father's warehouse business in Belfast before my parents went to Moody, so he had a keen business sense. Growing up, his family raised cattle, rabbits, and chickens, so he had a love for animals and farming since his childhood. In addition to his teaching responsibilities, my father helped with automobile repairs and other maintenance work on the mission compound. My father often reminiscences about his treks to surrounding villages on weekends to preach the Gospel. Although they recall working with some interesting characters and some times of hardship, they have fond memories of their first mission station and loved to tell us about Roni.

Since going to Nigeria in 1992, I had always wanted to go to Roni – the place where my parents began their missionary journey. In our early years we were caught up in establishing our own ministries; then the children came, and they always had weekend activities, so it was hard to get away. I determined in our last term in Nigeria that we would set aside a weekend to drive to Roni and see the place that had been so important and influential in shaping my parents as career missionaries. At Roni they clearly demonstrated determination to stick it out in a difficult place.

After being in Nigeria a few years, I wanted to honor my parents and learn about their first assignment as missionaries, so Dorothy and I, with our driver Kingsford, set out for Roni. Our excitement began to build Friday afternoon after a 7 ½-hour road trip from Jos when we saw the road sign "Roni" as we approached this small Muslim town in the northern Sharia state of Jigawa. We had left Jos early and, after a quick lunch of Lebanese *shwarma* in Kano, we picked up Yahaya, a tall Nigerian man who was a former student of Roni Boys School and would serve as our tour guide for the afternoon. We tried to time the trip to avoid the inevitable road closures when mosques along the main road closed the highway to allow worshippers to safely get to and from the Friday afternoon prayer time. We still ran into cordoned off roads in two villages and managed to drive around one road block but waited patiently at the other until prayers were finished. It was an amazing sight to see hundreds of men and boys bowed and kneeling in submission toward the east as the call to prayer sounded from the mosque loudspeakers. Cars and trucks were stopped with passengers kneeling on the road in reverent prayer toward Mecca.

This scene was a stark reminder of the enormous task still before the church to proclaim the liberating love of Christ to the millions in northern Nigeria who have not yet acknowledged Christ as the true prophet and Messiah.

We were also amazed at the hundreds of miles of newly planted farms with the freshly dug soil planted after the first rains. I was surprised to see a number of tractors working the farms, and the farther north we drove there were also paired oxen pulling plows. Men and women planted the seeds by sticking either their toe or heel into the ground to make a small depression where they dropped a seed, then covered the divot, and stepped forward to plant another seed. This is paradoxically the hungry time of the year as families have finished last years' grain stores and wait patiently for the new harvest. Living in the city we often forget both the enormous size of Nigeria and the reality that most still live in rural areas without either utilities or thriving churches.

With an estimated population of 5 million people, the 1000-year-old city of Kano is the largest city in northern Nigeria. The enormous number of people on the streets was overwhelming. We stayed in a hotel overnight and after checking out, we headed north for the 1 ½-hour trip to Roni. The topography changed from fertile farms to more rocky harsh land populated with goats and donkeys. The influence of Islam was everywhere — from the architecture of the houses to the attire of the people — and the prominent mosques in the center of each town and village. Even the worn political posters from the April elections declared this as Muslim territory, and evidence of Christianity was scarce.

After entering the small town of Roni, we turned right at "the" intersection and followed a long wall until we came to a gate with a sign "Girls' Computer School." This is the place where my parents began their missionary careers in 1951. At that time the school was an agricultural school for street boys to teach them basic farming skills. It was run by SIM and later turned over to the ECWA church. In the 1970s the school was taken over by the government and is now an Islamic school for girls. Three of the school male instructors gave us a tour, and it was amazing to us that in the middle of the bush, there was a school of 1,000 female students learning basic computer skills. We were skeptical until they showed us the classrooms that had a small laptop in a cellophane bag on each desk and, indeed, they were teaching basic computer courses.

It was difficult to reconcile the general impression that Muslim communities do not support education for girls, especially Western education with computers and advanced technology. Yet, in the middle of northern rural Islamic-dominated Nigeria was a school of hundreds of veiled girls learning the 4th century law of the prophet Mohammed and the 21st century rules of computer code. It was also desperately discouraging to realize that the Christian community had not been able to sustain the school against government takeover and that the Christian community had been so persecuted it was now almost extinguished. Our respect for the remaining Christians and pastors deepened, but it was disheartening to see how much work remained to spread the Good News of the freeing message of Christ to this generation steeped in a religion that enslaved them in spiritual darkness.

We drove to the adjacent church property and former missionary compound. Yahaya, our guide, met some former classmates of his who were living on the Mission compound, and they gave us a brief tour of the property. All the buildings were in disrepair showing years of neglect and wear. The small church was meeting in a classroom building, but they were proud of the new larger church they were building. We enjoyed seeing the house where my parents lived, the water tower my father built, the clinic where my mother ran a medical outreach, and a few other notable structures.

We met only the pastor's wife who was living in my parents' house because her husband had traveled. She was a radiant Christian woman who welcomed us warmly. It was a tremendous encouragement and a humbling experience to meet the Christians on the compound dedicated to being a witness for Christ in this strongly Islamic community. We were sorry we did not have gifts for them but thanked them for their faithfulness serving Christ in this place. We stopped briefly at the house of a retired pastor in Roni and then headed back to Kano. The pastor shared how challenging it was to be a witness for Christ in this hostile Muslim environment. There were probably fewer Christians today in that community than in 1950 when my parents were stationed there.

After my older sister Sharon was born in Jos in April 1951, she contracted malaria and was struggling for her life. My parents got permission from SIM to take her to London for treatment, so my mother took her to the Great Ormandy Street Hospital in London. She survived her case of cerebral malaria, but when my mother returned with her to Nigeria, the Mission Director, Mr. Playfair, asked my parents to move from Roni to Jos, so my father could take over the bookshop literature ministry of SIM. Having run his father's business in Belfast, Northern Ireland, my father had business experience. There were three bookstores when my father started, and over the next 15 years he expanded the ministry to more than 30 bookshops all over Nigeria, including several bookmobiles that took Bibles and Christian literature to remote areas.

On Sunday morning before heading back to Jos, we visited the ancient indigo dye pits in the Old Town of Kano. This dyeing operation has been going on for 600 years, and it was interesting to see the deep well pits which were filled with dark blue indigo dye into which the cloth was dipped to make the distinctive dark blue cloth. Women first tie the cloth in various places to make a pattern, and then the cloth is dipped in the dye pits to produce the tie dye appearance. To attain the nice blue color, the fabric is hand-dipped for six hours. We met an old man who had been dipping fabric for more than 50 years. After the dyeing, the cloth is then ironed.

Because in the ancient days they did not have either electricity or coal to make irons, they ironed the cloth by beating it with a large, flat wooden hammer until it was shiny. We ended the tour by buying a few shirts and then spent another two hours wandering around the cloth market. As the largest cloth market on the continent, this market is the entry point for all of the cloth sold in West Africa.

After a delicious pizza lunch in a restaurant that looked like a bamboo resort in the South Pacific, we headed for Jos and arrived without incident before dark. We were exhausted from the heat of Kano, the many hours on the road, and the morning walkabout in the market. It was a wonderful reminder of God's abundant blessings to us, the faithfulness of His servants laboring in a challenging environment in northern Nigeria, an insightful look into the past as we saw where my parents ministered 60 years ago and the enormous challenge the church faces in the north.

We were grateful for the Lord's protection on the roads, the privilege of meeting some wonderful people serving sacrificially in His name, and our responsibility to support them. It was terrific to see the place my parents had started, and I felt the weekend excursion allowed me to close the circle in my own understanding of the hardships they faced, the sacrifices they made, and the commitment they had to reach the lost for Christ.

MODERN MISSIONARIES
SALEH AND PAUL

Saleh Husseini

When we first met him he was wearing the traditional baban riga gown of northern Nigerian. He was a big, tall man with a scruffy beard and imposing voice. He instructed us about Islam and the Koranic schools throughout Nigeria. There are thousands of these small schools, or, more accurately, apprenticeship programs, where boys as small as six years old learn about Islam and memorize the Koran.

Devout Muslim families consider it a high honor to give their eldest son to their Islamic faith, so they send him to live with an Imam, or Koranic scholar. Their son lives in the Imam's house with 20 other young boys until he is about 16 years old and has memorized the entire Koran. He then returns as a highly respected man in his village and often is elevated to the role of Koranic scholar. The conditions in the Koranic school are harsh since the Imam cannot provide enough food, clothing, and medical care for these boys. The boys are sent out into the streets to beg for food every week. They often get sores on their legs, malaria, parasites, and other illnesses.

These were the boys that pulled at Dorothy's heart and for whom she began the Gidan Bege ministry to help them with food, clothing, medical care and the Gospel. Such was Saleh Husseini. At a workshop at Miango on Islam and strategies to reach Muslims with the Gospel in May 1995, Saleh showed us the scars on his legs from the sores he had as a boy begging for food on the streets. He was raised in a Muslim home, and, after receiving his college education, he began teaching at a university in a predominantly Muslim area of Nigeria. Through interactions with Christians, he put his faith in Jesus Christ and had a profound conversion experience. With his deep knowledge of Islamic teaching, the Koran, and Arabic, he became a powerful apologist for the Christian message and strategies to reach Muslims with the Gospel.

Because of his influence in Dorothy's compassion for street children, Saleh always had a special place in our hearts. Even though he lived and ministered in the far north of Nigeria, whenever he visited Jos he stopped in to give us an update on what God was doing through his ministry.

On one visit, Saleh told us about his outreach to Muslim "seekers." In addition to the 200 Muslim converts whom he was discipling, there were hundreds of moderate or nominal Muslims with questions about Christ and the Christian faith living in a major metropolis controlled by strict Sharia Islamic law. They could not go to a church or Bible study because of the risk to their families and their own lives. They sought out Saleh because he knew their faith, was well respected, and most importantly was trusted in the community. He openly discussed with them the claims, person, and work of Christ.

During the riots in his city in 2008, a mob of Muslims went to his house looking to kill him and his family. The mob had already caused widespread carnage in the city, burning vehicles randomly, and targeting houses of Christians. As the wild, angry gang approached his house, ready to burn it to the ground, Saleh managed to escape with his family out a back door and their lives were spared. They came back later to find all they owned destroyed by the house fire set by the irate mob. He is among many in Nigeria we consider true heroes of the faith. They risk their lives daily for the cause of Christ.

After we had returned to Nigeria from furlough one year, he was bringing his daughter to school in Jos and wanted to greet us and welcome us back to the country. After the usual Nigerian greetings, we asked about his family and were horrified to hear the story of how his son had been murdered while in university. His son was a strong believer in Christ and was doing well in school. Saleh had led a young man who was a Muslim to Christ, but the boy had to leave his family because of persecution. The boy's parents then arranged for a group to attack Saleh's son and murder him "so he would know what it was like to lose a son." It was a horrible tragedy and a strong statement on the cost some Christians are paying to be a witness for Christ in this country.

Even though the family was still struggling with grief and confusion, Saleh shared with us how God had given him the grace to forgive the killers of his son. If God could forgive him of his worst sins by dying for him on a cross, Saleh felt he must forgive the man who murdered his son. He spoke to a group of Christians in a northern city and gave his testimony. Afterwards, an elder in the church came up to him and told him he had also lost two children because they were Christians. The elder had been planning for years for a way to get revenge on the murderers. He had been making weapons and working on the perfect plan for the revenge murder. He was dumbfounded to hear Saleh share how he had forgiven the attackers. The vengeful man then repented of his own vindictive plans and brought the weapons to the church as a sign of his change of heart.

A few years later Saleh shifted his focus to the rural villages in the north of Nigeria where there are very few Christians. Most of the villagers believed in "folk Islam." It is a syncretistic belief in both Islam and animism so is mainly a corruption of Islamic teaching. Saleh was encouraging the few Christian missionaries stationed in these far-flung, predominantly Muslim areas. Interestingly, they have been thrilled by the spiritual Christian revival sweeping many remote areas. In one village the missionary had led three people to Christ. They wanted to build a small mud hut with a thatched roof as a place for prayer and worship in the village. Prior to this, word had gone out to all the northern Nigeria chiefs that if they allowed Christians to build a church, the government would not bring electricity to their village, or build them a road or a school. Subsequently, the chiefs were under a great deal of pressure to discriminate against the Christians. This missionary decided to build the prayer hut on his own property in spite of the threats. With the little money he and the new converts could scrape together, they built the walls of a mud hut and were planning to put on the thatch grass roof.

People in the next village heard what they were doing and, because they thought if that village did not get a road, school or electricity because of the Christian prayer hut, they would not either because they were further away. So they came at night and completely destroyed the hut. When the chief heard about it the next day, he called the villagers together and demanded to know who had done this. "This is not our custom. We welcome strangers as a blessing even if we do not believe what they believe." No one in the village admitted to destroying the hut until one person finally raised his hand, "I saw some young men from the next village doing it." The chief was furious that the neighbor village chief had not approached him in the proper way if the prayer hut offended him.

So the village people determined it was an act of war and decided they would attack them with their bows and arrows and destroy something of value in that village. The Nigerian missionary stood up in the meeting and said, "Please do not do that. That is not the way we do things as Christians. We have forgiven them and even if we do not rebuild, it will be okay. Revenge is not the answer. I will try again, but please do not attack them." The chief then wisely answered the people by saying, "I know what to do. I know how to irritate them in the best way. We will all convert to the religion of the missionary and build a church right in front of my palace." So that is what they did.

The whole village "converted" to Christianity and began coming to church. They knew nothing of what it meant to be a follower of Christ, so the missionary had an amazing and challenging responsibility to tell them the life of faith in Christ and the whole Gospel story. They even invited the neighboring chief and villagers to come and worship with them.

What an amazing story of courage and faith! We are humbled by what God is doing in Nigeria and hope we can be an encouragement to pioneers like Saleh and others who are on the frontlines of this battle for souls. In spite of persecution, hardship, and attacks, he and his family are faithful in disciplining men and women into the Kingdom of God through the proclamation of the saving blood of Jesus.

Paul Ushie

When we went to Nigeria in 1992, Paul Ushie was a resident in the family medicine program at Evangel Hospital. Throughout his training he became know as the "evangelist" or "missionary." On ward rounds, in the clinic, and everywhere Paul went, he was telling people about Jesus. He was always concerned about the spiritual health of our patients and often stopped on rounds to ask patients if they knew where they would spend eternity. His boldness was humbling and convicting, reminding us of our real mission in medical missions.

Dr. Paul Ushie was born into a family of animist idol worshippers. When his father the chief died, living slaves were buried with him to accompany him to the afterlife. His aunt then raised him. The new chief who succeeded his father became a Christian. Subsequently he threw his kingly gowns and adornments into the village pit latrine as a symbol of his turning from idolatry and decision to follow Christ completely. After he came to Christ as a young man, most of Paul's family became believers in Christ, and today they do not worship idols in his village.

During his family medicine residency at Evangel Hospital, Paul received a vision from God to reach with the Gospel a remote unreached tribe of naked people in eastern Nigeria. He made several trips to these remote people and was shocked at how primitive and uneducated they were. Steeped in animism and Islam, they had never heard of Jesus or the Good News of His death on the cross for them. They had desperate medical needs and were completely underserved as far as immunizations against preventable illness, understanding healthy practices like drinking clean water and the importance of breast-feeding infants.

Paul's vision materialized when he had the opportunity with his wife to begin taking medical teams including an evangelist to these remote people. He offered free medical and surgical care from the back of his truck serving thousands of people. After completing his Family Medicine residency, Paul became a senior attending physician or consultant at Evangel Hospital and began making two to three trips a year to the mountain people. Eventually the village leaders offered him a building to set up a clinic and a place to store his medical supplies and equipment between trips. We were excited to be able to help raise some funds to help him. He reported after every trip amazing numbers of people who had responded to the Gospel.

The needs were so great that the trips to the tribal enclave became more numerous and burdensome. Paul quit his job at Evangel and went into fulltime missionary work. On one trip 48 people prayed to commit their lives to Christ. Many are turning to the Savior because of the emptiness and despair in their other faith traditions. Many faced severe persecution for following Christ. One Fulani man who made a profession of faith in Christ had his new bride taken away from him by his family.

As more converted to Christ, Paul began bringing some of the converts back to Jos for additional schooling and medical care.

Because of the limitations of what he could do medically and surgically in the bush, he brought many to Evangel those who had more complicated medical problems. He also returned with a few who were being persecuted because of their conversion to Christianity. Each time Paul took a trip, he faced hardship, broken vehicles and generators, sickness, and attacks. He persisted through all this because of his commitment and passion to reach as many as possible of the lost in this tribe for Christ. We are so humbled by Paul's sacrifice for Christ to preach the Gospel and are honored to have had a part in helping him in his ministry to reach those who otherwise would have never had an opportunity to receive health care or hear of the hope of deliverance from the power of sin through Christ.

Two amazing men – Saleh and Paul – struggling and sacrificing to communicate God's love to the ends of the earth with humility and boldness. Both impacted us, and it was our privilege to know them and have a small part in encouraging them.

STARVING TO DEATH

When I first saw her in the outpatient clinic, she was staring at the floor with a look of despair on her thin, drawn face. Her companion said for months they had been going from one hospital to another throughout northern Nigeria searching for someone who could help her. With most of their earthly resources spent, Evangel Hospital was their last resort.

Six months earlier, Hanatu had inadvertently swallowed a lye solution that had permanently scarred and closed her esophagus. She was no longer able to swallow food, water, or even her own spit. She always had a rag in her hand to wipe the constant drool from her mouth. Because suicide or homicide attempts are the most common cause of caustic burns of the esophagus, I carefully probed her for a reason why she might have done this to herself. Over and over she assured me it was an accident that had ruined her life and her family. Her sad countenance resonated with her tragic story.

Even in modern Western medical centers, people who swallow lye face a tough road to recovery, but early intervention with medication to reduce the inflammation and esophageal dilations can sometimes prevent the most serious narrowing that leads to starvation or major surgery. One important caveat in surgery, especially in the developing world, is an understanding that people with poor nutrition don't heal well after surgery. They are more likely to have a major complication like infection, disruption of their wounds, or even death. So the first goal was to improve her nutrition before considering restoring her swallowing.

I admitted Hanatu to the female ward, asked for a blood test to assess her nutrition, and started intravenous fluids to rehydrate her. We first attempted to give her nutritious liquids by mouth, but, as she said, she really was not able to swallow anything. I wanted to get a better idea how tight the stricture was to see if we could dilate a tiny hole to make it large enough to pass a feeding tube into her stomach.

In the Operating Room, I tried to gently pass the gastroscope down her throat to see where the blockage was and how tight it was. This information would help us plan her treatment and possible surgery. I knew surgery for this condition was daunting and hoped we could find a narrowed portion we could enlarge with the esophageal dilators. But that was not to be. I found the esophagus completely closed quite high in her neck with no sign of any opening we could enlarge. I wasn't sure how long the stricture was but knew the option of a minor procedure had vanished.

Throughout the early days of her hospital stay, I wanted to be sure the chaplains were counseling Hanatu and was pleased that early in her hospitalization they had recognized her depression and had been visiting her daily.

With her becoming more malnourished every day, I knew we needed to intervene and make a way for her to build up her strength and improve her immunity in preparation for a much larger operation. So we took her to the Operating Room and under a general anesthetic made a small incision in her upper abdomen, found a segment in the upper part of her small intestine, and placed a red rubber tube through the skin and muscle of the left side of her abdomen in the small intestine. We sewed the hole in the intestine around the tube, so it would not leak, fall out, or be pulled out unintentionally.

There are many nutritious drinks available in the United States for dietary support of patients. Some are designed to deliver specific ingredients like vitamins, protein, and calories based on the illness while others advertise their flavor, absorption in the intestine or reduced side effects like diarrhea or gas. We started Hanatu on the kwash pap used for malnourished children to help her gain strength. The nurses gave her the diluted, then full strength kwash pap, and she began to gain strength and noticeably improve. This definitely bought me some time to research and prepare for her surgery and improved her chances of recovery. I knew she would need several weeks of the feedings to reach our goals, so I began to do my own homework.

There are several different operations for this problem, but all essentially boil down to removing her diseased esophagus and replacing it with a healthy section of intestine. The controversy was focused on whether the operation should be done by opening the chest or tunneling behind her heart and the choice of the best substitute to replace her damaged esophagus.

This was going to be a big operation and one I had never seen before, much less done in Africa. So I emailed a thoracic surgeon missionary colleague working in Kenya and a few other surgeons and decided on an approach for Hanatu's operation that I thought we could do with the lowest risk of complications.

An important part, of course, is to prepare the patient for the operation. This meant both physical and psychological preparation. I knew the chaplains had been visiting her and was encouraged that she was emotionally much brighter by the time she was physically strong enough for the surgery. I explained the possible complications, including the risk of dying in the Operating Room or after the surgery, and she was still committed to going ahead with the surgery.

There is no question that in spite of my years as a surgeon working in Africa, there are still cases that make me nervous. I prepare well but pray hard that things will go well – for the benefit of my patients and God's glory. So when Hanatu was in the Operating Room before the nurse gave her the Pentothal to go asleep, I prayed for God's wisdom and for a good outcome.

Dr. Joel Anthis began his part of the operation in the neck to free up the esophagus, and simultaneously I opened her abdomen. I had decided to remove her esophagus without opening her chest by bluntly dividing its attachments behind her heart through the hole in the flat diaphragm muscle that separates the chest from the abdomen. I also freed up the stomach from most of its attachments leaving it supplied by a single artery. I pulled out the diseased organ, and then passed the stomach up to the neck through the tunnel where the esophagus originally lay. We then sutured the stomach to the healthy proximal esophagus in the neck and closed both the neck and abdominal incisions. The whole team sighed in relief, and we thanked God after the three-hour, smooth, uncomplicated surgery. Hanatu was taken to the intensive care unit and settled down for the night.

The biggest worry in these cases is a leak from a hole where the stomach was sewn to the esophagus. This can be a devastating complication. I made sure she was on good antibiotics and started the tube feedings right away to keep up her nutrition and support her immune system.

After a week, I wanted to get an x-ray with Hanatu swallowing a radio-opaque fluid, so I would make sure she didn't have any problems. Well, there was no radio-opaque fluid available, so I removed the tube from her nose that went into her stomach and allowed her to drink some water. The nurses were instructed that if that went well, she could add juices and soup.

The next day, instead of seeing a depressed, downcast woman, Hanatu wore a huge smile on her face. She thanked me profusely, and her mother came dancing in the ward singing in her language. Everyone was laughing. The nurse told me she was saying, "She was so grateful she wanted to 'back me.'" Small children are carried by being tied on their mother's backs. So "backing" me was an expression of great affection and appreciation. What joy for all of us! What joy!

I was even more excited to hear the rest of the story from hospital Chaplain Enoch. He had been spending time with Hanatu, and although she was a Christian, through her suffering she had wandered from God in her despair. Even before the surgery she had rededicated her life to following Christ, and after the surgery joy flooded her heart. She had hope and a future after desperately seeking help all over the country – her journey of suffering was over and she could rest and serve God with all her heart.

HILLCREST LIFE

One of the most significant decisions missionaries must face is where your children will attend school. Most agencies leave the decision to the parents. SIM had educationalists to discuss options for schooling children, but usually this focused on families going to places where home schooling was required because there was no other option. In the 1960s when I was growing up in Nigeria, most SIM parents sent their children to Kent Academy, a boarding school for missionary children. A few SIM families in Jos sent their children to Hillcrest School, which was a multi-mission school.

By the time we arrived in Jos in 1992, all the SIM families with children in Nigeria with few exceptions sent their children to Hillcrest. Some home schooled their children until they were in middle or high school and then sent them to live in a hostel in Jos and attend Hillcrest. Once our children were school age, our lives and social schedules revolved around Hillcrest School activities. We gradually got more involved until, by the time we left, we were totally immersed in the school activities and culture. When Marie started first grade in 1997, Dorothy began helping in the classroom. She continued helping while the twins were in elementary school. Later Dorothy became credentialed as a teacher, taught third grade at Hillcrest, and then became the elementary school principal. In addition to helping with our children's activities and programs, Dorothy and I served on many of the school committees. Eventually I was asked to be the board chairman and served in that role the last few years we were in Nigeria.

As a parent, I also felt deeply the concern of parents for a safe, Christian school environment in order to protect our children from the dangers of culture, and both the Nigerian and Western ungodly cultural influences. There were many situations that reminded us we lived in an ungodly world. In some cases, it was teachers behaving badly. At other times, children would bring a negative influence to the school. Clearly no one expected the pledge of the students and parents to behave in a "Christlike" manner would produce a utopian school, but there were times we were disappointed by the interference or neglect of parents in supporting the school's mission.

In spite of this, Hillcrest had an enormous impact on our family and was like the potter's wheel for each of our children. It was a place where they were shaped and molded by teachers, administrators, and their peers. The school itself also went through changes and was impacted by the leadership, the culture, and the political events in Nigeria. Having attended a mission boarding school (Kent Academy) as a boy, I understood the enormous impact this environment could have both in positive and negative ways on our children. We are thankful their experiences were mostly positive and helped them mature as young people physically, emotionally, and spiritually.

In 1942, the Church of the Brethren Mission (CBM), started Hillcrest School to provide a Christian education for the children of the CBM missionaries. Several years later other missions joined CBM, and the general framework of the governance was established. Participating missions or "Cooperating Bodies" governed the school and helped provide missionary teachers. The curriculum was designed to meet the needs primarily of the North American children and was intentionally Christian in focus. SIM became a

Cooperating Body and as such had representation on the Board and provided teachers to staff the school.

After some time the school opened admission to children whose parents were not missionaries. This allowed children from homes of local businessmen, diplomats, and nonparticipating mission agencies to attend. It further internationalized the student body to include Nigerians, Ghanaians, Lebanese, Germans, Irish, Asians, Canadians, Australians, and New Zealanders. Although the children and parents did not have to be professing Christians, they had to agree to abide by the conduct code and participate in the Bible classes and religious activities of the school.

As the troubles in Nigeria with political unrest and terrorism increased, it also became more challenging to recruit Western trained teachers to come to Nigeria. This finally led to the school hiring teachers directly.

The Board of Governors met twice each semester for two-day sessions. Although it was mainly to review school polices, personnel and finances, many other issues were discussed including the escalating security crisis in Jos, the hostels for boarding children, and accreditation. There were also four or five subcommittees that reported to the Board. Dorothy and I spent countless hours at the Board and committee meetings. Dorothy believed I had the spiritual gift of "Boards" so was pleased when I was asked to Chair the Board or the Subcommittees. I was interested in shaping policy and organizing important school documents, so they were accessible, consistent and reflected the values of the school.

Because the children graduating from Hillcrest were applying to mostly North American colleges and universities, it was also important to have U.S. credentialing. The school was accredited by the Middle States Association school accreditation organization in the United States and the Association of Christian Schools International. Teams from these accrediting bodies would visit every few years and review the governance, curriculum, polices, student life, recruiting and mission/vision of the school. Hillcrest gave the SAT and ACT exams and offered AP classes to help students gain entrance into Western universities. Graduates of Hillcrest were accepted into prominent universities across North America and Europe because of its high academic standards.

The school's calendar year was marked by significant events each month. As our children moved up through the grade levels, we became more involved in both their classroom activities and the many extracurricular programs. These times were important family events as well as much needed social interaction with other Hillcrest community families and stress-relieving therapy.

August – Back to School

The first week of school was a grand reunion as friends reconnected, checked out the latest fashions and phones from the United States, and met the new wild-eyed-in-wonder staff fresh off the plane. The campus was abuzz with the excitement of a new year as everyone shared news about their summer activities. A big issue every year was getting enough staff to begin the term. Often there was last minute shuffling and reassignments. Middle school kids were learning to move to different classes throughout the day; high school freshmen were adjusting to being at the bottom of the pecking order after being king-of-the-hill in middle school; seniors were spreading their wings as "top dogs on campus"; and new teachers were trying to appear confident as they took control of their classes. Our most memorable August was our return to Hillcrest in 2010.

After a grand welcome by the Nigerian staff we work with on the Evangel compound, Dorothy got a message that the Hillcrest superintendent wanted to see her. So we left the girls in charge of unpacking, David ran off with his friends, and I dropped Dorothy off at the school. I ran around town and did a few errands and when I got back, Dorothy was shaken as she shared the news that she had been asked to be the elementary school principal. Apparently in the recruitment for the second grade teacher, they received applications from two strong candidates and, since they also needed an elementary school principal to replace Linda Taylor who was leaving in December, the school administration decided to accept both candidates and ask Dorothy if she would be willing to be the elementary school principal. Dorothy had left the superintendent's office and found a quiet spot to cry until I arrived. This was a total surprise. She loves teaching and had been really looking forward to teaching third grade again, especially since she had big plans for the four boxes of third grade classroom materials she brought from the States. We discussed this proposal, prayed for the Lord's peace, and then went back and accepted the position. Now for David his school principal was his mother! Dorothy settled quickly into her new role and had a terrific year. She also enjoyed mentoring the new teachers and was thrilled to see them thrive at Hillcrest.

In our previous term in Nigeria from 2007-2009, Dorothy taught third grade, having just completed her teaching credentials in California while on furlough. She shopped in education stores for weeks before we left and filled several boxes with educational aids for her third grade classroom. Dorothy was an incredibly effective and loved teacher. She approached every subject with enthusiasm that was contagious to the kids. Writing class became "Boring to Better" with instruction on how to make a boring sentence into an interesting one. Studying whales meant making life-sized chalk drawings on the basketball court. When the focus shifted to American Indians, each student made a diorama of an Indian village complete with plastic toy horses, people and popsicle stick teepees. Human anatomy was not just learning the "knee bone" but the "patella." Her biggest challenges were dealing with children with behavior problems like anger management. In some cases the parents clearly contributed to their children's bad behavior, but in other situations the parents pleaded for help to manage their children at home. Dorothy rarely had to ask for the principal's help, but occasionally she reached the limit of her patience and sent the child to the principal's office. Having two years' of teaching experience helped her deal with these challenging youngsters when she became principal.

I normally taught Christian Apologetics one semester to the high school juniors and Biblical Ethics in another semester to the high school seniors. One graphic illustration I used to help the students understand the importance of discerning truth and the true Gospel was my "Prophet Pooh" lecture. I dress up as a goofy prophet who believes he has received a revelation from God in the form of the Winnie the Pooh stories. I challenge the class whether I am a real prophet or not and if the Pooh stories are really from God. It is a good exercise for them to learn how to discern truth from hogwash. They usually struggle for a bit trying to figure out what is going on but eventually understand the point and focus on asking insightful questions to determine if I am a truth teller or a charlatan.

August also included Open Houses for each school, so parents could visit their children's classrooms and meet the teachers, Parent Teacher Association got started, discipleship groups were formed by the school chaplain for after-school spiritual encouragement, and the extra-curricula sports programs kicked off in the middle and high schools.

September
On alternate years, a few of the Hillcrest High School staff and Christian adults in the Hillcrest community hosted separate sexual purity retreats for the high school boys and girls. On two consecutive weekends about 20 adults shared a biblical view of integrity and purity through testimonies and small groups and challenged the teenagers to honor God by staying pure until they are married and then faithful once they are married. It was a great opportunity to help young people with an important and increasingly challenging area in all our lives. The adults shared their own struggles and victories, and we pray it helps these teenagers understand a

biblical view of sexuality and make a commitment to purity in their relationships.

October

October 1 is Nigerian Independence Day, so during that week the school celebrated with a parade and special assembly. Each child could come in a costume of his or her home country or hero. Nigerian traditional dancers put on a dancing show, and some of the older children staged a fashion show of Nigerian cultural clothing, and a speaker focused on Nigerian culture.

Dorothy was teaching the third graders about Joseph in the Bible and the amazing land of Egypt. She gave each child a stuffed animal, which they "mummified" by taking the stuffing out of the brain through the nose and then made an Egyptian style coffin for their "mummy."

October is the month in their senior year our girls began the application process for college. Even though Hillcrest had a high school counselor who was helpful, with poor Internet and email it was extremely challenging gathering helpful information about various U.S. colleges. They also had to fill out the financial aid applications, which was even more difficult with our taxes being prepared by a U.S. tax consultant. All three girls applied to about four colleges and were accepted into every school they applied to. Marie chose Azusa Pacific University in Los Angeles to study child psychology; Heather chose Azusa Pacific University to study biology; Anna chose Seattle Pacific to study fashion design. Fortunately, we had visited all the schools they applied to on previous furloughs, so they had a sense of the campus environment, academic programs, student life, and Christian atmosphere in each school. They were excited to be accepted into their first choice colleges, and all received substantial financial aid.

November

The high school National Honor Society at Hillcrest arranged with the school administration to let the high school students help in a variety of ministries in the community for half a day. Most of the places they went were ministries to Nigerian children, including Gidan Bege (City Ministries) and a ministry to AIDS widows and their children. As a member of the National Honor Society, Marie played a big part in planning and organizing the afternoon activities.

Because Hillcrest was such a small school, our girls played on the four major school sports varsity teams – basketball, volleyball, soccer, and track. November was basketball tournament season. All our girls played on the girls' team or were helping their class sell drinks and snacks at the games to raise class funds. The school games were social events for the parents who spent hours watching the games, drinking coffee, and praying there would be no major injuries.

Historically the high school seniors put on a drama in the fall term, and the entire high school staged a musical in the spring term. Our girls always had major parts in these productions. As a family we usually went to all three nights of the play. With an international student body, some of the role assignments were interesting. Everyone had a great time rehearsing for the productions, which were a major source of entertainment in the community.

December

The Hillcrest community presented a Christmas musical program "Nine Lessons and Carols" every year that was a great introduction to the season. The auditorium was decorated with holly wreaths and lights, creating a Christmas festive atmosphere in the middle of Africa. Each school also had a concert highlighting the Christmas celebration.

Dorothy's special interest in teaching reading played out in her initiative to track reading fluency in her students. She discovered a number of interesting deficiencies as students went on holiday breaks, from students from homes where the parents were not English speakers, and families that had few children's books in their libraries. As part of Dorothy's subtle strategy to motivate kids to read she organized a reading contest every school holiday called "Can you read more than Mrs. Ardill?" After the school break, each class totaled the number of pages they had read, and displayed the statistics prominently on a poster outside her office. Dorothy gave out prizes for the top readers in each class and the elementary school class that had read the most pages. The parents loved it, Dorothy loved it, and the kids learned to love reading!

January

In January 2001 I was asked if I would be willing to teach the senior Bible class on Biblical Ethics. Since I had a personal and professional interest especially in biomedical ethical issues, I agreed and began to put together a one-semester course on the common ethical dilemmas of our generation. We covered a comparison of worldviews and a biblical worldview and then tackled the following subjects from a biblical worldview: abortion, reproductive technology, euthanasia, music, drugs and alcohol, homosexuality and pornography, war and civil disobedience, church/state conflict, ecology and the environment and wealth and poverty.

Most students have appreciated my teaching, and it has been a great privilege to have some input in their lives before they face these issues as freshmen in secular American universities! I have been especially encouraged by a few students who have made life-changing decisions during the year.

February

The elementary school had its Science Fair in February every other year (to give the parents a break!) The problem was it became a contest to see whose dad could make the best project! In January 2008 when he was in second grade, David started working on his science fair project, testing various water filters for water purification. The next year when David was in third grade, he tried to answer the question, "What food makes the most electricity? – lemon, potato, onion, or tomato? He placed four of each food in an egg crate, hooked them together in groups of four by wires with paperclips, and then measured the voltage for each food group. He learned that lemons make the most electricity. David was very proud of his experiment. (So is his father!)

March
Because the rains come in April, March is the end of track season. Marie and Heather competed in the long distance events. It often was very hot and humid, and heat exhaustion was a concern. We discovered that David also loved to run. An after-school running club was started for the middle school kids. One week David ran 10 miles and was hardly out of breath. He only stopped because no one else could keep up with him! Marie often invited David to run with her because he excelled in long distance events.

The first weekend in March is lots of fun with the elementary school Field Day on Friday morning. There was an obstacle course, water games (over, under with a pitcher of water, run and sit on a water balloon, etc.), bowling to knock over the pins, and a crazy game in the gym. The big prize is the privilege of being the first to go down the water slide (AKA our playground slide with a small pool at the bottom). In 2009 Dorothy and David's team, the Purple Knights, won; I am sure it was Dorothy's cunning strategy and David's speed and agility that won the day.

April
For weeks the junior class prepares the venue, menu and program for the Junior-Senior Banquet, which honors the senior class. The junior class uses the funds they have collected from the various class events since they were freshmen and puts on a big extravaganza to honor the senior class. It is the equivalent to the prom in most U.S. high schools, so it is a big event in the high school to close out the school year. The excitement around our house on Friday

evening preparing for the Junior-Senior Banquet is palpable. Our girls had bought dresses for this event years earlier when they were in the United States on furlough. The few who are couples in the class go together, but the rest either pair up with a friend or go alone. In 2008, Marie's junior class chose the theme of the *Phantom of the Opera* and transformed the school auditorium into a magical opera house complete with grand piano, chandelier, opera booths and a string ensemble playing the Phantom music throughout the evening.

May

May is the end-of-year activities in all three schools. The last big social event for the middle school is the eighth grade Banquet. Although not as big a production as the Junior-Senior Banquet, it is an opportunity for the eighth graders to dress up in fancy dresses and go with a date to a dinner in a nice restaurant. Sometimes the boys ask their dates a year in advance, so it can became quite awkward if things change during the year. It is hilarious for the parents but an important milestone for the eighth graders.

The last Sunday before graduation is the SIM Senior Tea and the Baccalaureate service. This Sunday was usually a big day for our family. On Sunday afternoon SIM hosts a Senior Tea to honor the SIM kids who are graduating from Hillcrest. The graduating students display their Memoir Book they have been working on all year in their senior English class. It is a wonderful compilation of essays and creative writing, recounting meaningful events in their lives. It is a very special time for parents to honor their children publicly with a short tribute to their son or daughter.

On the furlough before their senior year, I gathered pictures of Marie, Heather, and Anna from our archives and put together a PowerPoint slideshow about their lives. In 2012 for Heather and Anna we compared and contrasted them with all their unique gifts and abilities. We then encouraged them to stay true to the Lord and remember to write home once in a while!

Sunday evening is the Baccalaureate service. The seniors all dress up in Nigerian clothing in their class colors. Parents of the seniors participate in the service. The audience has to suffer through the parents of the graduates singing a song to them that is countered by the graduating class responding with a song. In 2005 and 2009 the graduating class asked me to give the Baccalaureate address. It was a real honor and special joy to be asked by the seniors, especially since Marie was in the graduating class in 2009.

The closing chapel on the last day of school was the final hurrah for the faculty and students before graduation. It was a time of farewells, recognition of departing students and teachers, and a prayer for safety in travel for the many going abroad over the summer holidays. The seniors were recognized and honored and they let out an enormous cheer after the closing prayer.

Before the crisis in Jos, the graduation was held on a Friday evening, but when we curtailed evening events because of security concerns, the graduation ceremony was moved to the afternoon. The seniors asked some of their parents to participate in the ceremony and chose their speaker. I was asked to be the graduation speaker in 2004, 2008, and 2012 for Heather and Anna's graduation. The class sponsors give small personal vignettes about each student that are thoughtful and insightful.

The changing security situation in Nigeria greatly affected the activities and programs of Hillcrest. Traditions were challenged, schedules rearranged, and there was a serious rethinking of everything the school did from its academic mission to the many social and spiritual programs. After each traumatic event in the community, teachers allowed time for debriefing students, counselors were available, and the administrators were sensitive to the unique needs of children in these stressful situations.

We are grateful for the opportunity Hillcrest offered our children to get a great education, grow spiritually and emotionally and provide them a firm foundation for the rest of their lives. They all look back on their years at Hillcrest with great affection and appreciation for the friendships, opportunities in sports, drama, service activities, music education, and leadership development. We pray Hillcrest will continue its mission to provide an excellent education for the children of missionaries serving in Nigeria.

SPARE TIME

Dorothy and I are both blessed with the vision to see needs around us and respond with ideas to help. We perceive needs as opportunities to do more. We are solution people, not problem-focused people. We are what some call "green light thinkers" who find out ways to make things happen and not "red light thinkers" who find reasons why things won't work.

We have both struggled with this at different times because often the right answer to a problem is to do nothing, or wait or bring others along with you instead of charging ahead with a solution. It has been especially difficult but important to understand in terms of the Nigerian culture, to know how we are perceived, how our ideas are understood, and how Nigerians solve problems. We have learned that, like people everywhere, if the Nigerians were not included in the problem-solving process, the solution would not be theirs, would lack their emotional and financial support, and would likely fail when we left the scene.

Another BIG idea I learned after a few years of heartache and pain working at Evangel Hospital is the notion of diversification. I love to do surgery and thoroughly enjoy the work and people at the hospital. However, there were many days when I could not do surgery because there was no water to wash my hands to do surgery, or there was no oxygen, or no clean sterile instruments packs or … or … and so on. This was exasperating.

After having this happen for a few years, I looked for things to do outside the hospital that I knew would be fulfilling and enjoyable when surgery was not possible. I gradually took on more responsibilities outside the medical work. There was great variety to these extracurricular activities, from teaching Bible classes to sitting on committees. It was not until years later that I realized how much happier I was, or rather how infrequently I was getting upset, when things at the hospital were not operational because of my outside activities. I could go to another responsibility that was fulfilling and not feel the day was a total waste of time. Diversification also allowed me to express my other gifts and contribute to a variety of ministries. Flexibility and adaptability were keys to survival. Getting the best training and education possible is important before going into missionary service, but in the same breath one must be prepared to do unexpected things for the greater glory of the growth of the kingdom of God. Let me tell you about a few things I have been involved in over the years.

Church

When we arrived in Nigeria, we were interested in attending a Nigerian church. We wanted to learn about the Nigerian church culture, develop friendships, and contribute to the church. After visiting several Nigerian churches, we developed several criteria for the "ideal" church. The main deciding point was the music. We preferred churches with the traditional African instruments like drums and percussion instruments. The churches with a singing group leading the worship and an electronic keyboard and microphones seemed to have, at best, mediocre music. The person playing the keyboard appeared to be learning to play during the Sunday morning church service – searching for the same key the choir and people were singing. More often than not, it turned into a cacophony of sound between the competing choir, congregation, and music group.

We also wanted to attend a church with a children's program. A few churches had children's activities during the morning service usually consisting of 50 small children packed into a small room to hear a Bible story. Our children were the only white children, so everyone stared at them and wanted to touch their white skin. Our children hated Sunday mornings.

We eventually decided to attend a small church about ten minutes from the hospital compound along a terrible road that was almost impassable in the rainy season. In fact, several times the road was so bad we had to abandon the car along the road and walk the rest of the way to the church. It was located in an area of the town that still had a village atmosphere and was surrounded by boulder hills typical of the Plateau State. The church was a concrete block building with a corrugated zinc roof and concrete block bench pews for about 300. The usual attendance for the early English service was about 70 youth, and the pastor was a seminary student working part-time. There were no other missionaries going to the church, and at that time they were using traditional instruments. They did not have a children's program, but Dorothy decided she would be willing to help start one.

Over the ensuing months we got to know the seminary student pastor and got involved in helping the leadership by teaching in Bible studies and Sunday school. We were always invited to their church functions, including several after-church lunches. The women cooked jollof rice and had various Nigerian dishes. They were hospitable to us, and we felt highly welcome. We have many good memories of this church including the humorous sermon about the Body of Christ with the illustration about the anus and how it felt unwanted by the other parts of the body, so it went on strike. The other body parts very quickly learned to appreciate it. Of course this was to illustrate the interdependence of members in the church, but it was still a funny and bold illustration for a morning church service.

Much to our regret, the church eventually raised funds for electronic musical instruments. They did not have anyone who could play the instruments, but the leaders believed, "If we have it, they will come." Sure enough, when they got the keyboard and microphones, young people who thought they knew how to play came to the church. Unfortunately, Sunday morning appeared to be their main practice time, and the learning curve was steep and painful to our ears.

Dorothy started a children's program, and for months she taught Sunday school to 50 – 100 small children in a dark, dirt-floor room in a building adjacent to the church. She asked the congregation several times for help and offered to train others to be Sunday school teachers. Most of the children didn't understand English, so even the value of her teaching was suspect. She photocopied coloring sheets and gave out crayons, which were rarely returned. Our girls got the same touch-and-feel treatment and, after a year of trying, Dorothy gave up trying to convince the church leaders of the value of the Sunday school program. The girls were not enjoying church, and more often than not I would stay home with the children on Sunday morning, so at least one of us would have some undistracted worship time. Eventually, we left the church and attended Hillcrest services for the rest of our time in Nigeria. This context was better for our children and still allowed us to help teach Sunday school classes, preach occasionally, and help with various activities and programs in which our children were also involved.

NEMI

NEMI, the Nigerian Evangelical Missionary Institute, was started by several Mission leaders in 1985 to serve as a multi-mission missionary training institute. Because many Nigerian churches did not have missionary training facilities and faculty, this initiative broadened the opportunities to train nationals for missionary endeavors. It is the flagship training facility for the Nigerian Evangelical

Mission Association, an umbrella organization whose mission is to facilitate the promotion of Great Commission initiatives throughout Nigeria and the African continent.

One of the elders at the small ECWA church we attended was a seminary student named Titus. I served as a mentor for the elders and so developed a close relationship with Titus. He was a member of the ECWA missions arm called EMS (Evangel Missionary Society). Through his seminary training he had been teaching and helping at NEMI and one day asked if I would be interested in teaching a class. Because of my schedule I did not think it would be possible to fit into the modular framework for their classes but offered to teach one afternoon a week. This fit in well with their weekly student chapel schedule, so I began teaching in September 1999.

Each week as I drove the 20 minutes to the school property outside of Jos, I was excited about the opportunity to impact these men and women who will be the new pioneers in the missionary enterprise in Nigeria and beyond.

The school was using a dangerously dilapidated building on a church compound near us. The roof was sagging and the ceiling had already fallen down in several places. There was one light bulb in the room, and the students sat on hard benches with coarse, wooden tables. The broken-glass windows were replaced with cardboard, and the chalkboard was so old it was difficult to either write on it or decipher what had been written. I began to teach the book of Acts every week to a dozen students. The students were from a wide spectrum of churches and denominations that all had one thing in common – a desire to learn to be a witness for the Gospel cross-culturally. None had formal seminary education but had been working in a variety of professions before God called them to become missionaries. Some already had missionary experience, but most were new to the idea of a career in missions. Some were being sponsored by their churches, so they had food and money for books. Others, unfortunately, had no financial help and struggled each term to pay the school fees and feed their families. A few came with their wives and children, but most were either single or came alone.

One afternoon after class, a student named Clement asked to talk to me about a personal matter. In Nigeria this usually means a person needs money and wants to ask privately. To my surprise this was not Clement's story. He related to me an incredible tale that started when he was about 16. As he said it, he "found" himself murdering a man and was sentenced to die. After eight years in prison his sentence was changed to life imprisonment. Some time during his imprisonment, he became a Christian and felt a calling to be a missionary. After five more years the Governor pardoned him and he was released. During this time his father had died and left an estate for his sons. When Clement contacted his older brother to discuss the estate, his older brother accused him of corruption and dishonesty and refused to share the inheritance with him. Instead, the older brother made it his mission to kill Clement.

Clement was living secretly in a city and was being discipled by a strong Christian pastor. Clement still felt called to be a missionary so was sent by his church to NEMI for training. While at NEMI, his older brother sent his son to poison Clement, but he narrowly escaped this assassination attempt. His brother did not know exactly where he was, but Clement feared for his life. He asked me if I could help. What do you say to someone with that kind of story? I encouraged him that God was still in control of his life even in the midst of this persecution. God was as able to redeem his brother from his hatred, as He was to deliver Saul when he was persecuting the Christians in the first century. I thought it best to involve a mature Nigerian counselor who could talk this through with him and work toward reconciliation with his brother. I referred him to a well-respected seminary professor with years of counseling experience who I knew would provide godly counsel.

Other students gave testimonies of being persecuted for their faith, undergoing incredible financial hardship, and remarkable sacrifices in obedience to God's call in their lives. It was a challenge to me, and I felt privileged that the Lord allowed me to open His Word to them each week. I sought to teach them how to study the Bible and discern God's truth, and to be encouraged by the wondrous story of how God built His church in the first century. Many events like those in the book of Acts are happening in Nigeria today, so each week we dealt with relevant and practical applications of God's Word.

Cephas is a Nigerian missionary working in a remote area of Nigeria whom I met when I was teaching at NEMI. He took my class on the book of Acts and kept in touch after he deployed as a missionary. The people he was living with were primitive, illiterate, and had a mixture of beliefs mingling African traditional religions with Islam. They had virtually no contact with the outside world and were living in great darkness. He started living with them, learned their language, and began developing trust. He realized the villagers needed a school, so he started a primary school and was teaching the children to read in the Hausa language. Later he taught them English, which would open many more doors of opportunity for them.

Cephas also met a woman he wanted to marry, but she was from a different tribe. After working for years to accumulate the high bride price and working through the cross-tribal issues, they were married. Every time he came to Jos he stopped at our house to give me a report. We gave him clothes and books and prayed with him. Cephas' example of humility, commitment to Christ, and an enthusiasm to share the Gospel with these unreached primitive people is amazing. I marvel at the courage and commitment of these Nigerian missionaries to go to these risky remote places with the Gospel.

In 2003 I read the incredible story of the modern Chinese house church missionary movement in the book Back to Jerusalem[8]. After

---

[8] Yun, Brother Yun, Xu Yongze, Peter, Wang, Enoch, Hattaway, Paul, *Back to Jerusalem*, IVP Books, 2005.

years of persecution by the Communists, the Chinese Christians have learned to endure and thrive under persecution. Three of the house church leaders were led by God to raise an army of 100 thousand missionaries from China to take the Gospel along the Silk Road back to every country between China and Jerusalem. The movement has begun sending Chinese missionaries who have been trained in China to endure hardship to reach the unreached in the many cities and villages between China and Jerusalem. It is really the heart of the 10-40 Window and presents a huge challenge to the church.

The church in Nigeria is enormous and has tremendous resources. There are more Christians in Nigeria than all the rest of the West African countries combined. Some of the largest churches in the hemisphere are in Nigeria, and the potential of a mobilized church for the missionary movement is enormous. At the annual meeting of the Nigerian Evangelical Missionary Association in November 2004, I challenged the 250 mission leaders in attendance to take the gospel to the 250 million unreached people between Nigeria and Jerusalem – to "Go Back to Jerusalem" with the Gospel of Jesus Christ. There are obstacles for the church in Nigeria to taking on this task including the widely preached prosperity Gospel, self-centered preachers, dependency on Western churches, lack of unity and cooperation between churches and denominations, and relegation of missionary service to the least educated and gifted in the church. These problems and issues must be resolved for the Nigerian church to assume the mantle of mobilizing the West African church to take the Gospel to North Africa, a region where Western mission agencies have failed to make much of an impact.

There was keen interest in this challenge in several of the mission agencies and denominations of NEMA. We are praying that the Holy Spirit will continue to burn with conviction in the hearts of hundreds of men and women the urgency of the mission to reach the lost in North Africa with the saving love of Jesus Christ.

Jaipur Mobility Workshop

It is estimated that in non-war zone African cities about one percent are disabled. In Jos with approximately 500 thousand people, there would be about five thousand disabled due to poverty, unemployment, and lack of medical and rehabilitation facilities to care for those with injuries and disabilities. In a country with enormous economic problems, there are little or no resources dedicated to helping the disabled. As a neglected group in every community, the emotional and spiritual needs among the handicapped are enormous.

There is also a culture of begging in many poor countries. Because of high unemployment many have no other option but to beg. In fact, begging provides pretty good income. Even when jobs or vocational skills are offered, they often reject these opportunities and prefer the income, freedom, and "working" hours of begging. This occupation of sorts is also desirable to women. In orthodox Muslim homes, women are rarely allowed out of their compound. A blind or crippled woman who is allowed out of the compound to beg has unusual freedom and social opportunities.

A missionary friend offered to take an amputee beggar to a hospital several hours away to get a prosthesis for him. She wanted him to be able to move beyond begging for his livelihood. After many trips and quite a large sum of money, the man finally got his prosthesis fitted properly. Several weeks later Dorothy and I were going up the steps into the main market in Jos and noticed the man who had been helped with a new prosthesis. He was sitting in his usual begging spot with his plastic bowl for donations in front of him, his hands out as he pleaded with passersby with his beautiful prosthesis sitting propped up beside him on the steps. I guess the artificial leg helped him "get to work," but his work was still begging!

Ever since coming to Nigeria in 1992, as a surgeon I have had to do amputations on patients because of trauma, serious infections, and tumors. I was not aware of any place in our region that offered prostheses. The nearest place was several hours away and required a large amount of money and an extended stay for the fitting. Most of the methods I had seen in the United States during my training required sophisticated technology and supplies that were not available in Nigeria. For years I searched for a solution.

While on a trip to a medical conference in Kenya in 1998, I visited the Jaipur Workshop. The Jaipur method was invented in India by a surgeon and a local craftsman. They used PVC pipe to make the leg and then attached a molded rubber foot. The process to make the leg was very simple, not requiring either high tech equipment or sophisticated materials. I carefully watched what they did in the workshops, determined to reproduce this in Nigeria for my patients.

Shortly after returning to Nigeria, I discussed the idea with several staff at the hospital and found an orthopedic nurse at Evangel interested in learning this method to make artificial legs. After discussions with the hospital management and the Kenya Jaipur Workshop, we sent this man to Kenya for three months to learn the technique. He came back and we set aside three rooms at the Gidan Bege site for him to set up a prosthetic workshop to begin making legs. Much to my disappointment, after nine months he had set up a nice painted office but had not made a single leg! He had wanted a stereo player for this office and a tea set for his break time. He needed soft drinks and a lot of other amenities before he could make a leg. Then just before we left for a one-year furlough, in spite of all the time and money we had invested in him, he quit!

I went on furlough to the United States very discouraged. While there I learned a lot more about how to make legs and got several helpful books and supplies from a few prosthetics companies. Determined to start again when we got back to Nigeria in one year, I came up with a different approach for the workshop. Upon our return, I decided it was more important to find a person with the right heart for this ministry than a person with the right training. You can train the mind, but it is a lot harder to change a heart. I asked Peter Fretheim, who was in charge of the Gidan Bege ministry, if he knew of someone in the ministry who would be a good person to train for this workshop. He recommended two men, Victor and Daniel, so we sent them to Kano, in northern Nigeria, for a two-month course in making artificial legs using the Jaipur method. They came back enthusiastic about making artificial limbs. We bought the necessary tools and equipment locally, and in a few months we began to work together to make legs. The first few I made looked pretty bad, but we sure learned a lot. Victor and Daniel kept improving and did a great job in running the Mobility Workshop at Gidan Bege.

The patients who came with an amputation were often depressed and had lost their jobs or source of income. Many resorted to a life of begging in order to survive because they could not afford the artificial limbs. Because of this I was determined to offer the legs at no charge. Many people were helped from all walks of life and all ages as their mobility improved. Because they often came for several visits in the course of the fitting and adjustments, we developed close relationships with them with many opportunities for counseling and witness to the saving and healing power of Jesus Christ.

Men's Accountability Groups

Desiring to help mentor and disciple several Nigerian men, I began a weekly Bible study with my driver Kingsford and several other men. It was a great opportunity to help him grow spiritually and to share some of the life principles God had taught me. We worked our way through the life of Christ in a "harmony of the Gospels" approach, and it was interesting to hear the groups' comments and insights. We discussed marriage, family, parenting, and life in Nigeria. I learned a great deal from him about culture, the church, Nigerian politics, Islam, and tribal beliefs. Kingsford told me he took our Bible lessons and shared them with his church youth group. He soaked up anything I shared with him from the Scripture and applied it to his family and life. We also enjoyed meeting his family and watched his children grow as he and his wife raised them in a godly environment.

I was also eager to get involved with men in Nigeria to whom I could be held accountable. Five of us began to meet together at 6:30 a.m. on Thursdays to ask basic questions about our thought lives, our devotional times with God, our marriages, families, and work. We committed to praying for each other, keeping the things we discussed confidential, and being honest with each other. Each week as we shared, it was wonderful to see how God answered our prayers and how the ups and downs of each member were balanced by the other members of the group.

After a few years, others expressed interest in joining us, so we split the group and each of us led another group. These groups were a great help to many men living in stressful situations with a variety of crises including death, serious illness, ministry failures, and family crises.

Writing

When I was a child at the boarding school Kent Academy, the dorm parents made us write to our parents once a week. Those letters I am sure were not very profound, but they left a lifelong impression on me – the importance of communicating with family. While on the mission field for 24 years, I faithfully wrote every week to my family and friends about our joys and failures, sorrows and successes. When Dorothy and I were dating long distance (she was in Chicago, and I was in Liberia), I wrote an airform letter to her every day for five months! Over years, I have learned both the fun and the discipline of writing.

In my high school days I learned the value of good writing. Mr. Lally, my high school senior English teacher in Belleville High School in New Jersey, gave us an essay topic each week. If we made one spelling mistake or grammar error on the paper, we failed the paper. I quickly learned the rules of grammar and spelling.

This was in the days before computers and spell checkers, so all my papers were typed on a manual typewriter, usually with "erasable bond" paper.

A few months after being evacuated from Liberia because of the Civil War, I had a two-week spell without many appointments. We were staying with Dorothy's parents in Maryland, and so I told them, "I am going to the basement for a while. Please don't disturb me unless it is an emergency." So for the next two weeks I buried myself in my notes, research, and journals, and wrote the book *Where Elephants Fight*, about our experience in Liberia. After many drafts and the help of several friends who were good editors, I printed the book in Nigeria and have been distributing it to friends and family members since. I enjoy writing and expressing my emotions and thoughts and have been fortunate to have opportunities to publish in a variety of forums.

My interests are so varied that I have also written on both missiology and medicine. It seems I always have a few manuscripts in various stages of completion, and occasionally a magazine agrees to publish something I have written. It is a certain thing, however, that if my livelihood depended on my writing, we would starve.

Pass It On

A few years ago a team from one of our supporting churches came to visit us in Nigeria. They had supported us for years, but no one from the pastoral staff or leadership team had visited us on the field. We were thrilled and did not lack things for them to do and see during their ten-day stay. One evening after a busy day of activities as we were reflecting on the many ministries we are involved in, the pastor asked if there was a common idea or thread we could see through our diverse ministries. After a second it occurred to me that in everything we are doing, we are involved in teaching, mentoring or discipling Nigerian men, women, and young people. It really struck me that we were impacting many for the Kingdom of God through direct didactic teaching, modeling, mentoring, and discipling.

It was affirming and reassuring that all the many things that crowded our lives and consumed our time and energy were indeed in line with our mission to pass to the next generation of Nigerians the skills, knowledge and vision the Lord had given us. So, if we are not doing whatever we are doing with someone else alongside us, we need to. We are not in this alone and have made it both a life-style and commitment to pass along to others what God has given to us.

THE CLEAR AND PRESENT
DANGER OF AIDS

Ladi was one of our very first volunteers in the Gidan Bege ministry. She had a great heart for people and especially enjoyed witnessing to women. She was instrumental in introducing the blind women in Jos to the Gidan Bege ministry and opening up Blindtown for Gidan Bege activities. So, Ladi was a special person in both the ministry and in Dorothy's life.

One day, Ladi was admitted to the hospital for treatment of a brain abscess. This is an unusual diagnosis and sparked some key questions. Dorothy went to visit her, and we began to pray for her healing. It came out during her hospitalization that she had AIDS and was dying. The next days and months were very difficult. Dorothy wanted to encourage her, but we realized that her situation seemed hopeless. During her visits, Dorothy would read the Psalms to remind Ladi of God's faithfulness and goodness. This was Dorothy's first personal encounter with someone with HIV/AIDS. It was a disturbing experience to see her good friend dying in front of her.

When Ladi was discharged, she went back to her village in Miango. Dorothy visited her and learned more each visit about the agony and heartbreak of this devastating plague. Dorothy learned Ladi was reaping the consequences of something she had done many years ago before she had become involved in ministry. We were in the United States when Ladi died, but her life and death made an indelible impression on Dorothy.

Another close personal encounter with AIDS happened in our house. We needed someone to clean the floors, windows, and bathrooms every day. Our friend Simon Khantiok from the hospital recommended Rebecca who was from his church next to the hospital. We interviewed Rebecca and her husband, and they seemed a good Christian couple. Shortly afterwards Rebecca started working in our house.

After about two years Dorothy noticed Rebecca seemed to be getting sick a lot and sometimes even found her lying on one of the bedroom floors taking a rest. Dorothy became suspicious, and so asked her to get tested for HIV/AIDS. Dorothy will never forget the day Rebecca came back with her results. She was HIV+. She wept with Dorothy and tried to think about her future through the blur and shock of this news. Dorothy immediately asked her to get her husband tested. Her husband was also HIV+ and, without prying too much, it appeared that maybe Rebecca contracted the HIV virus several years earlier during a surgical procedure done by a native or traditional doctor.

Dorothy tried to help Rebecca think about the implications of her death and advised her to leave something tangible for her children that would not be taken by the family or lost in the inheritance battle. Dorothy felt the best thing would be for her to build a house for her children, so at least they would have a place to stay after their parents died. So we started helping Rebecca and her husband with a house loan.

They were faithful in making their payments, but over the coming months, Rebecca became more ill and was unable to work. She had days of diarrhea, vomiting, fever, and other signs of infection. She would usually send one of her children to the house to tell us she could not come to work. She often went to local pharmacies or clinics for medicines, but we were not happy with the drugs and treatments they dispensed. We offered to help her with medical expenses, so we made the rule that we would only pay for medicines and clinic visits from one of our church clinics or hospitals. There were still many irregularities in drugs that were ordered for her, but at least we had some control and could address the problems.

She made heroic recoveries time after time in the coming years. Dorothy used the opportunity to learn firsthand from Rebecca what it was like for an African woman to have AIDS. Dorothy wept with her often as she began to realize the horrible stigma, the shame, and loneliness of this horrific disease. Dorothy also used her time with Rebecca to encourage her to educate her children about sex and AIDS. Dorothy learned a lot about the practical aspects of the disease and how the average Nigerian can cope.

One recommendation was to drink only clean water, take vitamins and an antibiotic once a day to prevent infections. These simple suggestions helped Rebecca survive as long as she did. We struggled over whether we should also help Rebecca by enrolling her in an HIV antiretroviral drug program. There were very few free programs and enrollment was difficult. The drugs were very expensive and required a high degree of compliance taking the medicines or the virus would become resistant to the medications.

We decided to see how Rebecca would do on the simple vitamin and antibiotic protocol first. She had heard about a local healer who had the "cure" for AIDS. Rebecca wanted to spend an enormous amount of money to buy this cure. We had seen many of these charlatans over the years and strongly discouraged her from wasting her limited resources. She ignored our advice and took the medicine on a loan plan of some sort, but it never helped her. She was still not very compliant and often ignored our advice, so we made the difficult decision to not pursue getting her on an antiretroviral drug program.

When we went on furlough in 2001, we did not expect to see Rebecca when we returned a year later. It was a tearful goodbye but, much to our surprise, she was alive and doing fine when we returned. She resumed working for us, but her health began to deteriorate to the point that she would be sick for weeks at a time. Dorothy went to visit her one day and was shocked to see how thin she was and how difficult it was for her family to even feed her. She had lost the will to live, and it seemed the family was just waiting for her to die.

One morning one of her children came to the house and told us the news we had been expecting for a long time – Rebecca was gone. Dorothy went to see the family to see how we could help with the funeral arrangements. Over the coming days it was distressing for us to see Rebecca's family and her husband's family quarrel over where she would be buried, where the funeral would take place, and who would get her things including the house we had helped them build. Dorothy went to the funeral and burial and did her best to encourage and support Rebecca's children.

We had several friends in the United States offer to help Rebecca's husband finish his house. As we inquired, we were disturbed to learn that the papers for the house were not in order, and her husband had not followed through properly in securing the house in the will for the children. We encouraged him we would help with the expenses to get the papers in order to guarantee the house would go to Rebecca's children. Again it was a painful reminder of the abuse of women's rights and the total neglect of the children at a time of great tragedy in their lives.

The many lessons Dorothy learned from her intimate relationship with Rebecca and Ladi served her well later in designing the Home-Based Care Program for HIV/AIDS families, including the need to care for the children, inheritance rights, home-based care to all in the community, and the importance of compassion to all.

When we left for our furlough in 2001, Dorothy had handed over the Gidan Bege ministry to the Fretheims and began to ask the Lord for His leading in a future ministry. While we were in the U.S., Dorothy began to learn more about HIV/AIDS in Africa and the various church-based programs around the world. We attended an HIV/AIDS conference sponsored by Samaritan's Purse called Prescription for Hope. It was a terrific experience for Dorothy and energized her to get involved in working with people living with AIDS upon our return to Nigeria. Her heart was to work with the children and women in a church context because of her wonderful experience with the Women's Fellowship group.

Over the course of the next 12 months on our home assignment in the United States, Dorothy began to formulate a plan to mobilize the women in the church to care for the widows and orphans in the church and community. Armed with prayer and these ideas, she excitedly returned to Nigeria in 2002 asking God to use her to help many suffering from the plague of the HIV virus. The statistics were staggering about the number who were infected in sub-Saharan Africa, the number of widows and orphans, and the projected numbers as the disease would spread.

Dorothy was curious to know how many widows there were in the local ECWA church she attended for Women's Fellowship. After they took a survey, she learned that in the group of 300, there were 80 widows. It was impossible to know how many of the husbands had died of AIDS, but clearly from the stories she was hearing, there were many. She also found out there were a number of orphans who were not being cared for by the church. Most were living in child-led households and barely surviving. Widows were often abused and taken advantage of in the society and even in churches. They usually lost everything they owned when their husbands died because the families would come and claim their own piece of the inheritance.

Then, forced to do dishonorable things to stay alive, some widows resorted to things they would never have considered if they had been financially taken care of and loved. So, how could the church in practical ways help the widows? How could they identify the widows and orphans and do a better job in caring for them in a holistic approach?

The Lord reminded Dorothy of an idea she first heard from a teacher at Hillcrest School many years ago. Since the women in the Women's Fellowship took up at least four offerings (passing the plate) during each Friday afternoon meeting, Dorothy wanted to come up with a tangible way to help the widows without the burden of another offering. Since each woman had to cook for her family every day, if a woman set aside a handful of grain (rice, wheat, corn) each time she cooked a meal and put it in a bucket, by the end of the month she would have a fair bit of grains set aside that her family would hardly notice at mealtime. If all the women in the church set aside a little, at the end of each month if they brought their "little" and put it together, it could amount to a large offering for the widows. Hence the "Widows' Bucket Project" was born. Dorothy offered to buy the women the plastic buckets if they committed to setting aside the grains.

She floated this idea to the Women's Fellowship executive, and they loved it. It was soon implemented in the church Dorothy attends for Women's Fellowship, and the first Friday collection was an amazing event. Imagine three hundred African women all dressed alike in their colorful church "uniforms" with small clear buckets balanced on their heads dancing their way to the front of the church singing praises to God in their Hausa language. It is a picture of pure joy if there ever was one. At the front they dumped the grains from their buckets into large grain sacks and sang their way joyfully back to their seats. Talk about giving with a hilarious heart!

Before distributing the buckets to the women, Dorothy had an opportunity to talk about HIV/AIDS to the women in the fellowship. She explained clearly what the disease was, how it was contracted, and how it was NOT contracted. She wanted to dispel the many myths about the disease and promote prevention measures. She concluded with a compassionate, biblical response to interact with those living with the disease. In each bucket were two pieces of literature about AIDS. One was a brief overview of the basic information everyone needs to know about AIDS to help the women remember her presentation.

Because the mothers were the ones most likely to discuss sex with their sons and daughters, she also gave them a pamphlet called "10 Great Reasons to Say No to Sex Before Marriage." This pamphlet is a culturally relevant piece of literature for teenagers which discusses many of the common questions teenagers ask about sex.

Dorothy did a survey a few months later and was amazed to learn that most of the women had shared the two pieces of literature with at least six other people including their children. The power of both the printed word and relevant teaching was awesome. Recently another SIM missionary woman created a culturally sensitive adaptation of Ken Taylor's book "Almost Twelve" to help parents prepare pre-teens for puberty. This booklet was added to the Bucket Project literature, so parents had another resource for their pre-teens and teenagers. There are so many folklore, lies, and misconceptions about sexuality and AIDS that education is a key element in the fight to curb this plague. A biblical approach is essential to promote the godly mandate for abstinence and faithfulness rather than the message being promoted of free sexual expression with "protection."

This project was so well accepted that Dorothy began to receive invitations to speak at other Women's Fellowship groups to present the Bucket Project. She realized she would soon be exhausted trying to go to every church in northern Nigeria with this idea, so she developed a different strategy. Every year Women's Fellowship groups from all over Nigeria get together for weekend spiritual life conferences. They camp outside at night on the ground with only the stars for a roof and, during the day, sit for hours under a makeshift, branch-covered shelter listening to the choirs from each church and being challenged by various speakers and preachers. At mealtimes the women form long queues and are served "mush" from large pots Dorothy affectionately calls "cannibal pots." At night they sing until the wee hours of the morning and then are up at the crack of dawn to ready themselves for the new day of activities. For most of the women who attend, it is the highlight of the year because they are away from their husbands and children and are having great fun with their friends in Christ.

Dorothy has attended these conferences for years and usually is given the VIP treatment – a room in a house somewhere near the conference with a pit latrine instead of just going to the "bush." She realized these conferences represented the leaders and key women from each church in the north – the cream of the crop! She asked the Women's Fellowship executive if she could have the opportunity to present the Widows Bucket Grain Project, give each woman a bucket with AIDS literature, and present a short drama about AIDS. One year she was given time to speak at six different weekend conferences.

Another element of the project was raising funds for the buckets. At each conference there were between 3,000 and 10,000 women! So for all the conferences each year she needed funds for 20,000 buckets! Dorothy appealed to our supporting churches in the United States with the condition that each church would send two women to help her distribute the buckets. It would signify a partnership or sisterhood between the U.S. church women and the Nigerian church women and would also convey to the Nigerians that this money was from concerned Christian women and not just from supposedly wealthy missionary women. Dorothy also gave several criteria for the U.S. women considering joining her – they had to be able to wear a head tie covering for three days, use a pit latrine, and sleep on the floor. So she waited to see what would happen.

Much to her delight, God provided not only the funds but several teams of women came to help her distribute the buckets at the weekend conferences. The American women who came were adventurous and brave and had a terrific time. Dorothy's mother came one year and was the only one to brave all six conferences with Dorothy. Remember they are sitting all day in the hot sun, listening to sermons, special music, and drama – all in a foreign language! The response from the Nigerian women was also thrilling as they saw the concern of the women in the American churches and began to understand that they had a responsibility in helping care for the hundreds of widows and orphans in their churches.

This project has continued and spread into other church denominations as well. Dorothy has spoken to Women's Fellowship groups in other churches and challenged them with the same opportunity for the women to care for their own and the children who are too often neglected. Her goal was to keep children and women from becoming destitute street people. This is possible through the power of the effort of organized women's fellowship groups throughout Nigeria. With over 4,000 churches throughout Nigeria, the ECWA denomination has a wide impact both geographically and culturally.

The other aspect of the AIDS ministry in which Dorothy has been involved is developing a home-based care training program for church volunteers. To her surprise, Dorothy learned that the Women's Fellowships have divided their constituents into areas surrounding the church. Each area was assigned a woman who is to know about the needs of the women in her area, visit the sick and report needs back to the fellowship leaders. What an amazing infrastructure already in place to expand the visitation to people living with AIDS! All they really needed was more specific training in caring for people with AIDS. So Dorothy and her colleagues at the counseling center, Spring of Life, began to put together a Home-Based Care workshop to train lay women in the basics of AIDS, the fundamentals of counseling and simple first-aid health care triage to know who needed to be sent to the hospital, who could be cared for at home and how to care for the sick at home.

The Spring of Life AIDS counseling team has offered this Home-Based Care workshop, and it has been well accepted and appears to be having an impact on the care of those living with AIDS.

We pray it will continue to grow as churches begin to train volunteers from other churches and spread the information from person to person.

For many years the HIV drugs were too expensive for most Nigerians. In 2004 the United States government under President George W. Bush's leadership began a program called the President's Emergency Plan For AIDS Relief (PEPFAR) to provide antiretroviral treatment to people who were HIV+ and living with AIDS in sub-Saharan Africa. Evangel Hospital became an approved site and eventually was treating 4,000 patients. Before PEPFAR the life expectancy of people with AIDS in Nigeria was two years. After patients received the medications, the life expectancy increased to ten years. Spring of Life counselors used to attend funerals of clients every week, but this decreased to almost none after PEPFAR started. It was an amazing medical and sociological phenomenon that was a game changer in Africa. We were thrilled to see so many children whose HIV+ parents would be able to raise them instead of leaving them as orphans.

From a national or global perspective, the battle against AIDS is still depressing and hopeless. The number of infected young people grows exponentially in spite of our best efforts. We liken the fight to the image of the sinking Titanic. We cannot stop the ship from going down, but we are in the lifeboats rescuing people by pulling them into the boat one at a time. Through a biblically based education prevention program as our first priority, we hope to curb the pandemic within the church. We also believe the only spiritual hope for a person in Africa with AIDS is in Jesus Christ. In spite of PEPFAR, the news about the future of an HIV+ person in West Africa is not too bright. The church can come alongside the hopeless and offer comfort, assistance to them and their family, spiritual and emotional acceptance, and help them prepare for eternity.

COUNTING THE COST

O ften when we were in the United States, friends com-
mended us for the sacrifices we made serving God in
Africa. They also expressed concern about the impact
on our children and all they are missing being raised in a developing world country. Indeed, I left the opportunity to work in a
lucrative surgical practice in an American medical system where
everything works (lights, water and phone), supplies and equipment are readily available, and there is generous compensation
for your efforts.

Certainly, living so far from home in Africa required many sacrifices. Being apart from our families was among the top costs. It
was especially difficult living an ocean away when a family member,
like a parent, was sick. Each time, we waited for news of our loved
one's condition and prayed we didn't have to make an emergency
trip to the States. There were several times when we struggled with
the decision when would be the best time to go home. It was a huge
decision because it involved the children, their school, the ministry,
and all our other commitments.

In 1992, after we had been in Nigeria for three months, we
received news that my father was diagnosed with prostate cancer. I felt like getting on a plane and going home immediately,
but I was encouraged to wait since my sister Sharon and my

brother John were available to help my parents through this crisis. My father eventually had treatment over a two-year period. It was not easy being so far away, but I appreciated my sister's faithful correspondence and phone calls. Several years later, Dorothy's father had to have emergency cardiac bypass surgery and be taken back for a second emergency procedure. Again we felt anxiously removed from this situation. Another time my mother fell and broke her hip and needed emergency surgery. I wondered, "Should I go by myself? If I take Dorothy, I must take the children. How long will we be away for and if we are away long, what about the children's schooling? If I leave, is there adequate coverage at the hospital and my other areas of responsibility?" Again I was pleased my sister and brothers intervened to help her, but each new situation produced lots of challenging questions.

Our family missed being physically close to our parents and relatives. My children have not spent as much time with their grandparents and cousins as we would have liked. They have missed spending holidays like Christmas, birthdays, and summer holidays together. Their grandparents have not attended their music recitals, important sports events, or the times they had leading roles in a school play or musical. They have not had opportunities to be spoiled at the shopping mall, treated to ice cream cones, or teased when they got new boyfriends. We were able to do some catch-up on building these memories when were in the U.S. for our home assignments, but they were few and far between compared to the pace of milestones in our children's lives. Our family missed seeing our children grow up, only getting a quick snapshot when we visited. Our children saw the changes in their cousins, aunts, uncles, and grandparents only every few years. We lived through the dramatic improvement in communication options from snail mail by international post to email with pictures, phone calls from a telephone booth at the phone company to a landline in our house, then cellphones and finally to Internet phone calls and video Skype calls from our living room. These advances made the world smaller, our family closer, and the loneliness easier to bear.

As far as other options, we didn't have the shopping, vacation or technology (Internet, cell phones) choices of our counterparts in the West. We didn't have the luxury of a variety of wonderful churches every week with great children's programs, fantastic music, and sound biblical teaching. We certainly didn't have Starbucks coffee and Krispy Kreme donuts – which we jokingly consider one of our greatest sacrifices!

The children also did not have the same school course options and extracurricular activities as their U.S. peers. When we came back to Nigeria from our furlough in the summer of 2008, we asked friends in the Jos community if they would be willing to teach our girls piano, give Heather trumpet lessons, and Anna flute lessons. They were good music students, and we wanted them to further develop the gifts the Lord had given them in music. The girls had been faithfully practicing all year and found it difficult to stay motivated without a qualified instructor. There are only a few opportunities to perform publicly, and that also made it hard to keep practicing. Although there were several capable music teachers in the community, unfortunately no one was willing to teach our girls. In spite of our pleading with several women who were excellent pianists, no one stepped up to help, so our girls continued without help and eventually lost interest in practicing. It was frustrating for us and a huge disappointment to the girls – a sacrifice we never expected they would have to make.

As I have reflected on this over the years, I believe we have made sacrifices, but some were easier to lay on the altar of serving God than others. Entertainment was an easy sacrifice. We did not watch local Nigerian television, so we were not inundated with morally bankrupt television shows and movies from the States or Nigeria. We appreciated the option to control the media our children were exposed to through control of the video player. Our children were not constantly bombarded with messages advertising more stuff, toys, and games they didn't need. Dorothy did not miss the soccer-Mom lifestyle of spending most of her day in the minivan taking the children to school, after-school activities, and church events. We didn't miss the individualism of most American communities that prevents people from knowing their neighbors or is suspicious that friendliness is odd behavior.

Professionally, I didn't miss the litigious American society that has discouraged and crippled many physicians and the associated enormous malpractice insurance premiums. I am thankful I didn't worry about billing health insurance companies hoping they will pay or looking over my shoulder worrying about the government or HMO oversight of my medical practice.

What we sacrificed was well worth the peace of knowing we were where God called us, to know Him, grow in Him and serve Him. As a family, we shared a rich, cross-cultural worldview. Our children had seen several African cultures and traveled in Europe, the British Isles, and the four corners of the United States. They developed lifelong friendships at the Christian school in Nigeria with children from around the globe. They loved to read and devour every book they could get including National Geographic magazines. There were sacrifices, but there were also many rewards. There is much to be said in favor of raising a family outside of the United States in another environment with a different perspective that allows us to maintain our family values and still serve the needy in Jesus' name.

I remember as I was preparing to come to Africa as a missionary, I asked my father for any last-minute advice. Did he have any suggestions to help me thrive in my missionary career? He said, "Remember, you are in a marathon, not a sprint." It seems we unconsciously pace ourselves for whatever assignment we face in life. We had an emotional tank that was normally full when we went each term to Africa. When that reservoir was empty from the stresses of living in Nigeria, we ran out of gas, we lost our motivation for the task, and it undermined our effectiveness, attitudes in relationships, and how we coped with hardship. If we planned a four-year assignment, at about the 3 ½-year mark we began to run low. Folk that came for one year and decided to extend for another year often struggled in that additional year because they did not have that much in their emotional reserve when they arrived.

Someone has said, "The problem with a living sacrifice is that it keeps crawling off the altar!" When we surrendered our lives, our futures, and dreams to God to go and serve Him in another land, we knew it meant giving up many of the things I have mentioned and more. When hardships and trials came, they were not a surprise, even though they were painful and trying. Some behavior by missionaries we considered unnecessarily risky and foolish. Sometimes those people paid the price for their poor decisions. However, when we suffered because of where we were or what we were doing in obedience to God's call in our lives, we did not doubt our calling to be there. We naturally wondered God's reasons for suffering but never His love or our need to trust Him.

After being evacuated from Liberia in 1990, we discovered the following quotes, which summarized our perspective on our circumstances.

> The fishermen know that the sea is dangerous and the storm terrible, but they have never found these dangers sufficient reasons for staying ashore.
>
> -Vincent Van Gogh

> Safety does not depend on the absence of danger. Safety is found in God's presence, in the center of His perfect will.
>
> - T.J. Bach

TAKING A BREAK

To survive the stresses of living the "marathon" in the Developing World, we recognized the need for regular time off from our hectic schedules. A wise adage often repeated to students going off to university is, "Work hard and play hard." This is certainly true on the mission field as well. Those who do not take time off for recreation end up taking it out on the rest of us. The underlying stresses of living in Africa and the additional tensions in ministry affect everyone's physical, emotional, or spiritual health. Some of our time off needed to be away from the irritations and the grind of life and work.

Early in our marriage, Dorothy and I began to arrange a date night to celebrate our monthly anniversary or "monthiversary" on the nineteenth of every month. In the early years of our marriage in Liberia, we scheduled an evening at a nice restaurant and would spend our dinner dates discussing our relationship. We had a checklist of sorts to review our strengths and weaknesses and give feedback. (Must have been my idea!) At first, it was helpful as we were getting to know each other after our short courtship. It was painful each month to hear how I had failed or kept repeating the same old mistakes month after month without making much progress. After a while it became apparent to both of us that the conversation each month was similar as we reviewed the litany of unchanged behavior on both of our parts. We realized there were some things we would have trouble changing and would have to learn to live with – like my not putting my socks all the way into the clothes hamper! This discovery was both liberating and depressing. I was finally free of the nagging guilt of having to change things that were difficult for me to change, but at the same time I had to accept in Dorothy those habits that I had enumerated each month.

The next phase of the monthiversary tradition was the decision to invite other couples to join us for our dinner dates. It removed the intense introspection and added a new dimension to our date nights. We had little social time with many of the missionary couples with whom we worked, so it was a wonderful time to get to know our friends better and have a relaxing meal together.

Another practice we started as a family when our children were young was to get off the compound for one weekend a month. With the constant stream of people coming to the door sharing their requests and problems and the hospital intercom and cellphone regularly ringing with patient issues, we needed to get away for some rest and recreation as a family. Unfortunately, the choices were limited as far as activities for the children, safe food and water, and a reasonable distance for driving. Driving on the roads in Nigeria was always fraught with danger from armed robbers, accidents from careless drivers, vehicle breakdowns in the middle of nowhere and harassment by police, local tax collectors, vehicle inspection officials, and army personnel at various checkpoints along the roads. Occasionally we went to a nice hotel in the capital city of Abuja, but we usually chose more modest escape hideaways.

One great activity in Jos was hiking in the amazing boulder-strewn hills and mountains in Plateau State. We would often organize groups of kids and young adults and trek to a nearby rocky hill. We usually hiked in the dry season because during the rains the grass was tall and snakes were a big problem.

Most of the hiking favorite spots had unusual names. Gog and Magog are a set of twin-peaked rock formations that look like giant, house-sized boulders in two big piles. The hike was mostly climbing through narrow rock caves and wiggling up narrow passageways between the enormous boulders, but when we got to the top, it offered a spectacular view of the city of Jos and was well worth the climb. Fortunately, I didn't have to play trauma doctor and all got back safely.

On Wednesday morning, January 1, 2012, Dorothy, Marie, Heather, Anna, and David joined a group who reenacted the bringing of the Gospel to Miango by the early missionaries by trekking 12 miles from Jos to Miango. This was a grand celebration of an historic event and involved wide, enthusiastic support from the Nigerian and SIM missionary communities. Along the way they stopped in a few villages for speeches by the local chiefs and musical numbers by the Women's Fellowship groups. In Miango there was a big celebration with about 1,000 in attendance and included a welcome by the paramount chief, six village chiefs, and rice and okra soup for all. David was honored twice for being the youngest person to complete the entire trek. The event even rated news coverage on the Plateau television news.

We needed at least one member of the family who could ambulate the next day, so I drove to Miango with our luggage for the SIM Annual Spiritual Life Conference and attended to the weary trekkers. Amazingly, David and Dorothy held up well during the long trek.

YELWA Club
I could not believe my eyes as I drove the van full of children onto the YELWA club property for a Saturday afternoon swim in the summer of 2004. The old colonial era, stone clubhouse that was built by the British tin miners had the roof completely torn off, and the naked beams and ceiling boards were exposed to the harsh rainy season winds and rain. The storms had already caused much

damage, and it reminded me of the war-torn carcasses of buildings I had seen in the Civil War in Liberia. What a shame. What happened?

During the British colonial era in Nigeria, large tin deposits were discovered in Plateau State. Hundreds of Europeans, mainly British, arrived and began mining, refining and exporting enormous quantities of tin. The YELWA Club was started in 1920 to provide a recreation club for the many British tin miners and their families who had settled in the Jos-Bukuru area. The club included a clubhouse with restaurant, bar and snooker table rooms, a large theater for drama productions, about six duplex cottages, and a swimming pool with playground and infant wading pool. In the center of the complex was a small, oval railway track about the size of a basketball court where a small steam engine train gave rides to the delight of children attending the Club Christmas party and other big events. The club was the center of social affairs for the British community in the Plateau area and the place where many business deals and connections were established in what today we would call networking.

I remember my father telling me when they arrived in Jos in the 1950s that it was not considered proper for the missionaries to join such clubs because of the drinking and other activities. My father looked at it differently. He knew his children loved to swim so saw joining the club as a wonderful opportunity for family recreation and an opportunity to develop relationships in the British expatriate community. In addition, my father was British and because he was running the SIM Bookshops in Nigeria, he knew many of the club members. What better way to improve relationships than to join the club? It would be good for the bookshop business, good for his family and might even be a good opportunity to share the love of Christ with people who were lonely and needed God's love. Like many expatriate families living overseas, several had problems in their marriages and with their children. Adjusting to life in Nigeria was challenging and, unfortunately, these problems often surfaced in behaviors like alcoholism and domestic abuse.

So we were the first missionary family to join the YELWA Club. We have some old 8-mm video films showing my sister, brothers, and me cavorting around the toddlers' pool and learning to swim. My sister was the little mother and was always trying to keep us out of harm's way. We would go as a family to the swimming pool every other weekend and during the summer months when we were home from boarding school at Kent Academy. All four of us children learned to swim there, and I have vivid memories of learning to dive from the springboard and getting up the courage to jump from the high dive into the deep end. The club was a "happening" place, and through it my father developed many friendships.

When we returned to Nigeria as a family in 1992, I was thrilled to learn the YELWA Club was still open. We quickly joined and went so often that if people wanted to know about the pool conditions, they would ask us. I enjoyed the swimming, the quiet environment, and beautiful tall eucalyptus trees that surrounded the pool.

We never imagined that things might change, but they did. A government VIP who had been trying to buy the club got tired of waiting for the court to decide the legality of the deal so sent in armed men and took it over. He then deployed carpenters to remove the roof and started renovations on the buildings. So when we drove onto the compound and heard the story of what had transpired that week, we almost wept as a family. We sought answers, but none were forthcoming. The hired help who had maintained the pool and grounds stopped working, and eventually the pool water became unswimmable and we were barred from entering the property.

We moved our swimming recreation to other places with clean, quiet pools and that sufficed until we left Nigeria. Although YELWA Club never opened to the public, it still has a fond spot in our family memories.

Miango

In the earliest days of SIM in Nigeria, Director Roland Bingham realized the need for missionaries to get rest, refreshment, and a break from the stresses they faced in their ministries. He began to look for a place to set up a "Rest Home" and decided on some property donated by the local chief in a village called Miango about 15 miles outside of Jos. In the early 1940s SIM opened the Miango Rest Home (MRH) as a place for missionaries to come for their annual vacation or recuperation from an illness. Shortly afterwards, the school for missionaries' children, Kent Academy, was opened next door, so parents could visit their children when school was in session and have more family time.

The Miango Rest Home sits nestled in between several low hills on about 100 acres. The entrance road to the main building is lined with flame of the forest trees that provide a gorgeous red canopy of flowers along the roadside. Inside the oval driveway is a grassy area perfect for volleyball, little kids' soccer games, and picnics. There are several tall palm trees that rustle in the breeze, and the many enormous mango trees provide shade and an abundance of mangos. Although mangos sound beautiful and delicious, their downside is the mess when the ripe ones fall on the ground and attract hordes of flies. The main building has an imposing, large red sloping roof that ascends to several lightning rod pointed spikes on the top. The administrative offices are on the right in front of the kitchen, and the left side of the building is the large dining hall and lounge.

Since there are no kitchens in the guest rooms, all the meals are served in the dining hall. The ten-person rectangular tables provide an opportunity to meet other guests from Nigeria and all over the world. Both Western and Nigerian dishes are served buffet style. This is one of the important reasons we like going to Miango. Dorothy enjoys not having to cook for the family when we are on vacation or just away for the weekend.

The large lounge has a piano and lots of couches and soft padded chairs facing a large fireplace. In recent times, satellite television and a video projector were installed, so guests could watch sporting events like the World Cup, Olympics, movies, or other programs. The walls of the lounge are lined with bookshelves, and off the lounge is a playroom with toys and a video player for the small children.

Spread around the 100-acre compound are the guest cottages, some of which are named after notable former missionaries. We have had several favorite houses over the years, but as our family grew we had to choose houses with more beds.

On the compound there is also a dental clinic where Dr. Steve Porter and his wife Ruth provide excellent dental care for missionaries and nationals from all over Nigeria. There are also two tennis courts, a miniature golf course, table tennis, and plenty of table games. At the mission school there are also basketball and volleyball courts, swings and slides, seesaws, tetherball and a large playground and a soccer field and track. The school also has a piggery and large chicken sheds that are big attractions for the children. They often had piglets, and our children enjoyed going to see both the pigs and chickens.

Hiking was also a favorite activity at Miango. There are two extinct volcanoes about a mile away, which were fun to hike and enjoy a panoramic view of the beautiful countryside. We also hiked to a local waterfall, rock hills, and the village of Miango for market day. The children loved hiking and enjoying God's outdoor laboratory. Miango and Kent Academy were great places for the children, and we spent many relaxing hours as a family in this safe and comfortable place designed for that purpose.

Dorothy and I realized we needed to schedule time away from our responsibilities in Jos, so we went camping one weekend a month in the dry season and went to Miango one weekend a month during the rainy season. For years we enjoyed our regular weekend breaks at Miango.

Camping at Kurra Falls
Conventional camping was not done by the missionaries in the early '60s in Nigeria when I was growing up in Jos. At the SIM Hostel

in Jos for high school kids, the dorm parents would take the kids from the hostel on a campout for a special treat about twice a year, but otherwise no families I knew of went camping.

When we returned to Nigeria in 1992, I was surprised to hear that there were a number of missionary families that went camping. In our first few months in Nigeria, Dorothy and I got a small, two-man tent and went for a weekend camping trip with our neighbors, the Baileys from New Zealand, and a few other families. We went to a place along a riverbed about one hour east of Jos. None the wiser, we packed up the few things we had for camping, including our tiny tent and the portable crib for nine-month-old Marie. After wandering around the bush for a while off the main road, we eventually settled on an area beside a stream where we thought it would be safe for our campsite. The stream was disappointingly shallow, but it allowed us at least to cool off. It had a large sandy bank and flat ground along the shore for our campsite.

We took foam mattresses and tucked Marie along the outside gutter between the edge of the mattress and the wall of the tent. For her naps during the day we set up the portable crib in the tent. In spite of the intense heat during the day and the flies and mosquitoes, we had a good time and actually wanted to go camping again.

Over the next few years we began to accumulate from departing missionaries everything you could possibly need for camping. A good friend of ours, Arden Keller, had a Coleman camping equipment business in Pennsylvania, so I contacted him and asked if he could help us with a family tent for camping in Nigeria. He gave us a beautiful large tent that we used for about ten years of camping in Nigeria. It was large enough for our growing family and durable enough to withstand the rains and storms that occasionally caught us early in the rainy season. Eventually we sold the tent because the girls wanted more privacy and their own smaller tent. We ended up with two smaller popup tents that were easier to set up and allowed the girls their own space.

Our favorite place to camp, actually our only camping spot, was at Kurra Falls. Back in the 1960s the British government foresaw the need for generating more electricity so built a series of large reservoirs to power a hydroelectric plant in a remote area on the southern edge of the plateau. One of the few sites along the 1½-hour trip was a tourist stop with a playground set up by the Nigerian government. Its main claim to fame was concrete seats in the shape of upward facing cupped hands that were set up all over the playground. The "hand seats" made for good pictures, but the place was too remote to generate any serious tourist business.

Along the road, we saw many villagers returning from gathering wood in the bush with enormous bundles of branches heaped on their heads. There were a lot of Fulani tribal people in the area with their herds of wandering cattle, large colorful straw hats, kaleidoscope colored clothes, long sticks for herding the cattle, distinctive facial markings and big grins. The road narrowed from a two-lane paved road to a one-lane, marginally paved, rough road that had lots of sharp turns, blind corners and dramatic ups and downs. The girls knew when the roller coaster part came and would raise their arms in the van and scream as if they were riding the big coasters in the U.S. amusement parks.

The upper series of lakes were the cleanest, and years ago someone had set up an area for camping. We would choose our traditional spot to set up our tent and then send the children out to gather firewood. We made a rule that we always went with at least one other family. In case there was an emergency or problem, we did not think it wise to be by ourselves. Sometimes there were a dozen other families and sometimes only two.

Although most of the surrounding countryside was savannah plains and rocky rolling hills, the campsite was in a wooded area about fifty yards from the water. The water level rose and fell dramatically depending on the time of year. At the lower end of the reservoir was the dam retaining wall that regulated the outflow of the water and directed it to the hydroelectric pumps. We cautioned all who came with us to never go near the outlet because of the danger of being sucked into the pumps. The water was always refreshingly colder than we expected.

At the far side of the lake was a group of rocky, boulder-covered hills that were great for hiking, so groups would either swim or boat across the lake or take a hike around the edge along the retaining wall. We usually took all the kids for a hike to the top of a small hill to see the spectacular view and enjoy the breeze. At the top you could see all the lakes in the reservoir system and marvel at this wonder of engineering in the middle of Nigeria. Occasionally we would see baboons walking along the retaining wall or wandering on the hills.

In addition to hiking, the main event was always the swimming. We brought Styrofoam noodles for floating devices, and inflatable boats and inner tubes to cavort in the water. The lake was several hundred feet deep in the center but had a gradually sloping bank that made it safe for the children to swim and play along the edge. In the dry season, there was a small peninsula that became an island when the water level rose. This became a favorite destination for the children to get away from the parents. The ground was quite rocky, so it helped to wear swim shoes that also protected from the occasional scorpions sunning on the rocks.

Dorothy was the self-proclaimed President of the Camping Club. She arranged who would bring the various meals and food ahead of time, so we could eat together for breakfast and supper. We set up a meal preparation and cleanup schedule. Everyone helped with the chores and allowed others to get some rest. Breakfast was usually eggs, bacon, and pancakes cooked over a campfire with the aroma of fresh brewing coffee drawing the reluctant out of their tents in the morning. Some went for an early morning dip in the cold lake, but most stayed in their sleeping bags as long as they could before the noise of the children made it impossible to sleep. At night, we always had a large meal together that was traditionally Irish stew or "campout stew," as it later was named, and spaghetti made from the unique sauces of each family combined in a big pot. The resulting concoction was delicious!

Dorothy organized the meal schedule and did a great job in coordinating everyone in the outdoor kitchen under a portable awning. After the evening meal we sat for hours beside the mesmerizing campfire telling jokes and stories and enjoying the crystal-clear, star-filled night skies. The children were busy making "doughboys" with their wooden sticks, and occasionally a generous person would donate the almost impossible-to-get marshmallows. The evenings were a wonderful time of fellowship as we got to know each other better through the stories and lively jokes.

A few in the camping club were seriously into the camping scene and brought various 12-volt appliances that ran off their car batteries. We had basic 12-volt lights that were safer than the kerosene or gaslights, but some dear friends brought their 12-volt video and television. That seemed a bit much to us because we were trying to get out into nature, not bringing all that stuff and noise with us. Of course, the exception was the short wave radio. Listening to the BBC or Voice of America (VOA) radio programs every morning had become a habit most of us had difficulty breaking. I remember the time when we were listening to the VOA at Kurra Falls and heard the verdict on the OJ Simpson case in the U.S. We were as shocked as the rest of the world as we sat in a remote campsite in Nigeria.

There was usually at least one memorable story after each campout, and these varied from interesting to wild. Usually the children from the surrounding villages would gather around our campsite and just sit and watch us like animals in a zoo. On a few occasions they got into our tents and stole items when no one was watching. A few of the missionaries started bringing their dogs, which took care of that problem. There were also sightings of snakes and other animals that were exciting as well. At night, we would hear noises outside our tents, and usually we figured it was local dogs on the prowl, but I am certain there may have been some wilder animals also investigating these intruders.

A few times in October when the rains were just starting, we would have tents blown down or leak terribly, so wet sleeping bags and clothes had to be dried out the next day. At night, we could often hear the trucks full of drunken villagers returning from their Friday night parties. At times the local Fulani herders directed their herds of cows right through our campsite and this caused a bit of a commotion. Rarely was anyone hurt during the camping weekends, and I can only remember one time in ten years when we had to leave early because one of the children developed a high fever. We were so grateful to God for the safe and fun times we enjoyed at Kurra Falls for many years.

On Sunday morning, we would have a short worship service then a last swim and lunch before packing to leave. It was a great outdoor worship experience and rounded out the weekend in a nice way. As we prepared to go, the crowd of village children watching us grew. As soon as we left, they scavenged the site looking for anything we might have left, including food. Sometimes we left food intentionally for them, but occasionally we left towels and a few other items unintentionally.

We had become so used to camping every month during the dry season that it was a terrible blow when we began hearing reports that there might be schistosomiasis in the lake. This parasite is carried by snails and can cause intestinal, urinary tract and neurological harm in humans. While we were on furlough in the States, a missionary from another mission became paralyzed from schistosomiasis thought contracted at Kurra Falls, so there was a renewed concern among all the missionaries about the safety of swimming in high-risk lakes. We doubted some of the reports since we had been swimming at Kurra Falls for ten years and none of us had tested positive for the parasite. Still, when we were on furlough in 2001, the mission doctors strongly advised us not to swim in fresh water lakes. The world epicenter for schistosomiasis is the middle belt of Nigeria – right where we were camping!

It took me months of wrestling the pros and cons, risks and benefits of giving up camping at Kurra Falls. It had become so much a part of our recreational time, and without the swimming it was not much fun to just camp there. Finally, Dorothy and I agreed we should probably not camp or swim there again.

Yankari Game Park, Bauchi, Nigeria

One of the few wild animal game parks in Nigeria is three hours east of Jos near the city of Bauchi. The Yankari Game Park was built in 1956 when Nigeria was under British colonial rule. It covers 870 square miles of savannah plains and includes several warm water springs including the Wikki Springs. Wikki Springs is about 40 feet wide and 12 feet deep at its mouth, which is the base of a tall rock cliff. The park is a refuge for over 50 species of mammal including more than 300 African bush elephant, olive baboon, patas monkey, tantalus monkey, roan antelope, western hartebeest, lion, African buffalo, waterbuck, bushbuck, and hippopotamus. Over 350 species of birds have been sited in the park.

The road from Bauchi to the Park used to be a dusty corrugated dirt road, which rattled you to the core. It is now a paved road, and the six-hour, round trip outing can be comfortably made in a day from Jos. At the entrance to the Park the guards ask for passport identification and then have a list of charges including a vehicle charge, a per person charge, and charges for each camera and video camera taken into the Park. The road from the entrance to the lodgings takes about 30 minutes, and it is not unusual to see lots of game even in this area of the Park.

For many years we had heard horror stories from families who had visited the Park with their small children. There are wild baboons and warthogs roaming the housing areas. The baboons are very aggressive, snatching food from your hand, jumping into vehicles to get foodstuffs, and opening the doors of the houses to rummage for food. We avoided going to the Park until we felt our children were old enough to not be so terrorized by the baboons. Armed with slingshots and rocks to throw at the baboons, we were instructed to go everywhere in pairs or groups and avoid going out of our houses at night.

In December 2006, we finally made a trip to Yankari and were thrilled at the amazing sight of a herd of about 50 elephants on the side of the road while we were driving into the park. We also saw several hartebeest and baboons. After negotiating with the hotel staff to get the three rooms we had reserved a month earlier, we settled into quite comfortable chalets built by a European company of high quality, imported furniture and materials. The houses were large round houses like Nigerian huts with a large living room area, two bedrooms, a bathroom, and a kitchen.

This beautiful location did have a few problems. The first problem was the intense heat in this part of the country. At Yankari the only relief during the day came by going into the spectacular warm springs river. At 7 p.m. the hotel management turned the generator on to provide lights and air conditioning to the houses and restaurant. Needless-to-say, we spent most days in the water, coming out only to go on a safari or to eat. The crystal clear water in the river comes straight out of the base of a vertical flat rock cliff and flows for about a quarter mile until it disappears beneath the jungle into the game park. The river then meanders through the park as the main source of water for thousands of wild animals.

Another problem was the aggressive nature of some animals. Near the swimming area of the river the baboons were incredibly aggressive and persistent. Someone stayed out of the water at all times to guard our things and especially the food from being taken by the baboons. Around the living quarters the baboons had learned to open the house doors, so they would barge in, cause mayhem and take whatever food they could find. Many families had their house broken into by the baboons while they were down at the river swimming.

We went on safari trips in the four-wheel-drive trucks provided by the Park. We saw more elephants on two other occasions in herds of about 50-75 animals. Although a bit scary, it was an amazing experience to see the elephants up close. We also saw waterbuck, bushbuck, antelope, a crocodile, beautiful birds, and monkeys. Another nuisance were the tsetse flies that bit through our clothing and left painful, itchy welts that lasted for days. Overall, the three days were a lot of fun, especially since the kids had their friends to play with in the river and during the evening hours.

After several more missionaries had frustrating experiences with the hotel management and the ongoing aggressive behavior of the baboons, we stopped staying overnight and only made day trips. Although a long drive for a day trip, it was a nice break from the stress of life in Jos. As the religious and political trouble in Nigeria intensified, we had to stop going to Yankari because it meant going through Bauchi, one of the strongholds of the Muslim terrorist activity in northern Nigeria.

Obadu

Another vacation spot we had heard about for years but thought it was too far to take young children was a cattle ranch in the highlands along the Cameroon border. A number of years ago a European man was flying over the range and noticed good pastureland on the plateau on top of the mountains, so started a cattle ranch. Eventually because of the cooler climate and fantastic vistas, Obadu Mountain Ranch resort was built as a tourist attraction and hideaway for the rich and elite. It included a Presidential Villa for the President of Nigeria, two incredible restaurants, and recreation facilities including tennis courts, miniature golf, horseback riding, a gymnasium, and organized hikes through the mountains.

In 2004 they built a huge swimming park at the base of the mountain resort and set up an amazing Austrian-built cable car system to transport guests from the resort on the mountain to the swimming park at the bottom of the mountain. The water park included a diving pool area, a lap pool, two water slides, a kiddy pool, and a picnic area along a bubbling brook behind the park. In 2009, we decided the kids were old enough to handle the long drive and enjoy the swim park, so we set off for Obadu with about a dozen single missionaries. It involved an eight-hour drive southeast to a mountain range close enough to see into the hill country of Cameroon.

Even though we went for the cheap plan and stayed in a local mosquito-infested half-star hotel, we had a wonderful visit! We are especially thankful our long road trip was uneventful with no accidents or car trouble either way. Unfortunately, it was too far to go often so we never went back.

Kenya

I joined the Christian Medical and Dental Association (CMDA) when I was a medical student in the 1980s. It has many ministries providing resources to physicians and dentists in the United States, but one of its most significant activities is running a two-week continuing education conference for missionary physicians and dentists to help them keep their U.S. medical licenses current.

The conferences alternate between Kenya for the Africa-based missionaries and Thailand for the Asian-based missionaries. CMDA invites top-notch physicians and dentists from the United States to give lectures in their respective fields of medicine and dentistry and also asks missionaries to present topics that in many cases are more relevant for those working in resource-poor settings. CMDA also invites a pastor or well-known Christian speaker to give a daily spiritual challenge. They facilitate daily prayer groups and organize a program for the spouses of the missionary physicians and dentists.

Probably the most significant benefit of the conference was the networking and encouragement of being with several hundred physicians in similar circumstances facing incredible hardship, overwhelming medical and spiritual challenges and emotional struggles of loneliness, stress, anxiety, and burnout. Some missionaries were new to the mission field while others had spent their careers in cross-cultural ministries and came for refreshment, renewal, and healing.

The conference in Kenya was held at a Baptist conference center called Brackenhurst in the hills north of Nairobi amidst the tea plantations. The setting at 7,000 feet was beautiful with mostly clear blue skies, old stone cottages surrounding a common dining room and meeting rooms in a quiet rural environment (no motorcycles, lorries or explosions!), surrounded by gorgeous plantations with thousands of rows of green tea bushes. It was cold enough during the clear, starry-filled nights for a fire in the fireplace and a light sweater. It was refreshing to the soul in so many ways.

I started going to the Kenya meeting when I first went to Liberia in 1986 and continued to go every two years when I was in Africa. Each time I went, I was facing different challenges, and the conference had a huge impact on me, refreshing me through the amazing music, spiritual messages, and encouragement of seeing friends from previous meetings in similar circumstances. The medical and surgical presentations always gave me new ideas, and I was even asked to give lectures at several meetings.

For one reason or another, Dorothy had never been able to attend the Kenya conference the 24 years we had been in Africa. We were determined that she would go with me our last year in Nigeria (2012), so we worked out the details for her to attend. At the conference I had great fun introducing Dorothy to my friends from all over the continent with whom I had this strange, intermittent relationship. There were several hundred doctors, dentists, nurses, and other health professionals from all over the continent working in a wide variety of facilities and ministries. There were also faculty from North America who brought updates on the latest gizmos, treatments and wonder drugs in modern Western medicine.

Although some of what they presented was not relevant for our practices in Africa, it was helpful to know some of the latest research and practices. The fellowship with like-minded medical missionaries was encouraging, and we enjoyed learning about what God was doing all over Africa.

Dorothy attended the special program for non-medical spouses and enjoyed sharing her experiences living in Africa (and being married to a missionary doctor!) On the weekend, we went on a walking mini-safari in a Nairobi park and saw hippos, giraffe, zebras, wildebeest, antelope, duiker deer, and monkeys. I had been to the Masai Mara Game Reserve, and Dorothy had been there when she was in Kenya a number of years ago at an AIDS/HIV conference, so we had seen the big game of those amazing parks. Dorothy enjoyed shopping at the Masai market (mostly tourist items, fruits and vegetables) in Nairobi and getting a tour of the tea plantation.

Since returning to the States, I have had the privilege of returning to the conference as a U.S.-based surgeon to give lectures. Because of the trouble that some African physicians had getting visas for Kenya, the increasing political instability, and the desire of some of the missionary physicians to bring their families, CMDA changed the venue to Greece in 2014. The conference in Greece had a record-breaking 500 attendees and was held in a beautiful hotel north of Athens.

South Africa

Sometimes the "Nigeria Factor" stress built up, so that we felt we had to get out of the country for a mental break. As the political situation in the country deteriorated and our vacation options decreased, we began to look for affordable vacation options outside Nigeria. We wanted to go to a place that was less stressful, free of the Nigeria Factor frustrations and that had recreational options for the whole family. I had been to Kenya a number of times for the Christian Medical and Dental Association meetings, Europe was pretty expensive, and we knew little about other African countries. We looked to South Africa as a possibility because we knew several missionaries working in Nigeria from South Africa who raved about the beauty, vacation options, and civility of their homeland.

On Friday, June 5, 2003, we flew to Lagos where we spent the night at the Baptist Guesthouse. We left for Johannesburg (Jo'burg) Saturday evening on a beautiful South Africa Airlines plane that not only transported us to another country but also seemed to transport us out of the stress and frustrations of Nigeria. After getting a connecting flight in Jo'burg to Durban, we rented a car and made our way to a cozy family Bed and Breakfast. Over the next week we visited the Umgeni Bird Park and enjoyed seeing many exotic African birds, took an early morning boat ride to see sharks caught in the shark nets along the coast (saw lots of dolphins but no sharks!), were enthralled watching the dolphin and killer whale shows at SeaWorld, were amazed at the modern stores and shopping malls full of Western goods and conveniences, relaxed at a Japanese garden, and ate delicious and inexpensive food in a variety of restaurants.

We took the kids to the Mitchel Park Zoo in Durban, had lots of time playing in the waves at the Durban beaches in spite of the occasional shark sightings, and had a terrific time at the Gold Reef City Amusement Park in Jo'burg on our way back to Nigeria. We also saw most of the big African animals living in the wild at the Uhlulwe Game Park north of Durban, crocodiles at the Crocodile Park, and were awed by the lions as we drove through the Lion Park in Jo'burg.

In spite of a few glitches in our travel arrangements, it was a restful and fun vacation. We realized South Africa is a First World country in Africa with Third World prices. The roads and utilities were beautiful and worked, the people were friendly and not as aggressive as West Africans, tourism is a vital and well managed part of the economy with enormous options including outdoor activities, safari parks, beaches, mountains and amusement parks for all ages. We returned to Nigeria refreshed but committed to return to the "land down under" on the African continent.

Our experience in South Africa in 2003 was so positive we made arrangements to go to Cape Town for Christmas in 2005. A good friend who lives there offered his house and car while he and his family were visiting their families in the States. We left Jos at 7 a.m. Sunday morning and drove to the domestic airport in Abuja. We arrived at about 10:30 and spent the next 1 ½ hours haggling with official and some unofficial airline agents to figure out how to get a flight to Lagos. After a few minutes, Dorothy urged me to "get in there and be aggressive too," so I did. (I usually do what she tells me!) Finally, the boarding agent, God bless him, acknowledged us and motioned for us to board. He made a space for the kids and Dorothy to get to the stairs to the plane. We then settled in for a calm flight to Lagos.

We had arranged for a driver to meet us and take us to the international terminal. I thought it would be prudent to get my return ticket then from Lagos to Jos for January 4 when we returned to avoid the chaos we had just been though. With Dorothy and the children patiently waiting outside in the intense heat and humidity of Lagos, I proceeded to the ticket counter and asked if I could purchase tickets for my family on January 4. The agent looked at me in surprise, "Oh, that is too far away. We cannot do that now. You must go to the main office to make a reservation, but that is closed today so come back tomorrow." I am not sure what possessed me to think I could buy a ticket in advance, but I guess it was a moment of weakness.

The flight got off fine and was a smooth six-hour journey to Johannesburg. We arrived at 5 a.m., hurriedly got our bags, got across to the domestic terminal, grabbed a little food for breakfast, and boarded the flight to Capetown. We were so thankful when we got off that plane and had finally arrived. Our host family's secretary met us and took us to their lovely home. The house where we stayed was on a golf course in a vineyard and was gorgeous, quiet, and extremely safe. We enjoyed the small, heated pool in the backyard every day and were thankful for the kind help of the house cook.

We went Christmas shopping at the largest mall in the southern hemisphere and the V&A Waterfront, had a wild time at the Ratanga Junction amusement park and a water park with water slides, enjoyed the stunning beauty of the Cape Horn coastline and

Chapman's Peak drive, swam with penguins at boulder beach, rode the cable car to the top of Table Mountain, wondered at the beauty of the Kirstenbosh Gardens at the Christmas Day concert, hiked up to the "eye" cave of Elephant Mountain, marveled at the diverse glory of the thousands of birds at a bird park and learned about the southern hemisphere night sky at the planetarium. The grocery stores were a "heavenly" shopping experience and rivaled anything back home in the States. It was truly an "out of Africa" experience.

My biggest adjustment was driving on the left side of the road. In spite of that fact we only had a few close calls, but Dorothy preferred to sit in the back seat instead of beside me!

We also had great times to relax at the house, went for rides on the golf cart, and unwound in the heated backyard pool. The weather was cooler than usual since it was their summer. Overall we had terrific weather, which seemed to be perfect for the specific activity we had planned for each day. It seemed the Lord both orchestrated our schedule and the weather!

Upon our return from our vacation in South Africa, we learned the shocking news that Justin Ward, the 4-year-old son of SIM missionaries in Jos, had drowned in an open well on their compound on New Year's Eve when we were in South Africa. He was buried in the cemetery where our little Aimee was buried in 1998. David played with Justin every day and Heather had a close relationship with him as a frequent babysitter. She was devastated when she heard the news and we all mourned with the Ward family during this extremely painful time.

Ghana trip

For years a senior tradition at Hillcrest was the Senior Trip. In the past the class had gone to Abuja for a weekend at a nice hotel, but in recent years Ghana had become popular. It was a huge logistics effort to get visas for the whole class, book the flights and hotels, and buses, and then organize activities while in Accra. Marie's class went to Ghana and had a great time and so, when Heather and Anna became seniors, they tried as a class to go someplace different, but none of the options they explored were as affordable and do-able as Ghana. Dorothy and I were delighted when we were asked to go as class sponsors.

We had never been to Ghana and were as excited as the kids to see this neighboring former British colony that was so similar and yet so different from Nigeria. The official class sponsors did all the hard work of getting the visas and organizing the transportation and flights, so our main task was to show up and keep an eye on the kids and help as needed.

The day of our departure finally arrived and turned into an interesting day. Here is the story from my journal.

Last Thursday (March 15, 2012) I woke with expectation and excitement. It was my birthday, and we were going to Ghana for a week with the Hillcrest senior class. Realizing it might be tough to pull off something before breakfast, I thought my family might try a surprise party on Wednesday evening, but that did not happen. I saw some icing mix in the sink and guessed at least they had made a cake. Breakfast came and went without any sign of a surprise celebration, so we loaded the car with our bags to go to the school where we would load the buses for the Abuja airport and our flight to Accra, Ghana. At Hillcrest we joined the 37 students and seven adult sponsors and loaded the vans and bus for the four-hour trip to the Abuja airport. Just before the school chaplain prayed for all of us, Anna asked me timidly, "Is it your birthday today?!" I said, "Yes," and she sheepishly said, "Happy birthday, Daddy." I then watched her tell my adoring wife the news. EVERYONE in my family FORGOT my birthday! Wow! (The only reason Anna remembered was because a fellow student asked her, "Isn't today your dad's birthday?!")

Dorothy, Heather, Anna, and David all forgot! After Anna announced it to the group, one of the teachers hurriedly went into her apartment, plopped a candle on a cookie, and rushed out to the parking lot with my "birthday cake." Everyone (including my embarrassed family) heartedly sang "Happy Birthday" before we piled into the vehicles. It was a memorable birthday but not for the usual reasons! (After the humiliation of forgetting my birthday on the 15th, Dorothy did remember our wedding anniversary on March 19 while we were in Ghana.)

We had a fantastic trip with the Hillcrest senior class. After the 1 ½-hour flight from Abuja to Accra, Ghana, we stayed for one night at a poorly managed hotel in Accra that had no water and had broken air conditioners. Ghana is much smaller than Nigeria, so the smaller population made the streets and public places seem almost abandoned compared to Nigeria. There also appeared to be more law and order, less chaos, and less garbage and litter. The streets were better maintained with fewer slums and more working streetlights and power in the country.

The next day we drove three hours to the El Mina slave castle on the coast where we had an interesting and sobering tour of a castle that was used to house slaves prior to their being sent to the New World. It was shocking to hear about the abuse, awful conditions, high death rate, and inhumane treatment of the slaves. We then went to a lovely resort on the coast called Coconut Grove. It was a beautiful resort nestled along the coast with comfortable luxury cottages on the beach, a fresh water swimming pool, terrific restaurant, 18-hole golf course, riding horses, and beautifully manicured grounds.

The next morning we went to the rope bridge canopy walk 120 feet up in the trees in Kakum Forest. On Monday we returned to Accra where we went shopping at a modern shopping mall and an arts and crafts market, played soccer with an international American high school twice the size of Hillcrest in soccer (and won!), and got a tour of the major sites in downtown Accra.

The trip home went smoothly until we were in Nigeria! About an hour from Abuja, our vehicles were stopped by the "nail boys" – young men hired by the local government whose job is to push boards with rows of nails in front of cars to stop them and demand payment for taxes to support their local government. Normally each year our drivers get all the stickers proving we had paid the taxes to the local governments along the journey, but this group would not accept our stickers, so we were detained for 1 ½ hours while our drivers negotiated with the police and local government officials.

The four-hour road trip was extended to almost seven hours. We are grateful we got back to Jos safely without other incidents. It was a great week for the students and a terrific experience for all of us.

Europe

For many years Dorothy and I had dreamed of visiting my relatives on my mother and father's sides of the family in Northern Ireland and going to Switzerland. The summer of 2008 was the last summer we would be together as a family since, after Marie's graduation in May 2009, she would be off to the United States for college. For months I planned the dream trip to Europe, including a week in Switzerland and a week in Ireland. It was challenging arranging from Nigeria not only the air flights to Europe and within Europe but also our hotel and land transport.

Everything seemed in order until I realized our re-entry visas had expired to get back into Nigeria! I was so stressed that they would not arrive in time I almost got an ulcer worrying that the huge trip-of-a-lifetime I had been planning would have to be canceled because of my oversight. Thankfully the visas arrived just in time, and we boarded the plane in Lagos for Frankfurt. Marie had gone to the States for a summer transition workshop for M.K.s returning from the mission field, so the plan was for her to meet us in Frankfurt, and we would go through Europe together.

We were thrilled to see Marie in the Frankfurt airport shortly after we arrived. We stayed for five days at the Beatenburg Bible Institute near Interlaken and stared in wonder each day at the magnificent beauty of the Alps. One of Dorothy's longtime dreams was to ski the Alps. As she sat contentedly on the guesthouse porch facing the Alps sipping a cup of coffee, she felt her dream had come true. We enjoyed going in a huge cable car up Mount Pilatus near Lucerne, hiking and scootering in the mountains, as well as doing a little shopping in the very expensive stores in Switzerland. It is a land of great beauty, fantastic chocolate, watches and clocks, Swiss army knives, mostly white Europeans, and cigarette smokers. Although we were busy trying to do everything on my carefully planned itinerary, we did slow down often to enjoy the beauty, great tasting food, and fun activities of Switzerland.

In Northern Ireland we stayed in a beautiful country farmhouse where a Christian businessman had renovated the stables of his estate into two apartments and a conference center. We were allowed to use both apartments and thoroughly enjoyed the slower pace and quiet beauty of the surrounding green pastures of rural Enniskillen. A peacock noisily greeted us each morning, and I conversed with the cows and rabbits on my morning walks. We enjoyed amazing hospitality from friends and family and tried to balance seeing some of the popular sights in the country and visiting friends and family. We had fun walking around the unique rock formations at the Giant's Causeway, balancing along the Rope Bridge, admired the skill and artistry of the craftsmen at the Tyrone Crystal Factory and Belleek China Pottery factory, learned at the Ulster American Folk Park, and climbed the fortress tower of the Carrickfergus Castle.

The whole family enjoyed visiting my Uncle Austin (my father's brother) and cousins and had a wonderful evening with about 30 of my mother's family who lived in the farming community of Clogher.

We came back to Nigeria rested and refreshed having many good memories and experiences as a family.

So as a family we have had many great breaks together during our time in Nigeria. I am grateful for the opportunities to play hard as we have worked hard serving God overseas.

THE ARROW MAN

We had just come back from our Christmas holiday break at Miango in 2004. Since we normally do teaching rounds with the interns and residents on Monday and Thursday mornings, I walked into the Intensive Care Unit looking for the family medicine residents so we could begin ward rounds.

I did not see any other doctors, but what I did see shocked me. Sitting upright in the second bed on the left was a Nigerian man with two arrows sticking out of the left front side of his chest. One arrow was moving rhythmically with each heartbeat. There was another arrow a bit lower entering the lower middle part of his rib cage. He appeared a bit anxious and fearful but certainly was not in shock or extreme pain.

I moved toward him and asked the nurses, "When did this man get here?"

"He came in last night."

"Why wasn't I called?"

"The residents thought he was pretty stable, so they decided not to bother you."

The nurses were casually doing their notes on the patient charts at the desk as if having a man with two arrows sticking into his chest was pretty routine.

I immediately assessed his situation more thoroughly and reviewed his x-rays. If you can imagine, he was so stable that the residents had time to send him down to the x-ray department in the middle of the night for x-rays. That means calling the x-ray technician, waiting for at least 30 minutes for him to come, waiting another 20 minutes for him to set up his machine, and then another 30 minutes to get the films developed. Needless to say, the x-rays were actually helpful. From the x-rays and clinical examination, I could see no evidence of a major lung injury or bleeding in either side of his chest. I was certain, however, from the location of the arrowheads on the x-ray and the pulsations of one arrow that one arrow was inside or beside his heart. How he had survived and not bled to death was beyond my comprehension!

Apparently Yahaya lived in a remote village many hours from Jos. He had three wives and was seducing another woman to be his fourth wife. She already had a boyfriend who was planning to marry her. When Yahaya did not back off, the enraged boyfriend and his friends attacked him with bows and arrows, shooting him four times, twice in the chest. For some reason he wanted to come to Evangel Hospital, but it took him four days after he was shot to get to our hospital. It is hard to imagine how he traveled that distance, especially in a taxi which usually packed in six people!

Since he was pretty quiet and stable, I took time to get adequate blood from the laboratory blood bank for a possible transfusion and prepared the nurse anesthetist and residents for the case. We don't often see chest trauma cases, so this could be a good teaching opportunity. Most patients with severe chest injuries die before they ever make it to the hospital.

Through an interpreter I introduced myself and had a discussion with Yahaya about his situation and explained how we could help him. Although he was clearly fearful, he agreed, so in the afternoon we took him to the Operating Room. With the help of Dr. Joel Anthis, I opened his left chest and saw the arrow going through his left lung into the sac around the heart. I carefully opened the sac and was amazed to see the tip of the arrow poking into the top left chamber of his heart. The heart muscle had made a seal around the shaft, and very little blood was leaking out of the heart.

I carefully placed a large, silk suture in the heart muscle around the hole. The plan was to pull out the arrow and then pull this "purse string" suture tight to close the hole. After a quick prayer, I made a rapid jerk on the arrow with one hand and pulled on the noose suture with the other. It sort of worked. I ended up having to put another suture in the heart muscle to finally control the bleeding.

I then directed my attention to the other arrow. The patient had no signs of a collapsed lung or bleeding in his right chest, so from the direction of the shaft I thought it must be in his abdomen. I made a small incision in the upper middle area of his abdomen and after reaching in to his abdomen discovered that the arrow was not in his abdomen at all! It was lying right on top of the diaphragm, the muscle that separates the chest and the abdominal cavity. To avoid opening his right chest and all the problems that procedure involved, I pushed the arrowhead through the diaphragm into the abdomen right over the liver and brought it out. It had a two-inch long head with razor sharp spikes and tip.

I was relieved and amazed he had done so well throughout the surgery and finished by closing his chest and abdomen after the arrow extractions. In cases that are tense or require intense concentration, I ask the anesthetist to turn off the music on the CD player in the Operating Room. But in this case we were ready for some stress relief, so I had the staff put on one of my favorite CDs –"The Best of the Beach Boys"–and toe-tapped through the rest of the case.

Yahaya had a surprisingly uneventful recovery in the ICU; unfortunately my next few days would not be so predictable. I had to leave the country in the coming days, but fortunately he did well. During this time the hospital chaplain visited my "arrow man" and learned he was a member of the Fulani tribe and not a Christian.

The Fulani are a strong Muslim tribe who have been resistant to the Gospel for years. The chaplain contacted a Fulani pastor and a missionary, Mark Gaddis, who knew the Fulfulde language. When Mark entered the ICU after the man had returned from surgery, Yahaya had fear written all over his face. He was terrified. After hearing the Gospel from Mark in his own language, Mark and the Fulani pastor led him to a personal relationship with Jesus Christ. He immediately exclaimed how peaceful he felt. Mark said he noticeably relaxed, his breathing slowed down, and there was a visible change in his appearance. Shortly afterwards Yahaya left the hospital with no complications.

Mark gave a good report several years later that Yahaya continued to follow Christ in spite of the pain of returning to his village and finding that all his wives had been married off to other men and all his cattle were sold. Apparently, the villagers thought he had died in the attack. He did get back a few cattle and one wife, but then faced tremendous persecution as a Christian. We praise the Lord for his healing, his trust in Christ, and his faithfulness in continuing to follow his Savior. What a wonderful outcome from such tragedy. I will always remember Yahaya as "The Arrow Man."

HOME ASSIGNMENT

At SIM, the general rule of thumb is that for every year on the field, you get three months back home on what was called "furlough" but is now called "home assignment." Because I wanted to get a job working as a surgeon in an American hospital every furlough, we chose the four-year home and one-year furlough" plan. This ongoing cycle of living in two worlds is not unlike what many military families experience. The whole family uproots every few years, finds a new place to live and go to school, work, and church, and tries to understand and cope with the new culture before it is time to go to another culture. It takes a lot of work to go in either direction and has the terrible aspect of always having to say goodbye.

We make good friends for a while, and then we leave and try to muster the courage to make more "best" friends. On the upside, we have friends all over the globe, understand a variety of cultures, and get pretty good at packing and maneuvering through airports and customs. We also raise flexible children.

Getting ready for furlough involves more than most people real-ize. Because we will be in the United States for a year, we must pack up our household belongings in Nigeria and put them in storage. This takes a lot of planning and work, which we begin six months before we leave. With a good plan, we are usually packed at least a week before our departure date, so we have a few days to say our goodbyes.

An important part of living in the Nigerian culture is proper goodbyes to the right people. We do our best to say goodbye by attending the farewell dinners, allowing time at our house for the constant parade of visitors the last week and taking care of financial obligations or commitments to Nigerians while we are away.

Preparing for our U.S. life is another part of the process of leaving. This involves making arrangements for a job, so I can get back into American medicine to update my skills and knowledge. We must find a vehicle and set up a place to live with furniture and the basic necessities. Our home churches, in whatever area we have settled for furlough, usually help us find a vehicle and a house and set us up with the basic supplies and groceries for the first week or two. This has been a wonderful blessing, allowing us the opportunity to get to know a lot of people in the church who brought meals during the first weeks. This is the closest we know of community when we are in the States and is a very humbling experience.

As we visit each church, we normally are asked to give a presentation about our work and ministries. This can be a sermon, lecture, slide show, video, or drama. During our first furloughs we used slides to show our house, the country, the hospital, and the people and so on. As technology improved and expectations rose, we showed either a video or a computer PowerPoint presentation of our life in Nigeria. These presentations take a lot of work to prepare, so the last six months before our trip we also put these together. It is a good opportunity to review what we are doing but is challenging to make something that will be relevant and interesting to an American audience.

Having been born and raised in Nigeria as a missionary kid –"MK"– I have many fond memories of our furlough trips through Europe and visiting family in the British Isles. I remember traveling all over the United States to our supporting churches but also having the great opportunity to see many of the wonderful sights and landmarks in America. There were both good and bad aspects of this nomadic lifestyle for our family.

It has been said that a man's identity is in his work, but a woman's is in her home. When we came to the States, I was fortunate to get work in Veterans Administration hospitals so was able to quickly get back to doing surgery. My adjustments were more in the areas of the abundance of stuff, driving by the rules on the clean superhighways, making decisions about what to order from a restaurant menu, and recoiling from the violence and immorality on television programs and movies. This was all "re-entry" stuff common to most missionaries returning from a developing country.

In Nigeria we had a Nigerian cook, a house cleaner, a gardener and a driver. Dorothy would not have been able to get out of the house if not for the terrific house staff. She would not have been able to start the street children's ministry, write curriculum for the HIV/AIDS program or teach at Hillcrest. Having help with the household chores in Nigeria, however, made it challenging for Dorothy when we went to the States for furlough. For starters, stateside cooking is a whole new challenge for the veteran missionary cook. Used to making everything from scratch, she had to re-learn how to cook with instant foods. When at a friend's house, one of Dorothy's friend's bragged she had made the pizza from scratch. Dorothy was surprised until she found out "scratch" in America means you buy a ready-made crust, pour on a jar of ready-made sauce, and add pre-shredded cheese and pre-sliced pepperoni! For Dorothy "scratch" means really making the pizza dough from yeast and flour, making the tomato sauce from real tomatoes and fresh vegetables, adding the only kind of cheese we can get in Nigeria, and slices of our precious pepperoni brought in by caring visitors! As a retort, her friend remarked, "I guess you make pumpkin pie by getting your own pumpkin?" To which Dorothy replied, "Yep!"

So it takes Dorothy a while to learn about quick meals and how to use a microwave to cook. One problem Dorothy faced, however, was that our family didn't like the instant foods. For example, we would not eat spaghetti made with the jars of sauce since it tasted so different from the real thing we were used to in Nigeria. This new way of cooking changed the way she shopped and cooked. In Nigeria our cook had the evening meal ready for us by 6 p.m. In the States, however, sometimes there was a conflict between helping with homework and getting dinner ready.

Shopping was another point of tension for Dorothy on furlough, especially grocery shopping. America is the land of abundant choices, so when Dorothy went to the local grocery store, it was paralyzing to look at entire aisles of bread or cold cereal and decide the color, brand, flavor, economy or family size, low or high fat, vitamin enriched and on and on. Just going in to get a loaf of bread became a major decision. Dorothy usually settled after a while on one kind of bread, one or two varieties of cereal, and so on, so she didn't have to go through the decision process every trip. Her first store trips took four hours, but by the end of furlough, she could be out of the store in 20 minutes.

An important aspect of furlough was visiting the various churches and financial supporters who supported us while we were in Africa. Our churches were scattered all over the United States, so for us to visit them all takes quite a trip. We always planned an elaborate plane, train, and automobile trip from Annapolis to New Jersey, Pennsylvania, New York, Michigan, Texas, Wyoming, Oregon, and California. For example this was one furlough trip:

> May 31 Leave Nigeria for SIM HQ in Charlotte,
> North Carolina
> June 5-25 Annapolis, Maryland
> June 26 Quakertown, Pennsylvania
> June 28 Bloomfield, New Jersey
> July 3 Farmington, Connecticut

July 4-17 Camp of the Woods, Speculator, New York
July 18 Grand Rapids, Michigan
July 21 Chicago, Illinois
July 22 Kansas City, Missouri
July 24 Dallas, Texas
July 27 Tyler, Texas
July 29 Comfort, Texas
July 30 El Paso, Texas
July 31 San Diego, California

We worked the trip stops around Sundays because most of the churches wanted us to be there to present our work in a Sunday School class, Bible study, or morning worship service. Most churches also fit us into a mid-week home group or a Sunday School class. After spending four years in Africa each term pouring our hearts into various ministries, it was difficult to hear the senior pastor tell us, "You have five minutes to tell us about the last four years of your work." We were excited about what we were doing and found it difficult to accept that what we had to say was not important enough to be heard for more than five minutes.

One exceptional church gave us so much time over a weekend, we ran out of things to say. We spoke at a Saturday evening barbeque event, a Sunday School class, twice in Sunday morning services, and then the Sunday evening service. By the end of the weekend we had little left to say and that was extremely unusual.

Being away from the American church scene for years at a time, we also see the differences between the African church and the American church. Music is a wonderful part of worship in all African churches. It is loud, boisterous, usually involved either traditional instruments or electronic off-key instruments, and is generally joyous and worshipful. Many times individuals spontaneously stand and perform a special number without feeling embarrassed or out of place. Although the services follow an order of service, they are generally more informal and less rehearsed than Western worship services. We noticed that in some larger churches, worship was a group of people watching a music performance by the professional worship team.

As we visited the various churches on our circuit, we usually stayed in the houses of friends or family. This seemed at first the best and cheapest option because it would allow us more time with friends we had not seen in a long time. We encountered several problems with this approach, however, which helped us modify this part of the furlough plan. For example, I am allergic to cats, and after staying in a few homes with cats and finding myself with itchy eyes and tears all night, we learned to ask before we stayed in a home if they had cats. Then we learned the hard way that some homes without children are not child-proofed and are not as much fun for our family. We asked if we could stay with a family with children near the ages of our children, even if we did not know the parents. We could get to know another new couple, and our children would get along famously with theirs.

I am a light sleeper and often get a sore back if the bed is not firm enough. I also liked a large firm pillow to avoid neck pain in the morning. In Nigeria we used to sleep on a waterbed until Dorothy began to have back problems. After her surgery we got rid of the waterbed. This is relevant because very few hosts and hostesses along the way asked us about our preferred sleeping arrangements. After a few sleepless and painful nights on hide-a-beds, we put the mattress on the floor and hoped the host didn't catch us in the morning. This worked fine as long as the hide-a-bed was not in the living room where the hostess would see our new arrangement when she came down for coffee at 6:30 a.m. We were most flattered and honored when the host and hostess offered us their bed, and they slept on the hide-a-bed in the basement. That's genuine hospitality!

In the morning at the breakfast table we met another "Americanism" – decaffeinated coffee. Dorothy is a Starbucks coffee drinker and managed to go an entire four-year term without running out by having visitors regularly replenish her stock. With so many adults switching to decaffeinated coffee for health reasons, we found it a remarkable trend in the States. So it was difficult to find a household where we stayed on our trips that served or even had in the house regular "leaded" coffee. So Dorothy brought a small jar of real coffee with us everywhere, so she could get her morning fix if the house cupboard was bare.

When we sat down for the evening meal in our host home, we also noticed a few other strange things. If they had teenage children, they seemed unable to communicate with their parents, much less with us. If they showed up for the meal, they said little and disappeared as soon as possible. Then the adults delved into "deeper" conversations – like sports team scores, stock market disappointments, their house renovation project glitches, or whatever. It was very frustrating to spend an evening with someone who never asked you about your ministry or work. We tried a few comments to get the conversation started about our ministry in Africa, but inevitably the host was not comfortable asking us honest questions about our work. Some people seemed afraid of missionaries. They thought we were super-spiritual and couldn't dialogue with mere mortals, or they were not really interested in anything outside their own little world.

Then there were the people who came up to us at church and asked, "Aren't you the ones in Algeria or Siberia?" In a good church with an active missions program it showed us either people still didn't pay attention or our message was not clear enough. After pouring out my heart for an hour at a supporting church and telling them the heart-rending story of our escape from Liberia, a man came up to me the next Sunday and said, "I was too busy and didn't make it to your presentation the other day. Could you give me the five-minute version?" Needless to say I was not pleased but graciously gave him the two-minute curbside version of the death-defying escape from rebel soldiers.

As I understand the American economy, there is an annual increase in the cost of living called inflation. This is reflected in an increase in the costs of goods and services and usually salaries. When most churches signed on as a supporting church with us, they committed to a certain amount each month or year that they would send to our mission towards our monthly support. Since our term was usually four years overseas, this amount was usually not reviewed until our next furlough. However, when we are on the field, the mission increased every year the amount we were expected to raise to keep up with the increased cost of living around the world. Since the amount the churches sent was fixed, the amount we needed continued to rise because our support was not keeping up with the mission's requirement. Interestingly, few churches asked if we needed more support when we were visiting them and none has ever asked about the idea of an annual increase in our support to keep up with the normal increase in the cost of living. We were certainly very grateful for the many churches and individuals who were incredibly faithful in supporting us. I wonder, however, if missions committees in churches consider the changing economic forces in the developing world that affect our standard of living and our buying power with the support funds we receive?

On our compound at Evangel Hospital we had a wonderful warm sense of community. We walked into each other's houses unannounced at any time of the day. We saw each other throughout the day and week and helped each other with a cup of sugar, a plumber's wrench, an extension cord, or a computer problem. We were indeed our own support group for everything we did. Although I would not say everyone was my best friend, we developed close friendships as we were involved on a daily basis with the joys and sorrows of our families and ministries. The children would play in and around our houses every day, and they became best friends more naturally and quickly than the adults. There was a great sense of community and kinship in our life goals and ministries.

When we came to the States, we faced the cold, cruel reality that life here was not like "compound life." Usually we didn't meet our neighbors until a month before we left. The children didn't play with the neighborhood children because we didn't know if they were safe, and we went to Wal-Mart for the things we needed, not to the neighbor's house. When we went to church, it was a hurried 1½ hours with a group we hardly knew and then back home for lunch. If we joined a small, mid-week home group for a Bible study, we got to know a few more people, but we saw them only once a week. So furlough was usually lonely emotionally for us as we stepped for a few months into a world that had everything but lacked the warm sense of belonging we enjoyed in our African home.

On a more positive note, there were many things we loved about living in America. Our first impressions were usually that it is a land of abundance and opportunity. We stood in awe when we stepped into a grocery store or Wal-Mart and saw aisle after aisle of food and goods with so many choices and a seemingly limitless supply of everything. We were also struck by the cleanliness of the streets, the sidewalks, and stores. In Nigeria, garbage is strewn everywhere, and there is no garbage pickup service in the city. In contrast, the cleanliness of America is striking. In addition, all the cars seemed new and were not limping along barely held together with string and tape. The front and rear car lights all worked and produced a beautiful kaleidoscope of light at night. One of our daughters was quite surprised to see red lights on the back of American cars since so few had them in Nigeria.

Here are just a few of the stateside impressions we have made upon our return:

- Driving is very quiet. No one beeps their horn to greet you or remind you they are passing.
- Air conditioning is too cold. We roll down the windows in the car and take a jacket to the mall, so we don't freeze.

- The streets and roads are smooth with no potholes. There are lines for lanes and traffic lights that work, so there are no men directing traffic at the intersections.
- We are not sure where people put their garbage, but it is not on the streets and in the streams and rivers.
- Motorcycles are very rare here and those driving them wear helmets and don't have an entire family packed on the bike behind them.
- Hardly any people live in America, and the only place we see large numbers are at the shopping malls and on TV at sports events. We did see a lot in the churches we visited and wonder where they all hide during the day.
- There are friendly people everywhere, but they don't wave at us or greet us unless we know them.
- We go into "shock and awe" mode when we step through the automatic doors of grocery stores. There is SO MUCH STUFF, so many choices of everything in any color or size you want.
- The houses have nicely trimmed lawns and gardens, but we don't see people in their yards enjoying them much.
- Out of habit we keep greeting African-Americans in Hausa, and they look at us quite strangely.
- In the American "markets" called malls, there is so much room for walking, and the stores are huge. We could pack in a whole lot more selling stalls and stands in the walkways and at least double the amount of merchandise on display.
- The church services are lively and worshipful and very orderly with only one offering. Very few churches have choirs and those that do rarely wear church gowns or robes. The services are short, only an hour, and then everyone hurries home.
- The lights have not gone off once since we have arrived, and there has always been water from every tap we have turned on. I have to admit I am enjoying leaving the water running

while I take a shower instead of turning it on and off and collecting the water in a bucket to use to flush the toilet. No one here has asked us to do that yet. (Maybe in California!)

- The TV has a lot of programs that are quite superficial and silly. Even the news is mostly about what is happening in America with little mention of what is going on in other places in the world.
- Computer Internet access is like lightning here, and we are enjoying the faster access and better communications. The phones work, voice mail lets us leave messages, and overall communication options are better.

For our children, amusement parks, Chuck E. Cheese's restaurants, and McDonald's were highlights. We loved the heavenly Krispy Kreme donuts, rich Starbucks coffee, and delicacies like filet mignon steak and lobster tail. In Maryland, we enjoyed delicious crab, in Texas the beef brisket barbecue, in California fish, and in Pennsylvania the great Pennsylvania Dutch shoofly pies of Dorothy's family. We certainly do not live to eat, but we did enjoy the wonderful food we discovered all over America.

As we traveled around the country on our visitation trip, few people entertained us in their homes. Usually we were taken to a restaurant. So we all gained weight over the year we were in the States, and when we returned to Africa we were "fat" or "fresh," as the Nigerians would say. It seems in Nigeria we ate less junk and fattening food and settled into a more active routine, so we could keep the weight off. Additionally, having a bout of diarrhea and vomiting every few months, from whatever the parasite of the month was, also helped keep off the weight!

Of course the most exciting and wonderful aspect of being back in the States was the time we spent with our families. We especially wanted our children to get to know their grandparents when we were here, and so we did our best to arrange time throughout the year with both sets of grandparents. Our children loved them all and enjoyed the time with family. It was a difficult thing for the grandparents and for us when we left, but we were grateful both families supported us in our ministry and we did not have to fight them to explain God's call in our lives. We know of one missionary family that for the entire ten years they were in Nigeria they had ongoing tension with their grandparents who thought they had stolen the children from them. They essentially resented or doubted their being called by God to Nigeria. We are grateful we did not have to deal with that and were especially privileged that our parents prayed for us and supported our life's calling.

Before we went to the United States, we made an effort to give the children some orientation about what to expect when they arrived. However, we could not cover everything as is illustrated in the following story. One Sunday in February 2011, before the Superbowl football game, we had a quick Skype call with Marie. She said she could not talk for long because she was going to be late for the Superbowl party at a professor's house. When we asked her who was playing, she shrugged her shoulders saying she had NO CLUE! We laughed and she did mention that the other MKs were going to bring a "real" football and play football (soccer) during half time. In Nigeria Anna also wanted to see a football game on satellite television, so we asked her what city the Steelers were from and what city the Packers were from. She had no inkling either! So to improve our children's cultural education, one evening together we watched a game rerun. Even knowing the ending, we had fun seeing the new amazing stadiums, the wow technology, the beautiful green field, sharp looking players, and a good football game. Dorothy kept cheering for the Steelers, thinking maybe she could change the result. One thing that really struck me was how foreign the half-time show was – seemed quite a spectacle and not exactly our style of entertainment. By the beginning of the fourth quarter, we were all so tired we came home and went to bed.

Normally during the year we were on furlough, we noticed a cycle of emotions. At first we were excited by everything we saw, smelled, and heard, and basked in the luxury of abundant choices. Everything seemed fantastic and America seemed a paradise of pleasures and fun. We did not think about Nigeria or the needs there and communicated little with those we left behind. This phase lasted about three months, and then we began to settle into a more normal view of America and developed a routine. We adjusted to the school and church activities and started building friendships in the community and church. For about six months we began to feel like "normal" Americans and almost fit in to the life and community where we lived.

At about nine months, we began to get irritated at some things in America like the narrow worldview or the self-absorption and shortsightedness of the American church and began to feel some disillusionment with the America we call "home." We also realized it was almost time to go back to Nigeria so started the process of disentangling ourselves from this culture. We made preparations to get rid of the furniture we had borrowed, changed our banks and financial arrangements, disconnected the phone and cable TV services, paid the last rent and utilities bills, and so on.

Planning for our return involved the very hard work of buying and packing all the things we anticipated we would need for another four-year term. Dorothy had a list of all the girls' clothes and shoe sizes, so she could get clothes and shoes for each of the children as they grew in the coming four-year term. We also tried to think what food and grocery items we would need, office supplies and books, gifts for the children's birthdays and Christmases, and other household items. It was a huge job and took a lot of preparation and time to purchase and then pack all these things. Each box we packed had to be a certain size and weight to meet the airline requirements, so it took careful packing to get the job done well.

While on furlough I also spent a part of the year collecting medical supplies and equipment to take back to the hospital. Often this involved contacting various medical supply dealers and negotiating the best or lowest price that we could afford. The suture, gloves, light sources and so on must also be packed along with our personal boxes, so they were ready for the planned departure date. We usually took over a two-car garage with all the stuff and boxes, and it became quite a production.

After tearful goodbyes to our family and friends, we boarded the plane and headed back "home." It was only when we were sitting on the plane that I began to relax and not worry if we had left something behind or forgotten to do something. Upon our return, we had to face the interrogation of the Nigeria Customs officers, but we were in familiar territory and prayed it would be hassle-free. Bathed in prayer from family and friends we returned to the place of our ministry with wonderful memories of our furloughs in the United States but ready to get back into the work again.

KINGSFORD USMAN ABUBAKAR

During the middle years of our time in Nigeria, Kingsford Abubakar was our driver and became an important part of our family. His father was from the Bugi tribe in the Bassa local government of Plateau State. Kingsford's grandfather was a Christian but so poor as a hunter that he did not have enough money to send his son to school beyond grade 7. He decided to send his son to live with a wealthy Muslim family, so he could attend school. Dorothy and I would meet Kingsford as a grown man and exemplary Christian, but his story began here, with his Christian grandfather's decision to send his son (Kingsford's father Francis) to live with a wealthy Muslim family.

One of Francis's classmates came from a rich Muslim family. This boy told his father about Francis's desire to continue in school. The father agreed that he would help, but that Francis would need to live with them. Kingsford's grandfather agreed. He sent his son to stay with this man's father who then adopted him into his family. Francis eventually became a Muslim and was given a new name. Eventually, he became a lecturer in English at the polytechnic trade college.

As is the custom in many Muslim families, Kingsford's father had four wives. The first, second and third wives had five children each and the last had three children. Kingsford was the first born of his father's third wife Hawa. Like his father, his mother was a teacher with a small salary.

One of his father's students was a young Muslim woman from Ghana. His father eventually married her as his fourth wife. She was his brother Mathias' mother. They had an unusual brand of Islam, much different than the Muslims in Nigeria. These Muslims joined the Christians in their churches for special occasions, and the Christians reciprocated by bringing food to the Muslims at Ramadan. Both sides were tolerant and moderate in their beliefs and had a friendly relationship.

After Kingsford was born in the Gada Biyu section of Jos near Evangel Hospital, his father was transferred to a secondary school in Kagoro. His father met a white man from England named Kingsford. They became such good friends that his father named Kingsford after the white man, Usman Kingsford Abubakar.

Kingsford attended primary school at Kagoro opposite the ECWA Bible College. Because Kagoro was a predominantly Christian area, there were not many Muslims. In his whole primary school there were only five Muslims. During his primary school, most of Kingsford's friends were Christians. He remembers them inviting him to the ECWA church. He used to sneak from the house to avoid his father and go to the church activities. He enjoyed going to church especially hearing the Zumuntar Mata women's choir.

Because his father was a teacher, he wanted all his children to be teachers. So after primary school Kingsford went to Teacher's College in Kafanchan where he was actively involved in the Muslim Student Society. After graduation in 1987, he started teaching in primary school. His father had been transferred to Saminaka, his mother's home. Interestingly Kingsford was also transferred to teach primary and adult education in the Central Primary School in Saminaka. Again he became involved in the Islamic society. However, the Christian influence of his younger years had left an imprint. Despite living in a predominantly Muslim area of the country, most of his friends in the school were Christians. In Saminaka the Christians invited him to play volleyball at the ECWA church.

He met a Christian man named Sunday whose father was a pastor. He began giving Kingsford Bible lessons several times a week. Kingsford then began having dreams and telling Sunday's father about his dreams. Sometimes he would dream fire was burning him. Sunday's father would say, "That is what the Lord is teaching you. When you die, you will go to hell because of the life you are living." Sunday's father patiently answered Kingsford's questions. Eventually Kingsford accepted Christ as his personal Savior but was afraid to tell his family.

After Kingsford's conversion, his uncle visited the family. Kingsford's father did not like him and did not want Kingsford to be friendly with him. His uncle was upset that all the children had become teachers who had low status and salary, so his uncle asked Kingsford if he would like to do different work. Kingsford was interested so, against his father's wishes, his uncle provided a new job driving a truck with a transport business. Meanwhile, his father was transferred to Katsina in the far northern state of Sokoto. His uncle then invited Kingsford to go to Jos with him. When Kingsford came to Jos, his uncle found him another driving job. His father sent word he had gotten him a teacher job in Katsina, so he could get back into teaching. However, Kingsford enjoyed the transport driving work. His responsibilities in the company had increased, and he was promoted to cashier and booking clerk in the business.

One of his cousins, Yusuf, was attending an ECWA church and encouraged him to go to the church programs with him. Because he had attended ECWA church functions earlier in his childhood and was familiar with the church, it was not new to him. At a crusade in Saminaka the preacher said, "There are so many people who have accepted Christ but are afraid to come out boldly. I am looking at you. I am seeing you. Don't be afraid. Come out. Matthew 10:33. All those who deny me I will also deny them in the presence of my father." Kingsford was convicted and decided to stop being a secret Christian.

Kingsford's older sister Aisha attended the School of Technology trade school in Zawan where she had a Christian teacher. The teacher's daughter was in Aisha's class and they became best friends. Through their influence, Aisha also became a Christian. After she finished her schooling, Aisha came to live with Kingsford and got a job with ECWA Community health. She was assigned to Biliri Kaltungo Bible College to be their clinic health worker.

Aisha was afraid of how her Muslim parents would react to her conversion. Her mother seemed more tolerant. Unfortunately, her father verbally abused her for a long time by threatening to stop her school fees and other support. Kingsford was also interested in telling his parents he was a Christian but wanted to see how his sister would fare before telling his parents.

When he returned to Jos, he wrote a letter to his father that he had given his life to Jesus Christ as his Lord and personal Savior. When his father read the letter, he gave it to Kingsford's mother and said, "Look what your son has done. I didn't want him to go to Jos because I knew that is what would happen." His mother wept. She wrote him a letter asking him to come see them. After getting the invitation, Kingsford asked his pastor, Reverend Zachariah, for advice. He met with him and told him to fast for one week. They fasted for one week, and then the pastor told him to meet with his father and mother and them tell the truth. By this time, some of his brothers and sisters had already given him a name. Whenever he was with them, he always said, "Let's pray." So they gave him the name "Me addua" which means in the Hausa language "Let's pray." Kingsford's older brother still calls him by that name.

When he went to see his parents, his mother was not happy. If she wanted to discuss something with the family, she would wake the whole family after morning Islam prayers at 4 a.m. to discuss the issue. So at 4 a.m. the next morning, they called Kingsford to discuss what he had done. His father's words surprised him. He said, "You have taken a decision. I remember when I too made a decision on my own to become a Muslim because of lack of money. All your uncles and aunties are Christians." God had been working through the fasting and prayer Kingsford undertook before meeting his father. His mother and father both accepted his decision in good faith.

When he came back to Jos, it was time to share the Gospel with the rest of his family. He then asked his father if his younger brother Matthias could come to Jos and stay with him. Surprisingly, Matthias was allowed to come to Jos. Kingsford wanted him to continue to go to school, but Mathias did not like school. He wanted to learn to be an electrician. So he went for a six-month course in electrical work and obtained a certificate. Then Mathias wanted to learn driving, so Kingsford taught him to drive. Early in the morning they drove the cars to the taxi park where the vehicles would load their passengers for the day. If they did not load, they would take them back. Mathias stayed with Kingsford in Jos and eventually became a Christian.

Another of Kingsford's sisters, Sarah, was named after his father's first wife. Sarah was still a Muslim and stayed with Kingsford. He extended kindness to her despite their faith difference. During the Muslim fasting time he gave her whatever she needed when she was fasting. One vacation Sarah visited Kingsford's sister Aisha and gave her life to Christ. The pastor in ECWA church Kaltungo Biliri wrote a letter to the pastor in the ECWA church in Jos for her. When she came with the letter for the ECWA church pastor about her conversion to Christ, she did not tell anyone else in her family. On Sunday Sarah went to the church early in the morning but did not say anything to anyone and sat down in the church for the worship service. Kingsford did not see her. When the pastor announced, "We have a new convert who came to us from Biliri. The pastor wrote a letter for her, so we will introduce her as a new member and welcome here. Her name is Sarah Abubakar." Kingsford was shocked, speechless, and very happy. Seeing his sister Sarah become a Christian was the greatest surprise in his life.

Of the eighteen children in Kingsford's family from his father's four wives, some are still Muslims, but many have become Christians. It is especially challenging for the women who married Muslims because they will not be allowed to convert. Kingsford is still burdened for these members of his family and continues to reach out to them in love with the message of the King of love.

Before his father passed away, Kingsford's father gave his life to Christ. Kingsford visited him when he was sick and spoke to him. "Why don't you accept Christ? If you accept Christ, your wife — my mother — will accept Christ as well. We will pray for you." Kingsford's mother sent for him to come before he died, and she told him his father wanted to give his life to Christ. They sent for a local pastor who led him to the Lord. During the burial ceremony of his father in 1999, his mother was deeply touched at the funeral. A month after his father's death, she gave her life to Christ.

Although he was working in the transport business and taking care of his younger siblings, his sister Aisha encouraged Kingsford to go back to school. After Aisha had finished her diploma in medical health technician, she told him, "Today if you and I work in the same place, I will earn more than you because I have a diploma and you have only a Grade 2 certificate. I am higher than you. Why can't you go back to school?" He responded, "If I go back to school how will Sarah and the others go to school because I am paying their school fees?" One of his friends also encouraged him to go back to school, so he went with his friend to buy the application forms. Kingsford applied for admission, but his friend who encouraged him withdrew.

Interestingly, Kingsford and his future wife were doing the same course in the Polytechnic College in Jos; she was in the morning section, and he was in the evening section. He saw her once during the exam week. After the exams in 1998, he took his motorcycle to check if the exam results were posted. On his way back home, he saw her walking to the school, recognized her and stopped to talk to her. She told him where she was living and that she was going to check her results. He told her they were not out yet. She replied, "One of these days I may get in touch to say hello."

On his way home he decided to check where she was living because a lot of girls give a fake address. When he found her house, he was told she went to the school, so he knew she was telling the truth. After three months he worked up the courage to go see her. Gradually they got to know each other and were married in 2000.

Kingsford continued to work for the transport business, but the director of the transport company was a fanatical Muslim who had made big donations to the mosque. He had been trying to convert Kingsford back to Islam since he knew he was from a Muslim background. He would give him gifts, trying to influence him. Unfortunately Kingsford had a motorbike accident before his final exams and broke his collarbone. When he was in the hospital, one of his coworkers told his boss he was going to school when he had the accident. His boss told him he had to make a decision: either work or go to school but not both. Kingsford told his pastor who went to talk to his boss, but he was still not convinced. Kingsford's pastor advised him to quit the job even though it was only three months till graduation and God would provide him with another job.

What he did not know was that God would place Kingsford into our lives. With the increasing traffic in Jos, the danger of the *achaba* motorcycle drivers buzzing everywhere, and my concern that Dorothy not get mixed up in the chaos of an automobile accident, we realized that a driver would be a great help to our family. We needed someone who could drive Dorothy and our kids to Hillcrest School every morning and afternoon (especially since Dorothy was working full-time), someone who could take our cook Regina to the market for the weekly shopping, someone who could be trusted to do errands around town, and, most importantly, drive us safely to out-of-town places like Abuja.

Being uncertain whom to hire, I approached Simon Khantiok, the nurse anesthetist at Evangel with whom I worked and trusted because he was a church elder. I asked if he could recommend a driver for us, someone trustworthy and with integrity. In a few days Simon came back to me and recommended Kingsford. Simon knew he was active in the church Youth Fellowship and was a man of integrity.

I called Kingsford for an interview and after asking him a few questions about his experience as driver and his Christian testimony, we hired him as our family driver. It was the beginning of our relationship with this amazing young man. Each day he carefully checked that our cars were safe to drive, the engine fluids were kept up, the belts were good, and the tires were safe to drive on. He took our vehicles to the mechanics regularly and kept our vehicles in great shape. It was a great relief to go downtown with a safe driver and not have to worry about hitting someone, finding a parking spot, and getting into an argument with a belligerent motorcycle driver. He drove our family thousands of miles over the coming years, and we even hired him out to other families looking for a reliable driver.

Kingsford became a jack-of-all-trades for us. When we left for a vacation or trip, he took care of our dog, Mowgli, and all David's pet rabbits and birds. Kingsford sometimes brought his family to stay in our house when we were away to keep an eye on the house. We trusted him with anything we owned and were glad to help him with some extra income as well. He made a little farm in our yard to grow some yams and enjoyed having some of the fruit in our yard as well.

When Dorothy began the Widows Bucket Project, Kingsford became her executive assistant and driver. He took full responsibility for the arrangements of getting the buckets, getting the vehicles we needed, purchasing the literature that was distributed and supervising the literature table at the women's conferences. After a few conferences Dorothy handed over the bookkeeping and logistics to

Kingsford, and he did an outstanding job of accounting for every penny that was spent, making sure everything was in order. He had incredible integrity and discipline in everything he did.

We saw great potential in Kingsford and knew that he was destined for much greater things than being our driver. He had enrolled in school to get his diploma in accounting because that was his area of professional interest. When there was a job opportunity in the SIM Treasurer's office, we recommended Kingsford with enthusiasm and were so grateful when he was offered the job. Although it meant losing him as our full-time driver, we knew it was a good career move for him. He started as the cashier and surprised everyone by breaking the three-month record of no errors in the cash count in the SIM office. He was well liked by all the staff in the office and the missionaries that came to the headquarters. He was given increasing responsibility and continued in his education, finally receiving his accounting diploma.

Kingsford continued to help us with driving on weekend trips and special occasions, especially the Widows Bucket Project on weekends. As our time in Nigeria was coming to a close, we offered to sell him our van at a discount and gave him a lot of our household furnishings to help him get set up in the new house he was building on the outskirts of Jos. We had fun visiting his half-completed house before we left and enjoyed the tour of his dream house using many of the things we left for him. He even took our dog, Mowgli, and was responsible for making sure all the arrangements we had made when we left were carried out.

We miss Kingsford and his family. He was a great friend who was humble and eager to learn and grow. I would also describe him as "faithful." During the rainy season, it rains heavily all day. The dirt road on the compound has lots of potholes, so not only is it a bumpy ride, but the car gets plastered with mud every day. Still every morning Kingsford started his morning with a bucket of water washing our van, getting it ready for the day. He is a living example of faithfulness. He applied the life lessons he learned and was respected and loved by all who knew him. He made our lives in Nigeria so much more enjoyable, our ministries more effective, and we felt privileged to have the opportunity to invest in a man with such integrity of character and love for his family and his Savior.

ROBBERY AT BAPTIST GUESTHOUSE

April 6, 2004

A couple working with the American Embassy in Lagos was in Jos for the week visiting friends. We invited Marty Larsen, his wife Janelle and their daughter Joyce over for supper one evening. After dinner at 7 p.m., I offered to take them back to the Baptist Guesthouse.

As we pulled into the parking lot of the Baptist Guesthouse through the unguarded open gate, nothing looked out of order. As Marty and Janelle were getting out of the right side of the back of the van, a short Nigerian man approached my door on the driver's side nervously waving a small handgun. He demanded money and asked where the Guesthouse safe was. I immediately raised my voice and tried to warn Marty by saying, "We have a problem here. Marty, we have a situation here."

I was trying to alert him, so he could get his pepper spray or at least get rid of his bags. However, he did not seem to notice me and kept talking to Janelle. By this time two men had come around his side of the car. Marty and Janelle thought they were guards coming to help with the bags, so they had handed them their bags before they realized they were armed robbers.

I got out of the car and threw the car keys on the floor. I now could see they had a Nigerian hostage. I later learned he was the gardener who had come into the compound unaware of the robbery going on. They made him lie down on the ground while I began to argue with the men that we were visitors and could not help them, I was not the manager, and we did not have keys or knowledge about the safe. I was not really scared at this time, but I do remember thinking that I could probably take out the smaller guy since he seemed nervous and was a good bit shorter than me. When I realized there were actually four men, and one was quite tall, I did not try to overpower any of them.

Part of my intention was to speak so loudly that any people who were in the Guesthouse would be concerned that there was something going on in the parking lot. The robbers kept looking around nervously as if they did not want to be discovered, so they kept trying to get us to be quiet. All along, they kept insisting we had the key to the safe. We kept insisting we did not. Marty and Janelle then began to pray loudly for the men. They pleaded in prayer for their safety. This seemed to get the men angrier. "This is not the time to pray," they said.

The small man with the gun asked me for my car keys, so I told him they were on the floor of the car. He went to get them and then put the keys in the car and tried to start the car. I had left it in gear, so it jerked forward a bit but never really started. I then got angry with him for trying to ruin my car. All along I was hoping someone inside would hear us but to no avail. The man then threw my car keys into the bushes, and I never found them.

They kept asking for money, so I said there was some in my wallet. The short man with the gun then took my wallet, began looking at each paper in it, and then threw them on the ground. He eventually found my backup $100 bill and threw the rest on the ground.

The men were getting more agitated. We could not help them, so they told us to lie down on the ground. Up to this point, we had been standing arguing with them, and they were either poking us with sticks or just pushing us back. When we were on the ground,

Marty began to say he was feeling sick and nauseous. He sort of sat up and did not lie flat. One of the men with a long stick then hit him on the back and broke the stick. Marty groaned and fell flat on his stomach. Janelle called out for the men to stop hurting her husband, and she rushed to help him. She was then hit on the shoulders and driven back. I moved over to cover Janelle and Joyce, since Marty was to my left at the end of the van lying in pain on the ground. Janelle, Joyce, and Marty then began praying aloud as I prayed silently.

It seemed that the man who had first approached me was still nervous and unsure of himself. I could talk to him without getting him upset. The tall man was angrier and eventually took charge of the operation. They all held their guns like they were as afraid of them as we were. The men were quite disorganized and were often yelling at each other, trying to make up the plan as they went.

About this time another van pulled in the parking lot and was stopped by two of the men. Janelle called to them to turn around and go back, but this made the men angrier. They pulled Devon Harrison (missionary ophthalmologist from Kano Eye Hospital) and two Nigerian men from the van and forced them to lie on the ground. I heard one of the men say something about "being on a mission." When Devon was pulled out of the van, one robber said to another, "Is this the man?" To which the other robber replied, "No, it's not him."

Later Devon recalled that an Assemblies of God missionary contractor was staying in the Guesthouse and had brought payroll funds to his room that day. We later wondered if the men had knowledge of this and had come specifically for his money. In spite of the commotion, no one in the Guesthouse seemed to notice what was happening in the parking lot. They again asked Devon for the safe keys, and he told them the same thing we had. They went through his bags and took about N 80,000 (~$500) he had from the hospital and some personal money. He was thrilled later to find they had not taken his ophthalmoscope and $2000 eye instruments.

The men then said they were going to go into the Guesthouse, and Devon pleaded with them to leave the women and children alone. Two of the robbers began to break down the Guesthouse door since they could not get anyone to open it. They kicked the door in and made the loudest sound of the night. A missionary was sitting in the TV lounge and was caught by surprise. He was brought out and made to lie on the ground with us. About this time it began to dawn on me that if I continued to argue with the men and they got angry with me, they could either take me as a hostage or they could shoot me. I would be of no help to others if I was shot, and it seemed I was not making any progress in convincing them, so I decided to lie down quietly.

I felt very vulnerable lying on my stomach and feared for the first time getting shot in the head or back. I prayed silently and asked the Lord to protect us from injury. The pressure seemed to be off us since the action turned to the Guesthouse. I looked up and saw one man with a gun sitting beside the guard hut and another roaming around. I later learned the robbers had tied up the guards first, and so the two guards were bound in the guard hut. One armed man was guarding them and us in the shadows. I then knew I could not run, and the best plan was to stay quiet and out of harm's way.

At this point, we were not sure what was happening inside the Guesthouse. We were all lying on the ground with the vehicles between the building and us, so it was difficult to see what was happening. They could not see us, and we could not see into the building. The two who had gone inside ran first to the first floor apartment with a light on – Number 1 – Devon Harrison's room. They burst in the door and totally shocked Laurie, her friend Shannon and their kids. They demanded their money and jewelry, so Laurie moved the children into the bathroom and gave the robbers her money and some jewelry. They then wanted to take Laurie with them but for some reason changed their minds. After they left, she quickly locked the door and hid with the children in the bathroom.

Greg O'Neill and his family (SIM Miango Conference Center manager) were playing a table game in their upstairs room when they heard the men kick in the front door. Greg looked out the curtain, realized it was a robbery so moved the beds in front of the door, and quickly put their children Aimee and Josh into the attic through the ceiling door. He then had the presence of mind to call a few mission people in Jos on his cellphone. This started a chain of telephone calls to various SIM and Baptist missionaries and the police. Greg then remembered his car alarm so pushed the remote button, and his car horn began to blare.

By this time, we heard the men leave the Guesthouse building and move to the back of the compound and leave. They had gone to some of the boys' quarters houses and then climbed up a gate and over the back wall. As the car horn was blaring, they went over the wall and were gone. We all lay still for a few more minutes until the coast was clear. I saw a few Nigerians moving about the boys' quarters and thought it was the robbers, but it was the gardener's family. We then got up, and I went inside to see if anyone was hurt or if they had managed to get into the safe.

After a few minutes, I asked the gardener if I could use his cell-phone to call Dorothy. I let her know briefly what had happened and that I was okay. Just a few minutes before I called, Chuck Truxton at Evangel had gotten a telephone call about the robbery. Chuck came over to our house to check on us, realized our van was gone, and then asked Dorothy where I was. He and Dorothy then knew I was in the middle of the robbery, so Dorothy called the kids and told them, and they prayed for all of us.

Back outside, I tried to recover the contents of my wallet. I was sad to see the small zipper pocket in the wallet had been opened, so I feared my wedding ring was taken. Marty saw something shiny on the ground. We found my ring. I then began walking around the compound looking for Marty's bag and anything else they may have left.

About this time, the police Commissioner showed up with six policemen. We explained what had happened, but the Commissioner only wanted to know who was in charge of this compound. We explained that the manager did not live here and the Baptist missionary in charge was not here. Finally, the Baptist missionary leader, Mike Stonecypher, arrived. The police Commissioner then rebuked him that it was our fault. Because we had not notified the police of our presence, they could not provide protection.

We could not believe what he was saying. At that point I was so angry I left the conversation and walked away. He did not want to talk to anyone involved or get a report but only wanted the person in charge to report to his office the next day at 9 a.m. I was disappointed he did not want to hear what had happened, look for evidence, or even offer sympathy.

Later that night the police apprehended one man and brought him to the Guesthouse. Marty recognized the shoes he was wearing and made a positive ID on the man as one of the four thieves. SIM Director Phil Tait and SIM Deputy Director Bill Foute went around to the compound in the back and looked for anything the men might have dropped along the way. A few things were found in the compound, but unfortunately, they got away with Marty's bag with his Pocket PC, digital camera, money, and documents. I later found out that the three letters I had given him to mail to the U.S. from the U.S. embassy were also in the stolen bag. I called Dorothy's father to notify Merrill Lynch that a check was stolen. I then notified them to change our bank account and freeze the check I had written.

We went to the police station on Friday for the Larsens to give a report of their stolen items, but the Commissioner was not there because it was Good Friday. We eventually went to the police headquarters where they had a holding cell with about 100 prisoners. We met the Inspector assigned to the case, and he told us they had one man in custody. He mentioned there had been more than one robbery that night and asked us to come back on Tuesday to give the police report.

I did not sleep well for several days. It was hard to stop replaying the tapes in my head of what happened. Did I do the right thing? Should I have said or done something differently? Did I act appropriately? And so on. I think I was most fearful when it finally occurred to me I might have gotten hurt.

I was reminded of the critical lesson of the importance of trusting God for our protection every day. We are so thankful no one was shot or seriously injured. This robbery created a stir in the missionary community, and everyone began talking about ways to improve security on our compounds and in our houses. What we did not realize at the time was that this incident foreshadowed more serious events to come and one that would change our lives forever.

RECONCILIATION

Ladi was a teenager when her parents married her off to get a handsome dowry to help support their poverty-racked existence in northeastern Nigeria. Their village was in a desert-like region in a solidly Muslim stronghold now under the siege of the radical Islamic Boko Haram group.

Shortly after her arranged marriage, Ladi became pregnant. Like many young girls married too early, her pelvis was too small to deliver a baby, so after three days of agonizing and life-threatening labor, the unborn child in her womb died. After the delivery, Ladi was unable to control her urine because of the damage done during the prolonged and traumatic labor.

She had a vesico-vaginal fistula – a condition from which many women die and most are abandoned because of the stench of urine from them. Their husbands no longer want them in the home, so they are forced out without their children and with no way to support themselves. Many resort to prostitution to stay alive, and so the condemnation of their society increases. Some victims return to their parents and hope they will help them, but usually that means they are given a hut on the edge of the village and someone takes them a bit of food each day. They are the "unclean" lepers of our day who are abandoned by their families, villages, tribes, and religion.

Ladi heard of a place in Jos where she might get medical help for her urine leaking problem – her fistula. But that was a ten-hour drive away, and she had no money, no way to earn it, and no support from her family. What was she to do? How could she possibly get to that place for help? Her parents and family had been unwilling to help her with any money for the trip, abandoning her alone in her misery. She finally found some vegetable seeds and began a small vegetable garden. Selling her small produce she was able to cobble together enough for the public transportation fare for the 10-hour journey to Jos.

When sitting on the buses, she was put in the back compartment with the luggage and animals because of her offensive odor. She endured the humiliation by clinging to the hope that there was help at the end of the trip. After arriving at Evangel Hospital, she was lovingly cared for by the fistula program staff and was assessed to have a complicated problem. She eventually underwent two procedures but was still not quite dry. She had nowhere to go while she waited, so the Gidan Bege City Ministry staff were contacted. They allowed her to live in a small room at the ministry center and began caring for her. She came to faith in Christ as her only hope and optimistically hung on to the dream she would one day be completely healed. Ladi also visited the other fistula women in the hospital and shared the message of hope in Christ and how she had been delivered from a hopeless situation.

While waiting for her third surgery, Jacob, a staff member of City Ministries, asked Ladi if she would like to return to her village and tell them about Jesus. She had been severely wounded by her family and the villagers. But Ladi's heart had been healed as well, and she was eager to return to her people with a team from City Ministries to tell her Muslim neighbors and friends about the new hope she had in Christ.

With a film and evangelism team, Ladi joined the City Ministry outreach group and made the long journey home. When she entered her village, all the people were shocked, thinking she had died on the journey when she left them. When her parents arrived, they fell at her feet, a sign of submission, and begged her forgiveness for their egregious transgressions. She told them about her medical care, the love she had received, and the new hope she had in Christ. Although not completely healed physically, she had a new heart and joy in her life. As a result of her testimony and the work of the team, many came to faith in Christ during the few days the team visited her remote village. The team plans to return for follow-up discipleship when the security situation improves in the area, and hopefully Ladi will join them and stay with her family to walk with them along the new path they have chosen with her.

THE SHOT HEARD ROUND THE WORLD

I t was dark and quiet about 7:30 on Monday evening January 3, 2005. I was working on email in our office sewing room. On the back porch, Dorothy and our children were entertaining a Nigerian family we had over for dinner. Dorothy was telling Lydia Itapson about her work with AIDS widows and orphans.

From wherever we were in the house, we all heard a loud bang, like an explosion, coming from our neighbor's house. The Naatzes had recently bought an old go-kart, and I thought maybe there had been an explosion with the gas tank while they were working on it. Then we began to hear some other noises from their house like people talking loudly or yelling. I waited a few seconds to see if there was any clearer indication of a problem.

Dorothy saw the flash and must have heard more than I did because she immediately called to me through the window connecting the porch to the sewing room, "Bill, you need to go over there and see what is going on." I quickly ran out the front door in the dark with Dorothy a few steps behind me. On her way out, Dorothy paused for a second to tell the kids to stay in the house.

Our two-car garage is detached from the house and has large metal doors that we usually close at night to slow down thieves interested in our vehicles. That night the doors were open, so I ran around the open door in the dark onto the laterite dirt road that connects the houses on our compound. Immediately I saw the silhouettes of two dark figures only a few feet in front of me coming at me at a full run. I could not see who they were but tried to move left to get out of their way. Suddenly I saw a huge white light accompanied by a large explosion coming from the figure on the left. Instantly I felt an incredible searing hot sensation in my left upper arm that was the most excruciating pain I had ever felt in my life.

I realized I had been shot and when I grabbed my left arm I felt warm blood pouring out. I cried to Dorothy, "I've been shot. I've been shot." I tried to apply as much pressure as I could to stop the bleeding and kept on moving toward the Naatzes' house. Dorothy was a few paces behind me around the corner, saw the bright light, and heard the explosion but did not see me getting shot. She grabbed my right arm and helped me into the neighbors' house. Later she looked at the metal door and saw a large dent in it where a clump of pellets had ricocheted after going through my arm. Had she been any closer to me, she might have been hit as well.

As we entered the Naatzes' living room, strangely no one was there. Firmly gripping my painful left arm I awkwardly lay down on the floor to keep from fainting and told Dorothy, "Get something to wrap around my arm as a tourniquet." She grabbed a towel from a stack of freshly folded laundry on the table and tied it around the upper part of my left arm to slow down the bleeding.

I moved all of my fingers and wrist and still had feeling in my hand so was encouraged that none of the major nerves or arteries had been injured. In that instant I remembered another missionary who had been shot by armed robbers who attacked his vehicle on the road out of Jos. He had been shot in the armpit area, was left on the side of the road by the thieves, and bled to death.

The Naatzes had barricaded themselves in the back for protection, so the door to their back bedrooms was locked. We called to them asking for help. Their 18-year-old son Elias came frantically running out of the bedroom with blood squirting from his right arm. I was settled on the floor with the shirt tourniquet on my arm, so Dorothy put a cloth tourniquet on Elias' arm as well. She ran back to our house to tell the kids what had happened and to get the van keys to take me to the hospital. She cried, "Help! Help!" as she ran back to our house, hoping to draw the attention of others on the compound. By this time the Naatzes were blowing whistles and had set off the house alarm.

As I lay on the floor in extreme pain, I learned that the armed men had walked in Naatzes' back door, pointed sawed off shotguns at them, and demanded their money, cameras, cell phones, and computers. The family cooperated, but the robbers began discussing taking one of the Naatzes as a hostage and going to the other houses for more loot. Elias kicked one of the thieves to distract him, and one of them shot at Elias, grazing his right arm with a few of the pellets and breaking a window behind him.

This was the first explosion we had heard, and it forced the thieves to flee the scene prematurely with whatever things they had gathered. I ran into them in their flight from the house toward the red car they had waiting near the guard hut at the corner of our property. Apparently they had driven onto our compound earlier in the day to check out the situation. They returned after 7 p.m., drove right past the security guards at the hospital entrance, parked the car in the dark near our house, tied up the night guard, and then proceeded to the Naatzes' house.

Because Dorothy told the girls to not leave the house, 14-year-old Marie had locked the front door. Dorothy had to yell until Marie let her in. Our children and guest Nigerian family had gone to our "safe room" – the hall bathroom with the steel-plated door and barred window – and were anxiously waiting with tears in their eyes for word from Dorothy about what was happening. Dorothy ran in the house with blood all over her hands and told them, "Daddy has been shot in the arm, and I need to take him to the hospital. Stay here for now." She grabbed the car keys, got the van out of the garage, and pulled up in front of the Naatzes' house to help Elias and me into the van.

By this time, several of our neighbor Nigerian doctors had heard alarms and came to help. We were both holding our mirror-image wounds to reduce the bleeding and pain. By this time, the Naatzes' house alarm was blaring, they were blowing whistles, and Rick Naatz was on the phone telling the mission leaders and local police that there had been an armed robbery on the Evangel compound and that Elias and I were injured. Lydia, our dinner guest, called her husband who also notified the police. Dorothy raced the van to the hospital, blaring the horn all the way down the road to scare off any lingering thieves and announce to the compound we were in distress.

Upon our arrival at the hospital, I was taken in a wheelchair into the Operating Room area. One of the Nigerian doctors was taking me to the recovery room area, but I insisted on being put in the main Operating Room immediately. I was frustrated that those attending me did not seem to be doing the "right" things quickly, so I began barking orders to them. "Draw blood to type and cross me for several units of blood in case I need a transfusion. Then get a large bore IV going and call the nurse anesthetist to put me asleep. Remember, don't put me asleep until you have the blood ready." Dorothy helped bring Elias into the Operating Room area. In the midst of the chaos every doctor on the compound showed up when the alarm was raised. Rick Naatz was a laboratory technician so notified the missionaries around Jos that we needed A+ blood donors as soon as possible. Several people showed up within minutes to donate, so there was plenty of blood if we needed a transfusion.

Simon Khantiok, the nurse anesthetist, got an IV line in my right arm quickly and proceeded to put me asleep with ketamine, so they could stop the bleeding and treat the wound. Dorothy was holding my hand at the time, but I remember vividly a horrifying vision as I was being put asleep. I saw a bright green ray of light that was collapsing down on itself like a folding yardstick. On each beam of light was a filmstrip with parts of my life. I felt like I was looking at my life as if it had all been imagined. None of it seemed real. I tried to move and stop it but felt pinned down and completely helpless. Dorothy said I cried out, "I see the light. Help me. Help me." It was a horrifying experience because I was powerless, certain I was dying. Then my mind went blank and the next thing I knew I was groggily looking at Dorothy and the nurses in the ICU. Dorothy was unable to watch the surgery, so she had gone outside and prayed feverishly for Elias and me.

While I was being prepared for surgery, things got exciting back at the house as a crowd of missionaries and Nigerians who had heard the shocking news gathered from all over Jos came to lend a hand. The police eventually showed up. Our children stayed in the house until both of the Naatz twin boys came over and told them it was safe. Arrangements were made for the children to spend the rest of the night at a friend's house on another compound, but they stopped at the hospital on the way to find out how I was doing. Dorothy told them I was doing okay in surgery and was pleased the children were in good hands and going to a "safe" place for the night.

Apparently after the robbery someone called the hospital front gate to alert the guards that the thieves' car was on the way out of the compound. Rumors abound as to what happened next, but the car was not stopped and none of the thieves was ever caught. Every day after that for the next week the guards came to salute me in my hospital room, I suppose as an act of contrition!

After I woke up from the surgery in the ICU, although groggy, I felt much better. Dorothy stayed with me and after a while noticed my bandage was still leaking a lot of blood. She alerted the doctors and later in the evening I was taken back to surgery to stop the ongoing bleeding.

I was moved to a private room the following day since I was more stable. Over the coming days, missionary nurses took turns staying with me night and day to help with my medications, bathing, wound care, and other needs. I will forever be grateful to Jean Garland, Jill Tait, Ruth Robertson, and Linda Ward for their kindness to me in this sacrificial way. Dorothy stayed at a safe and quiet friend's house and got some badly needed rest each night. The girls were okay with their friends, but David seemed the most upset and stayed with Dorothy for a few nights.

There were many people from the Jos community who came to visit including missionaries, business people, and Nigerians from local ECWA churches and every ministry in which we were involved. The Governor of Plateau State came twice to visit me. Because I was being given ketamine anesthesia every morning for my dressing changes and taking so many pain injections, I do not recall many of the visitors who came or the events of the first week after the shooting. Dorothy later told me about the visitors and many of our conversations, but I have no recollection of those days. I remember being in pain, seeing my children a few times (although they say they came to see me every day) and some moments during the nights with the special duty missionary nurses taking care of me.

Seeing our children was a highlight of each day through the first week. I was sad that David was reluctant to come near me. Since I was consuming most of Dorothy's time, she was thankful others stepped in to take care of the children. The annual SIM conference was being held at Miango later in the week, so it was a relief to her the children would be busy and well cared for at Miango by SIM families.

Even though the doctors had taken an x-ray of my left upper arm early in the week looking for a fracture, they had not seen any broken bones. I was still in great pain every time I moved and especially when they took me to the Operating Room for a dressing change. Finally on Thursday they did another x-ray and saw that my upper arm had a fracture. This helped explain why I had been in so much pain, especially when I was moving the arm or getting in and out of bed. They applied a simple plaster splint and kept my arm in a sling with the wound well bandaged.

The primary Nigerian doctor taking care of me was leaving town to get married, so I remember requesting another Nigerian surgeon, who worked primarily at the university teaching hospital, to come and take over my care. He was not available all the time, so Dr. Joel Anthis, the ENT missionary surgeon, was in charge of my care. Joel was uncomfortable with this role, especially since my pain was not being controlled with the drugs available in Nigeria. Dorothy took some pictures of my wounds, and after showing them to me, I was not happy with what I saw. I figured I would need either a muscle flap or at the least a skin graft, so I began to explain to Joel how to do a skin graft ON ME! Seeing this turn of events and the inadequate pain management, Joel and Dorothy agreed that they should begin preparations to evacuate me out of Nigeria by air ambulance as soon as possible.

Dorothy and Joel came to tell me about this decision, and in my drug stupor my response was, "I think you are way overreacting. Even if you do have to send me out, Dorothy does not need to come with me." Wow, was I ever wrong and out of touch with my own condition! Finally after 45 minutes Dorothy gave up trying to convince me and let Joel explain it to me from a medical standpoint. I finally agreed, and they began in earnest the complicated process of a medical evacuation. They needed to call our local mission leaders, then the United States SIM administrators, then the insurance company, and finally they would contact an air ambulance service in Europe to fly an ambulance jet from Germany to pick me up.

The decision was made to send us to London for my immediate care. Marie, Heather, Anna, and David were already out at Miango for the SIM Annual Spiritual Life Conference, so Dorothy went to tell them the news. They were understandably upset. We had peace about leaving the children because we knew Dorothy could not manage the children and take care of me. The children were being well cared for by the many missionaries who loved them and us.

Dorothy expected the children to follow us to either England or the United States in a week or so depending on my situation. Dorothy asked Erin Rigsby, a young single missionary nurse working in the Gidan Bege ministry, to be "surrogate Mommy" for the children while they were at Miango. Dorothy also wanted Erin to accompany the children to the U.S. when that time came.

The air ambulance was scheduled to arrive at 7:30 Sunday morning, but there was a looming problem. During the dry season there is a hazy dust called "harmattan," a very fine dust that blows down from the Sahara Desert in the north and hangs like a dense cloud over the northern part of Nigeria for months. This dust fog often makes it impossible for small aircraft to land, and it was so thick that there was great concern that the air ambulance would not be able to land at the Jos airport (45 minutes away).

We would then have to go by road to Abuja (a four-hour journey) and this did not look very appealing since I was already having trouble handling the pain. There was also a concern about getting approval from the Nigerian government for the air ambulance to land. So the entire SIM Nigeria missionary family began to pray on Saturday that the harmattan would lift enough for the plane to land and that permission to land would be given.

I was loaded into the front of the most comfortable vehicle they could find, and we headed to the airport without knowing if the air ambulance would be able to land. Earlier Dorothy had asked the air ambulance staff by telephone if she could accompany me on the jet, and they said, "Maybe." So she packed two small carry-on bags with essential things for us, and we headed to the airport. Terry Hammack, an SIM missionary who was helping coordinate the logistics of the air ambulance rendezvous, called the Jos airport tower authorities to see if they knew of the flight. They had heard nothing, so Terry called Abuja and asked them to notify the Jos air authorities to expedite the arrival of the plane.

God answered our prayers! The harmattan lifted and the plane was given permissions to land in Abuja and then Jos. As our vehicle pulled onto the tarmac of the Jos airport, we heard the sound of the air ambulance landing right in front of us. The German doctor and technician on the flight were debriefed on my condition, and then they lifted me onto the stretcher and Dorothy sat in a jump seat in the back of the plane. Dorothy remembers finally relaxing a bit when the medical staff conversed in German about how to care for me, and I did not jump in to tell them what to do! I remember meeting the flight crew but have little recollection of the entire flight, which stopped in Algeria, Germany, and then on to London. I do recall in Germany that after we had refueled and were speeding down the runway, we heard several alarms start screaming from the cockpit. The pilot immediately put on the brakes, turned the plane around, and we ended up taking another even smaller jet to London.

Upon our arrival in London on Sunday evening, Dr. Peter Jackson, a former SIM missionary doctor who had helped SIM with many medical evacuations over the years, met us with an ambulance and swiftly moved us to a private hospital near Gatwick airport. We had just come through a week of hectic activity, an evacuation on a private ambulance jet, tearfully left our children, and were struggling with uncertainty and my pain. Needless to say Dorothy was exhausted and her stress level was very high. One of Dorothy's funny memories of the London visit was her first conversation with the nurse. The ambulance staff had just moved me from the stretcher to the bed, there was an exchange of medical information, I needed pain medication, and Dorothy was trying to be helpful yet not be in the way of the busy staff. The nurse calmly looked at Dorothy, smiled, and asked in her classic British accent, "Would you like a cup of tea?" Dorothy was flabbergasted. She thought to herself, "Can't you see my husband is in distress and I am exhausted? Why on earth would I need a cup of tea?" She caught herself when she remembered that in the land of Queen Elizabeth, the troubles of the world are best treated with a cup of tea. We soon learned the importance of tea when it was offered to us at 6:30 a.m. with breakfast,

10:00 a.m., 12 noon with lunch, 3:30 p.m., 6:00 p.m. for dinner, and again at 9:00 p.m. before bed. What a civilized addiction!

We learned later from Dr. Jackson that in his search for a private hospital that could attend to me quickly, he was promised only one night at the Gatwick BUPA Hospital. He decided to take the one night offer and pray they would not kick me out the door. Of course, our stay was never challenged the entire week, and we are grateful to God for opening the door that first night.

The surgeon Dr. Jackson had wanted to care for me was out of town visiting his ailing mother-in-law in Scotland. When he arrived on Tuesday, he took me straight to surgery. My arm had two holes – an entrance wound where the shotgun pellets had entered my arm and an exit wound at the back of my arm. Incredibly, if the wounds had been on the inside of my arm, I could have lost complete use of my arm with nerve injuries or even died from bleeding from the main arteries to the arm and hand. A few inches more and it would have entered my chest and killed me. Does God guide bullets? More on that later.

Mr. Colin Stone (senior surgeons or consultants in the United Kingdom are called "Mr." and not "Dr.") decided to connect the two wounds on the upper part of my arm to clean out the dead muscle and bits of clothing and shrapnel still in the wound. He then applied a more substantial plaster splint to stabilize the broken arm bone. That was the only procedure I had all week in the London hospital because the main goal was to get control of my pain and help me get strong enough to board a commercial flight to the United States for definitive treatment and rehabilitation.

In the coming days with the daily full English breakfast of sausages, bacon, beans, eggs and toast, the delicious lunches and dinners and the encouragement of my wife and visitors, I began to gain both emotional and physical strength. I was in bed most of the time but eventually managed to get to the bathroom, so I could shave and do my teeth. Because we had come from an outside hospital, especially from Africa, I was in isolation and was not permitted to leave my room for the entire week.

On my last day in the London hospital I was allowed to walk down the hospital hall with the help of Dorothy and the nurse. I was glad to be out of the severe pain and felt especially glad to be out of the intense stress and in a place where I trusted the medical care and was not orchestrating my own medical care. I know Dorothy was glad to be able to hand me over to someone she knew I trusted to take care of me.

It was wonderful to have visitors during our week in London from some dear former SIM missionaries who were now working in London, a Nigerian nurse who had worked in the Evangel Operating Room a few years ago, and an SIM United Kingdom administration couple. The Jacksons were very kind to Dorothy and invited her to their house several times to email, do some shopping, and get a break from hospital life. Since the weather was colder than in Nigeria, Dorothy bought sweaters for both of us and a few other necessities.

For the past 10 years, we had sent a weekly email family newsletter to several hundred people. It was originally to let our immediate family know how we were doing, but the list of interested friends grew until it was going all over the world to individuals and churches who were interested in praying for us. Late on the evening of the shooting, Dorothy sent a brief email letter to the weekly list with the subject, "Bill shot by armed robbers." Over the next weeks she managed to carve out time every few days to give an update to the praying and watching world.

We received hundreds of responses to these bulletins. Most were short and had words of encouragement, but some had detailed questions that needed a response. Every few days Dorothy would read to me the list of those who had written, and she occasionally printed out entire emails for me to read. I was not only emotionally and psychologically unable to deal with correspondence, I was physically incapable of getting my hands up to the keyboard. After about six weeks I finally was strong enough to use the keyboard and began to read over 600 emails we had received after the incident. It was amazing to see the number of emails, knowing there were hundreds praying for us around the world.

By Saturday, I was strong enough to get up and sit on a plane. So Dr. Jackson took us to Heathrow Airport, and we headed for Los Angeles and the next phase of treatment. He had arranged for a wheelchair to take me through the airport, but as the security people passed the security wand over my left arm, it began to buzz. I lifted up my sleeve and told the guy I had been hurt and showed him my bandage. It did not occur to me until a few seconds later that the shrapnel in my arm was setting off the alarm! We boarded the flight and were delighted to be in Business Class with larger seats to stretch out for the flight.

For the last few nights at the Gatwick hospital, I had felt some chills at night but was not sure why. After about five hours of the ten-hour flight, I began to feel the chills again, and severe back pain began to bother me. I was not sure if it was because of a wound infection or if I was having a bout of malaria. Anyway, in spite of being in Business Class, I was miserable for the last five hours and was determined to be admitted directly to a hospital upon our arrival in Los Angeles.

To our delight, Dr. Bob and Sally Zirschky from Oregon met us as we came out of Customs in the Los Angeles Airport on Sunday. I was in a wheelchair and was so weak and uncomfortable I could not contain my tears. I was exhausted from the flight, relieved to be in America and happy to see Bob, an orthopedic surgeon who knew us from several trips to Jos. He wheeled me to the car and said we should not make any decisions about going to a hospital until he had a chance to look at my arm wound in Carlsbad. He gave me some pain medicine for the 1 ½-hour car trip, and we headed for my parents' house in Carlsbad on the famous Los Angeles freeways.

The reunion with my parents was emotionally overwhelming. I was so incredibly weak, emotionally exhausted, and relieved to be "home" that I barely made it into the bedroom. I cried and cried as my parents embraced me with deep affection. My brother Jim and my sister Sharon were also there to encourage me. Later in the day, Bob changed my dressing, and they were all shocked at how deep and bad my shotgun arm injury was. It was clean and bleeding, but there was a huge chunk out of my upper arm.

It was also the first time since the accident I had really seen the wound, and it was disturbing to me as I imagined the difficult recovery ahead. Bob was pleased the wound was not infected so speculated my fever on the flight was probably a flare up of malaria since my immune system was weak after all I had been through.

During the week I was in London, a counselor from Ghana came to Nigeria to help with post-crisis counseling for anyone involved in the robbery. We are grateful she had an opportunity to meet with each of our children. We anticipated the children would follow us to the United States in about two weeks but had to work through the approval process with SIM and the insurance company. Dorothy had told the families caring for the children approximately when the children could come to the U.S., so the children had psychologically been prepared to spend a few more days with friends. We knew they were well cared for and that was very reassuring.

In Nigeria, as the discussion was unfolding about the timing of the children's trip, the insurance company insisted they leave for the United States as soon as possible. So on Sunday morning about the time we were leaving London, the SIM leaders came to the children as they were getting out of Sunday School and going into church and told them they had two hours to pack, and then they would be leaving for the United States. This came as a big shock because they would not be able to say goodbye to many of their friends or get the homework they would need to keep up with their classmates.

Several missionary women helped the children pack their bags, and a kind Lebanese friend in town brought them hamburgers for lunch from his restaurant. Erin Rigsby, the SIM nurse who had been helping the children at Miango, was also notified of the abrupt evacuation and she prepared to leave. Erin and our four children went to Abuja on Sunday afternoon for the early Monday morning British Airways flight to London and then on to Los Angeles Monday evening. So instead of expecting the children later in the week, we were suddenly surprised to learn they would be arriving on Tuesday.

My sister was working as a pain specialist nurse for a group of orthopedic surgeons in San Diego. When she heard about the shooting and the possibility we might come to California for treatment, she asked her surgeon friends to recommend the best surgeon to help me. Sharon asked Dr. Balourdas if he would be willing to help. He agreed to see me on the Tuesday after I arrived.

On Tuesday my father drove Dorothy and me to Dr. Balourdas' office for my first appointment. After looking at the wound, he said he was pleased it was not infected, but it would need some muscle repair and wound closure. He applied a new dressing, a better plaster splint, and sent me home to prepare for admission for surgery the next day. I was encouraged and optimistic we were on the road to recovery, glad to be in the hands of a competent surgeon.

Sally Zirschky stayed in Carlsbad after her husband went back to Oregon on Sunday evening. She wanted to encourage Dorothy and help her shop for some things she needed. Bob needed to get back to Salem, Oregon, for work, but when he heard the children were coming on Tuesday, he flew back to San Diego in time to rent a van and drive Dorothy to Los Angeles International Airport to pick up the kids on Tuesday morning. We were all excited to see the children, and it was a great boost to see them after spending so little time with them when I was sick in Nigeria. I think it was also good for them to see me not looking so critically ill.

Wednesday morning Dorothy and I went to the outpatient surgery center. It was still painful to move my arm, but the staff were very gentle and kind. After coming from our little Operating Room at Evangel in Nigeria, in spite of my anxiety, I was awestruck being in an American operating room with its fully stocked shelves, clean floors, and stacks of monitors and equipment – all working!

For the first surgery, Dr. Balourdas decided the wound was not clean enough to close, so he applied a vacuum dressing device to clean the wound and reduce the swelling and secretions. In applying this treatment I needed to be admitted, which was a big change of plans for Dorothy. She had counted on being able to take care of me at home and coordinate the supervision of the children. If I was admitted to the hospital Dorothy wanted to stay with me, but then who could take care of the children? So, in a rare "needy" moment, Dorothy called her parents in Maryland and asked if they could come and help take care of the children while I was in the hospital.

They had been planning to go to Pennsylvania for the weekend but cancelled their plans because of a large snowfall and the cold weather. By the next morning, Thursday, Dorothy had not heard from her parents and was a bit concerned. In fact, they had been up late that night booking flights and getting ready and were on the first flight from Baltimore in the morning. They called Dorothy about 10:00 Thursday morning, and Dorothy asked them when they were coming. They said, "We're in Phoenix and will be in San Diego in a few hours." Wow! It was less than 24 hours from the time Dorothy called them in Maryland until they arrived in San Diego. They rented a van at the airport and checked in at a hotel five minutes from my parents' house.

In the coming days, they were a terrific help with the children, treating them to a fantastic day at SeaWorld, taking them swimming at the hotel pool, helping them at the library get online to do their emails, going shopping, taking them for walks in the neighborhood, and keeping them preoccupied and happy.

On Friday I went to the Operating Room again for my second surgery to close the gaping wound in my left arm. I had been on so many medications that I had trouble thinking clearly afterwards but was relieved this initial phase of my recovery was over. Dr. Balourdas took a few patches of skin from my left thigh for a skin graft. Much to my surprise I was discharged the same afternoon, so Dorothy's parents came to the hospital to take us home. What a wonderful feeling it was to be home and on the mend. I thought the worst was over.

WHEN THE OTHER SHOE DROPPED

After coming home from the hospital, I stayed in my parents' extra bedroom. Dorothy's mother stayed with the children at the Guesthouse on the SIM retirement village compound at night, and occasionally David went with her father to the hotel.

One afternoon we came across the Bill Gaither Hymn Sing program on the television. A group of famous Gospel singers were dressed in turn-of-the-century costumes singing old hymn favorites. Two songs that brought tears to my eyes were "Day By Day," a long time favorite of mine since the time Aimee died, and "He Giveth More Grace." These songs comforted me often in the coming days as I faced even more pain and suffering.

While I was in the hospital after my skin graft operation, I experienced several side effects of the medications I was on and often felt like I was suffocating. I had intermittent mid-abdominal pain with a terrible acid feeling that increased every day. I tried taking antacids and milk products to relieve the pain, but the burning got worse. After I was discharged, I continued to have terrible nausea and could not take any liquids or food. By 10 p.m., I began vomiting and the burning was unbearable. The dry heaves continued until 4 the next morning when I was absolutely exhausted, getting dehydrated from so much vomiting, and having unbearable, searing stomach pain.

I admitted I needed to go to the hospital, but we were not sure if I should go to the hospital where I had the surgery, which was about 45 minutes away in San Diego, or go to a nearby hospital in Encinitas. We tried to call Dr. Balourdas but could not reach him, so we decided to go to the hospital where I had the surgery. They would at least have my hospital records.

The SIM Retirement Village host, Jerry Fawley, drove Dorothy and me to the hospital Emergency Room. With my eyes closed to shut out the world around me, I curled up in agony in a fetal position, holding my stomach and moaning in severe pain. The nurses were quite attentive, trying to help me as quickly as they could. Since I had just come out of the hospital, my veins for an IV were difficult to find, but the nurses were eventually successful. Unfortunately, it was the change of shift for the doctors and nurses, so the first Emergency Room doctor wanted to get a CAT scan of my abdomen and so left me to suffer without any medication.

A while later, the day shift doctor came to see me and agreed with me that my pain was probably a stress ulcer or gastritis so gave me a terrific IV drug to stop the nausea and an antacid cocktail of drugs to drink to stop the abdominal burning pain. A short while after taking these I began to feel much better and could finally relax in the bed and get some relief from the excruciating abdominal pain. I was afraid at one stage I had a perforated ulcer but was encouraged when the pain was relieved quickly with the strong antacids. It's difficult to turn the doctor part of me off.

I did not want to go back to the house without feeling significantly better, so the doctor was gracious enough to let me stay until I was sure I was okay. Dorothy called my parents and by 10 in the morning they arrived, and I went home to recover from a stress ulcer as well as my arm injury. The instructions for my recovery included a bland diet, more medication, and rest.

Over the next several days, I began to feel better and was regaining my strength. Robin, the occupational therapist, was a great blend of graciousness and firmness in getting me to move my arm and stretch out the painful scars that were settling in so I could regain the movement and strength in my arm. She assigned exercises for me on my road to recovery.

I had been taking sleeping pills since the shooting in order to get adequate rest and to cope with the nightmares. I noticed when I was in bed at night that my lower back began to ache. I assumed it was either the soft bed or tiredness from being in bed for three weeks. I started using various pillows to support my lower back, tried stretch exercises, and eventually asked my mother for a heating pad.

Over the last weekend in January, we were delighted by a visit from many members of our family. Before the shooting, my cousins from Ireland, Ken and Beulah Robinson, had planned a trip to the United States to visit their son Timothy, who was studying at Dallas Theological Seminary. They visited my brother John in Tyler, Texas, and then flew to California to visit my brother Jim, my parents, and us. My brother Jim and his family, my brother John from Texas and the Zirschkys from Salem, Oregon, also came for the weekend. It was a packed house, especially at meal times. Even though I did not feel very sociable, they were a great encouragement. Stories and jokes about life in Ireland abounded in a "who can top this" competition. The laughing was almost nonstop and was great therapy. I was still very weak and needed frequent naps but was pleased that I was not in the hospital during their visit.

Bill Schmidt, an SIM pastor-at-large, was also in Carlsbad and stopped by to see us. Bill and Eunice had come to Nigeria a few years ago to speak at our annual SIM spiritual life conference. They had lost an adult son, and we had lost Aimee, so there was an instant kinship from our common grief experiences. They encouraged us to consider going to a place called Link Care in California for family counseling after I was physically stronger. We had begun thinking about getting trauma counseling, so this was a helpful recommendation.

I was emotionally exhausted and physically weak but felt the need to connect with God. I asked my daughter Marie and my father to read the Bible to me to help focus my thoughts on God and not so much on my own circumstances. My Dad read from the Psalms, but eventually he got into the chapters where the psalmist David talks about his enemies and "the terror by night." That was not what I needed to hear, so I asked him to read from the New Testament. Even in prayer, if people recalled the incident and thanked God the bullet didn't injure my arm more severely or hit me in the chest and kill me, it was still very hard for me to hear the story retold. Every time there was any mention of the incident, I relived the events in my mind over and over. I was not ready emotionally to process the crisis and tried to keep that closet of memories in my mind closed.

One passage of Scripture I reflected on was the pruning of the vine in John 15. The passage suggests God prunes the branches He wants to bear more fruit. So He is not pruning unproductive vines as much as the ones He knows can bear more fruit. The problem is that pruning REALLY hurts. It is painful to be under the knife and have the Master cutting parts of our lives out. The branches don't know which ones need pruning – only the Master knows.

Dorothy's parents returned to Maryland after two weeks. They were a terrific help, especially with the children. They had arranged for us to stay in the hotel after they left because Dorothy's sister, Sue, had a vacation time-share in the same hotel, and they gave us two weeks of their time-share allotment. I was ready for a change, and it would give my parents a break. So we moved into the hotel on Tuesday, and it proved a terrific boost for our family. We could spend more time together as a family, and the children could swim every day in the delightful children's pool. We had a beautiful room overlooking the Pacific Ocean complete with TVs in every room, a fantastic pool with a water playground for kids, a hot tub, workout gym, and picnic area. I was so pleased they were happy and enjoyed hearing their tales of fun and adventure every evening. I was getting stronger and even ventured out to an electronics store to get a few things, so we could do email from the hotel. I still had fresh wounds on my arm and leg so was not able to go swimming or enjoy any of the five hot tubs in the hotel.

One evening when I was resting in my bedroom, I was watching an episode of M*A*S*H, a television comedy show about the medics in the Korean War. The story revolved around a soldier who had been badly injured, needed abdominal surgery, got a serious infection, and was dying. He needed a blood transfusion. His best buddy in their combat unit was also in the hospital with a minor injury but would not leave the side of his seriously ill friend. He offered to donate blood, but when his blood was examined for compatibility, he was found to have leukemia. The doctors urged him to go immediately to a specialist hospital in Seoul, Korea, for expert treatment. But the soldier insisted, at the risk of his own life, on staying at his wounded buddy's side until he recovered.

The background story was the surprise visit of the regional monsignor to the M*A*S*H chaplain. Having been up all night with the wounded soldier, the chaplain was totally unprepared for his important sermon on Sunday in front of the visiting church dignitary. So for his sermon he told the story of the two soldiers – one willing to sacrifice his own ambitions and needs for the other. Of course, the monsignor was impressed with the chaplain's sermon, and the wounded soldier pulled through his medical crisis. The chaplain's closing statement, "It's not about me" brought me to tears. It had a stunning impact on me as I sat contemplating my circumstances. My whole world had been about "me." I was convicted to think more of others and think about how God would use this for His glory. It's not all about me.

My backache continued to get worse through the first week we were in the hotel, and by Thursday I was in great pain. Strong painkillers and hot packs on my lower back were the only things that helped. I finally realized I was passing a kidney stone so asked Dorothy to take me to the nearest hospital to confirm this and to get more painkillers. We went to the Emergency Room at Scripps Hospital in Encinitas. Once again I found myself sitting on a hospital stretcher in a flimsy gown waiting for someone to take pity on me and give me some relief from my pain.

The pain was excruciating, and I was not coping well having been in and out of the hospital so much in the past four weeks. The Emergency Room doctor finally gave me an injection, and I felt some relief. They did a CAT scan and confirmed I had a kidney stone on my right side that was quite low and "should pass on its own." So I was sent home to drink lots of water, take my pain pills, and hopefully pass the stone. They also gave me the name of a local urologist for follow-up.

Well, the next 24 hours did not go well. I was barely able to tolerate the pain even with the strong pain medicine. I was also unable to eat or drink because of the overwhelming nausea, so it was difficult to even take the pain medications. Then I started vomiting and the pain became unbearable. Finally on Friday afternoon, February 4, 2005, I was in such severe pain I asked Dorothy to call an ambulance to take me back to the hospital. With the sirens blaring, I was taken back to the hospital and put back into the flimsy gown to wait for someone to help me. I was in agony that had been going on for hours even before going to the hospital and could see no end in sight. This was one of the lowest points for me. I felt so alone, so helpless. I cried out to God to help me and bring some relief, but God did not seem to be there, be listening, or care. His silence stunned me.

I begged for pain medication, but the nurses said they could not give me any injections unless I had an IV line. So they began sticking me to get an IV line. I told them I was difficult to stick because most of my veins had been used in my previous hospitalizations. They paid no attention to me and began sticking me. I also begged for them to use a local anesthetic but was told, "We don't do that in the Emergency Room." I was not happy and after sticking my right arm six times, they decided to try my feet and so stuck me a few more times. Finally they sent in their "best" nurse, and she was able to eventually get in an IV after I was in tears from the soreness of the kidney stone and the many vein sticks.

I finally got some relief and was whisked back to x-ray to confirm the location of the kidney stone. The doctor on duty planned to load me up with pain medication and send me home again to tough it out. I begged him to find a urologist who would admit me and evaluate me. I had not been able to pass my previous kidney stone in Nigeria and wanted to get help with this one. Eventually the Emergency Room doctor located Dr. Butler, a urologist, who agreed to admit me and evaluate me the next day for possible surgery. I was so relieved to be admitted even though it was another setback on my road to recovery.

I could not believe I was having so many problems after the gunshot wound: first the ulcer, then the kidney stone. God seemed very, very far away and my suffering was beyond what I could handle. I was completely exhausted physically and emotionally and had no reserve to handle any more pain. I felt like a failure spiritually for not being strong, and a wimp for being so unable to handle even the slightest pain. I was praying for a miracle that didn't happen. So I thought, "Can I ever expect a miracle if it didn't happen at my neediest hour? Does God really hear our prayers when we suffer? Why on earth would He remain silent?" I thought, "I would never let my son cry in pain for hours and days if I knew I could help him and relieve his pain."

It seemed to get back to the basic apologetic argument, "Why does God allow pain and suffering in the world?" Only later did I accept that God was working out His plan through my suffering even though it was a painful mystery to me. God allowed His Son to suffer for me to the point of death and never intervened. I MUST accept the suffering and know God still loved me and had a purpose, which was a mystery to me. God is God and I'm not!

On Saturday morning Dr. Butler showed up at the hospital and agreed to do a procedure that afternoon to get the stone out. I was anxious about having more surgery but relieved to know the stone would soon be out. I was also encouraged to learn Dr. Butler was a Christian and seemed interested in our background as medical missionaries in Nigeria. Dorothy called the family to tell them the news, and we settled in to prepare for the next surgery.

I was pleased to wake up after the surgery and know the stone was gone. Dr. Butler had evaluated both sides and had cleared both sides of stones. He left small catheters in the ureters, which he said he would remove later in the office. I was not feeling like going home that night so stayed overnight until I was feeling a little stronger. On Sunday morning we got the okay to go home, packed up, and headed back to the hotel. My parents had taken the children to church, but we had a great reunion when they arrived back from church in the afternoon.

The last time the children had seen me I was being loaded into an ambulance, so it was good for them to see me feeling better and stronger. I was so tired of being sick, so tired of pain, and so tired of feeling isolated and separated from my family. I wanted to start getting stronger and recovering from the arm injury but kept suffering setbacks that were hindering me from recovery. I thought, "Maybe this time I will be able to stay out of the hospital for more than a week!"

When Dorothy and I finally made it to church together, we knew it would be hard to hold back tears during the music part of the service. The song that really got to me was the phrase, "Let the weak say I am strong." I felt very weak but could not say, "I am strong." So many phrases about the Lordship of Christ and praising Him were not where my heart was as I nurtured a broken heart, clinging to the only hope I knew, the promise of God's faithfulness and presence. I didn't feel like praising the Lord as the church songs implored. I needed my faith and trust in God restored before I felt like praising Him.

Even more disturbing were the television services with the "health, wealth and prosperity" preachers. One man in great health and dressed expensively said with a big grin, "I will praise God in every circumstance." I thought, "If only you knew what I have been through. If you had been through suffering and pain, would you feel and say the same thing so glibly?"

In reading an issue of Discipleship Journal on suffering, the first line of the article was terrific. It said, "God loves you and has a difficult plan for your life." That was exactly how I felt. As I reflected on the last 15 years of my life, there have been many difficult times – Liberia, reassignment to Nigeria, hepatitis, twins' early years, Aimee's death, David's traumatic birth, diabetes, armed robbery and now a shotgun wound, ulcer and kidney stone!

I struggled with doubts about my own spiritual progress. "Was I learning what God wanted me to learn through these trials? Had I grown spiritually? Did it keep happening because I am not learning? Was I leading my wife and children through these difficulties as a spiritual leader? Why after all I've been through did I feel so weak and impotent?" Through this last blow I felt like a failure and a spiritual dwarf.

I received a wonderful little card from Sally Zirschky quoting 1 Peter 5:10. "And after you have suffered for a little while, the God of all grace, who called you to His eternal glory in Christ, will Himself prefect, confirm, strengthen and establish you." These words were a great comfort. Suffering would only be for a little while. The God of grace promised to strengthen and establish me. I felt so weak, with dim hope for the future. This glimmer of hope was a blessing.

We had only a few people visit during my early post-operative days since most people thought we needed the privacy and quiet for recovery. Pastor David Hall from my parents' church came by one afternoon to drop off the Volvo station wagon the church was allowing us to use. He was very encouraging, but in our conversation, one small phrase spoke to my heart. He said that in the time of trouble or crisis "God is always there behind us with open arms to catch us when we fall." What comfort because it assumes we will fall but not completely.

The kidney stone and ulcer days of agonizing pain were more discouraging to me than my memories after the shotgun injury. After my injury, things seemed to be happening that were "God things" to help my recovery, but through the ulcer and stone hours I felt helpless and abandoned. I had become quite depressed at a perceived absence of God in my painful moments. Yet, I felt I MUST believe. Even though it was not obvious to me or visible to me, God was there. He was allowing me to suffer but ready to catch me when I fell. I thought I was not a steadfast Christian, was not a strong father, and had not projected triumph, victory, and praise through my suffering. Rather, I had been beaten down completely by the pain and loneliness to a point of despair and complete discouragement. It was humbling, terrifying, and depressing. Maybe that's where God wanted me to be.

I thought of the biblical character Job and his tragic circumstances. He certainly had a greater loss than I in terms of his family and resources. The verse that haunted me was, "Though He slays me, still I will trust Him." It is not "Though He allows Satan to slay me" or "Though He allows circumstances to slay me" but "Though HE slays me." Is God really the one who slays? Is God the one who attacked me? Somehow we want to fudge and mention God's permissive will by explaining that God allowed us to suffer, not made us suffer. The overriding message was Job's trust in God. That was my goal – to renew, re-establish my trust in God in spite of or through my circumstances.

As I was emerging from the injury, the ulcer, and kidney stone, in my grief and weakness the best picture I could visualize from my perspective was one of me riding the crest of the wave of missionary success. We had lots of great things happening – crisis pregnancy ministry, VVF program, and *Back to Jerusalem* missions movement. Dorothy had the training workshops for home-based care of HIV/AIDS patients and the Bucket Project weekends. We were all healthy and happy. We had a wonderful vacation before Christmas at Yankari Game Park and a great time as a family at Miango for Christmas.

Then it seemed that as I was walking along with God, He stuck out His fist and smacked me in the face and knocked me flat on my back to the ground (gunshot wound). Then when I was down and bleeding, God kicked me in the stomach (ulcer) and as I recoiled and took another breath, He walked around me and kicked me in the back (kidney stone). It seemed so cruel and unfair and pushed me to the limit of my physical and emotional resources. I was empty, beaten, exhausted, and bankrupt in my heart. It challenged my trust in a God who was good and loving.

I told Dorothy again, "I would never do that to my son." Her quick response was, "Yes you would if it would prevent him from danger ahead." Wow! There's at least one reason why God MIGHT have hurt me to protect me. I did trust Him, but this sure was confusing and challenged my foundational trust in Him like nothing I have ever experienced. I DECIDED to still trust Him but knew it would take a while until I FELT like I trusted Him!

I asked myself questions, "Has my suffering been 'for Christ's sake,' or am I just being dealt some hard circumstances? Has my pain been the attacks of Satan in spiritual warfare or just 'bad luck'? Was the attack in the scheme of Satan to get us out of the ministry in Nigeria or is that over-spiritualizing the incident?" Elbert Hubbard puts it this way, "All that counts is not our medals and trophies and diplomas but our wounds and scars." Are my scars "for Christ"? The pain, depression, grief all seemed from Satan. The despair and helplessness didn't seem from God although I knew He could use them to draw me closer to himself.

Suffering and pain had drawn me closer to Dorothy and hopefully would draw me closer to God – now that I was through the main pain phase I could read the Bible again and be encouraged.

On one of my morning walks with Dorothy I asked her about the "Why?" question regarding suffering. God choosing us for trials seemed to have nothing to do with our spiritual state, work performance, or ministries. He seemed to want to teach us something. Through this trial I felt my response had been poor, but had I learned anything? Did I trust God more? Did I feel more intimate with God? Did I know more about Him and His character? Would I get to the point I could praise Him and thank Him? Those questions were only the beginning...

DOROTHY'S TURN

fter the armed robbery incident in January 2005, my arm wound was painful for months and the broken bone was healing. After I recovered from the kidney stone incident, in mid-February we decided to go to a Christian counseling center called LinkCare in Fresno, California, for trauma counseling for two months. This proved to be a difficult emotional journey for all of us. I was struggling with PTSD after the shooting, and David was so traumatized from hearing about the details of the event, that he regressed to the point of not being able to go anywhere alone. Each of us had individual counselors, Dorothy and I had a pastoral counselor, and we had a family counselor. Through many tears I recalled every detail of what happened, and then the counselor helped me understand how God fit into this tragic picture. I felt the healing was well underway in my heart and mind, we got David "back," and each of the girls had a counselor who met them where they were in processing the situation. Overall it was a time of healing, reflection, and realignment spiritually, which helped us so we could return to Nigeria in time to allow the children to finish out the school semester at Hillcrest that had been so abruptly interrupted.

However, shortly after getting to LinkCare in Fresno on February 14 (Valentine's Day), Dorothy started complaining of lower back pain. She had struggled with lower back pain on and off over the years, but it usually responded to a heating pad, back massages, and exercises. So that was the plan. This time, however, the pain didn't improve. Dorothy tried a variety of pain medications and muscle relaxants, but it kept getting worse. Since it would require a physician's prescription to see a physical therapist, we decided to see if a chiropractor could help. I was quite taken aback watching the adjustment by the chiropractor. Dorothy had several sessions and seemed a bit better. Through this she was given all sorts of advice from both professionals and well wishers, and finally she settled on alternating hot and cold packs to her lower back. We also took turns giving her back massages in an effort to help her feel better.

She continued with several more chiropractic treatments through the middle of April when we left Fresno for Carlsbad, California, where my parents lived. In fact, she felt well enough and pain-free enough to return to Nigeria. Our trip involved getting on a plane for the 10-hour trip to London and then another six-hour flight to Abuja, Nigeria.

Amazingly she had no pain on the trip from California to Abuja. We then took a four-hour ride in our van to Jos. After arriving, her back began to hurt again. She tried rest, medications, massage, and prayer to no avail. The pain began to ease in her lower back but became worse in her hip in a sciatica distribution down her thigh.

Dr. Cindy Anthis decided to try a few days of round-the-clock Valium to break the muscle spasm. Dorothy slept a lot that week, and finally after about five days she stopped taking the Valium to see if the muscle spasm in her back was broken. Unfortunately, the throbbing had not improved. Dr. Anthis began to correspond with an SIM physician in the United States, and he recommended a short course of steroids. After that approach Dorothy had mild relief, but the pain essentially was so incapacitating she spent her days and nights in a recliner chair, only getting up to go to the bathroom.

One afternoon I heard Dorothy calling out for help from the bathroom. I was certain she had fallen, so rushed to help her. Dr.

Anthis had started her on an anti-depressant in addition to the Valium and steroids. She was to take ten tablets of the steroids the first day, then eight, then four, two and so on in a tapered schedule. Dorothy had looked at the six pills of steroids and thought they looked funny before she swallowed them. Then in horror she realized she was about to take six Valium tablets – a lethal dose! She pleaded with me to remove all the medicine from her reach and asked me to give her the right pills each day. Quite a scare!

Two of our supporting churches in Maryland had sent a team to visit us during the summer. Lori Giblin was a physical therapist on the team and had come with her husband and one-year-old daughter. She wanted to bring her daughter to our house each day for a nap. It proved to be a great time to help Dorothy with physical therapy as well as needed friendship and encouragement. Lori was able to arrange for a friend in the States to send a back traction apparatus for Dorothy. She tried it for a few days and initially it seemed to help. Dorothy would get strapped in this device, and it would literally begin to pull her apart, stretching open the spaces in her backbone. Unfortunately it made the pain worse, so Dorothy stopped using it.

I had been trying to manage our home, orchestrating the children's activities and meals as well as my own responsibilities at the hospital. I didn't want the situation to continue indefinitely because of uncertainty about Dorothy's diagnosis and unrelenting pain. We wanted to get x-rays of her back, but because the Evangel Hospital machine was not working properly, I had to take her to a little place downtown that had a functioning machine. The films showed a loss of disk space in several of the lower vertebrae and severe degenerative disease of her lower spine. Basically Dorothy's lower back looked like the back of an old woman. Finally, somewhat in desperation, I wanted some outside expert advice. I sent digital pictures of her x-rays with an email report of the story of her pain to the SIM physician in Charlotte and Dr. Duke Sampson, a neurosurgeon friend of mine in Dallas.

On Monday evening May 30, 2005, I received an email from Dr. Sampson saying he thought Dorothy had a herniated disk and needed to come to the States for evaluation and treatment. Armed with that email I was now convinced we had tried conservative measures long enough, and it was time to go to the U.S. for expert care. I walked over to Dr. Truxton's house and showed her the email. She agreed and gave me the approval to contact the SIM-USA medical office and begin the medical evacuation process. "Here we go again!"

We contacted Dorothy's sister Sue and asked her to line up a neurosurgeon in the Annapolis area. Dorothy felt more comfortable going to Maryland because her family and we had supporting churches there. After hearing Dorothy's story of progressive pain, the doctors at the SIM Charlotte medical office agreed with the evacuation plan. They wanted to check on the insurance situation with the Maryland physicians. It took another two days to find out if the Maryland surgeon would accept the SIM insurance. We were willing to go to Charlotte for the surgery but thought Maryland would be better from an emotional support and postoperative recovery point of view.

Finally on Wednesday, June 1, 2005, we got the okay from SIM to go to the States. The neurosurgeon, Dr. Solomon, in Maryland not only agreed to see Dorothy but also would do the surgery pro bono! Wow! I called the evacuation insurance company, and they began the process of arranging the flights. They also wanted to send a nurse to accompany Dorothy on the journey.

A few times we had discussed with the children the possibility of Dorothy going to the States for treatment. We pondered whether we should take the children but thought it would be best for them to stay in our house with an adult while I accompanied Dorothy. We asked two college student women, Saralynn and Rebecca, who were visiting for the summer, if they would be willing to babysit the children for a few weeks and they enthusiastically agreed. So that evening we told the children we would be leaving again!

On Thursday morning about 8 o'clock we got a call from the insurance company that we would be leaving for Abuja that afternoon in order to get the early Friday morning flight. That was fast! On Tuesday and Wednesday I had started making a list of things to take and had thrown a few things in a bag, but now we needed to pack in earnest. When the kids woke up, we told them we were leaving that day. The girls were sad, but David was excited he would get more sleepovers at his friend Hunter Fretheim's house. He didn't seem to understand what was really going on. After getting most of my packing done, I went to the hospital with David to see a few patients in the clinic. I told the surgery team I was leaving and said goodbye to the Operating Room staff before heading home to finish packing. I then spent some time with each of the children to tell them how much I loved them and would miss them. Saying goodbye to them was the hardest part for me, and I fought to hold back my tears.

We then gave Sarah and Rebecca a quick tour of the house and let them know about the lights, power switches, water, and so on. A few of the hospital staff came to say goodbye, but we had not told many people we were leaving, so we had very few visitors. Simon Khantiok, from the Operating Room, brought over a wheelchair I had requested in case we needed it in Abuja.

Terry Hammack from the SIM office came after lunch, and we packed our bags and the wheelchair in the SIM Mercedes station wagon. Terry was driving to Abuja because his son was returning to the U.S. for college. Just after getting off the plateau about one and a half hours down the road, the Mercedes began to jerk so much that we had to stop. After trying several things it became apparent the car would not make it to Abuja. So we used our cell phone to call Jos and asked someone to bring another car, so we could make it to Abuja. I was most worried about Dorothy with this delay, but she seemed reasonably comfortable propped up in the front seat of the car with her pillows strategically positioned. So we waited patiently for about four hours for the other car to arrive.

We made it to Abuja about 8 p.m. (seven hours after we left Jos) and aimed for the Sheraton Hotel where the insurance company nurse was waiting for us to help her prepare for the trip. I was glad we had brought the wheelchair since our hotel room was as far as you could get away from the elevator to our room, and Dorothy would not have been able to walk that distance. The nurse from Holland was a terrific help and called for five good pillows from room service to prop Dorothy up in the bed, so she was reasonably comfortable for the night.

We got up at 4:30 a.m. Friday to get ready to go to the airport. Much to our surprise, at the airport we were taken to the first class lounge, which was quite nice. The airline had arranged for Dorothy and the nurse to fly in the first class section, and I was in the economy section. The nurse graciously offered his seat to me, so I was thrilled to be with Dorothy in the nice first class section for the entire flight. The seats reclined to a flat position, so Dorothy could find a comfortable reclined position. In London we were pleased they had a first class lounge which had drinks, snacks, a business center with newspapers and a nice bathroom, so we could get a shower and freshen up. I also managed to squeeze in a free, ten-minute massage! I figured there was no point in both of us being miserable!

Although our flight to the States was late leaving Heathrow Airport in London because of rainstorms, we had a good 7 ½-hour flight to Washington Dulles International Airport and arrived late Friday night. I pushed Dorothy in the wheelchair through Customs and Immigration, and after the big doors beyond the Customs desk opened, we were both thrilled to see Dorothy's parents waiting expectantly in the crowd. We thanked our nurse and headed for Annapolis.

Dorothy's sister, Sue, had arranged for the MRI scan to evaluate Dorothy's back on Saturday afternoon. Although it was quite painful for Dorothy to lie down flat in the machine, she toughed it out. It was obvious that she had a pronounced herniated disk at the third lumbar vertebra level (L3) with degenerative changes at L4 and L5. Dorothy jokingly asked the x-ray technician, "Is my pain all in my imagination?" The tech replied, "O No, sweetie!" We stopped at the surgeon's office to drop off the x-rays and get pain medication for Dorothy.

Dorothy found that the recliner chair at her parents' house was the most comfortable place for her, so she spent most of her time day and night in that chair. She had access to books, the phone and television so was okay for the time being. I went to church on Sunday, and her brother Bob and sister-in-law Ellen came over for a visit. A few other friends also came over to see her, but she was not in any shape to have too many "greeters."

On Monday afternoon we went to the neurosurgeon's office. Dr. Solomon was very kind to squeeze Dorothy into his schedule at the end of the day. It was quite late when he saw her, but after examining her and looking at the MRI, Dr. Solomon wanted to admit Dorothy into the hospital that evening and plan for surgery the next day at Johns Hopkins Hospital in Baltimore. Everything was all happening quite fast now that we had arrived in the United States. I was so thankful we had made the decision to leave. She could not stand straight or walk very far without extreme pain. I was even more grateful that Dorothy was in the hands of a well respected expert in his field.

We came back to the house and packed a small bag for her hospital stay. I planned to stay with her in the hospital room. We drove to the hospital in Baltimore, and she was admitted to her room about 9 p.m. After getting Dorothy settled, I hooked up the computer to the phone line, so I could use email and let folks know how things were going. I slept on a narrow, uncomfortable, stretcher-like cot next to her.

Both of us slept poorly with the constant interruptions of the staff checking to see if Dorothy was still alive! They were good about checking the neurological status of her legs, which was appropriate with her spinal cord problem. The anesthetist came to see her on Tuesday morning, June 7, and although he was a shy man, we pulled out of him that he had been to Kenya on a missions trip in the past. The Operating Room staff came with a stretcher at 10:30 a.m., and I went with her to the Operating Room waiting area. I prayed with her before she went in and then anxiously looked for a spot to wait and pray. Much to my surprise, in the waiting room were two women I knew from Dorothy's parents' church. The husband of one woman was also having surgery, and they were waiting for him. It was comforting to be with friends during this tense time. We had lunch together and expectantly waited for news of our loved ones.

Shortly after returning from lunch Dr. Solomon came out of the Operating Room to tell me the surgery had gone very well. The piece of disc they removed that was impinging on her spinal cord was so big he suggested we give it a name! He was pleased and expected her to have a good recovery. I was thrilled and quickly called our families with the exciting news. When I got into the recovery room to see Dorothy, she said she had not been nervous and remembers telling the anesthesiologist about her AIDS work in Africa before falling asleep. Never miss an opportunity! Amazingly she was also pain-free. The severe shooting pain down her leg was gone, and the feeling and strength in her toes had already improved.

She was brought back to her room about 30 minutes later and was looking even better. A few hours later she was able to get out of bed, and we took a short walk in the hallway in the evening. By the next morning she was doing so much better that after the neurosurgery resident came by to check on her, we called Dorothy's parents to come and pick us up.

For the next three weeks Dorothy began the slow process of recovering her strength and stamina. For a month she was not allowed to bend, lift or twist, so I still had to help her with a lot of activities. She began taking walks in the hallway of the condominium building and gradually built up, so she could take walks in the neighborhood with me. Her first visit with the neurosurgeon ten days after the surgery confirmed our feeling that she was doing fine and would continue to improve. A few weeks later Dorothy was doing so well that we drove to Pennsylvania to attend a women's conference in Hershey the weekend before I left for Nigeria. It was a great encouragement to her, and the Lord used the speaker, music, and fellowship to continue His work of healing in her heart.

About 2 ½-weeks after the surgery I returned to Nigeria, and by that time Dorothy was able to do almost everything on her own, including driving. Her parents went on a trip to Europe, so she moved in with friends for about two weeks before moving back to her parents' house. My trip back was fine except that on the flight to London our plane was struck by lightning before landing in Heathrow Airport. No damage was done, but our next plane had also been damaged by the lightning which caused a four-hour delay while they looked for a suitable aircraft to take us to Abuja. Never a dull moment!

Dorothy's last visit with the neurosurgeon was about a month after the surgery, and he agreed she had recovered enough to return to Nigeria. She called the insurance company to schedule her trip back to Jos. I was calling her and sending emails daily, so I knew how she was doing and she knew how we were coping in Jos.

Dorothy had planned to use the summer to read a number of books on suffering and trials and process all we had gone through as a family. When she began to have the back pain, it put her own processing on hold and even exacerbated the stress and emotional pain. So, although she had more time to read because she was on her back, the additional stress made it difficult to really work through the issues of our trauma as a family. The uncertainty about whether she would need surgery, the return trip to the States, and her physical agony piled on top of her residual stress from the first six months of the year.

After the back surgery Dorothy began again in earnest reading and praying to come to grips with the suffering and pain we had been through. We talked often about what we were thinking, and I realized we would arrive at that point of peace in our own way. It was helpful to talk about our struggles, but we individually wrestled with different aspects of the uncertainty. About ten days before she was to return, I noticed a big difference in the tone of her voice on our phone calls. I knew she had peace and had come to terms with God on all He had allowed us to go through. The sparkle was back in her voice, and I knew she was ready to face the stresses of family life and ministry in Nigeria again.

Throughout the trauma of the last six months, I had been receiving most of the attention because of my physical and emotional needs. Dorothy was in the provider and caretaker role, and it took a long time for her to let down her guard and acknowledge she also had some emotional and spiritual needs. She was about a month behind where I was emotionally when we returned to Nigeria in April.

Her trip back was pleasantly uneventful and the family reunion was fantastic. She brought back more gifts for the children, and there were lots of whoops and screams as we opened the boxes and passed out the gifts. During the next days there was a constant stream of visitors welcoming Dorothy back. They were thrilled she was better. Over and over our Nigerian friends expressed their amazement we had returned to Nigeria after all we had been through. We were pleased it made a statement about our calling to serve the Lord here and our commitment to help the Nigerian people.

It was great to sit at the dinner table as a family for the first time in months. We thanked the Lord for His healing and for His help through the trials we had faced this year. Each of the children fared well emotionally through the pain and separation, and we are grateful there was no evidence of emotional scars in their hearts from our ordeal.

We faced the future knowing suffering more intimately as we shared in "His suffering." We were heartened by the host of friends on both continents who loved us and cared for us. We were more committed than ever to God's calling in our lives to serve in Nigeria and believed each of our ministries was vitally important for the growth of the Kingdom of God. We believed that Satan would have had the victory had we not returned. We felt God had more work for us to do in Nigeria. Both of us were determined to move forward together trusting God with our family, our ministries, and our futures.

While strolling through a Christian bookstore in Fresno, California, a picture caught Dorothy's eye. It was a huge photograph of a lighthouse in a storm. The waves surrounding and engulfing the lighthouse were enormous and about to crash around the solid rock pillar. Casually standing outside the door of the lighthouse was a man who seemed oblivious to the impending tidal wave. The picture encapsulated our experience through the storms in our lives. God had been our fortress and shelter in the midst of potentially soul-sinking waves. I managed to find the picture as a poster, and it hung nicely framed in a prominent place in our living room as a constant reminder of God's protection and faithfulness through the storm.

When I was in the hospital in January 2005 after being shot, the children went to Miango for the children's program at the SIM Annual Conference. David learned the song "Be Strong and Courageous" from Joshua 1:9. He learned it so well he sang it constantly on the plane trip home with his sisters and Erin Rigsby. He then sang it several times a day for weeks after we were reunited as a family. Little did he know how powerfully the message of that song spoke to our hearts in the days after the trauma. The song verse was displayed beside the lighthouse picture as another reminder of God's promise to never leave us.

"Be strong and courageous.
Do not be terrified.
Do not be discouraged.
For the Lord **of** God is with you wherever you go."
Joshua 1:9 (Our son David's version)

PRO-LIFE EVANGEL

Within the first months of our arrival in Nigeria in 1992, I was appalled to hear a significant number of stories about women admitted to Evangel because of complications from abortions done in the community. Some came because of bleeding problems, but many were admitted with serious infections or perforations in their vagina, uterus, and intestines from botched abortion procedures. Several died and many were left unable to ever get pregnant again.

The family medicine residents reported that many women came to Evangel asking for an abortion because they trusted us to do a good job and not mess it up. We explained because we were a Christian hospital that believed in the sanctity of all human life, we did not do abortions. We then proceeded to try to convince the woman to keep her baby without being able to offer professional counseling, adoption services or assist her through her pregnancy. We had no idea what happened to these desperate women after they left the hospital. It seemed we were doing so little to help them, and in fact we were.

In spite of the fact that abortion is illegal in Nigeria, there are as many abortions performed in Nigeria per adult woman as in the United States where it is legal. Doctors in private clinics perform most of the abortions, but unfortunately many are done in awful conditions by midwives, nurses, community health workers and anyone else who wants to make some quick money. We were shocked in 2003 to learn that 26 percent of the girls in the ECWA church youth fellowships had been pregnant, and 22 percent had undergone an abortion procedure. These figures were alarming.

A biblical view of sex is often not taught in homes or churches, so young people learn from their peers which often results in a shameful pregnancy or a sexually transmitted disease like AIDS. Church leaders thought discussions about sex and pregnancy from the pulpit were inappropriate. Generally, Christians were embarrassed by their "wayward" daughters and knew no other option than abortion.

Being a general surgeon and not an obstetrician/gynecologist, this topic was out of my scope of practice and training but weighed heavily on my heart. In 2004 the Lord urged me to do something about this catastrophic problem, so I began looking into what it would take to begin a crisis pregnancy ministry in Jos. While we were in the States for a few weeks' holiday, I visited crisis pregnancy centers in Maryland and California. The first comment from one of the counselors in the center in Annapolis, Maryland, was "If you are starting a ministry like this, be prepared for an attack by Satan – this is his territory."

Upon our return to Jos at the end of the summer, I put out an email inquiry to the missionary community in Jos and was surprised at the terrific response I received from many who thought this was a wonderful and long overdue idea. I then asked a number of Nigerian staff at the hospital, and they also were excited at the potential of this ministry to women in crisis.

In October 2004, we had the inaugural meeting of the Pro-Life Evangel ministry to share our vision to make abortion a rare event in Jos by providing services to women in crisis pregnancies. Amazingly, 70 Nigerian hospital staff and seven missionaries attended the first meeting. We divided into six committees to begin working immediately to shape what this ministry would look like. We decided to be a primarily volunteer-driven ministry which would provide counseling for women in crisis pregnancies, help for those who wanted to keep their babies, adoption for those who could not, and education and awareness in local churches and the community about this important problem. These groups began to meet, and it became clear an immediate need was to have a workshop, so the ministry would have trained counselors for clients. Plans crystalized for the first workshop to be held at the hospital in February 2005. On January 3, 2005, when I was injured in an armed robbery and was evacuated to the United States for medical care, we wondered if this was the satanic attack about which we had been warned. The committees struggled with whether they should proceed with the training workshop or wait until my return. The missionaries thought the group should wait, but the Nigerian staff encouraged the group to press on in my absence – so they did.

The two-week workshop to train counselors and volunteers for the crisis pregnancy ministry was a resounding success. The hospital provided office space for the new counseling unit, and we began looking for a director and volunteer counselors. Although we began the ministry at Evangel in Jos, we anticipated it would grow to a national outreach because the needs were everywhere, and there were concerned Christians in every part of the country who would embrace this ministry to women and children in crisis.

As the Pro-Life Evangel ministry became known in the community over the next two years, many amazing things happened. We received generous gifts from abroad and locally, including a set of fetal models to show women the size of their babies, an ultrasound machine from a crisis pregnancy ministry in Dallas, Texas, knitted baby caps and sweaters from a church group in Michigan, videotapes to educate men and women regarding pregnancy and sexually transmitted diseases, baby supplies for new mothers who had chosen to keep their babies, and food for the mothers as they waited to deliver.

During this growth phase we set up an Advisory Board, hired a Director (Grace Dankyau), had our first baby cared for by missionary foster parents (Mike and Barbara Blyth), and our first baby adoption by a Christian couple who were childless and longing for a child to love. We became affiliated with a major pro-life organization in the States called Heartbeat International and sponsored the director Grace Dankyau to attend the Africa Cares for Life conference in Durban in September 2005. (It is a well-organized crisis pregnancy ministry in Southern Africa.)

As part of the media and marketing effort, we created two color pamphlets in English and Hausa. "What You Can Do Today That Will Change Tomorrow Forever" was about abortion and the ministry of Pro-Life. The second brochure addressed the basics of pregnancy, complete with pictures of embryos and fetuses at several stages of pregnancy. In Hausa it was called "Ina Da Ciki," which translates, "It is inside," an interesting euphemism for pregnancy. These were a great help increasing awareness about the various aspects of the ministry.

Justina Kuzasuwat, a chaplain at Evangel Hospital, had been instrumental in the beginning of the counseling and vocational rehabilitation programs in the vesicovaginal fistula ministry to women with childbirth related injuries. She developed a keen interest in the crisis pregnancy ministry as well and eventually was transferred to help as a counselor and then dorm parent for girls needing a safe place to stay during their pregnancy. She also began an aggressive outreach and education initiative to present the importance of abstinence in government schools, church youth groups, Girls Brigade units, church councils, university campus groups and Women's Fellowship conferences. These were wonderful opportunities to provide clear information about sexuality, the consequences of immorality, the horror of abortion and the hope offered by Pro-Life for women in crisis pregnancy situations. It helped educate pastors, youth leaders, parents, church leaders, and young people. Although there was little financial support in return from these outreaches, it was an important aspect of creating awareness about the ministry and provided a biblical perspective on abstinence and sexuality.

Another crucial development was the establishment of the transition house for girls who had nowhere to go during their pregnancy because their families had threatened or abandoned them. Most were not married and had no means of support. Justina and her husband Yusuf were the first dorm parents for the "Miriam House." She brought her vast experience in counseling and training in sewing and other vocational skills. Many girls came and went from the Miriam House over the ensuing years. On Wednesday, August 12, 2007, I was invited to the ceremony for a half dozen girls graduating from the crisis pregnancy house. They were ready to go back to their families and community after a period of time being counseled and discipled in the Miriam House after the delivery of their child. Each girl gave her testimony of how she had come to the House and how it had impacted her life. Holding her precious baby whose life had been spared death by abortion, one girl tearfully recounted how she had been thrown from her home and threatened by her father and how the ministry had helped her save her baby and rescued her from the threat of her father.

In 2007, the relationships between the staff in the Pro-Life office began to unravel, and the next two years were turbulent. The director went on maternity leave and later resigned, so it was unclear who was in charge. Eventually the hospital medical director took over. There were disagreements between the staff regarding accountability, and a few of the babies rescued from abortion died as newborns from either infection or ignorance of their mother.

The hospital was complaining about the ministry's failure to pay the bills of the clients. In spite of our best efforts to be clear that this was not "our" ministry but an Evangel Hospital ministry, we were perceived as the major funding source for the entire ministry. Funding became complicated and resulted in problems with the hospital management.

Despite the hospital and ministry's financial concerns, Pro-Life Evangel continued to rescue babies from certain death by abortion. Many challenging situations came up regularly with babies abandoned at the hospital, babies brought to the ministry who had been found on the street, babies born of HIV mothers, and, unfortunately, some who died from pneumonia and dehydration.

We also celebrated victories:

- A 25-year-old female student was referred for counseling because she wanted to terminate her 7-month-old pregnancy. She was counseled, gave her life to Christ, and decided to not get an abortion.
- Another 25-year-old woman was brought to the counseling office by a relative. She was confused and shocked after an ultrasound showed she was six months pregnant. She rededicated her life to Christ and decided to keep the pregnancy.
- A 27-year-old male student living in Abuja came for help because his 19-year-old girlfriend was pregnant. He was looking for a place to keep her because her parents wanted her to get an abortion. He was counseled and promised to bring his girlfriend to the Miriam House for the rest of her pregnancy.
- An HIV+ blind woman came into the office after being raped and was now eight months pregnant. She was counseled and decided to keep the baby. The staff gave her some food to help her and encouraged her to come back for help and follow-up.

Despite these encouraging victories, the financial situation of the crisis center was still complicated. While we were in the States, I received an email asking me for funds to support the ministry. I made it quite clear that I was not the sole fundraiser and had no plans to bail the Pro-Life hospital out of debt. When we returned to Nigeria, we were still met with the question, "Did you bring the money?"

The Advisory Committee and hospital management expected us to return with a large sum of money to pay for the entire debt to the hospital even though I had never promised that. This misunderstanding was never cleared up. The hospital maintained the position I had started a ministry that was expensive and expected them to take it over without their initial commitment and blessing. To their credit the hospital had paid the staff salaries, but there was much more to the ministry, including the outreach events, hospital expenses and caring for the girls at the Miriam House.

Because of many problems, we eventually closed the Miriam House and never opened the transition house on the compound because of the uncertainty of the hospital's commitment to the ministry and the lack of funds. I had intentionally weaned my financial support of Pro-Life to help the Advisory Committee and hospital management understand the need to raise funds from other sources, but this never happened.

When we left Nigeria in the summer of 2012, I was encouraged by the faithful commitment of the Director and volunteers in the ministry. Every month they reported 10 to 15 women who had either accepted Christ as their Savior or rededicated their lives to follow Christ. Although the vast majority of women kept their babies or their families took them, we continued to have babies given over for adoption. There was a group of three or four missionary families who served as foster parents. Since Plateau State did not allow foreign adoptions, and foster parents were not eligible to adopt, missionary families were perfect foster parents. We also had a list of couples wanting to adopt. We had an organized screening process for couples wanting to adopt, including a home visit, extensive interviews, and references. It was incredible to see the radiant joy in the faces of a childless couple when their child was given to them for the first time at the ceremony. It made it all worthwhile.

Another amazing encouragement was the support of teams of Christians from churches in the United States who came to the ministry to help with counseling, spend time with the girls in the

Miriam House, and bring donated clothes and supplies for the ministry. Support also began to grow from Nigerian churches, Women's Fellowship groups, and youth fellowships. We had visitors from around the country asking about the crisis pregnancy outreach, including other churches, missionaries, and church leaders. The ministry was unique in northern Nigeria, and we hoped it would serve as a model for other organizations to launch their own ministries to women in crisis pregnancies.

LESSONS IN EDUCATION

I n the early 2000s ECWA began an initiative to open a Christian university called Bingham University as an alternative to the government universities in Nigeria. They had been plagued with strikes, which had paralyzed the educational mission and prolonged the course work. The universities have been fortresses of occultist tribal practices making them a hostile and unsafe environment for Christians. In addition, the overriding religious and indigenous bias of each university makes it almost impossible for Christians to gain entrance into universities in the north of Nigeria and for nonindigenous students to gain admission in states outside their home region.

The goal of the ECWA leadership was to establish a university with a Christian worldview, free of tribal and regional bias, where the staff and students would not go on strike and non-Christian practices would not be tolerated. This was a long overdue, good idea.

ECWA began building a large university campus on donated property near Abuja, erecting the buildings and infrastructure for the undergraduate programs, and then seeking accreditation. In their initial charter, the university was asked by the Nigerian Graduate Medical Council to start with a medical school. The basic science classes were offered on the campus in Abuja, but the dream was to build a teaching hospital on the campus in Abuja, so they could also offer the higher level classes on campus as well.

When it became apparent that the hospital was financially impossible, the administrators started looking for a location where the upper level medical students could do their clinical rotations. They approached several government hospitals, but they were expensive, unaffordable options. After unsuccessfully pursuing a number of government teaching hospitals for the Bingham medical students, the administrators set their eyes on Evangel Hospital with the intent on taking it over as the teaching hospital for the Bingham University Medical School.

I had a meeting with a retired SIM missionary Jim Kraakevik in 2005. He was a professor of physics at Wheaton College in Illinois before coming to Nigeria in the 1960s to teach in the SIM Bible schools. He was a brilliant educator and was well liked in the mission and Nigerian church community during his tenure in Nigeria. It was because of this respect and his impressive track record as an educator that the ECWA leadership solicited his review of the proposed graduate medical school, the curriculum, and overall plans of Bingham University. Jim showed me a photocopy of the Bingham University medical school curriculum, which was essentially a copy of the University of Jos medical school courses.

In late November 2008 an executive from Bingham University came to Evangel to discuss the proposal to use Evangel as the teaching hospital for the medical school. Questions were raised about whether Evangel would be the permanent site, the nature of the relationship between the University and Evangel, the role of Family Medicine in the medical school curriculum, and our concern about the goals of the university.

Because the Bingham administrators were based in Abuja, we had little communication with them over the coming months. During the summer of 2009, all the SIM missionaries were away. In mid-July 2009 while on furlough on our trip across the United States visiting our supporting churches and family, we received the following news, "ECWA Executive and Bingham University Council today agreed that ECWA Evangel Hospital should be taken over by Bingham University to become Bingham University Teaching Hospital."

The hospital would no longer be considered within the medical department of ECWA but become directly accountable to the University. This had obvious implications in terms of communication between Bingham University, the hospital administration and the physicians, accountability to the ECWA medical superintendent, and the relationship of the hospital with the other medical institutions in ECWA. The new chairman of the hospital board was Dr. Daniel Iya, a close friend and supporter of the "missional" goals of the hospital. Unfortunately, when he was asked by the ECWA Executive to appoint a medical director who was not recommended by the hospital board, Dr. Iya resigned. The ECWA Executive promptly appointed a new board chairman and their choice for medical director.

Upon our return to Nigeria from our furlough in July 2010, we noticed a number of changes in the hospital and administration. Equipment and buildings had been put in place to satisfy the needs of the medical school for accreditation but which had little utility to the hospital. Part-time medical school faculty members were hired for pediatrics, obstetrics, and internal medicine. The family medicine physicians who had been competent and committed teachers, clinicians, and mentors in these disciplines were re-assigned to the outpatient department. The family medicine physicians were demoralized as a result of this decision and some left Evangel. Although I was offered additional part-time surgical faculty, I maintained we were adequately staffed and did not need more faculty. I was also asked to be the Chairman of the Department of Surgery but declined.

By March 2011 there had been no obvious compromise or discussions with the Bingham University leadership regarding the concerns expressed by the SIM missionaries working at the hospital.

The SIM Director and I met with the ECWA Executive to outline our concerns about the changed direction of the hospital, the poor communication with the Bingham leadership, the shameful way the Nigerian Family Medicine consultants were being treated, and our hesitation to provide additional SIM personnel support. The ECWA Executive gave us an audience, but there was little assurance change would be forthcoming.

Another sign of the change in focus of the hospital was the directive by the hospital administration to eliminate support for the Pro-Life crisis pregnancy ministry in the hospital. Support for this ministry would probably not continue because the Bingham leadership had told them that resources must be directed to clinical activities that would be income-generating. Against the advice of the hospital board, the medical director made a commitment to the Pro-Life Advisory Committee of continued support.

Bingham University medical students arrived in April 2011 and settled into several buildings renovated as dorms and classrooms. They began showing up in the hospital for their clinical duties, and the hospital faculty were asked to give lectures. The Nigerian family medicine physician in charge of the residency program offered to help with lectures but was told in no uncertain terms he did not have the qualifications to lecture to the medical students! When the students rotated on surgery, we were given no curriculum or expectations for evaluating them.

Over the next six months, the situation in the hospital continued to deteriorate. Some of this was because of the declining number of patients after the terrorist activities in Jos and the restricting of Muslims to travel to the Christian areas of the city. The lack of diesel fuel to run the generators caused frequent power outages, even in the middle of medical emergencies. There were increasing incidences of shortages of medications, x-ray films, and lab supplies. The roads and buildings on the compound were not maintained and became more neglected. Trash that was to be incinerated because it was medical waste piled up in front of the incinerator building and was visited by dogs and vermin. Payment of salaries for the staff became more and more delayed.

By February 2012 the situation at the hospital had become so dire that the ECWA Executive formed a committee of committed community Christian leaders to review the overall management of the hospital. The committee interviewed about 25 key figures in the community and hospital, including the ECWA and SIM leadership. Meeting almost weekly for three months, the recommendations from the review committee were incisive in delineating the problems that led to the current state and solutions for recovery, including redefining the hospital relationship with the university and medical school.

On the positive side, once the medical students arrived on the Evangel compound, I enjoyed giving lectures and supervising their activities in the hospital. They were young and impressionable, knowing little of the political storm that had been brewing about their education.

Another unintended consequence of the diaspora of Evangel doctors was that the Family Medicine physicians who left Evangel became actively engaged in other exciting venues of ministry. Dr. Joshua Sule began his own Christian clinic with a stated goal of reproducing the "old Evangel" as a lighthouse to care for the poor, a place of witness and provide excellent medical care to the community. Dr. Aboiyar is an ENT surgeon at a sister hospital in Jos and has a huge referral practice in the community. Dr. Gidado is the medical director at the state government hospital and is having an enormous impact on the quality of care and serves as a godly role model for the Family Medicine residents at Plateau Specialist Hospital. Dr. Ahmed is the medical director at the local government hospital in Keffi and again is in a key position of leadership in his community. The men and women trained as Christlike leaders at Evangel continue to have an impact throughout Nigeria. When we left Nigeria, there were only two SIM physicians still involved in the clinical activities of the hospital and giving lectures to the medical students.

In summary, I was extremely concerned that the reputation of the hospital, church, SIM and Christ were at stake with the poor planning process and philosophy behind converting Evangel Hospital to the Bingham University Teaching Hospital. Men who had a different vision for the hospital were dissembling the original vision of Evangel. Knowing the history of Evangel and having invested 20 years of my life in ministry serving all who came, letting go of the hospital ministry was emotionally draining and spiritually challenging as I watched the University plan unfold. Dorothy often reminded me, "This is their hospital and their university, not ours, so let them do with it as they will. They are the ones who will be accountable for its failure or success, not us."

This painful chapter in my life changed me as I learned to trust in God's sovereign plan as He builds His church, not mine! It will be interesting to see God working out His purposes for building His church in Nigeria and the unfolding narrative of the medical ministries.

ROOTS

The current violence in Nigeria can be viewed as community level criminal activity and as another theater where
global religious and cultural battles are being waged. The
increased access to modern weapons has fueled both dramas and
produced unspeakable carnage in the country. Nigeria was ranked
14th in the Fragile States Index 2015 survey by the Fund for Peace in
its evaluation of failing states.

When we arrived in Nigeria in 1992, the biggest security threats
were petty thievery from neighborhood boys or the occasional thief
who wandered onto the compound. The robbers were unarmed
and appeared to act alone at night. We made certain our outside
doors had good bolt locks and the window bars were secure, and
we employed watchmen armed with bows and arrows to patrol the
compound at night and on weekends. We were not afraid to walk
around the compound at night, and the children often played capture the flag and other night games.

In the southern part of Nigeria there had been reports for years
of armed robber attacks along major roads. Weapons were more
available in the Southeast because of the insurrection by tribal
groups waging war against the government over oil money. In the
Southwest we knew there was more crime, including armed robberies, in the big cities like Lagos. Over the next decade, weapons

began to move north, and we saw the crime wave of armed robberies move north along the major roads coming from the south.

The strategy of the robbers was to have three groups positioned along the target zone. The middle group would step onto the road in front of a target vehicle. If the vehicle tried to back up to get away, the first group would attack. If the vehicle tried to speed up, the last group would attack. The usual operation was to steal phones, laptops, cash, and other valuables and not harm the civilians. Often large luxury buses were stopped, and the entire group was fleeced. Those who tried to flee the scene were mowed down with machine guns. This began the era of dangerous traveling, not just from reckless and speeding drivers but also from roaming groups of armed robbers. Some of the attackers were from Chad, and when they were being pursued, they fled into the deep bush or across the border to Chad.

Missionary Bob Wandersee got caught in an armed robbery along the road on August 7, 1998, and died as he lay alongside the road from a gunshot wound to his upper arm and chest. This created great concern in the missionary community, and we became more concerned about traveling outside Jos, especially to the capital Abuja. We avoided traveling at night, early in the morning, or at dusk because of the fear of being attacked.

The Nigerian army launched several campaigns to catch these robber gangs but had little success. One approach the army and police used was to set up checkpoints along the most dangerous positions of the road. Although this helped deter the robberies along that stretch of the road, it also set up a series of extortion points when every driver was hassled for a bribe in order to pass the police or army checkpoint. There was controversy in the mission community whether it was morally acceptable to pay them or if that would ruin the witness of the missionary community. Some missionaries offered water, bread, Christian tracts, and other gifts to build good will with these government workers for their service to protect the citizens of the country.

Eventually the guns made their way into the gangs in the cities in the North, and they became a part of the robberies in the Jos community. Many Nigerians were attacked, and eventually missionary compounds were also targets because of the perception that the white people were wealthy and had lots of cash and valuables. My first encounter with violence was in April 2004, when I was a victim of a robbery at the Baptist Guesthouse. Fortunately, no one in the Guesthouse or in our group was harmed except for a friend being hit with a stick while we lay on the ground. Incidents like this increased with an escalation of accompanying violence. Some Nigerian guards were killed, missionaries were physically attacked, and one missionary woman was raped during a robbery. This resulted in another ratcheting up of our security measures with stricter protocols for the guards screening guests coming into the missionary compounds, stronger and higher gates and walls, lights and security cameras, a reduction in nighttime activities, and an increased sense of fear and insecurity at night.

Then on January 3, 2005, we experienced an invasion of the Evangel Hospital compound, and I became a victim of the increasing gun violence in Nigeria. As a result of that armed robbery, the Mission raised the height of our cement block compound wall, added razor wire on top, installed a ten-foot-tall steel security gate with guards, improved the security lighting on our end of the compound, hired more guards to patrol at night, and secured a dog to serve as our early warning system.

This ready access to weapons, explosives, and technology like cell phones also fueled the larger conflict between the major tribes and religious groups in Nigeria. The tribal and religious conflict in northern Nigeria has its roots in events centuries ago. The thousands of tribes throughout West Africa were largely animist. There were fierce tribal rivalries and territory disputes for centuries. Outside geopolitical influence began with the advent of the Muslim crusades from the North in the eighteenth century and the Christian missionaries from Europe and North America colonization along the coastal ports in the late 1800s. These two religious movements were in a grand chess match over the West African territories prior to the colonial powers slicing the land somewhat arbitrarily into countries. Unfortunately, the region was partitioned with north to south borders, so each nation had northern Muslim influenced tribes and southern Christian influenced tribes. In Nigeria these met in the Middle Belt state of Plateau, and Jos was the epicenter of the conflict zone. The British were so concerned about the fragility of the country that they initially forbade the Christian missionaries from entering the North to evangelize for fear of a religious war. It was not until the missionary societies gained permission from London that they were allowed to enter the North and then only to work in clinics to treat leprosy patients. The other strategy of the British was to use the existing tribal leaders to govern the territories. They empowered the chiefs to enact the wishes of the crown, thus maintaining the status quo among the tribes. During the transition of independence from Britain in 1960, the British turned over leadership of the military to the northern Muslims whose influence in the military has been visible ever since.

Because of the geographic polarization based on religion, the tribes in those areas were also associated with either Islam or Christianity. In Nigeria it is generally believed that if you are not a Muslim, then you are a Christian. It is a cultural designation more than a comment on your personal beliefs. This sweeping assumption stands today even though on an individual or village level it may not be the case. For example, if you were Berom by tribe, you were a "Christian," while Hausas are considered "Muslims." The background historically of animism tainted both, so "folk Islam" and syncretistic Christianity were common.

Plateau State became a melting or boiling pot for the conflict between the Christian tribes, the Muslim tribes, and the animists. In Plateau State there are three indigenous tribes who consider themselves the original inhabitants and owners of the land. These tribes were receptive to the early Christian missionaries and, although animism is still a religious force in the community, these tribes are now considered Christianized. Muslim Hausas immigrated to Plateau State centuries ago from northern Nigeria. During the days of British colonialism, the Hausas were also invited to help with the tin mining operations in Plateau State. Now there are several generations of Hausas in the state who call it their home. This claim has been a foundational tenet in the current tribal conflict. In many Muslim families there are four wives with each husband, so they have large families, and their numbers increase rapidly allowing them to become a major political force in the region.

An additional tribal element was the presence of the southern tribes like Igbos from the Southeast and the Yorubas from the Southwest who also settled in Plateau State. Generally political alliances were along religious lines, not tribal identity. Most of the Igbos who had immigrated to the North from eastern Nigeria fled during the Biafran Civil War in the 1960s. Since then thousands have returned and set up homes and thriving businesses throughout the Middle Belt and the North. They are considered a Christian tribe aligned with the Plateau indigenous tribes. Most Yorubas are Christians, but there is a sizeable Muslim population among the Yorubas.

There are both moderate (Darika) and radical (Shi'ite and Isala) sects of Islam in Jos. Occasionally there are disagreements between them and violence erupts. In recent years, the Hausa Muslims in Plateau attacked and killed many of the Yoruba Muslims because they thought the Yorubas had revealed their "secrets" to the Plateau indigenes. Since that attack of one Muslim group against another, the Plateau Yoruba Muslims have surprisingly sided with the Plateau Christian indigenous tribes rather than the Hausas. The Hausa call these people "mainfika" which means *untrustworthy*.

This conflict has also had serious political fallout. Depending on who is in power at the national level, Plateau State has had a strained relationship with the federal government. This has impacted funding to the state, implementation of the army in times of unrest and violence, and initiatives by the federal government to assist with the tribal and religious conflict in Jos. The Governor of Plateau State has historically been a Christian who understands the religious and political battle in Jos. Because they are not indigenes, northern Muslims who have immigrated to Jos have felt politically impotent. The Governor has made a number of political decisions to decrease the influence of Muslims in the state and protect the Christian communities.

An ongoing issue throughout northern Nigeria has been the persecution of Christians and destruction of churches by Muslims. Regularly churches are burned, pastors and their families slaughtered, and university students killed for taking a stand as Christians in Muslim-dominated schools. Many of the surviving Christians flee to Jos, and often the victims of the violence end up at Evangel Hospital for treatment. Because the government authorities and army are often influenced by Muslims, Christians were often left unprotected and repeatedly harassed and persecuted.

The most disturbing and unsettling development in Nigeria in this decade is the rise of the radical Taliban-style Muslim faction called Boko Haram. The group leader wants to take his people back to a more pure Islam, rejecting Western education, government, and authority. He has embarked on a campaign based on oppression and violence including the introduction of suicide and car bombers, devastating use of explosives and unimaginable atrocities against men, women, and children. His targets are the Nigerian government, including the police, army, schools and government offices as well as Western and Christian institutions and organizations.

The actors (groups aligned by tribe and religion) are in place at any opportunity for a violent drama with the indigenous Christian tribal groups pitted against the northern Muslim tribes. The churches and mosques are used for political propaganda and campaigning with the pastors and imams stirring up hatred of the opposition and calling their groups to arms.

The spotlight for this drama is focused on the stage of the city of Jos. It is a key city and Plateau a critical state in the battle for Nigeria. Plateau is a stronghold of Christianity in the North, and if it falls to Islam, other states will follow. The indigenes know this and have seen what has happened in the northern states now under Sharia law. There is religious oppression of Christians, oppression of women, economic poverty, and a culture of violence. The Christians have vowed to fight till the death to prevent this from happening. Many of the disturbances were incited by political rallies and elections or government actions like raising the price of petrol. Because the Evangel Hospital compound surrounded a polo field that was used for Christian crusades, political rallies and trade fairs, trouble often started just over the wall of our compound. Consequently, we were directly impacted by the street violence when injured civilians were brought to the hospital for treatment and the predictable invasion of the police and army to quiet the crowds and shut down the neighborhood.

This battle for souls has been going on for a long time, and the end is not in sight. Both sides are fighting for survival, both sides are using violent methods, and the infusion of radical suicide bomber ideology has irreversibly changed the formula causing widespread destruction of human lives and property. There is no easy solution. In spite of reconciliation efforts initiated by factions from each side, the majority on each side of the religious divide is unwilling to compromise toward a peaceful resolution. We continue to pray for a miracle and "the peace of Jos."

IT'S TIME TO GO

The Jos North local government where we lived was a politically contentious area because of the long-standing rivalry between the Muslims and Christians. Even though it was where most of the Muslims lived, there was still a 2:1 majority of registered Christian voters. Consequently, the Christians always won the elections and the Muslims responded with violence and riots. On Thursday, November 27, 2008, an election to select the local government officials was scheduled. Anticipating violence, the governor called for military personnel to monitor the city and restrict all motor vehicle travel. We were confined to our compound and did not hear any gunshots or violence the whole day.

At 1:30 the next morning, however, Dorothy and I were jolted awake by the sounds of cheering and yelling coming from the market near the hospital. These were not the cheers of a football match victory or the policemen marching exercises. Simultaneously we realized it was a reaction to the election and we started to get nervous.

The Muslim political party understood they had won the election but heard the governing Christian party was manipulating the results. This sparked their anger and the demonstrations began. By 6 a.m. we heard chants and gunshots from both our neighborhood and downtown near the mosque. Then I noticed a huge pillar of smoke from a building near the main mosque. Because of the gunfire, by 6:45 a.m. we decided we would not send the children to school and called around to make sure everyone on the compound had operational walkie-talkie radios. Dorothy called Hillcrest and asked the principal to find a substitute teacher for her third grade class.

I went to work at the hospital at 7:45 a.m. and decided to drive in case I needed to leave in a hurry. When I got to the Operating Room, the staff were already taking care of half a dozen wounded who had been brought to the hospital. Over the next few hours more and more wounded arrived until we had treated about 25 people. One man had a forearm fracture from a machete, another had a fractured kneecap from a gunshot wound, one man had a badly crushed ankle fracture, and many had small pellet wounds from homemade shotguns. Because we did not have time to get involved in any major surgery, we sutured the lacerations after cleaning them but then only splinted the bone fractures. We cancelled all the elective cases for the day, not certain what lay ahead in terms of the trauma burden.

When I went to the Emergency Room, the scene was chaos. All the beds had injured patients, but the staff could hardly move because of all the concerned visitors and friends who had piled in. I asked one of the family practice residents to get things under control while I checked out other areas of the hospital. There was pandemonium at the front gate as well. The two guards at the front gate were having a great deal of trouble controlling the people forcing their way through the gate. Finally they managed to get enough control to only let in the injured. A large, loud crowd gathered on the street outside the front gate. As people came from downtown with news of what was happening, people began yelling and running in panic back and forth along the road raising the level of anxiety of everyone. Someone started burning tires right in front of the hospital as part of the protest.

The most frightening sight was the growing number of huge plumes of dark smoke from buildings around the city that were being burned. The roving mobs heard the Muslims had lost the election, so they marched to the main mosque and began burning buildings in that area. The angry crowd then burned another market, lumberyard, and huge grain market to the ground. Eventually there was a wall of smoke and huge billows of flames along the horizon from buildings that had been torched. Some of the smoke columns were so dark and fierce they looked like fuel depots on fire.

Along the Zaria Road, the Christian mob burned all the cars in the used car lots owned by the Muslim Alhajis because they believed these rich Alhajis had financed earlier riots. In another part of Jos the Muslims attacked and burned churches, killing several pastors. The pastor of ECWA Tudan Wada got out his gun and began firing at the mob and turned them away. When the Muslims in Tudan Wada area burned several churches, the Christian mob mobilized. They burned to the ground all the houses in the Muslim section of Tudan Wada. The Muslims managed to get some of their women and children into buses to move them out of the area. On their way out a Christian mob stopped the buses and dragged the women and children out and beat them.

There was at least one amazing event that day. Some of the Christians and Muslims who had been in the reconciliation programs after the 2001 riots agreed to not participate in the fighting and not attack each other's neighborhoods. At the Transition House (TH) where the Gidan Bege boys lived, people in the community trusted them so much they brought their valuables to the boys to keep through the crisis! These boys who had been the worst thieves on the streets were now being trusted with people's valuables! When the fighting started, some of the TH boys went out and brought injured Muslims into the compound and began to care for them, and amazingly none of the boys went out to join in the fighting. In the past they would have been part of the mob destroying Christian homes and churches.

At the hospital I kept going back and forth between the Emergency Room and the Operating Room trying to help them make decisions about patient injuries and helping them keep better order. By 11 a.m. I thought things had settled down and seemed more under control. If the situation deteriorated, however, I wanted to be sure the back gate of the compound could be opened in case we needed to leave in a hurry. After about 30 minutes, we finally found the keys for the back gate. When I began that discussion over the walkie-talkie radios, Dorothy helped the kids pack their "flee bags" knowing evacuation was a real possibility.

At 11:30 a.m., the situation at the front gate began to deteriorate. When an armored police truck came flying by the hospital, the crowd of armed youth fled to the side streets until it passed, and then they followed it to the Gada Biyu area. The Muslim mob apparently had moved, so the Christian vigilantes were in pursuit. A few minutes later army vehicles brought wounded to the hospital, and the front gate crowd again went into a panic. The two security men struggled to keep the pushing crowds out. It seemed only a matter of time before they lost control of the gate and the mob would rush onto the compound, including "bad" folk coming in to cause more trouble. As I watched the boys with sticks and clubs on the street moving around like a swarm of bees ducking in and out of the side streets, the panic rising in the front gate crowds, the resurgence of new casualties brought in every few minutes, the growing number of buildings going up in smoke and the volatility of the situation, I decided it was time for us to leave the compound.

I called the missionary men on the walkie-talkie and asked them to come to the front gate to see what I was seeing. They came, fortunately with Paul Chaga, our Nigerian security consultant and friend. Standing on the front steps of the hospital they could see the smoke from the burning buildings all around town, the panic of the crowd at the front gate, and the inability of the guards to control the situation. They agreed it was time to go. I called the houses where our families were anxiously waiting and told them we had decided to evacuate. After packing their flee bags, we would meet in our vehicles at the back gate. Mike Blyth called the SIM Niger Creek compound on the 2-meter radio and told them we were on our way. I then told the O.R. Nurse Supervisor Simon Khantiok and Dr. Chima, the Medical Director, we were leaving because of concern for the safety of our families.

At the house my family was sitting quietly in the living room surrounded by their bags. They had a change of clothes for four days, and Dorothy had packed our important documents, passports, a few pictures, medicines, and toiletries. I was amazed, but I should not have been, knowing how many times we have gone through this drill. I packed the car, turned off the water heaters, fed the rabbit and dog, and then locked the house and gate to our yard. We met the other missionaries at the back gate of the compound.

When we pulled out with Rick Naatz in the lead van and our Toyota van in the rear, it was amazing how much it was like the time we left the ELWA compound Liberia in 1990. The area was deserted of people except for the makeshift checkpoints set up across the road constructed with benches, wood, and rocks by Christian vigilante young men. They were armed with rocks, sticks, and pipes and approached our caravan shouting and waving their weapons as they carefully checked every vehicle trying to get past their checkpoint. They were spaced about 200 yards apart from the Evangel gate to the police barracks near the prison a mile or so away.

We also noticed lots of people lined along the walls of their houses anxiously watching the deserted road. All cars, trucks, and buses had been pulled over to the roadside, so there was no traffic except for our four vehicles. We slowed at each checkpoint and did not have trouble getting through except for one checkpoint when Rick slowed down and his van stalled. As he was trying to get started, a man approached his vehicle with a large rock in his hands. Rick got going in time just before the rock thrower, who was aiming for the windshield, let loose. We were thankful there was no other trouble. At the Hillstation junction a mile and a half up the road the checkpoints stopped, the crowds thinned out, and the road was deserted. Shortly after that we turned into the Niger Creek compound in the Tudan Wada area where several missionary friends met us and gave us our house assignments.

Along with the other Evangel men, I went to the SIM Director Phil Tait's house, and we debriefed him and Bill Foute, the Deputy SIM Director, about what had happened during the morning that prompted us to leave. We heard how widespread the unrest was around Jos and the number of buildings and churches burned and people killed including a pastor. Christians had burned a Tudan Wada mosque. There was lots of damage in Tudan Wada, so about 70 Nigerians came to another SIM compound called Apollo Crescent looking for refuge. During the afternoon we continued to hear more tragic news from around town. I felt affirmed we had made the right decision to get out of harm's way at Evangel and leave to a safer area.

The next day, Saturday, November 29, we awoke to random gunshots in the Niger Creek neighborhood. Over the next two hours the sounds of gunfire continued but seemed to move downtown. Later there were a lot of sirens that seemed to be going to the Evangel area and on downtown followed by sounds of mortars or big guns.

Around 10 a.m. we heard the governor had enforced a 24-hour curfew with no travel allowed. Our decision was made – we were not allowed to travel, even to go and look around the Evangel area. There was a compound security meeting at 12:30 p.m. at Niger Creek for an update. The mission leaders asked who was interested in going to Abuja with the U.S. embassy escort vehicle on Sunday morning. We knew that the Tudan Wada area around Niger Creek still had violence, and there was ongoing confusion about the curfew restrictions. The SIM security team thought it was okay for us to go back to Evangel in the afternoon.

At 1 p.m., Don Sampson, Chris Lemanski, Rick Naatz, and I drove back to Evangel. There was very little traffic and no checkpoints, but army and police vehicles and personnel were everywhere along the road. There were four burned motorcycles in the road and several stores at the polo field roundabout were burned. The streets were very quiet with only a scattered few pedestrians. We dropped off Chris Lemanski and Rick Naatz at their houses, and Don Sampson and I went to the hospital to see how the patients and staff were doing.

Dr. Chima, the Medical Director, said they had treated around 200 from the riots and five dead bodies were brought in. We did rounds and found two men with gunshot wounds in the ICU. One was shot in the abdomen and needed surgery urgently. In the Private Ward was a man with a left shoulder shotgun wound who had a large hematoma swelling, but we decided to wait on him. The wounded filled the hospital.

The rest of the missionaries drove back to the Niger Creek compound. After the surgery on the man shot in the abdomen, I quickly drove back to Niger Creek. It was quiet again on the way back, and I got back just at the 6 p.m. curfew. Dorothy did not re-lax until I was back with the family. Minutes after I pulled in, Jay Tolar heard gunshots outside the SIM Apollo Crescent compound gate. Apparently an army truck was driving by and a civilian car passed them. Because it was two minutes after the curfew, the army men shot up the car. No one was injured, but I am glad I was in the gate at 6 p.m. sharp! The family was glad I was back and we headed for the potluck supper. It was a quiet evening, and I slept better.

On Sunday morning, we again woke early to the sounds of ran-dom gunfire. Those sounds settled down and it was a quiet morn-ing. We also heard rumors that the Muslims had targeted several of the large churches for attacks during the morning worship services. We were all still on high alert. Some families in our group decided to take the offer to go to Abuja, which was out of the danger zone. Hillcrest School administration made the decision to evacuate all the kids in the hostel to Abuja in a bus and travel with about 11 other vehicles.

We had a meeting of the Evangel missionaries after lunch and decided we would all go back to the compound. The kids were disappointed because they were having so much fun with the SIM hostel kids, but we did not believe this was enough reason to stay. Around 4 p.m. we left and were pleased the road was quiet with no checkpoints and less military presence than before. After we got back to our house, David wanted to go out and play. You know you are on the mission field when your mother replies, "That's fine, David, but if you hear gunshots, please come inside!" In the evening to lighten the mood in the house, we put up our Christmas tree and decorations and enjoyed Christmas music and hot cider.

Although school was closed, we carried on with our normal hospital activities until Wednesday when we met with two missionaries on the SIM security team at 12:30 p.m. They had been receiving a lot of "intel" that reprisal attacks were being planned, and the SIM Pharmacy, Challenge, and Evangel compounds were in high-risk areas. They asked us to go to the safer area of Miango either Wednesday afternoon or Thursday morning. Each couple had a short meeting, and we decided to go at 4 p.m. that afternoon with the Naatzes and Sampsons. The Mitchells, Lemanskis, and Blyths would follow on Thursday morning.

We came back to the house and told the kids we had been asked to go to Miango for safety reasons. Marie was upset because she had wanted to go to Kagoro with the SIM hostel kids to spend time with her boyfriend Dwight and his family. Later she heard the SIM hostel kids were going to Miango also and all was well! I went to the hospital in the afternoon before leaving and told Dr. Chima and Simon, the OR Nurse Supervisor, that we had been asked to leave because of the risk for our families and they understood. We packed the car again and left around 4 p.m.

We took the long way to Miango through Vom because it avoided the hotpots of Gada Biyu. There was a major army checkpoint in Bukuru and then another at the Vom road turnoff. At the Vom checkpoint the army officer asked if we were afraid. Surprisingly, he said we should not be fearful and let us through. Otherwise, there were no problems and we got there in 1 ½ hours, just in time for supper.

By Friday, we heard life in Jos was quieter with no new rumors of attacks. There was even less of a military presence and the markets were getting back to normal. In spite of the apparent normalcy, several hospital staff cautioned me to stay in Miango because of the potential danger. Dorothy expressed her anxiety over the situation, and how she had been thinking about going to the United States for Christmas. She was discouraged at how poorly she was coping with the stress.

The Police Commissioner for Jos was replaced twice during the crisis, and the new one was a Muslim. The Commander of the army barracks near Jos was also a Muslim. This was worrisome, especially since we heard the Muslims were apparently still planning reprisal attacks. We were cautioned to stay on alert through the Christmas season because there might be attacks during the Christian holiday. We were advised to be ready at a moment's notice to leave in the event of more trouble. We had our flee bags ready and our evacuation list handy, but we kept praying that it would not happen.

Apparently on Sunday the Muslim Mullahs had a "Curse Walk" around Jos saying something bad was going to happen to the city because of what happened this time. "About a thousand lives were lost while property worth about billions of naira were destroyed in the mayhem." (Guardian 5 Dec 2008) More importantly, the Muslims lost the election and they threatened revenge. I have heard of Christian "Prayer Walks" around a city to pray for repentance and conversions, but this was my first time hearing of a "Curse Walk."

We are grateful no missionaries were victims of the unrest in Jos. We mourned with our Nigerian colleagues who lost loved ones during this skirmish. The mission leadership and missionary families learned a great deal through the evacuation. Communication improved, policies were refined, and prayer increased. With civil unrest from the elections, uncertainty and anxiety about reprisal attacks and kidnapping of a missionary, it was clear things had changed, and the security environment in Nigeria had deteriorated to a new low demanding more vigilance, caution regarding travel, more robust perimeter security for our compounds and houses, and a plea for God's protection to continue our efforts to be His witnesses to the nations. Little did we know that worse things lay ahead.

Jos gradually returned to a new normal with everyone more sensitive to loud sounds, groups of people running, or rumors of trouble. Dorothy's indicator of normalcy was when the women who sweep the edges of the streets resumed their work. Activities at Hillcrest also resumed, including nighttime programs. By the spring of 2009, we were preparing for our one-year furlough, so our focus turned to planning for our U.S. travels, housing, work and family matters.

When we went to the U.S. in the summer of 2009, we certainly were ready for a break from the stress, looked forward to helping Heather and Anna begin their college search, and spend much needed time with Marie who was starting college in Los Angeles. After traversing the U.S. visiting our supporting churches, we settled in San Diego where I worked at the Veterans Hospital and Dorothy found substitute teaching jobs in the community public schools. Heather and Anna toured colleges they were interested in and re-established friendships from their last time in the States. David took up trampoline and gained a few friends in the church youth group. We enjoyed spending quality time with family and made preparations for our last term in Nigeria.

On August 11, 2009, Dorothy read a disturbing note on the social media site Facebook from the son of a missionary in Nigeria whose physician father had just been shot in the arm during an armed robbery and kidnapped from their mission home in south-eastern Nigeria. With an injured arm Bob Whittaker had been taken hostage to an unknown location. Dorothy mobilized the missionary and Jos community networks from our house in San Diego to help Bob's wife and son get through this crisis.

Eventually the local Nigerian church leaders paid the ransom demanded by the kidnappers, and Bob was released. He was flown to the States for treatment of his injured arm, postoperative physical therapy, and rehabilitation. This event was another milestone intensifying our security concerns in Nigeria. Although foreign businessmen and diplomats had been kidnapped in the far North and in the oil rich East, this was the first time a missionary had been kidnapped for ransom.

In spite of the violence in Nigeria we planned to return. In spite of the ongoing reports of violence in Nigeria and against all reason, we believed God wanted us to return to Jos for one more two-year term to allow Heather and Anna to graduate from Hillcrest School. After two years we planned to return to the U.S. to help care for my aging parents. With the changes at the hospital and the deterioration of the security situation in Jos, the timing for our future final departure in the summer of 2012 seemed right. So in July 2010 we boarded the plane in Los Angeles for Nigeria with our usual truck-load of boxes one last time.

THE ATTACK

While we were still in California, we kept in touch with our friends in Nigeria and closely followed the international news reports on the Voice of America and BBC. 2010 began with more sectarian riots in Jos. Christians attacked Muslim neighborhoods and Muslims attacked Christian neighborhoods. A Muslim gang ransacked our electronics repairman Joseph's home and workshop, stole everything of value in his workshop, and then burned it to the ground. He lost all his tools, inventory, and equipment. He was visiting a family member in the hospital when the attack occurred, so no one in his family was hurt or killed. Marvelously, a Christian stranger gave him a house to live in until he could get back on his feet. We were amazed at his attitude of acceptance and trust in God's care for him. "Not to worry," were his remarks after losing everything he owned. With five children, four of whom needed school fees, in addition to food, clothing and the necessities of life, he was trusting God each day to meet their needs.

As the rains came over the next several months, tempers cooled down with the cooling weather. This was a common pattern, so we welcomed the rains for not only for the water but the added benefit of a calmer city. We returned to Nigeria in July 2010 in time for the start of the new Hillcrest School term for Dorothy, Heather, Anna, and David.

Unfortunately, the underlying sectarian animosity in Nigeria was till smoldering with outbursts of trouble and unrest every few weeks. The break in the U.S. from the stress and tension was helpful, but we quickly got back into hyper-vigilance mode with our senses alert for sounds of trouble and our evacuation bags packed by the door.

When the rains tapered off in the fall, the number of violent incidents rose. The Boko Haram group remained active in the northern states with additional bombings. During the October 1 Nigerian Independence Day celebrations in Abuja, the Boko Haram group detonated explosives in several cars near the celebration venue where there were many Nigerian government and foreign dignitaries. Sixteen people were killed and 50 injured in the blast. The bombing was another signal to the government that the arm of Boko Haram was long and could reach with impunity into even the heart of the capital city. It was also a stern reminder to the missionary community to avoid large public gatherings, which were easy targets for the terrorist groups. We wondered how long until Jos became a target. We didn't wait long.

December 24, 2010, Christmas Eve, was a day that changed Jos forever. Around 7 p.m. men from the radical Muslim group Boko Haram detonated explosives in wheelbarrows in two busy markets filled with holiday shoppers — four bombs in Gada Biyu, only a half mile from Evangel Hospital, and another one on the other side of the city. The terrorists set the bombs near bars during the Christmas season to have the maximum human carnage against those violating the anti-alcohol and anti-Christian dogma of the Islamist extremists. There were several reports that the group responsible was the Boko Haram sect of radical Muslims. Because the Christians had killed many Muslims in the 2008 riots in this area, some believed this was a revenge assault. On Christmas Eve they also attacked churches in Maiduguri and police stations and prisons in Bauchi. Apparently, of the three people who were later arrested making explosives, one was from Chad and two were Nigerians.

We were at Miango when the bombs went off. Marie was visiting us from college for the Christmas holiday. Everyone was horrified and panicked to know if anyone they knew was injured or killed. We called everyone we knew in desperation for news. Fortunately no one we knew was unaccounted for; no staff or their families were injured at the market. The Lees and Naatz missionary families were at the Christmas Eve service at Hillcrest and could not return to their homes, so they stayed at Woyke House for the night. With Dr. Lee and I both off the compound, there was no surgeon at the hospital. Because of the travel restrictions, I could not drive into Jos that night to help. The Evangel senior doctors and residents handled the mass casualties well and operated on the injured until late in the night. They admitted 36 injured people, and 16 dead were taken to the morgue. The only children admitted were a boy with a thigh fracture and multiple leg lacerations, a child who later died from his injuries, and a child brought in dead.

On Saturday, Christmas Day, I enjoyed a few hours with my family opening gifts and then went in to the hospital with Dr. Bob Whittaker, a visiting obstetrician (he was the missionary doctor who had been kidnapped a few years ago). We met Dr. Adam Lee and did rounds on all the patients. It was awful to see the large number of innocent people who had been injured in the explosions. We turned the VVF Ward into a trauma ward for 20 patients. One very sick woman who had surgery for a gunshot wound colon injury died shortly afterwards in the ICU. The final mortality report included 80 dead in the city and 189 injured. The horror of the attack began to settle in, and we were keenly aware that the isolation of Jos from the terror of Boko Haram was over.

On Christmas afternoon, we lined up the cases needing x-rays, labs, and surgery for the next day. On Sunday morning, Bob and I drove in from Miango and began the enormous task of working through the injured cases. He was a terrific help with the dressing changes and wound inspections while Adam and I did the major operative cases. One man had a gunshot wound damaging his bladder and rectum so we did a colostomy. Unfortunately, he died the next morning from infection and shock. Governor Jang and the Minister of Health visited the hospital while we were doing ward patient rounds. They offered to help, so we had a short committee meeting of several department representatives and made a wish list of medical supplies we needed. We finished our work at the hospital in the afternoon and drove back to Miango.

Monday morning Bob and I drove to Jos from Miango again after breakfast. After our two-hour ward patient rounds, Adam and I did three more orthopedic cases. The blast from the bombs caused enormous damage to flesh and bones creating a major surgical challenge to save the limbs and restore function. The Minister of Defense and the Police Chief of the Criminal Investigation Division also visited the wards. They did not stop to talk to us, but the police did leave several men who began interviewing the patients to hear their stories and glean whatever intelligence information they could about the bombings.

We finished in time to get back to Miango for supper. I was getting tired of the one-hour drive each way, the stress of the cases, and the awfulness of these war wounds. Many of the blown out bones were almost beyond repair. One woman needed a below-the-knee amputation (BKA) because of a crushed leg, one man needed bilateral BKA, but the family took him elsewhere, two men with destroyed feet also needed BKA, and another man with a popliteal artery injury needed a BKA. After getting back to Miango, I watched a movie just to have temporary relief from the onslaught of emotions and fatigue. I was angry, discouraged, and could not stop from going over each patient in my mind.

On Tuesday, we did two more orthopedic procedures for bad leg fractures. The OR staff was getting slower and slower, and the residents were tired from the large amount of work, especially the huge number of patients needing wound dressing changes. About 3 p.m., as we were getting ready to go back to Miango, we heard shouting from a crowd along the road. It went on for 15 minutes before Kingsford told me they had caught some of the fake soldiers in a neighborhood near the hospital. These Muslim men dressed in phony army uniforms had caused mayhem, killed Christians randomly, and pilfered wherever they went. The shouting from a youth gang moved along the main road toward the police barracks, and suddenly there were gunshots. We ran back inside worried there might be another round of mob chaos and gunfire.

After some consultation with Kingsford, we drove back to Miango. There was a large number of the mobile police along the road and lots of people curious about all the commotion. Along the way we saw a group of soldiers and some taxis stopped beside the road just past the army barracks. Then a large number of young men on motorbikes and on foot hurried toward the barracks. We later learned some Muslim Fulani cattle tribesmen were harassing people along the road, and the running people were coming to deal with them. These small attacks and counterattacks went on for days around Jos.

Generally the regular police did not have adequate weapons to deal with the attacks on police stations and prisons, so they were hesitant to intervene in these incidents. The Christians preferred the mobile police force because they had more powerful weapons and was less corrupt than the street police force. The army was brought in at the request of the governor when there were riots and unrest. Although the army had big weapons and were willing to use them, they often fired indiscriminately, sometimes even singling out Christians. This caused resentment in the Christian community in Jos, so much so that Christians wanted the army to leave. One of our Nigerian friends, Paul Chaga, expressed a popular street sentiment. "We would like the army guys to all leave and let us take care of the problem. If the Muslims want a fight, we'll fight them."

Another frustration was that after the fighting, any who were caught by the army in these incidents were taken off to prison in another part of Nigeria. When everyone had forgotten the incident, these troublemakers were either let go because someone had bribed the prison officials or they were quietly killed, so they didn't disclose who was behind them. The Jos Christians were tired of the way this had played out over the last few years and wanted in their own way to permanently clear all the Muslims out of Jos. It was said that there used to be this kind of back-and-forth violence in Kaduna until the Christians gave the Muslims a real thrashing and then the Muslims quieted down.

This malicious bomb attack rocked the Jos community and changed forever the perception that Jos was not a target of the Boko Haram, that innocent civilians were not their targets, and that the Middle Belt was not a focus. No one was beyond their reach, civilians were fair game, especially Christians, women and children, and Christian holidays were good days for attacks since the number of killed and injured would be greater.

There was an enormous escalation again of security measures to now defend against explosives from car bombs, explosives thrown from motorcycles, and suicide bombers. The hospital instituted more scrutiny of vehicles coming into the compound. At Hillcrest, the security committee recommended a complete change in where vehicles parked at the compound. Vehicles were completely restricted from coming onto the school property beyond the public parking area during community events like concerts and sports events. A bomb-proof parking lot was built away from the classrooms near the main road, and car barriers were placed around the perimeter of the classroom areas. New parking stickers and procedures were implemented, night events were rescheduled to the afternoons, extreme caution was used in screening visitors to the compound, we instituted bomb threat drills, and the school hired Secret Service moles to roam the school during normal school hours.

The army set up sandbag-walled bases throughout the city to defend their personnel and resources. Cement pillars were placed around government buildings to prevent car bombers, roadblocks were set up around churches every Sunday, so traffic was diverted during the morning worship services, and our mission organization established red zones in the city where we were not permitted to go. We were given maps that marked out in red the Muslim areas of the city where we were never allowed to go. This had a huge impact on our freedom to move around the city and visit friends in the "red zone." The Imams in the mosques on Fridays warned the parishioners that if they went to a Christian hospital they would be killed. Our city became a divided city with the red line along the Bauchi Road separating the Christian and Muslim areas of the metropolis.

On another serious note, we heard from several sources of Muslim radicals' plans to attack Christian and missionary institutions and churches. One source was a Muslim convert we knew quite well who had maintained his relationships in the Muslim community. He showed us a map of the city with Christian targets marked for bombing. This informant's information seemed more credible when there were threats in the coming days on several occasions against the hospital and even more worrisome threats against Hillcrest School. The mission and school administration took these threats seriously.

There were also ongoing violent attacks in the villages south of Jos between the nomadic Muslim cattle herders, the Fulanis, and the local tribal groups in the small villages. The Fulani do not own land so must get grazing rights from landowners to move their cattle around the country. Often there is hostility between the Fulani and villagers with the villagers stealing the Muslims cattle, villages being burned by the Fulani in retaliation, and many innocent people being killed in the attacks. Fulanis would come to a village at night and shoot off their guns. Curious villagers would run outside to see what was going on and then be mowed down by the waiting Fulani attackers.

A Christian physician friend of mine who became a state senator attended a large funeral of villagers in his area who had been attacked by a band of Muslim Fulanis. The Fulanis attacked again during the funeral, and he was killed in the melee. It was impossible for the army to defend every village in the rural areas from these random attacks. Reprisal attacks against "Christian" villages were occurring elsewhere in the country as well. Cletus is an Operating Room nurse whose family is from Benue State, just south of Plateau State. Fulani Muslims burned his village to the ground, destroying every building as retaliation for the violence in Plateau State against Fulanis.

Life changed for everyone in the Jos community. Although no one resisted the changes, as inconvenient as they were, everyone regretted the loss of freedom and innocence we had enjoyed for so many years. Our circle of movement was getting smaller, and we developed a lingering sense of "dis-ease" that we were more vulnerable than ever wherever we were and whatever we were doing. All these events increased the baseline tension and stress for everyone. We were all on edge, on high alert for sounds of gunfire or explosions, not sleeping well and vigilant for any tidbit of news that would change our activities, our driving around town, our security at home and work, and the safety of our children at school. This was the new normal.

Even though tension in the city eventually reduced, one day at school Dorothy heard a loud noise during the school chapel and immediately thought it was gunfire. It turned out to be a soldier firing in the air to quiet the crowd queuing for petrol at the filling station and then throwing tear gas canisters at them. Fortunately it did not escalate into a bigger problem or cause an explosion at the station. Now she knows what exploding tear gas sounds like!

INCREASING INSECURITY IN THE "HOME OF PEACE AND TOURISM"

"You know you are a missionary in Nigeria when …
- The first thing you think of when you hear a loud sound in a rainstorm is not lightning and thunder, but 'Is it a bomb?'
- Your son knows the difference between the sounds of firecrackers, gunshots and cars backfiring."

- Dorothy Ardill

The motto for Plateau State is "The Home of Peace and Tourism." The irony of this played out almost daily in the violence, unrest, and tension in Jos and the surrounding villages. There were also almost daily stories of individuals from both sides of the conflict being attacked because of their religious affiliation. A gang of Muslims attacked a Christian pastor taking a Muslim convert on his motorcycle to his village. They threw gasoline on the two men, but before the mob could ignite the fuel, the men escaped on their motorbike. 2011 proved to be another year of increasing turbulence in Jos.

In January the Hillcrest Board decided to close the school because of the increasing violence and after a Ministry of Education mandate. This increased the anxiety and uncertainty of parents, teachers, and students. Teachers made homework plans for the children to complete at home during the unplanned break and tried to keep in touch the best they could. This hiatus lasted two weeks, and then classes resumed with teachers trying to play catch-up, rearranging their curricula to fit the compressed schedule. It was one more additional stress for our family since Dorothy was the elementary school principal, I was teaching high school Bible classes, and our children had to figure out their homework on short notice.

In preparation for the upcoming elections in April, the government set up a new voter registration process in January to reduce voter fraud. Eligible voters had to show identification, sign registration documents, and have their ten fingers inked. If they had less that ten fingers or no hand, they had their arm or hand photographed. Quite a system! Christians were urged to vote to keep the Muslims from getting a majority in Jos and installing Muslim leaders. One Anglican pastor told his parishioners, "If you don't register to vote, you cannot take Holy Communion!" Dorothy asked a Nigerian teenager who lives on the Evangel compound if she was 18 and planned to vote. "No. The churches heard that the Muslim youth were being registered to vote, so the churches started forcing their youth under 18 to register to vote as well!"

Political rallies continued to be a flashpoint for trouble. After a January 2011 political rally there was widespread shooting around the city, a house was burned, and 20 injured and 14 dead were brought to Evangel. Most of the injured had minor stab wounds, two died after surgery, and one had devastating chest and abdominal wounds. The next day there was more violence in Jos and neighboring Bukuru.

Some Muslims joined with the Igbos from southeastern Nigeria to form a new political party headed by the former President Buhari. The party delegates planned to meet at a hotel in Jos for their primary, but because the Muslims were uncomfortable gathering in a Christian area of town, the venue was moved to the Muslim quarter.

At the meeting there were more Igbo delegates than Muslims, so an Igbo won the election. The Muslim Hausas were so upset they went on a rampage. They blocked several roads and trapped a group of 40 Christian Igbo men in the market and killed them. Up until this incident the Igbos had stayed out of the conflict because they believed it was between the Plateau tribal groups and the Muslims, but this brought them into the conflict with their arsenal of heavy weapons. They were now clearly aligned with the Plateau Christian tribal groups. Knowing a number of Igbo staff at the hospital, this incident was pivotal in the angry engagement of the Igbos in the tribal war in Jos.

Every time there was a riot or mob activity, the government would deploy army personnel at strategic junctions. The perception by the Christian community was that the army soldiers were being positioned around the city to protect the Muslims after they attacked Christians. Many believed that if the soldiers left, the Muslims would not attack because they knew the Christians outnumbered them. Because of the Christian reprisal attacks, a Special Police Force commanding officer brought a team from Abuja to "deal with the Christians." He was caught by the army and taken back to Abuja for prosecution. A few days later, twelve large luxury buses of soldiers arrived in Jos to replace the current group. It was apparently a better mix of Muslims and Christians. Barricades were set up around the city, and we knew we were under siege. At every checkpoint we prayed the soldiers would not hassle us and for the most part, they let us through quickly. Occasionally a smart aleck taunted us for fun.

Unfortunately there are abundant stories of the deplorable abuse of power by the army soldiers. A Muslim driving by the University of Jos on a motorcycle stabbed a university student. When the students gathered in protest, the army came and began shooting at the crowd of mostly Christian students. They told the Christians to stand to one side and the Muslims on the other side and then shot the Christians! Mobs began taking to the streets in protest against this kind of military action. They burned houses and petrol stations. We often could hear the yelling crowds from our house and could locate the action by the large columns of smoke rising along the Jos horizon.

That same morning, a soldier shot a boy who was brought to Evangel, but the child died on the Operating Room table. The watching crowd attacked the soldier who was brought to Evangel. When the parents of the slain boy saw their dead son at the hospital, they went crazy and wanted to go to the ICU to kill the soldier who shot him. Fortunately, we were able to stop them. I was fearful others might attempt to come and kill him. Over the next several hours we finally made contact with the Air Force Hospital, and they took the soldier out through a back door of the hospital. We did surgery throughout the day on several more innocent bystanders shot by soldiers. The unrest spilled into other parts of town, and by the end of the day three gas stations, a mosque, and several houses had been burned. Again the army did not help but seemed to escalate the already tense situation. In contrast to the chaos and violence, there was a peaceful demonstration downtown by Nigerian market women pleading for peace.

February 15 was Mohammed's birthday, so it was a federal holiday. In the market, several Muslim men in town got into an argument. When a Christian policeman tried to intervene, they killed him. When word of this spread to other areas of town, including our area of Gada Biyu, there was more violence. In one reprisal a "Christian" gang attacked the car of a Muslim policeman who was trying to get into the Evangel Hospital compound for safety. He was dragged from the car, killed, and his car was burned. Fortunately his family escaped. Many who had been injured with knife and gunshot wounds in the melee were brought to the hospital for treatment and surgery.

A Christian man was walking home when he came to an army checkpoint. Not wanting to be harassed, he dodged into the adjoining neighborhood to bypass the soldiers. He did not realize it was a Muslim neighborhood until he was attacked and beaten terribly because he was a Christian. He was admitted to the hospital with arm, leg, and ankle fractures and multiple bruises and lacerations. Everyone in the city was on edge and the slightest incident provoked violence that spread like fire in a tinderbox. By this time armored army vehicles and helicopters were patrolling the city several times a day looking for trouble situations. We stayed close to home only leaving to go to school.

At the end of March, two preventive incidents occurred. A truck loaded with bomb-making materials was intercepted trying to get into the city, and the police uncovered three bomb-making workshops with explosives in an affluent area of the city named "Millionaire's Quarter." We were thankful at least some carnage had been averted.

A Muslim politician, known for violence surrounding his political gatherings, held a huge rally on the polo ground beside our compound on a Saturday to raise support for the April election. We were expecting trouble so packed our flee bags in the morning and prepared for possible evacuation. Tanks, armored vehicles, and soldiers surrounded the area. The mostly Muslim crowd from the northern side of Jos gathered in the afternoon. By 4:30 p.m. when the crowd was worked up to a shouting frenzy, there were gunshots. In panic the crowd tried to disperse from the polo grounds. The soldiers had lined the main exit street from the polo ground to protect the Muslims from Christian youth who began throwing rocks at the Muslims. The soldiers fired at the Christians. Not surprisingly, several bystanders were killed. A soldier on a pedestrian bridge over the road fired at a civilian standing in a church parking lot, hit him in the neck, and killed him. The Christian youth mob became more inflamed and rushed the bodies of those killed and injured to the Evangel compound. Overwhelmed and afraid, the military men posted in front of the hospital gate ran for their lives. About 30 "Christian" men barged through the gate and then into the Operating Room and wards demanding to know which patients were Muslims or they would burn down the hospital.

The hospital staff were amazingly brave and cajoled the mob into leaving the hospital. "If you are Jesus people, why are you trying to kill Jesus people?" The youth mob left the Operating Room but demanded the body of the Christian man who had been shot, so they could parade it through the town. After about an hour of "discussions" and negotiating with the hospital senior staff, church leaders, police and army, the mob dispersed.

The first of three elections were scheduled for the first weekend of April. Elections are divided into local, state and presidential or national offices. All schools were to close, and each Saturday would be a "no movement" day with restrictions on all travel. Once again, we prepared to evacuate if necessary because of trouble in the Evangel Hospital area of town. On the one hand we liked the generally quieter day, but we were also concerned about post-election reprisal violence. The elections scheduled for the first two weekends were postponed for one reason or another. We were naturally frustrated we had cancelled all our plans and school activities but thankful for a quiet weekend. Nigerians were amazingly tolerant of this disorganized process, but our roller coaster of emotions was stressful. The last of the three planned weekend elections was held on April 26. Voters voted at the polling stations by placing their thumbprint on their ballot beside the candidate of their choice. In spite of it being the Easter weekend, there was no violence in Jos and it was surprisingly quiet — a miracle some said. We were greatly relieved.

As a result of the peaceful elections, tensions subsided. Life returned again to "normal." People were no longer afraid to come out of their houses, so there was a big increase in traffic, especially motorcycles, an increase in patients coming to the hospital, and more market activity.

About an hour away in Kaduna State, however, there was violence with reports of over 500 people killed because of the unrest.

Several serious gunshot wound patients were brought to Evangel Hospital for treatment. There was also a bombing in the northern city of Maiduguri, the heart of the terrorist movement. Elsewhere in the North more than 80 churches, some mosques, markets, houses, and vehicles were burned. Much of this was a reaction to the Christian candidate for president, Goodluck Jonathan, winning the election. Although we grieved for those families impacted by the violence, we were again grateful Jos stayed quiet.

On May 31, the newly elected President and state governors were sworn in. Since Jos is the capital of Plateau State, there were ceremonies for the state legislators and governor. We heard sirens and helicopters all morning as dignitaries paraded around the city, but there were no outbreaks of violence. We began to feel the tight, wound-up spring in our stomachs begin to relax now that the tense election days had passed. It seemed, perhaps, that the troubles might be behind us ... at least temporarily.

In spite of the summer rains, bombings continued in many northern cities. In July, a terrorist detonated a large bomb at the Police Headquarters in Abuja, and several bombs were thrown into crowded bars and restaurants in Maiduguri. In August, a suicide bomber drove a vehicle into the UN Headquarters in Abuja resulting in 18 dead and many injured. This was the first major attack by Boko Haram against a foreign humanitarian organization. With the stated purpose to oppose Western education, Boko Haram continued to make the point no one was beyond their reach – not the police, not the army, and certainly not humanitarian organizations.

The Abuja bombing ignited revenge killings in Jos between the Muslims and the Christian vigilante groups. Groups would make roadblocks in their section of town and harass vehicles trying to pass if they were on the "wrong side." Going into a Christian area, each person was asked to recite the Bible verse John 3:16. Those trying to enter a Muslim area were quizzed about Mohammed's mother's name or asked to recite the Islamic creed. Failing the test meant certain death on the spot. The injured and dead from these skirmishes were brought almost daily to the hospital. As the community temperature heated up with more unrest, so did our anxiety and caution.

At the end of the Muslim feast of Ramadan, August 2011, we expected trouble from the Christian quarter. "If the Muslims spoiled our Christmas (2010), we will give them trouble on their holy day." Although Tuesday and Wednesday of that week were declared national holidays to commemorate Ramadan, trouble began Monday morning. In Islam, holy days start when the Imam first sights the moon. Apparently the radical sect Imam in Jos had seen the moon earlier than the other sects, so they planned their Salah (holy day) on Monday instead of Tuesday. Armed with guns and knives seemingly looking for a fight, a group of men in this sect arrived at their mosque in a Christian area near Evangel. When the Christian youth gangs saw the group of Muslim men approaching their mosque, they attacked and slaughtered the Muslims, dismembering and beheading them. On their mosque property they stuck at least one head on a stake with a cigarette in his mouth. The gang violence escalated with burning of cars and motorbikes along the road until by noon there was chaos in the streets around the hospital. Then military vehicles arrived on the scene and came screaming into our compound carrying the injured from the fighting. Again we were on high alert and I was back in the Operating Room.

Some moderate Muslim groups had begun preparations at the polo grounds for their Muslim celebrations on Tuesday and Wednesday. They also encountered local Christian vigilante groups, and fighting ensued. Mobs rushed into the hospital compound again with those injured by machetes, guns, and other weapons even in the hospital parking lot! By the end of the day we had 86 injured and 12 dead. Four patients with major chest and abdominal gunshot wounds had surgery. I operated on one man who had been stabbed in the back and had an injury to his kidney. He died on the Operating Room table because we ran out of blood to transfuse him.

During the chaos in the hospital treating all the injured, a Christian mob heard there was an injured Muslim in the Emergency Room, so they came and took him and beat him to death in the hospital parking lot! It was a horrible day as the stories poured in of atrocities by both sides against innocent people. The shocking evil deeds by both factions were sickening.

Fighting continued for days in various parts of Jos. In retaliation Muslims killed a pastor and his daughter from an Assemblies of God church in the Muslim quarter. Downtown stores were looted during the mayhem, and much of the city was in lockdown by the military. By Friday, things had cooled down a bit, but our anxiety increased even more when we heard of credible retaliatory threats against churches during Sunday morning worship services. Missionaries were advised to not attend Nigerian churches. On our way to Hillcrest for the Sunday morning service, we passed military men guarding the streets and entrances of every church, and security men were wanding people coming into church for worship. I thought, "My, has it come to this – being strip-searched to go to a place of worship!?"

The neighborhood around the hospital was now considered very dangerous with threats by the Christian vigilantes to kill any Muslim found in the streets. The same was true for Christians in Muslim areas of town where they were not welcome. Tensions were extremely high throughout the city and mission community. Hillcrest cancelled school and the weekend staff retreat at Miango. We found ourselves on edge again, listening for bombs, riots, and news.

In September, a gang of Muslims was scheming to attack a Christian vigilante group but was held at bay by the army. After the Muslims then proceeded to kill two army men, the soldiers started shooting at the Muslims and let the Christians attack the

Muslims as well. About 40 died in this skirmish. Fearing looting and attacks, the Igbo businessmen with electronic and appliances stores began emptying their stores along the main street near the central mosque. Law and order was being maintained by the barrel of a gun.

On September 11, we feared attacks in memory of the New York 9/11 attack. The day was quiet until 8:45 p.m. when we heard two explosions and then gunfire coming from a market between our house and Hillcrest. Terrorists in cars had thrown two bombs into crowded outdoor restaurants. Amazingly, only a few people were injured, and no one was killed. A few of the injured came to Evangel, but none had serious wounds. There were more attacks by Muslim Fulanis in the villages south of Jos as well. Up to 17 were killed in one village alone! As we had heard before, the attackers dressed in military uniforms to deceive the villagers. The carnage continued and we wondered how long we could function in this stressful environment? I heard the rumors and reports but was most distressed to see the human toll of mangled bodies, slaughtered corpses, and distraught families.

Although we expected more trouble on October 1, 2011, Nigerian Independence Day, we were pleased it was a quiet holiday weekend. The President vowed to root out the Boko Haram terrorists and deployed large numbers of army personnel and military vehicles to Jos to take control of the city. Through all this we made every effort to protect our children, keep school programs going and maintain normal activities as much as safely possible.

Again in December we heard three explosions from the other side of town. The terrorists threw bombs into a crowd watching a soccer game in an outdoor viewing area. One person was killed and about a dozen injured. Most of the injured went to the government hospital on that side of town, so we only got a few of the injured with minor wounds. We continued to warn missionaries to avoid public gatherings and stop nighttime traveling. The travel restrictions, widespread fear, and apprehension by Muslims reduced the number of people coming to the hospital, so our surgery workload decreased except for the trauma patients from the violence.

On Christmas Day 2011, a Boko Haram sympathizer threw a bomb into a Roman Catholic Church in Abuja resulting in 40 people being killed, including one policeman. A motorcyclist attempted to throw a bomb into a church in Jos, but the bomb landed outside the building. The government finally banned motorcycles on Saturday and Sunday in Jos because they were often used in the attacks. In spite of a few arrests, the attacks continued unabated throughout the country. Fortunately, our Christmas at Miango was uninterrupted and joyful.

Much to everyone's amazement, on January 1, 2012, the President lifted a government fuel subsidy, doubling the price of fuel. This created economic panic in a time of heightened tension in the country from the terrorist attacks. The labor unions threatened a nationwide strike in protest. We stocked up on food and essentials in anticipation of a potentially paralyzing national strike. The nationwide labor union eventually went on strike closing all the airports, most public and government services, and some private businesses. The unions threatened to also stop all oil production (the main source of income for the government) and NEPA (electricity) if their demands were not met to restore the fuel subsidy. There were large demonstrations and protests, some of which turned violent, in major cities including Lagos and Abuja. The streets of Jos were quiet as people chose to stay home fearing more violence. Within ten days, the President reinstated some of the fuel subsidy, and the strike and demonstrations were called off. The nation sighed in relief and tensions eased immediately.

Our family in the United States commented many times that we seemed to live from crisis to crisis. They were right. Although many of the missionaries were on antacids and antidepressants, we were also on our knees praying for God's protection and wisdom each day. We regularly discussed if we needed to leave but wanted to stay if possible until the end of the school year, so Heather and Anna could graduate from high school.

In spite of the fact that the northern city of Kano is predominantly Muslim, Boko Haram set off 30 bombs simultaneously in the city. The death toll rose to 160 with horrific pictures of the devastation and carnage of buildings and human lives. Hundreds fled the North and came to Plateau State, hoping it would be safer for Christians.

There was a lot of discussion in the Christian community about a biblical response to the violence. The positions of pastors ranged from revenge and retaliation to dialogue and reconciliation. Historically, Roman Catholics have been more inclined to negotiate and dialogue with Muslims. In contrast, the president of the mostly Protestant Christian Association of Nigeria (CAN) made inflammatory statements regarding the churches' appropriate response to Islam. Some missionaries were engaged in discussions to reconcile the opposing factions.

There were more rumors in February 2012 of an attack against Hillcrest School. The Board considered closing the school but decided to stay open but improve the security at the school. These were difficult decisions since the school needed to take every reasonable precaution to ensure the safety of the children, teachers, staff, and school property.

At the end of February on Sunday morning as worshippers were gathering for the service in one of the largest churches in Jos, a suicide car bomber drove into the church. The Hillcrest Middle School principal and her family were in the parking lot and saw the bomb explode. Fortunately they were not injured. The blast could be heard in the far reaches of Jos, destroying the front of the church building. Windshields of cars in the parking lot and windows on buildings a few blocks away were blown out. The driver of the car actually rolled out of the car before it detonated. He was caught as he fled the scene and killed by the crowd. The repercussions of this evil act rippled throughout the city. Several hours later a few Muslims walking in a Christian area of the city were attacked and killed in revenge.

The next Sunday morning two men drove a car filled with explosives into St. Finabar's Roman Catholic church in a suburb of Jos called Rayfield as the congregation gathered for services. A dozen were killed in the incident and another dozen Muslims killed in reprisal attacks by Christians. Several Hillcrest families were at the church, but no one was injured. With Hillcrest families affected directly by the bombings in their churches, it had an enormous impact on the students and their parents. The school encouraged teachers to allow children to share their experiences, offered counseling, and was considerate of those needing time off. The tension in the city was very high with these recent bombings with widespread fear of going to any church or public gathering. There were more threats against the school, so the elementary and middle schools were closed for the week, and the high school students had a reduced schedule of classes. All extracurricular activities were cancelled except for practices for the end-of-year high school musical.

The Lutheran mission decided to evacuate its two missionary families out of the country. This was a major decision by a foreign mission group that rattled the community and caused everyone to ponder again the wisdom of staying in this risky environment. Some wanted to close Hillcrest, but most felt closing the school would compound the trauma for the high school students, especially those graduating. We also struggled with the desire to stay, so Heather and Anna could participate in the end-of-term activities like the musical, banquet, and graduation events. We prayed fervently each day for God's wisdom to make good decisions regarding our safety and continued presence in the country. There were also regular updates from the Mission leaders regarding security precautions in the city.

The next Sunday, as a precaution, Hillcrest cancelled the morning worship service. The governor reiterated his edict that no cars would be allowed to drive or park in front of churches on Sunday morning during the services. Motorcyclists were forced to walk their bikes near churches. When we drove to church the following Sunday, we had to weave our way through a frustrating gauntlet and maze of diversions and military and vigilante checkpoints on our way from Evangel to Hillcrest to avoid driving in front of a church. Our normal 10-minute drive to church extended to 45 minutes. We decided to not let the terrorists keep us from worship because of fear.

We anticipated that the Easter holiday weekend would be tough, and we almost made it through uneventfully. In the evening a motorcyclist threw a bomb into a crowded bar and injured several people. The destruction in so many places was extremely sad and depressing, especially since we saw little progress by the government to stop the terrorist actions. Courageously the Nigerians kept going about their business, fearlessly unintimidated by the radical thugs.

On May 22 the government authorities arrested a group of Boko Haram followers running a bomb-making factory in Jos. Much to the surprise of the authorities, they found not only 19 bombs but hollowed out Bibles that the terrorists were planning to use as bombs to be carried into churches! Carrying bags and purses into church had already been banned. Were they now to forbid Bibles?

We were thankful that in April and May 2012 Hillcrest end-of-term activities were held safely during daylight hours, including the musical, banquet, baccalaureate, and graduation ceremonies. We continued our preparations for our final exit from Nigeria, had sales or giveaways for the rest of our belongings, and said our good-byes to friends and co-workers in the many ministries in which we were involved. The SIM community had an encouraging and humorous farewell party for our family. Many in the hospital visited and expressed their appreciation for all we had done to help them over the years. We knew we would never see most of these friends again, so it was a painful and tearful time. We were humbled at the crowd that came to say goodbye as we left on the 4th of June for the Abuja airport to fly to London and the United States. We were exhausted — emotionally and spiritually spent — thankful the term ended well, especially for our children, and expectantly looking forward to what lay ahead. Our families, friends, and supporters in the States let out a big sigh of relief when we boarded the British Air flight to Heathrow airport – out of the danger zone of Jos and on to the next chapter of our lives.

LOSSES

Leaving by definition involves losses. Some things are worth losing. Some things are difficult to lose. In most geographical moves, it is a combination of both. Dorothy calls leaving our "happy-sad" time with a complicated mix of emotions. Some people or circumstances we could not wait to get away from, while others we dreaded and wished it was not so, especially when we realized it would be the final goodbye. Reflecting on our departure from Nigeria several months before we left, I am thankful my thoughts changed from remembering the difficult things to cataloging the good things and friends I would sincerely miss.

I will miss my unique role as a missionary surgeon. I went to Nigeria primarily because I believed God called me to work as a surgeon at Evangel Hospital. Twenty years ago I had a limited understanding or vision of what that would mean. Over the years, I have logged thousands of hours doing surgery procedures with the anesthesia staff, Operating Room staff, residents, interns, and students. Several of these relationships are deep friendships where there was trust, openness, and accountability. I knew I would miss those special men and women who helped me mature as a surgeon and as a Christian because of their honesty with me, their love and concern for my welfare and my family, and their instruction about culture, faith, and life. They were patient through my mistakes and times of anger and frustration. They cried with me through the crises we faced as a family. They rejoiced and laughed at times of God's blessing in our lives, especially the births of our children. The memories of their faithful friendship will endure in my heart and have made a profound and permanent mark.

Because of my role as a surgeon and often the only general surgeon, I had a wide range of responsibilities in the Operating Room and hospital. I appreciated when staff asked for advice on both hospital and personal matters. In my leadership role, I sought ways to teach those around me principles of good patient care and surgery as well as lessons in leadership and spiritual living. I relished teaching rounds with the residents on the surgical wards and the opportunities in the Operating Room to teach a resident or intern how to sew, do a procedure, or evaluate a patient. Although I will continue to teach surgery and endeavor to influence those around me toward deeper spiritual living, I will greatly miss the constellation of opportunities afforded me at Evangel as a leader.

I will miss the unique problems presented to me as a surgeon at Evangel. As a general surgeon trained in the United States, I had some exposure during my residency to a variety of surgery subspecialties. In spite of my efforts to prepare to be a general surgeon, I was in for a surprise. As I met challenging surgical problems in pediatric surgery, urology, plastic surgery, vascular surgery, orthopedics, and gynecology, I learned case by case to do more and more procedures and developed skill and confidence in a wide range of surgical procedures. At times when I tried a new procedure and there were complications, I would retreat for a while until I had the courage to try again. Much of this was out of necessity because I had nowhere to refer these cases, and knew if I could not help these patients, they had no options. Anytime there was a specialist visiting Jos, I would line up cases for them, not only to help the patients but also to teach me how to do these unfamiliar cases. Over the years as I grew in confidence and competence, I thrived on the new challenging cases that showed up almost every week in the clinic.

When on furlough working at veterans hospitals, my scope of practice was much more limited. I was known as the "missionary surgeon from Africa." This reputation sparked interest by the residents, students, nurses, and other physicians. I had opportunities to give presentations on our surgery and the challenges of working in a resource-poor environment. While in the States, physicians and people working in medically related professions often asked me how they could help with equipment or resources. I was amazed at the generosity of many and their excitement being able to help me in our work in Africa. I will miss the interesting and challenging surgical cases, the faith and skill-stretching procedures and the opportunity to teach others how to work through these challenges as well as the unique role of the missionary surgeon.

I will miss my opportunities to teach. My involvement at Hillcrest School was a gradual process, like stepping into the shallow end of a pool and moving toward the deep end. When our children started in the elementary school, Dorothy began helping in their classes as a teacher's assistant. I attended the usual concerts and school programs but otherwise was not very involved. Around 1999 I was asked to teach the high school Biblical Ethics class. Someone asked Dorothy if I would be willing and interested, and she thought I would enjoy it. Indeed, for the next decade I thoroughly enjoyed studying and preparing the lessons, presenting the material, getting to know the students, and improving my skill as a teacher. I was also asked to teach Apologetics and had a similar positive experience. Some years the students were more challenging, as far as classroom behavior, but fortunately they were the exception. I especially enjoyed teaching all three of my daughters, knowing the lessons would help prepare them for the spiritual challenges they would face in university. Being in the classroom I had a better understanding of the issues my children were facing. The questions and doubts of the students forced me to further develop my own understanding of the subject matter. Occasionally at a graduation, an alumnus would corner me and thank me for the class and how it had helped them in college.

I was also asked to serve on the Hillcrest Board of Governors. This was a big commitment of time and gave me a better understanding of the workings of the school, its policies, and who the influencers were in implementing the mission and vision of the school. Serving on the Board also allowed me to use my "gift of Boards" in a leadership role to help move the school in a certain direction or avoid pitfalls in other areas. I found out I had the ability to listen to a discussion, quickly discern the key issues, clearly state the problems, and then move the group to a solution or action plan. I will miss the opportunity my Hillcrest leadership responsibilities offered to influence the lives of the students and teachers.

I will miss simple things about Nigeria. Being born and raised in Jos and serving there for 20 years, it is my "home." The sense of familiarity and belonging are strong, and leaving my home is hard. I will also miss our house where I raised my children, although I will not miss the termites that invaded the bedrooms and bathroom. I will miss the tree house we built for the children in the front yard, the many fruit trees in our yard, the play centers and sandbox we built for Marie.

I will miss Nigerian food. I love the tropical fruit we had year round like mangoes, guavas, pineapples, oranges, and bananas. Situated in rocky hills on a plateau, Jos was a beautiful region, especially when the rains brought the rich green grass, cleaned all the trees and streets and cleared the deep blue skies. I will also miss the smell of the first rain after five months of dry, dusty, hot weather. I treasure our swimming trips to the hotel pools, our weekend jaunts to the Yankari game park outside Bauchi, the amazing Wikki hot springs, and the swimming pool at the Hilton in Abuja.

I will miss the community of missionaries. Even though there were a dozen different mission societies represented from all over the world and across the denominational spectrum, there was a special kinship and brotherhood among the missionaries. This happened both on the compounds and in the larger missionary community. We shared our joys and sorrows. With so few social and cultural opportunities, we all went to the school sports activities, concerts, plays, and ceremonies. We worshipped together at the Hillcrest Chapel and often went on vacation with each other to Miango, Yankari, Abuja, or Obadu. These strong bonds of friendship were most evident during times of crisis. Expressed in tangible ways with food or meals or in words of comfort or encouragement, the community responded to tragedy in amazing and creative ways. I am sure a similar community develops in American neighborhoods and churches with time, but the bonds of the Jos community are an aspect of living in Nigeria I will sorely miss.

We will miss the travel we did during furlough to see family and friends scattered across the United States. During furlough we travelled for the first two months. In most churches we were given opportunities to speak in Sunday school classes, the Sunday morning worship service, in home groups and with mission committees. We enjoyed seeing our friends who were praying for us and supporting us financially so faithfully. Our identity as missionaries was something we were proud of as we represented these churches in Africa as part of their Kingdom vision. I will miss the ongoing support and contact we have had with this scattered community. I will miss the opportunities to tell them what God has been doing through us. I will miss the fun of traveling around the country, building great family memories. I will miss these aspects of being a "furloughing missionary."

I will miss the unique richness of being a missionary in a poor country. Missionaries often hear words of sympathy for all the sacrifices they have made to serve in poor countries. Few missionaries are honest enough to enumerate the many blessing of being a missionary. In addition to the sense of community, the richness of learning about and living in another culture, the benefits of raising children away from the decadence and materialism in North America and the education from traveling around the globe, there are a few other benefits. We have been humbled by the generosity of our family, friends, and churches. People have given us vehicles, furniture, clothes, hotel rooms, and loads of other freebies. Many places offer missionary discounts and scholarships. For all these things and more we were grateful.

Finally, we will miss being dependent on God for every provision. It is true there are sacrifices and hardships being a missionary. We have faced a number of crises as a family as well as the daily threats of illness from tropical diseases, harm driving on the roads, civil unrest or terrorist violence. All these take a toll on body and soul and shaped our view of God and His character. Daily we prayed for water, electricity, safety, and peace and were thankful when God answered our prayers. Our faith in Him was tested, our trust in Him deepened, and our confidence in His love and sovereignty grew. We learned to suffer and sometimes learned the reason why. We learned to endure frustrations and develop patience. We learned to not take for granted arriving at our destination safely when we got in our car.

We learned God's healing power from illness and His grace to handle pain. Were it not that we lived in Nigeria, we would have missed these lessons in faith and a richer understanding of the character and plan of God. Although I do not want to revisit any of the painful moments in my past, I admit I have grown closer to God through them. Living in the United States where life is easier and basic needs are instantly met, I have less dependence on God and develop a self-sufficiency removed from the intimacy of being on my knees daily for my "daily bread." I will miss the growth from these life lessons that was afforded me living in Nigeria.

PARTING THOUGHTS

Summer 2012

Each home assignment when I was a child returning from Nigeria with my parents, we traveled through Europe, crisscrossed the United States visiting churches and family, enrolled in public schools, and got involved in the church youth group. The places we visited had a spectrum of climates, ethnic variety as diverse as the planet, and both Western and African cultures. We enjoyed Pennsylvania Dutch shoofly pie, berries in Salem, Oregon, barbeque brisket in Texas, grits and greens in North Carolina, fresh crab from the Chesapeake, corn on the cob in Illinois, fish and chips from Northern Ireland, and pounded yam and egusi soup from Nigeria.

Through the challenges of traveling abroad, adjusting to different cultural expectations, figuring out jet lag and time zones, and learning to be flexible through our mistakes and missteps, our family matured with a world perspective and cultural sensitivity few in the States possess.

For Dorothy and me, Nigeria was a wonderful place to raise our family. There were interesting recreational opportunities, it was a child-friendly environment, and at an early age our children were exposed to young people from around the world. One afternoon one of our girls came home from school saying there was a new boy in her class who spoke with a different accent. We tried to learn more, but that was all we got. When Dorothy visited the classroom later in the semester, she discovered the new child spoke with a stutter, considered by the other children as just another accent.

The families in the Mission and Nigerian community took care of each other. We didn't think twice about our children playing all over our compound day or night as long as they came home for meals and bedtime. That approach changed as the security situation deteriorated but, overall, we felt safe raising our family in Jos.

We also suffered as a family. When someone in the Mission community was hurting, we all felt their pain and mourned with them. When our family had the trials of losing Aimee, getting sick, being injured, or being evacuated, the rest of the missionaries in Jos came alongside to comfort us, take care of our children, or liaise with the Mission on our behalf. My children saw many suffering people in Nigeria on the streets, in the market and in the hospital. They also suffered watching us go through difficult times and being without parents for periods of time. They saw us pray, weep, and appeal to God for help. They saw God's miraculous answers as well as His perplexing silence.

Being in Nigeria we learned to trust God for our daily needs like water and electricity as well as dare to ask God for the miracles of healing, the character to endure, and the balm of comfort and contentedness. I do not think we would have learned these profound lessons had we stayed in a quiet Western suburban community without the challenges and seismic events we faced in Nigeria.

We considered it a privilege to work alongside Nigerians in every venue where we ministered and functioned. Nigerians are gracious, friendly, forgiving and caring. They wear their emotions on their sleeves, and are equally willing to discuss their opinions about politics, religious beliefs, or culture. This cultural permission provides an open door for dialogue about the mundane and the intimate, the personal and the political. It created an environment conducive for close bonds of friendship and loyalty.

I am profoundly grateful for the men and women God brought into my life who influenced and changed me: people who taught me lessons about culture and my mistakes; friends who modeled trusting God and real worship; colleagues who shamed me with their commitment to prayer and whose prayers were biblical and God-honoring; co-workers who modeled sacrifice in ministry and trusting God to meet their needs even in times of crisis; hospital staff who courageously stood up to the "Christian" gangs looking for Muslim patients during the unrest and chased them out of the hospital; articulate, gracious, professionals in many disciplines who restored my hope for the church and the nation with their bold witness, clear thinking, and integrity; Nigerian missionaries with a vision and commitment for the lost who have paid a high price for their stand as Christians. Many ministered to me when I was injured and ill. Many visited us with their concerns, so we could pray for them and help them. We were surrounded by many with gigantic faith that humbled us and prompted us to greater trust in a sovereign, loving God. I consider it a great privilege that the Lord allowed me to know these saints and be influenced by them.

In the hospital, at Gidan Bege, in the AIDS ministry, in Women's Fellowship and at Hillcrest, Dorothy and I found people of character, humility, eager to learn and take on enormous challenges, trusting in God's provision each step of the way. We learned much from the spiritual hunger and desperate desire of Nigerian Christians for the presence of God in their lives. They taught us a great deal about living with suffering, managing with little, and trusting God to provide for their every need. Their prayers brought us into God's presence as they pleaded for the Sovereign Lord of the Universe to intervene in the desperate and tragic events in our lives. Although we were sometimes perceived as God's answer to their personal problems, we learned to redirect their pleas toward heaven where the All–Sufficient One reigned.

We found people of vision, courage, temerity, integrity, and Christlikeness. We were honored to work alongside those who helped us on our journey, holding us up when we were weak, pointing the way when we could not see the path, and grabbing the baton from us in ministries we initiated but needed a second generation champion.

Dorothy and I felt called to serve God as missionaries. We heard of the medical and spiritual needs and believed our training and experiences equipped us to serve. I thought I would provide surgical skills and care at Evangel Hospital, mentor the residents in training, and evangelize the lost. Dorothy went to Nigeria thinking her assignment would be in the laboratory, training the medical technologists and modeling Christ to them. Although we did some of those things, our job descriptions changed, our ministry focused shifted every few years, and we ended up doing a lot we never anticipated or wanted.

Yet, the more important lesson was not what we gave to Nigeria, how we helped thousands with surgery or food, or even the Christians we helped grow in their spiritual maturity. In her book Give Me This Mountain, missionary Helen Roseveare quotes a fellow missionary Jack Scholes:

> If you think you have come to the mission field because you are a little better than others, or as the cream of your church, or because of your medical degree, or for the service you can render the African church, or even for the souls you may see saved, you will fail. Remember, the Lord has only one purpose ultimately for each one of us, to make us more like Jesus. He is interested in your relationship with Himself. Let Him take you and mould you as He will; all the rest will take its rightful place.[9]

---

[9] Roseveare, Helen. *Give Me This Mountain*. Grand Rapids: W. B. Eerdmans, 1966. p. 80.

The fundamental lesson was God "moulding" us in His image. He could not have done that anywhere else, only in the crucible of Jos. Learning the lessons of God's amazing provision for our needs, the miracles of His healing and spiritual transformation, "fellowshipping with Him in His suffering," and learning to trust His plan and purposes above all — those were the reasons God wanted us in Africa. We answered a call from Him to go, thinking we would be serving others. But we learned our service was ultimately to Him as He "moulded" us to be more like Him in our perspective of others, our perception of the needs around us, and trusting He was unfolding His plan in Nigeria, even if it did not resemble our plan for the church.

I am generally organized and love to plan well ahead, including contingencies and a backup strategy. Evidence from the biblical and historical records strongly suggests God also has a plan that He unfolds often in a slow, difficult, and painful way. Rarely do the dots connect in a straight line. While the evangelical church often claims that "God has a *wonderful* plan for your life," my experience has often showed us that "God has a *difficult* plan for your life!" Studying God's track record with the Israelites and pondering His pattern in my life, I believe it comes down to trusting that God is good and His plans for us and the building of His church are perfect. It is usually not our way, our blueprint, our strategy, but it fulfills His goals and desires and as such is perfect.

God has planned a direction for the events of history, but He also has a specific goal for me to fulfill in this drama. Part of the fun and challenge is discovering our gifts and abilities and how we can use them to fulfill our part in the play. Finding the will of God is the perennial question of young Christians but is never more real than when one faces an overseas assignment as a missionary.

Amazingly, it was not until the last years of our ministry in Africa that Dorothy and I recognized two key common features in the ministries in which we were involved. The first was the observation that our focus had been on helping the marginalized–the vesicovaginal fistula program, empowering HIV/AIDS widows with information and home resources, facilitating a sewing program for widows in the Gidan Bege ministry, the crisis pregnancy outreach, and the expansion of the hospital chaplaincy staff to include female chaplains reaching the women in the hospital environment including mothers, wives and patients. So Dorothy and I have the gift of "seeing" – the disadvantaged, marginalized, and needy — and discovering ways to help them on a path to fulfill all that God has in store for them.

Another gift I discovered was teaching. Having struggled through years of college, graduate school, medical school, and residency with instructors who were poor communicators and awful teachers, I determined that I would learn to teach in a clear, simple, concise way, so anyone could understand. Even the most complicated concepts can be presented in understandable well-illustrated ways. So it was a great joy for me to find around every corner in Nigeria opportunities to teach – residents at Evangel in the family medicine residency program, students in the NEMI Bible school, high school pupils at Hillcrest, and my own children — algebra, driving an automobile, or life lessons. The Nigerians with whom we were engaged were eager to learn and appreciative of the commitment and sacrifice we had made.

That being said, I also realized year after year as missionaries went on furlough or Nigerians were transferred to other posts, that no one is indispensable, including me. Pridefully we think our role, whether as leader or follower, is vital to God's plan and key to the success of the project. Yet, God will fulfill His purposes with or without us. He may have a different purpose for us than continuing to do the same thing over and over. He may want to allow a ministry to die or a project to change direction. Change becomes acceptable as we rest in God's sovereignty and His power to alter our circumstances if it pleases Him. Sometimes He wants us to go through the crisis to learn, while other times He rescues us from the crisis. We are at the same time critical in obeying His call on our lives and dispensable according to how He moves us on the chessboard of history.

Learning to hold to our dreams and plans lightly, then, is important in having peace with the idea that God is in control. We learn humility through sacrifice of our agendas and taking on the role of the servant. I am learning to serve others and God. My best instructors have been my wife and my children. You quickly learn in marriage and as a parent that, "It is not all about you." Serving others for the acclamation or praise does not last long, so service becomes focused on Christ and the affirmation, "Well done, good and faithful servant." Serving does not come easy. It involves letting go of dreams, financial rewards, personal acclaim, and sometimes even health and life.

Serving sometimes involves suffering and trials. At times it is because we live in a fallen world surrounded by other sinners. Our difficulties may also be because of our sin or bad decisions. Other times it is because of the unwise choices of others. No matter the cause, through suffering we learn to depend on God. We realize our every breath comes from Him, and we understand in a unique way the suffering of our Savior. As Dorothy and I reflected on the death of our baby Aimee, even if God had given us an answer to the "why" question, it would not have satisfied us or helped us with our pain. So sometimes it is best to just not know.

The cemetery at Miango was built behind the Kirk Chapel in 1953 as a place for SIM missionaries throughout Nigeria to bury their loved ones who died in Africa. Since then, there have been 51 people buried there with over half being children under the age of two. The deaths occurred between 1928 and 1998. The causes of death range from natural death of old age, to stillborn births, deadly infections like rabies, polio and Lassa Fever, traumatic circumstances like automobile and airplane accidents and drowning, victims of the ravages of cancer, and in some the cause is unknown.

This cemetery is hallowed ground — ground soaked with the tears of grandparents, parents, sisters, brothers and friends. In the quiet, the wind blowing through the eucalyptus trees whispers the stories of those who have gone before. It is a history book and a family journal. It is the resting place of sacrifice and a memorial of suffering. It is the stepping off point for eternity and a place of solemn anniversaries. The living only visit, but they all leave changed with a clearer view of the present.

Having gone to the SIM boarding school Kent Academy since I was six years old, I have attended many of the funerals and burials of the residents of the cemetery. Some were people I knew well, like Beulah Herr, my dorm mother at the school. Some were parents of my friends, like Gordon Pullen who died of rabies from a dog bite. Over the years, I learned the stories of many buried there from family and friends. Since we have been in Nigeria, we have taken our children and visitors to Miango many times. Each visit to the cemetery I recall the stories of the people in the cemetery. The children ask innocent questions, and it provides wonderful teachable moments to talk about death and heaven. Little did I know on those tours how important this cemetery would become to Dorothy and me.

We continued to visit Aimee's grave over the years, and it surprised us that time did heal our wounded hearts even though we still have clear memories of this event. For weeks before we left Nigeria I had been thinking about my last visit to her grave. I knew she was in heaven and often wondered what she was like, her personality, what she looked like, and all about her, but the tangible connection with her was the cemetery grave. I had wondered for years how others had done it. One family left three. I was only leaving one. I wanted to do it with the rest of my family but ended up doing it with just one daughter. I knew it would be emotionally tough, but the deep feelings erupted into tears. I did not know her very well, but the final goodbye ripped at my heart in a profoundly sorrowing way.

We were so busy in the final days of our time in Nigeria that Dorothy and I were not able to visit Aimee's grave together. I realized when I took Heather to the dentist at Miango two weeks before we left that it was my last time going to Miango. After we were finished with the dental appointment, we walked to her grave, and as I gazed for the last time at her little cement-bordered plot covered with small white rocks and anchored at the top by the brass headstone plate, deep from within rose the wave of sorrow I had thought had gone years ago. I sobbed quietly as I hugged Heather and prayed again, thanking God for Aimee and how much I had learned and grown through her coming into my life. After a few moments of quietness I said, "Goodbye, Aimee," and we walked out of the cemetery for the last time. It makes me long for heaven–to see her and tell her how much I love her. Even as I write this now with tears in my eyes, a lump in my throat and heaviness in my chest, I know I will never forget Aimee, the inconsolable pain of losing a child, and the mystery of love.

As we close the Nigeria chapter in our lives, we are grateful that God called us to serve Him there. We are humbled by the Nigerians and missionaries with whom we had the privilege to work. We thank Him for the successes we enjoyed in ministries, projects, surgeries, and changed lives. We loved raising our family in a developing country, which they will always call "home." Most of all we know it was the crucible where God wanted us, so He could mold us to be more like Him.

LOOKING AHEAD

June 2012 to the present

The changes we faced leaving Nigeria involved almost every aspect of our lives–family dynamics, finances, work, church involvement, ministry activities, social relationships, recreational options and spiritual formation. Transitioning from one place to another involves looking back in reflection and looking at what lies ahead. I had mixed emotions looking ahead, both fear and anxiety.

David was disappointed to leave Nigeria and Hillcrest with his close friends, committed teachers, Bible instruction, sports, music activities, and the nurturing Christian environment. He jumped right into seventh grade at a public middle school in California with 3,000 students. He had only a few friends from our neighborhood, instructors with a secular worldview, and peer pressure from non-Christian kids.

His transition to the seventh grade was amazingly smooth. Although he did not make close friends right away, with his affable personality he adjusted well and was not intimidated by the school size. By the end of ninth grade we decided to transfer him for tenth grade to a smaller charter school where a number of his friends from the church youth group attend. He loves all the church youth group activities and leaders, and this has been a great blessing. They challenge him spiritually and he is making good life choices. He has also blossomed as an athlete in almost every sport he undertakes. He picked up where he left off in trampoline in a local tumbling and trampoline club and did well. He made it to the U.S. Trampoline and Tumbling National Championship competition in Kansas City, Missouri, in July 2013 and placed second in double mini-trampoline and third in trampoline. At the end of ninth grade his enthusiasm for gymnastics waned, and he surprised us with his next adventure. Like his grandfather, he expressed an interest in rugby, of all things, and has been excitedly going to every practice and game of a local youth rugby club. He is not intimidated by the giants coming at him and even became a certified rugby referee. He spends his free time either skate boarding or biking – anything as long as it is outdoors, high speed, and demanding physically. He is still unclear about his career aspirations, but we are excited to see where God directs him with his enormous energy and creativity.

In 2012 Heather started her freshman year at Azusa Pacific University. This would be Heather's first prolonged experience in an entirely new culture away from her twin sister. Marie was on campus with her for a year and helped her navigate the tricky waters of college life. Heather quickly got involved in the Third Culture Kids Network and soon was everyone's friend on campus. Her passion for fitness and sports also flourished with her involvement in extracurricular campus sports. She played the piano for a Sunday School class of elderly people at a church near campus and made a commitment to attend the worship services every Sunday. Her major is Exercise Science – a career focus that resonates with her passion for health, fitness, and training. She also has found a business opportunity to sell products that promote fitness and well-being, and this has provided both income and focus for her that resonates with her academic goals. She continues her involvement as a camp counselor and mentor for children during the summer months.

Anna went the farthest for college, Seattle Pacific University (SPU) to study her passion — fashion design. Several of her classmates from Hillcrest also attended SPU, so she immediately had friends. She looked forward to big city life, the cultural opportunities and branching out on her own. She learned the practical side of the fashion industry making costumes in the drama department and working summer jobs in children's retail clothing stores. She received school recognition for her dress designs and has been accepted to attend the Fashion Institute of Technology in New York for her senior year in the fall of 2015. Anna uniquely integrates African fabric into her fashion designs, which reflects her love for her "home" – Nigeria.

Having spent the second semester of her junior year in college in Chile, Nigeria, and Spain in a study abroad program, Marie returned to familiar ground at Azusa Pacific University for her senior year and then graduated in May 2013. After interviewing at several post-graduate psychology programs, she settled on a PhD program in child psychology at Alliant University in San Diego. She has been living with us to reduce costs and loves her classes, admires her advisor and mentor a great deal, has been creative in seeking part-time job opportunities, and was selected as the Alumnus of the Year in 2015 from the Psychology Department of Azusa Pacific University. We have thoroughly enjoyed having Marie live with us – helping us laugh with her fresh perspective on life in America and her creativity with children.

Leaving Nigeria, Dorothy faced enormous life changes as well. As the elementary school principal at Hillcrest she was in a position of leadership and influence. She also left a legacy with her ministries in the ECWA church women's fellowship, the programs for HIV/AIDS widows and orphans, and the street children outreach. At the house she had a Nigerian cook who made most of the evening meals, a Nigerian woman who cleaned the house and did laundry, and a driver to help her get around town. Coming to the States she faced a new way of living without a cook, cleaner or driver. She also did not have a job lined up in teaching or school administration. She wanted to focus on helping David in his adjustment and being available for the girls in college.

In addition to being the taxi driver for David to his many sports, social and church engagements, Dorothy found part-time work for one year as a substitute teacher in our school district and then took a full-time job as the elementary school science teacher in a charter school that caters to home-school families.

Although I have worked in Veterans Administration (VA) hospitals every furlough, I was anxious about jumping back into the practice of modern surgery. I felt woefully unfamiliar with management of sick patients in the ICU and current surgical techniques. I was also anxious about the additional responsibilities of committee work and other assignments that will come with full-time status at the VA. I looked forward to being in an Operating Room with electricity and water every day, seemingly unlimited resources, and reliable equipment. I was excited about the opportunities to teach and mentor residents and medical students and ways to express my faith as I rekindle previous friendships. I prayed the Lord would give me opportunities to be a witness for Him by word and deed as I deepened my relationships with colleagues and staff.

Over the past two years I found favor with the administration of the VA and was promoted to Chief of the Section of General Surgery and Associate Chief of the Surgical Service. In addition to these administrative responsibilities, I have enjoyed teaching residents and medical students from the University of California San Diego School of Medicine.

After two years living in southern California, Dorothy and I are beginning to feel like this is our new home. We are both sleeping better, are less anxious, and less on edge. I remember a few weeks ago realizing it was okay to laugh. Dorothy says we were like frogs in a pot of boiling water that were about to be cooked when we were pulled out. We are just now getting back to a normal temperature after our stressful years in Nigeria. We still do not feel we have landed completely, being unsettled about having few friends with whom we can share and little involvement in local ministries. As we wait for healing and strength, we are enjoying God's blessings of family, safety, and having enough to meet our needs each day.

Many times during the last two years we have been grateful we were in the States to help our girls with issues they have faced from boyfriend problems, to financial issues like student loans and credit cards, attending important school events with them, and helping them through some of their current challenges. We are still open to ministry opportunities here but have not felt ready. Many ask when we are going back to Nigeria or overseas. We answer that God wants us here for now, and we are content in that limited view of the future.

We are thankful for the opportunity we had to serve God in Africa for 24 years. We are thankful He brought us safely back and for the joy we have being with our children in this stage of their lives, helping my parents in their final years, being a living witness of God's grace in the school in Vista and the hospital in La Jolla, and learning to trust Him through this quieter chapter in our lives. We were honored to receive the Christian Medical and Dental Association's *Servant of the Year* Award in May 2015.

As I said in my acceptance remarks, "The rewards of missionary service are many and include a peace that I obeyed God's call to serve, phenomenal professional surgical challenges, incredible residents and students with an insatiable appetite for learning, amazing friends and supporters, an international band of prayer warriors, and a sense I made a difference in the lives of some. The revealing in heaven will be interesting. Finally, I am still learning to humble myself, serve others, and trust God in every circumstance."

Made in the USA
San Bernardino, CA
21 February 2018